Crises in the
Economic and
Financial
Structure

Lexington Books/Salomon Brothers Center Series on Financial Institutions and Markets

The Deregulation of the Banking and Securities Industry
Edited by Lawrence G. Goldberg and Lawrence J. White

Exchange Risk and Exposure
Edited by Richard M. Levich and Clas G. Wihlborg

Securities Activities of Commercial Banks
Edited by Arnold W. Sametz

Mergers and Acquisitions
Edited by Michael Keenan and Lawrence J. White

Crises in the Economic and Financial Structure
Edited by Paul Wachtel

Option Pricing
Edited by Menachem Brenner

Financing and Investing in Hi-Tech
Edited by Fred B. Renwick

The Emerging Financial Industry
Edited by Arnold W. Sametz

Crises in the Economic and Financial Structure

Edited by
Paul Wachtel
New York University

LexingtonBooks
D.C. Heath and Company
Lexington, Massachusetts
Toronto

Library of Congress Cataloging in Publication Data

Main entry under title:

Crises in the economic and financial structure.

Proceedings of a conference sponsored by the Salomon Brothers Center for the Study of Financial Institutions, at the New York University Graduate School of Business Administration, on Nov. 5–6, 1981.
Includes index.
1. Depressions—Congresses. I. Wachtel, Paul. II. Salomon Brothers Center for the Study of Financial Institutions.
HB3711.C69   338.5'42   81–48391
ISBN 0–669–05360–0   AACR2

Published simultaneously in Canada

Printed in the United States of America

International Standard Book Number: 0–669–05360–0

Library of Congress Catalog Card Number: 81–48391

Contents

Introduction

Structural crises have been a common and recurrent theme in economic and financial history for more than a decade. This almost universal concern with the theme suggested that a conference on crises would be a useful way of improving our understanding of the topic. It is as an outgrowth of that conference that this book came to be. The ideas and discussions presented in this book were first expressed at the Conference on Crises in the Economic and Financial Structure held at the Salomon Brothers Center for the Study of Financial Institutions of the New York University Graduate School of Business Administration on November 5–6, 1981.

The wealth and variety of material covered in this text exemplify the difficulty of obtaining an understanding of the crises in recent economic history. The causes and consequences of structural crises are difficult to discern because of the enormous diversity of crisis experiences. There are few common causal strands to unite the various crises experienced by the world economy in recent years. Although the phenomenon is a common one, each occurrence tends to be unique.

The task, then, of this book is to search for those common threads among the crises situations that have typified economic experience in the recent past. To do this, I invited a distinguished group of economists to address a series of particular crisis-prone areas or issues. Thus, we have a series of both descriptive and analytic chapters on four topics that will enable the reader to draw out the common threads of understanding that will better prepare us to withstand and adapt to the next crisis situation.

A word of caution is in order. Although analyses of the underlying situation often start from the perception that the economy is in a state of crisis, this may well be an exaggeration. The public may be too quick to assume that our economic difficulties go beyond the current recession and that, unless the government intervenes in some unknown way, the U.S. and perhaps the world economic condition will deteriorate. Although economic problems abound, *crisis* may be an exaggeration. Instead we observe various difficulties or episodes that necessitate structural change or arise when structural change is not readily forthcoming. Furthermore, we often discover an enormous resiliency of economic institutions in the face of crises. That is, the economic structure frequently exhibits an ability to adjust to crisis or to absorb the shocks and respond to change.

Thus, there are two possible conclusions that can be drawn from the coming discussion. One is the pessimistic reading, which makes the word *crisis* give rise to doom-and-gloom predictions. The other is the optimistic reading, which gloats in the ability of the economic system to respond to crisis. The chapters that follow will help the reader reach his or her own conclusions.

In this introduction I will conduct a preliminary investigation of the elements that unite the chapters and hopefully send the reader on to his or her own exploration. First, I will describe the four areas chosen for examination. The list is hardly an exhaustive one, but it does illustrate the broad range of topics to be considered. After describing the problems that led to the choice of topics, I will attempt to pinpoint some of the commonalities and differences among the chapters. The very first chapter in the book by Allan Meltzer will provide a starting point for this discussion. Meltzer's topic is an analysis of the underlying theoretical forces—risk and uncertainty—that may generate crises. Finally, a brief description of each of the chapters in the book will attempt to illustrate the concepts. The book is divided into four parts representing the following crisis-prone areas of the economy: (a) Monetary control, (b) Bankruptcy, (c) International finance, and (d) Market bubbles.

Which Crisis and Why?

An overview of the book will show which crisis areas are discussed and the motivation for choosing them.

Monetary Control

Structural changes in the financial industry in recent years have raised the possibility that the monetary sector is uncontrollable or that there is a crisis in our ability to make monetary policy. The crisis stems from the innovative acumen of an industry that rapidly responds to economic incentives by innovating activities that circumvent any undesired policy or regulatory controls. A crisis in public policy emerges since policymakers are unable to control the monetary sector as they expect to be able to do.

Before this crisis of monetary control is acknowledged as a problem several questions must be answered. First, is financial innovation a new phenomenon? Second, are policymakers really unable to respond to the macroeconomic situation? These questions are addressed by Richard Sylla and Thomas Mayer in their respective chapters. Sylla demonstrates quite convincingly that financial innovation is hardly new. The reader can only marvel at the revolutionary structural changes that took place in the eighteenth and nineteenth centuries. The current situation cannot be anymore revolutionary except that we expect policymakers to create a stable environment. Mayer provides a vivid description of how policymakers grapple with the vicissitudes of the modern economy. His behind-the-scenes description of the policy debates within the Federal Open Market Committee are often comic and often tragic.

Bankruptcy

The phenomenon of bankruptcy is an old one, which may however play an important role in contemporary economic crisis. Traditionally, we can view bankruptcy as a means of avoiding inefficient uses of resources. It is a market mechanism that moves resources away from inefficient activities and can, thus, be viewed as a healthy means of fostering growth. However, the emergence in recent years of bankruptcies of major economic organizations poses the threat of crisis. Although efficiency criteria may dictate that bankruptcy is appropriate, the disruption of economic activity that comes in certain instances may place an unfeasible burden on the economy. Two contemporary instances of this phenomenon are discussed. Jack Guttentag and Richard Herring discuss the case of the thrift industry. By any appropriate, if not conventional, definition large numbers of thrift institutions should be bankrupt. However, if these institutions were to cease operations or be liquidated there would be severe pressures on the ability of the financial system to function. Similarly, Thomas Ho and Ronald Singer discuss the merits of government loan guarantees to prevent the bankruptcy of a large real sector firm (the Chrysler case). In this case, the macroeconomic employment effects of bankruptcy create a crisis that may warrant government maintaining the corporation. A third example of the bankruptcy of a large economic unit having detrimental effects on the economy is the case of a country, which is the topic of Jeffrey Sachs's chapter in the next part of the book.

International Sector

The international arena has always been a fertile source of crises, and developments in the last decade have not changed this. Since the first OPEC price shock, observers have expected that an international crisis would have a serious impact on the workings of the world economy. However, the striking characteristic of the international economy has been its ability to adjust to structural change without debilitating crises.

Two chapters in this part deal with two distinct aspects of the issue— real sector adjustments in the industrialized countries and the financial adjustments and pressures on LDCs. The chapter by Knut Mork explores the effect of OPEC oil price shocks on the U.S. economy with econometric model simulations. Jeffrey Sachs investigates the financial fragility and near bankruptcy of the less-developed countries that have amassed enormous external debts to finance their fuel purchases. These debts have placed a severe burden on the entire international financial system. International cooperation has enabled countries to avoid default or bankruptcy in most instances since such a crisis could disrupt international trading relations.

Further insights into these issues is found in the chapter by Henry Wallich, a member of the board of governors of the Federal Reserve System, on the topic of the role of central banks in an environment of recurrent international financial crises. Governor Wallich discusses the burden that country debt rescheduling places on the central bank that simultaneously plays the roles of the bank supervisor and the lender of last resort. Risk in international bank lending is also the topic addressed by a panel of bankers whose remarks are included here.

Market Bubbles

In the last part of the book crises of a different sort are discussed, that is, the emergence of market phenomena that lead to the malfunctioning or disruption of economic activity on a particular market. Market bubbles, or the speculative explosion of prices, can lead to widespread crisis when the bubbles occur in a market that is important to the overall economy.

Although economic historians have examined incidents of market bubbles and runs on institutions before, there is little literature that formally defines the concepts. My interest here is to provide an appropriate definition of the phenomenon. The chapters by Robert Flood and Peter Garber and by Olivier Blanchard and Mark Watson should help define these phenomena. Flood and Garber summarize the theory of the formation of price bubbles and discuss the application of the theory to the issue of gold monetization. The possibility of speculative bubbles under a gold standard is of importance in determining whether a gold standard would be a stabilizing influence on the world economy. It is interesting to note that the gold standard is often suggested as a response to the problems of monetary control discussed above. However, if such a system were subject to the destabilizing effects of price bubbles there may be no advantage gained. In their chapter, Blanchard and Watson discuss how the presence of a speculative bubble can be detected. In the final chapter, Kenneth Garbade discusses a particular situation where regulatory authorities have intervened to prevent speculative bubbles. The efficacy of the margin regulations as a means of preventing stock price bubbles is Garbade's topic.

A Definition of Crises

Although examples of crises are legion, the economics profession does not have a framework for dealing with the topic. Hence the problem of definition is an important one. The groundwork for such a framework is found in Allan Meltzer's chapter, which utilizes a typology initially introduced by Frank Knight. Knight made the distinction between risk and uncertainty. Risk emerges because outcomes often differ from their expected value—but with a known or calculable probability. Uncertainty, however, is due to unpredictable changes in the distribution of outcomes. The distinction is important because economic units can prepare themselves for the consequences of risky outcomes but not for uncertainty. We can then associate our conception of economic crisis with the uncertainty of outcomes. A crisis may emerge when there is a shift in the underlying distribution of outcomes of economic events.

This typology is useful for analyzing crisis situations. For example, the OPEC oil price shocks can on one hand be viewed as a simple relative price change (an incidence of risk) or on the other hand as a structural shift in the microeconomy (an incidence of uncertainty). The distinction is subjective but clearly we will define crises as situations that are viewed as incidents of uncertainty. More formal modeling of crisis situations makes explicit use of the distinction. For example, a price bubble is defined as a discrete shift in the process that generates prices.

Some Conclusions

In this introduction, I will briefly look at the conclusions that can be drawn from the chapters in this book. That is, do they suggest that the topics examined are really crises or are just normal incidents of uncertainty? Furthermore, what do they conclude about the ability of the economic structure to respond to or deal with crises? By and large, as we will see, the authors here seem to suggest that although crisis—in the sense of structural change—does exist, the economic structure exhibits an ability to adjust. In fact these adjustments take place quickly enough so that crises seem not to inhibit the growth in economic well-being.

The consequences on the monetary system of economic crises can be simply summarized in one word in Sylla's view: innovation. That is, financial crises have not been debilitating because the financial system responds with both product and process innovations. Sylla cites numerous examples extending over several centuries of innovative responses.

Thomas Mayer concentrates on a much narrower time span, only two years, and is not nearly as optimistic. Mayer presents a copious case study of the process by which monetary policy is determined in this country. He uses the minutes of the Federal Open Market Committee to examine the monetary policy process during the recession of 1973–1975. He finds that the policymakers' response to and understanding of the problems that emerged during that long and deep recession were at best confused. In the face of one of the major macroeconomic crises of the postwar period, policymaking was unfocused and unable to differentiate between risk and uncertainty. Mayer searches the minutes in vain for a cohesive conception of monetary theory and its relationship to the events of that period. However, the behavior of the Fed cannot be viewed so much as inept but rather as reasonable responses to a difficult situation. In fact, as the nature of the crisis became clear, policy did shift to an appropriate response. The Fed cannot be blamed for lack of perfect foresight.

A somewhat different policy problem is addressed by Jack Guttentag and Richard Herring. Their subject is the insolvency of financial intermediaries, a crisis that might in part be due to regulatory policy and also requires a regulatory response. Guttentag and Herring detail the difficulty in determining the solvency of institutions in an insured and regulated industry. They, also, argue that rational use of regulatory powers can go a long way to mitigating the consequences of the crisis at hand. Here we have an example (perhaps due to a long history of improper regulatory incentives) of a crisis that would in fact affect the functioning of the economy. That is, there is reason to doubt the resiliency of financial markets in the face of widespread bankruptcies of thrift institutions. However, Guttentag and Herring do leave the impression that regulatory policy leaves room for optimism.

A more problematic area for government policy to avoid bankruptcy is the issue addressed by Thomas Ho and Ronald Singer. The bankruptcy of a major employer has macroeconomic effects that are undesirable. The issue is when and whether the government should impose a trade-off between efficiency considerations and employment in the face of financial crisis. They conclude that there are instances where government loan guarantees are warranted—but are not entirely sure that the Chrysler Corporation is such an instance.

The resiliency of the macroeconomy to a severe crisis is the topic of Knut Mork's chapter. Surely the loss of all Persian Gulf sources of oil can be considered to be an incidence of Knightian uncertainty. Mork uses econometric simulations of a world energy model to explore the consequences of such a structural change on the U.S. economy. His conclusion is that although a severe recession would result, it would be temporary and over a five-year period the macroeconomy would be able to adjust remarkably well to this disastrous crisis.

An additional note of optimism is found in Jeffrey Sachs's extensive analysis of LDC debt in the 1980s, which includes a historical evaluation of national defaults over the last century. Sachs finds that there are strong indications that defaults can only be avoided by debt reschedulings that seriously increase the riskiness of bank exposure. He concludes, however, that the prospects are good for the international community emerging without any crisis that will halt the workings of the financial system. Although bank exposure may at times be excessive and country debts often overly burdensome, the international financial system will continue to finance trade and investment for the world economy.

Governor Henry Wallich in his remarks on regulation and debt rescheduling shares Sachs's optimism. He notes that the international banking community has been very successful in recycling funds to LDC lending. However, Wallich is also mindful of the limits of this process and suggests that regulatory authorities might express such a view. In his discussion, Roger Kubarych expresses a different point of view about international bank lending; he is less satisfied with the viability of the current system.

A chapter that focuses on international bank lending is also relatively optimistic. Laurie Goodman finds that although various measures of country risk suggest that the situation is serious, it appears that the nightmare of paralyzing defaults is unwarranted. Her optimism is shared by the other panel participants, Arturo Porzecanski and H. Robert Heller.

The chapters by Robert Flood and Peter Garber and by Olivier Blanchard and Mark Watson discuss and make use of some analytic frameworks for particular crisis situations. Their topic is the phenomenon of a market bubble or the speculative movement of a market price away from the so-called fundamental value. Most earlier research on these topics has been anecdotal. Flood and Garber show that a price bubble or a run on supplies can emerge when the market price depends on its own rate of change. In such a model, the solution for the path of prices can undergo a mean shift or an incidence of uncertainty that generates a bubble in an otherwise stable model. As an illustration of the technique they model the conditions necessary to maintain a viable gold standard; that is, one that could resist a run on government gold stocks.

A more fundamental question is posed by Blanchard and Watson. They ask whether bubbles actually exist. The question is the fundamental one posed by this book. That is, are crises a class of situations that differ from the normal ebb and flow of economic events? After providing a precise definition of a bubble, Blanchard and Watson can state what price movements would look like in the presence of a bubble. One of their tests is suggestive of the existence of bubbles (in stock prices) and the other is not (in gold prices).

Long before bubbles became a topic of formal research, policymakers were concerned with the phenomenon. Kenneth Garbade analyzes a particular regulatory initiative to inhibit speculative bubbles. That is, margin regulations were introduced almost fifty years ago and the regulation has been used with the intent to inhibit stock price bubbles. Garbade analyzes the development of this interpretation of Congress's intentions. He also examines the evidence on such bubbles and the effect of the regulation. He concludes that credit-financed stock positions can give rise to price bubbles, but that the practical significance of this phenomenon in the United States is doubtful. In a rather cautiously drawn conclusion Garbade states that he finds it difficult to conclude that the margin regulations are not warranted. That is, they may inhibit bubble-type price movements.

Conclusion

In lieu of a conclusion, it is hoped that at this stage readers will go on to those chapters that are of interest to them. An introduction should whet one's appetite not satiate it. The reader can draw his or her own conclusions about whether the word *crisis* has been used appropriately. In fact, the summary above might well suggest that our topic has not been crisis but, instead, the resiliency of the economy as shown by the optimism of researchers addressing a wide variety of issues.

Acknowledgments

Appreciation is due to Sidney Browne for preparing the index and assisting in the preparation of the manuscript. I would like to thank Arnold Sametz, director of the Salomon Brothers Center for the Study of Financial Institutions and the members of the center staff for making possible the Conference on Crises in the Economic and Financial Structure. The center has had a long-standing interest in the issues of structural changes and crises. In fact this book evolved through a continuation of interest in these topics found in two earlier conference volumes: *Understanding Capital Markets, Volume II: The Financial Environment and the Flow of Funds in the Next Decade,* edited by Arnold W. Sametz and Paul Wachtel (Lexington Books, 1977) and *Financial Crises: Institutions and Markets in a Fragile Environment,* edited by Edward I. Altman and Arnold W. Sametz (Wiley, 1977). One can presume that as the economy continues to weather various storms they will be monitored by additional research activities and our conference programs will keep abreast with the crises and changes that take place.

Part I
Monetary Crises

1

Rational Expectations, Risk, Uncertainty, and Market Responses

Allan H. Meltzer

The incorporation of rational expectations into economic models is widely recognized as one of the more significant advances in economic theory during the past decade. The advances are methodological—improvements in the methods economists use to derive the implications of dynamic models and the treatment of unanticipated changes. Many of the substantive benefits of the methods remain in the future, however. The reason is that the models used to illustrate rational expectations typically endow people with more information than they usually have.

With few exceptions, current models that incorporate rational expectations use Edmund Phelps's (1970) island paradigm. The principal problem that people solve arises because no one can distinguish between aggregate and relative prices changes at the time changes occur. Publication of aggregate data provides the relevant information after one period, and this removes the difference between anticipated and actual events.

An older tradition in economics is associated with the classic work of Frank Knight, *Risk, Uncertainty, and Profit* (1921), but is prominent also in John Maynard Keynes (1921, 1936). These authors distinguish between risk and uncertainty. In the terminology of Knight, the island paradigm is a model of insurable risk because the unforseen changes that occur are drawn from a distribution with fixed mean and variance. There is no reason for opinions to differ about the outcomes anticipated for tomorrow or for the more distant future. Hence there are no opportunities for profit—economic profit—and no force driving entrepreneurs to excel at their specialized task—interpreting current events, divining their implications for the future, and profiting from their specialized ability.

The Knight-Keynes tradition is an alternative model that can be combined with the method known as rational expectations.[1] John Muth, who developed the method, applied the principle of economic efficiency to the use of information. Muth (1960, 1961) reasoned that accurate information

As always I owe a debt to Karl Brunner for his stimulating and insightful comments. Alex Cukierman made several helpful suggestions, tried hard to get me to clarify my thinking, and helped me to do so. Earlier, William Beranek urged me to relate Keynes's and Knight's views about uncertainty.

3

about the future is scarce. Not only are we uncertain about events that have not occurred, but we are uncertain about the correct interpretation of events that have occurred and about their implications for the future. The best we can do, according to Muth, is to use the best confirmed hypothesis to separate the essential *facts* from the inessential, to interpret observations (or facts), and to draw their implications.

Muth's work eventually produced an important change in the way economists introduce expectations into hypotheses. The old method, and its fruitful application is well illustrated by the work of Milton Friedman (1957) that stimulated Muth's contribution and numerous other applications. There, expectations are formed without regard for efficiency in the use of information or optimality of forecasts.[2]

Robert E. Lucas, Jr. made the second major change in method by joining rational expectations to general equilibrium theory. In a series of pathbreaking papers, beginning with Lucas (1972), he recognized that the information available in all markets must be consistent. Bringing expectations into general equilibrium theory requires people to act on the same beliefs when they are buying goods and bonds, selling services, and increasing or decreasing real cash balances. As Lucas (1980) later wrote, it is no longer acceptable modeling practice to introduce free parameters, representing expectations, into the equations of an econometric model to reproduce the past and forecast the future of the economy. Expectations must be consistent with the implications of a general equilibrium model and must either use available information or explain why it is not used.

The importance of Lucas's contributions can be judged both by the dominant role of his methods, models, and insights for the current generation of economists and by the negative reaction of an impressive list of general equilibrium theorists. The achievements of general equilibrium rational-expectations models are surveyed in several places, most recently—and insightfully—by McCallum (1980) and from a very different perspective by Brian Kantor (1979). The principal objections of some general equilibrium theorists are familiar also. Kenneth Arrow (1978) and James Tobin (1980) discuss a number of assumptions used in rational-expectations models that are inconsistent with observations. Everyone does not have the same information or access to information at the same costs. Tastes and opportunities differ. Aggregation is neglected. Forward markets do not exist for all contingent claims.

Many of the criticisms are too sweeping. One or more applies to all general equilibrium theory—indeed all economic theory, micro as well as macro. The particular reason for citing these standard assumptions in criticism of rational expectations appears to be that Arrow and Tobin claim that they are principal causes of disequilibrium in product and labor markets. If people learn at different rates or have different opportunities or information, some can be fooled. There is nothing in the method known as rational expectations that makes these standard assumptions more objectionable when applied to information than to markets for other goods or services. The fault lies in the model not in the method that requires expectations to be consistent with the best confirmed model.

My criticism of rational-expectations models is not a criticism of the method of bringing information into general equilibrium theory. By emphasizing the role of information, rational expectations has forced everyone to model some aspects of the process by which new information reaches the markets and to be clear about what is known and unknown, by whom and when. This is a step forward—I would say a long step—from the earlier tradition of deterministic models that relied on errors in the equation to rationalize our dependence on econometric estimates of parameters.

The gain from using the method is limited, however, by the quality of the models with which it is used. In the following section, I discuss the information people have available and, following Knight (1921) and Keynes (1921 and 1936), distinguish between risk and uncertainty. I relate uncertainty to stationarity and propose an alternative to Phelps's (1970) island paradigm.[3] The nonstationary model seems consistent with price-setting behavior in many markets and, I suggest, offers an explanation for this behavior and other commonly observed institutions and practices.

Risk and Uncertainty

The framework used most often to derive or test propositions from models in which expectations are rational follows Lucas (1972). Lucas combined Samuelson's (1958) intertemporal model with a key insight of Phelps's (1970) island paradigm to show that neutrality is temporarily disturbed if people cannot distinguish, on impact, between real impulses or shocks that change relative prices and monetary impulses or shocks that change only the absolute price level.

The innovative feature in recent work is not the discovery that money is neutral. Rigid wages and incorrect beliefs or misperception of future prices have long been used to explain why monetary changes have real effects and why the real effects persist at times. Recent models differ from their predecessors by incorporating the source of misperceptions within the model explicitly. In the island paradigm, spatial separation on *islands* raises the cost of acquiring accurate information about relative and absolute price changes to a level that is high when new information enters the system, then falls rapidly.

Discussion of rational expectations models often criticizes the assumption of islands or, more usefully, the posited cause of lags in the receipt of information. Usually, the criticism runs, people can have more information than the model allows. My criticism of current, rational-expectations models is that they endow people with too much information, not too little. Information is drawn from distributions with fixed means and constant variances. Everyone believes that the expected values of real variables (or their rates of change) are constant. Further, people know the rules governing the behavior of the money stock (and other policy variables).[4]

Frank Knight was a pioneer in the analysis of information and the role of information in economic decisions. Knight (1921) believed that the search for economic profit drives the economy. Profits occur because changes are predicted imperfectly. For Knight imperfect knowledge is a consequence of change: "Changes in conditions give rise to profit by upsetting anticipations and producing a divergence between costs and selling price, which would otherwise be equalized by competition" (1921, p. 198).

Knight classifies probabilities into three groups (1921, chapter 7, especially pp. 224–225). A priori probabilities are derived mathematically. The probability that a die or a coin toss will produce a particular value is an example. Knight thought that this type of probability is least important for economics and business. Empirical probabilities rest on classification of instances and are not derivable from mathematical laws or principles. A main reason for distinguishing empirical from a priori probability is that Knight wanted to emphasize the greater amount of judgment involved in classifying events or instances to form distributions where the laws governing the classification are not as well known as the laws governing (say) the probabilities of heads or tails in a coin toss. The distinguishing characteristic of the third class is that "there is *no valid basis of any kind* for classifying instances" (1921, p. 225, italics in the original).

Knight recognized that the three types of probability differed in degree. In practice, classification is neither certain or impossible. But, Knight wanted to distinguish sharply two types of errors. One is the error made when assigning events to classes. The other is the error made in basing decisions on the ability of particular individuals to classify events correctly. Business decisions are made by managers or entrepreneurs, and the success or failure of a business depends on the correspondence between actual outcomes and the outcomes anticipated by managers or entrepreneurs.

Knight assigned the term *risk* to uncertain events for which the distribution of outcomes is known either a priori or by classification. He restricted *uncertainty* to events for which the distribution of outcomes is unknown and the basis for classification is tenuous.[5] The classification of events as risky or uncertain is not immutable. People learn to group (classify) events, and they identify people with the ability to make correct decisions about uncertain events. In these, and other (1921, p. 239) ways, uncertainty can be reduced. But it remains as a source of profits, or Marshallian quasi-rents, to decision makers who forecast correctly the direction of change in the mean value.

J.M. Keynes discussed very similar issues at about the same time. In his *Treatise on Probability* (1921), Keynes described the *weight* of a probability as a relation between evidence and the confidence or degree of belief in the probability assigned to a particular outcome. Probabilities are subjective. The lowest weight is placed on *a priori* probabilities and the weight rises as evidence accumulates. Whenever people gain confidence in their beliefs but believe that an event is less probable, the weight increases as the probability of an event declines (1921, p. 72). In Keynes's terminology, a person who becomes almost certain that an event will not occur places a high weight on a very low probability.

Years later, in his *General Theory,* Keynes distinguished between *very uncertain* and *very improbable* (1936, p. 148) by referring to the discussion of weight in his *Treatise on Probability.* He used the distinction to explain the difference between a risk premium and a liquidity premium. The former produces more income; the latter may yield greater utility, a sense of security or confidence, but less income. A well-known example is the nonpecuniary yield that French or Indian peasants receive from the (alleged) practice of holding wealth in gold or silver during periods of stable or falling prices. The peasants are *uncertain* about the durability of noninflationary or deflationary policies, so they pay to reduce uncertainty. Keynes (1979, pp. 293–294) gives a similar example.

Keynes never refers to Knight, but there is no doubt that he made the same distinction between risk and uncertainty. At one point, he uses reasoning very similar to Knight's to explain the difference between uncertain and improbable. Keynes (1973, pp. 113–114) wrote:

> By "uncertain" knowledge, let me explain, I do not mean to distinguish what is known for certain from what is only probable. The game of roulette is not subject, in this sense to uncertainty; nor is the prospect of a Victory Bond being drawn. . . . The sense in which I use the term is that in which the prospect of a European war is uncertain, . . . or the position of wealth-owners in the social system in 1970. About these matters there is no scientific basis on which to form any capable probability whatever. *We simply do not know* (italics added).

Keynes argued that in practice, people ignore uncertainty. They act *as if* the distribution of expected returns is fixed. Expected values are computed on the assumption that future outcomes are drawn from a stable distribution of returns. People know that distributions are *not* fixed, but they have no better choice than to act as if they are. In Keynes's words, (1973, p. 114) "[T]he necessity for action and decision compels us . . . to behave exactly as we should if we had behind us a good Benthamite calculation of prospective advantages and disadvantages, each multiplied by its appropriate probability, waiting to be summed.''

Neither Knight nor Keynes appears to reject the key assumption of Muth's rational expectations—that individuals act as if their subjective probabilities are identical to the distribution of outcomes required for a general market equilibrium. Knight stresses that the probabilities that people use to evaluate risk are obtained from observations and adjust as information changes. Keynes's emphasis on weight, and his observation that the assigned weights change as information changes, have a similar implication.[6]

The critical difference between these earlier works and current models is that Knight's and Keynes's discussions of uncertainty recognize nonstationarity. Their world is subject to change in ways that cannot be foreseen or predicted from the distribution of past outcomes. These changes are the cause of profit (and loss) for Knight, and the attempt to minimize cost and maximize profit in a world of uncertainty is a principal reason for organizing business firms, delegating power of decision, centralizing decisions, and compensating executives. Keynes, too, linked uncertainty to the form of economic organization but drew very different conclusions about business decisions.

Stationarity and Uncertainty

At a purely formal level, we can assign prior probabilities to any event or to the timing of any event that we can imagine. The expected value of any occurrence can be computed, in this formal sense, and decisions can be described as a choice between expected values.

An alternative, and possibly more useful, way to think about economic decisions is to distinguish between risk and uncertainty and to treat uncertain events as (unforseen) changes in the mean of a distribution of outcomes. The mean of the distribution becomes nonstationary in a sense to be made more precise in this section. People make decisions by assigning (subjective) probabilities to outcomes, but the only outcomes they consider are drawn from stationary distributions. As in Keynes and Knight, there is no basis for assigning probabilities to some occurrences or, if one prefers, for placing much weight on the assigned probability.

A simple model illustrates the point. Suppose that the process governing a variable X_t is

$$X_t = A_t e^{\alpha(t)t} u_t \qquad (1.1)$$

where t is time, A and α and u are random walks with, using $ln\ u$ for illustration:

$$ln\ u_t \sim N(0, \sigma_u^2).$$

If A_t and $\alpha(t)$ are constants, $ln\ X_t$ is expected to change at a constant rate through time. If X is real income, for example, real income deviates randomly from a constant, *stationary* trend. In any period, there is risk of departure from trend, but the risk is constrained by the knowledge that the trend is constant. A diversified portfolio of investments can be made in period t with full knowledge of the return expected to accrue to the owner in period $t + j$.

The expected value of the logarithm of X looking forward to t at $t + j$ is not a simple random walk around a trend, however:

$$E\ ln\ X_{t+j} = E\ ln\ A_{t+j} + E\alpha_{t+j}(j - t). \tag{1.2}$$

By assumption, A and α are random walks, but from equation 1.2:

$$E\Delta ln\ X_{t+n} = E\Delta ln\ A_{t+n} + E(\Delta\alpha_{t+n}(n - t) + \alpha_{t+n}) \tag{1.3}$$

Changes in A augment or reduce the level of X but do not change the system's trend. They appear as one-time or *permanent* changes in the level of X. Changes in α alter the trend rate of change. As people look forward in time, the difference between actual and expected X increases (or decreases) continuously following a change in α. It is no longer true that a diversified portfolio of investments will yield a predictable return if held long enough. Nonstationarity introduces the kind of uncertainty discussed by Knight and Keynes.

To summarize, X_t changes in three ways. There are transitory, random deviations around the trend line, given by u_t. There are, also, permanent changes in level, $\Delta\ ln\ A_t$, and permanent changes in growth rate, $\Delta\alpha$. People cannot observe A, α, or u directly. All they know is the history of X and the information they extract from the best available estimates of A and α. Muth (1960) used a model with permanent and transitory changes in level to show that the optimal forecast of a variable like X_t is a distributed lag of current and past values of observables.[7] A model incorporating unanticipated permanent and transitory changes in level and growth rate adds another source of error and incorporates many of the standard issues that economists discuss. Permanent changes in growth differ from permanent changes in level. Transitory changes in growth are persistent (or permanent) changes in level; transitory changes in level are treated as random changes.

Suppose we compute the optimal forecast of $ln\ X_t$, $E\ ln\ X_t$, and find, later, that the forecast is low. Call the observed error, $ln\ X_t - E\ ln\ X_t$, $ln\ \epsilon_t$. A single observation of ϵ_t is not sufficient to distinguish permanent from transitory changes or changes in level from changes in growth rate. Obviously, it is a mistake to equate $ln\ \epsilon_t$ with $ln\ u_t$. Even a series of observations, $\epsilon_t < 0$, stretching over several periods can be insufficient to determine with precision the type of change that has occurred. Knowledge that the conditional forecast of X_t is unbiased and efficient assures that we do not waste information but does not assure that we avoid persistent errors. Until we decompose $ln\ \epsilon_t$ into $ln\ u_t$, $\Delta\ ln\ A_t$, and $\Delta\alpha$, we must be prepared for errors that, with hindsight, appear to be correlated.

Every economist who uses market data discovers the substantial difference between dating past and current turning points. On the charts, accelerations and decelerations of money, income, prices, and other variables—or changes in their direction of change—often have sharpness and clarity that is absent at the time the changes occur. Even if every observation is drawn from a distribution with constant mean, large random deviations create opportunities for profit and loss.

The variance of the distribution of $ln\ u_t$ is a measure of risk. The larger is the variance, $\sigma^2\ ln\ u$, the greater is the risk that at time t the actual observation will differ from the expected value by a given amount. The difference $\sigma^2\ ln\ \epsilon - \sigma^2\ ln\ u$ is a measure of uncertainty. On the usual assumptions, $\sigma^2\ ln\ u$ is constant. Inspection of equation 1.2 suggests that $\sigma^2\ ln\ \epsilon$ is an increasing function of time; the variance increases as we look farther into the future. In period $t + j$, for large j, the risk element is insignificant; $\sigma^2\ ln\ \epsilon_{t + j}$ is dominated by uncertainty.

Figure 1-1 shows the effect of a reduction in α at period t_0 and an increase in A at $t + j$. The solid line is the actual path of X. If there is no uncertainty, and the mean is constant, the expected value is fixed permanently; X follows the broken line. Repeated sampling produces estimates that remain within sampling error of previous estimates, and the variance of the estimates is constant.

Permanent changes in level or growth rate produce nonstationary means.[8] When large changes in the mean are relatively frequent, people have difficulty identifying the mean. The critical ability is, as in Knight, an ability to classify events into drawings from a fixed distribution or changes in expected value. In my example, this involves making a correct inference about the expected value of the outcome or, more specifically, classifying an observation as a drawing from the distribution of $ln\ u$, $E\ ln\ X$ unchanged, or as a change in $E\ ln\ X$. Further, changes in $E\ ln\ X$ must be apportioned into permanent or transitory changes in the rate of change of X. The farther one looks into the future, the larger is the potential error of confusing $\Delta\ ln\ A$ and $\Delta\alpha$.

Keynes's examples of uncertainty about wars or the future of capitalism are extreme examples but fit the distinction between shifts in expected value and drawings from a distribution with a stationary mean. Prior probabilities can be assigned to these events, and the frequency distribution of wars per decade can be drawn. As the event approaches, typically more informa-

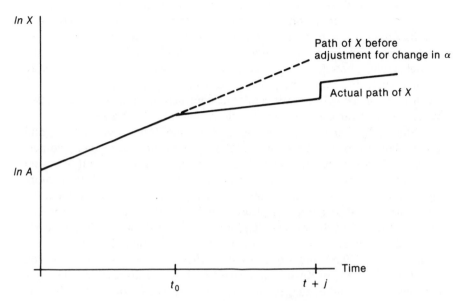

Figure 1-1. A Model with Uncertainty

tion becomes available. As Knight suggested, our ability to classify events may improve; in Keynes's terms, the weight on the probability may increase as the time between present and future shrinks.

There is, of course, no reason why every event becomes more certain as it approaches. Contemporary history offers many examples of wars, revolutions, earthquakes, and other shocks that are neither more nor less probable just before they occur. The model implies, however, that there is less uncertainty about near-term than about more distant events.

The forecasting problem does not end when an event occurs. The duration of most shocks is uncorrelated with time of occurrence. To paraphrase Keynes, we simply did not know how long the hostages would remain in Iran, how long the Shah would retain power, when the anchovies would return to the coast of Peru, when rainfall would end the California drought of the midseventies, or how long the Federal Reserve will continue any particular episode of inflationary or disinflationary policy.

Applications and Evidence

The standard model of rational expectations, described for example in McCallum's (1980) survey, ignores uncertainty and nonstationarity. Emphasis is on the confusion between changes in relative prices and changes in the price level. No student of economics has to be reminded that confusion between relative and absolute prices is important for economic theory and for its application to actual economies. But, a considerable amount of sophisticated, analytical work of very high quality should convince us that a model in which people know the correct expected values one period after an event occurs, and know the policy rules followed by governments, is difficult to reconcile with prewar economic contractions that lasted about two years and postwar economic contractions that last about a year.

Stanley Fischer (1977), Edmund Phelps, and John Taylor (1977), and others have proposed the existence of wage contracts to explain the persistence of recessions. Prices fixed by contracts are *sticky,* so all prices do not adjust to shocks at once. If wages adjust to new information more slowly than prices, real wages move countercyclically, and profit maximizing firms expand and contract procyclically. Cargill's work (1969) for Britain and the United States suggests, however, that this pattern is not clearly stamped on the real wage changes for the past century. Earlier work by John Dunlop (1938) and Lorie Tarshis (1939) and tests of the wage-lag hypothesis by Reuben Kessel and Armen Alchian (1950) reach similar conclusions. These studies suggest that wage contracts cannot explain the persistence of business contractions.

Two additional features of business cycles provide evidence about persistence. One is the length of cycles whether measured from peak-to-peak or from trough-to-trough. The other is the length of expansions and contractions. The National Bureau of Economic Research chronology provides estimates of these data for all the business cycles since 1854.

One of the most regular features of peacetime cycles is that on average there are four years between peaks and four years between troughs. The averages for twenty-four peacetime cycles—ten peacetime cycles under the gold standard (1879–1919) and five peacetime cycles between 1945 and 1980—differ very little. In contrast, there is a notable difference in the lengths of expansion and contractions. Under the gold standard, cycles are evenly divided between months of contraction and months of expansion. Since 1945, peacetime expansions are one-third longer[9] and peacetime contractions are less than one-half their average length under the gold standard. The average peacetime expanson has lasted four times as long as the average peacetime contraction in the five most recent peacetime cycles.

Under the gold standard, the government had a smaller role in the economy. Tariffs were the principal source of revenue. The monetary "rule" was widely known—gold movements determined the quantity of money. Prior to 1914 there was not central bank, and monetary intervention by the Treasury was limited, as Phillip Cagan (1965) has shown. Tenure rules for employees, wage contracts, severance payments, and firing costs were almost certainly less important, since more of the labor force was un-skilled and there were few unions to negotiate contracts. In contrast, the years 1945 to 1980 cover a period in which the monetary standard changed from Bretton Woods to fluctuating rates. Many currencies shifted from in-convertible to convertible and back again. The roles of government and labor unions expanded.

Were the rules clearer and the contracts less restrictive in the later period? This seems implausible. If so, the standard rational expectations model—with or without fixed nominal wage contracts—cannot now be reconciled with these facts about the comparative length of expansions and contractions. Fixed nominal wages are not a necessary condition for fluc-tuations of the type observed in the United States and other market economies.

Friedman's (1957) model of a wealth maximizing consumer, who chooses to allocate consumption and leisure between present and future, is not a model of constant expected income. Muth's development of rational expectations was stimulated, in part, by his interest in finding an optimal method of forecasting a variable like Friedman's permanent, or expected, income that is subject to shocks. He developed a model in which permanent changes occur but cannot be identified immediately. I suggest that this model, with rational expectations, captures part of the distinction between risk and uncertainty and is a more relevant model of the business cycle. Lucas's (1977) discussion of business cycles, unlike his formal models, takes a similar view of cycles.

The model with risk and uncertainty views wage and other contracts not as a cause, but as a consequence of fluctuations in the level and growth rate of economic activity. Workers do not enter implicit agreements or sign contracts that measure (or create) periods of unemployment without receiv-ing some benefit in exchange. The benefit from entering contracts is not very large where there is no uncertainty about the possible outcome. The comparative benefit from fixing wages or hours is not very large if all draw-ings are made from a distribution with fixed, known mean and constant variance. The benefit of an employment contract is reduced when everyone knows the expected value of lifetime earnings. For example, if real income, X_t, is drawn from equation 1.1 with constant A and α:

$$X_t = Ae^{\alpha t}u_t$$

Let A and α vary, as above. There is now uncertainty in addition to risk. Contracts and agreements can be analyzed as arrangements for reducing costs of acquiring information, of sharing the costs of variability, and as ef-ficient (or inefficient) arrangements for reducing the costs of variability to the minimum inherent in nature and in social arrangements.

Contracts and agreements are not the only reason for suggesting that the model with risk and uncertainty directs attention to issues that cannot be addressed in a model in which there is only risk. Some of the following questions suggest topics that can only be addressed where A and α are permitted to change.

Do Japanese consumers and producers believe that the observed growth rates of real income for the past twenty years have all come from the extreme right tail of the distribution they sampled in the previous hundred years? Do Europeans, Brazilians, or Koreans believe a similar story? Do the citizens of these countries believe that their growth rates can remain permanently above the rates in developed economies? Does anyone believe that the relative size of government or the expected future tax rate is constant, or that the growth rates of real tax burdens in Organization for Economic Cooperation and Development (OECD) countries are constant? If these, and other expected values are not constants, the stochastic process used in standard rational expectations models misses some of the principal uncertainties that most of us face as consumers and producers. These choices include decisions to change saving and consumption in response to changes in permanent income or to shift the allocation of portfolios between financial and real assets when there are permanent changes in the perceived rate of inflation.

Market Responses

Some goods and services are sold in fixed price markets, some in auction markets. Labor markets are commonly cited examples of fixed price markets, but retail grocers also post a price and allow purchasers to choose the quantity.[10] Indeed, retail transactions in developed economies are typically made at prices posted by the seller.

An economic rationale for the widespread use of price-setting markets, looks to the comparative advantage of buyers and sellers in acquiring or processing information relevant for announcing (or posting) prices. In the absence of the auctioneer, who calls prices at random, some pricing mechanism is required. The method or approach emphasized in rational-expectations models suggests that the choice of an institution or person to set prices would result from optimizing behavior. The problem is that the island paradigm provides no basis for making a choice of this kind. Everyone has the same information about the mean, and everyone knows that the mean is stationary. If we all draw the same balls from the same urn, there is no room for specialized information.

Frank Knight was an early expositor of what might have been called the economics of information. In Knight (1921, pp. 237–263), he argued that discussions about what is to be produced, how much, and when, require a pooling of information about the many individual decisions that, when aggregated, constitute a demand curve. Pooling gives rise to firms (productive units) as an efficient arrangement even in the absence of economies of scale in the production process.

A critical point of Knight's argument is that firms reduce uncertainty for consumers.[11] In principle, people can contract in advance for the goods and services they want, but this happens rarely. Individuals are less certain about the magnitude and timing of their own future purchases than firms are about market demand. Knight appeals to the law of large numbers to explain the firms' advantage (1921, p. 241).

A single firm's ability to reduce uncertainty by pooling differs from insurance. Both depend on grouping, but insurable risks must be measurable and susceptible to prior classification. Firms' (noninsurable) decisions possess a greater degree of uniqueness, according to Knight, so decisions require more use of judgment by the businessman when assigning subjective probabilities and computing expected outcomes. Errors of judgment tend to cancel, but only after the fact. The tendency for errors to cancel is weaker for business decisions than for insurance because groups are less clearly defined and decision makers are active for only a short period. Knight mentions *moral hazard* (1921, p. 251) as one reason why outsiders have difficulty classifying the risks in individual decisions before decisions are taken.

Instead of classifying risks, the market system relies on specialization to reduce uncertainty by concentrating information. Knight discusses several types of specialists, including speculators, entrepreneurs, and managers who centralize information in different ways. Each specialist relies on subjective evaluation of events that are not easily classified into risk distributions.

Knight's discussion lends itself to a view of the business firm as a unit producing or purchasing inventories today for future sale. Or, to put the point in a more contemporary way, production for inventory is a social arrangement that shifts uncertainty from individuals to collective units and, by pooling, reduces the social cost of bearing uncertainty.

Knight's argument for firms is consistent with several different methods of pricing. Consider the pricing of consumer goods. In Oriental bazaars and supermarkets, sellers hold inventories that they resell to final consumers. Prices in the bazaar are negotiated; in the supermarket, prices are posted by the seller. Price setting is not ubiquitous. The problem is to explain which prices are set in advance and which are set in auction markets or in bilateral negotiation. Knight's distinction between risk and uncertainty is useful.

I conjecture that prices are set where costs of acquiring information differ for buyers and sellers. One party to the sale internalizes the cost of gathering and processing information. Reasoning similar to Knight's argument about the advantages firms have in setting future production suggests that it is less costly for firms to acquire the specialized information relevant for pricing products. Once prices are posted, the least cost method for the buyer to acquire information about prices is, periodically, to shop at more than one store.[12]

Compare pricing information at the Oriental bazaar and the supermarket. A trip to two or three supermarkets provides a considerable amount of information about the prices of each of the goods in the buyer's market basket and, simultaneously, comparative information about the relative cost of the buyer's basket if purchased from different sellers. A trip to the Oriental bazaar provides none of this information. Buyer and seller negotiate each price, and there is no way to extract reliable information about prices at other locations or prices of other goods without purchase. Further, the buyer cannot know whether the price he pays is the minimum price at that location. Even after the trade is made, the buyer remains uncertain about the seller's reservation price and must incur relatively large costs to determine whether he is a victim of price discrimination. Moving to the next stall does not give the purchaser an array of prices or comparative costs and provides no information about the reservation price of other suppliers.

Price setting reduces the marginal cost of acquiring information for both buyers and sellers. The supermarket hires purchasing agents who acquire information about prices, thereby converting the cost into a fixed cost and spreading the fixed cost over a large number of units. In a competitive market, this lowers the marginal cost to the buyer of the product.

If the mean of the distribution of prices is invariant, everyone learns the mean value, so the expected price is a common reference point. When there are permanent and transitory changes affecting the level and growth of demand and supply, price setting is a low cost—and perhaps an optimal—method of disseminating information about market conditions. Firms have an economic incentive to set (or announce) prices where they have a comparative advantage in acquiring information relevant for pricing. Posted prices reduce buyers' uncertainty. Where the frequency of price changes is relatively large, and some changes are permanent, demand shifts from sellers that negotiate price to price setters.

We should find price setting as a dominant solution where opportunities for reducing marginal cost differ for buyers and sellers. In markets dominated by professional traders, buyers and sellers have similar costs of acquiring information, so prices are not set in advance. The purchasing agent for the supermarket, in the example, buys some goods in auction markets but sells all goods at preset prices. Retailers of diamond rings buy diamonds in markets where prices are negotiated and sell rings in a set price market. In the market for existing houses, neither buyer nor seller has, uniformly, a lower cost of acquiring information or an opportunity to internalize the cost.[13]

These examples suggest that mechanisms for minimizing the cost of Knightean (or Keynesian) uncertainty become important when we want to predict price and output changes in individual markets. The stochastic structure of current rational-expectations models does not distinguish between risk and uncertainty, and the economic structure does not distinguish price-setting firms from firms that negotiate prices or buy in auction markets. Where these distinctions influence the magnitude and timing of price and output changes, the current generation of rational-expectations models will make larger errors than market analysts who use less explicit models or economists who distinguish transitory and permanent changes.

This conclusion about firms is little more than a restatement of Knight's argument about managers, entrepreneurs, and other people with specialized knowledge or the ability to make better than average decisions under conditions of uncertainty. It is not a general conclusion, however.

Defining rational expectations as the expectations consistent with, or generated from, the best available model sidesteps an important issue. Economists do not use the same structural model for all events. The usual economic model tries to capture the aspects that are considered most relevant to a particular problem. There is a reason to believe that managers and speculators do not differ in this respect from economists.

The less explicit, often idiosyncratic, models that managers or speculators use to classify events and analyze their effects are unlikely to be comprehensive general equilibrium models. When the mean of some distribution changes permanently, their models, like ours, are apt to ignore the information that is outside the (changing) set of events deemed relevant in the past. Generally, this set expands and contracts. Events that are uncertain at one period become more predictable, more readily classified, and more subject to systematic analysis and prediction. For example, at the beginning of an inflation, firms may ignore inflation. Later, many internalize the monitoring cost and learn to predict (or buy forecasts of) inflation.

When large, permanent changes in the mean occur, economists' models have no clearcut advantage over the speculators, managers, or entrepreneurs because the models do not distinguish permanent changes in mean values and deviations around a fixed mean. The disadvantage can be reduced without abandoning rational expectations. However, it is not clear why, whether, or perhaps when economists can be expected to learn faster than entrepreneurs and managers about the proper classification of uncertain events.

Economists may have no particular advantage in treating uncertainty in individual markets, where they compete with specialists and yet have an advantage with respect to aggregates. To realize this advantage more fully requires, at a minimum, the use of rational expectations models that incorporate uncertainty and gradual learning.[14]

Conclusion

I have been asked to write about the role of shocks in relation to economic models, particularly rational expectations models. I have argued that there should be no issue about the use of rational-expectations models in economics. As is often true, the issue is the type of model that is most appropriate.

Economists have not settled on one model with known parameter values. There is no agreement on the specific form of the utility function, or other functions, used in our analyses. Frequently, the professional skills of an economist are best displayed in choosing the model most useful for a particular problem. To speak of rational expectations as expectations consistent with the most reliable model is to ignore or neglect a significant part of an economist's professional role—structuring the problem.

The current generation of rational expectations macro-models ignores uncertainty in the sense of Knight and Keynes. I treat uncertainty as a shift in expected value following a shock to either aggregate demand or aggregate supply and claim that this usage is consistent with Knight's and Keynes's treatment of uncertainty. A simple model of trend distinguishes between risk and uncertainty and illustrates the point.

Most current rational-expectations models treat prices as if set in auction markets. I suggest that the incorporation of uncertainty, and the distinction between permanent and transitory changes, helps to explain the prevalence of types of pricing. Firms set prices under conditions of uncertainty where costs of acquiring information can be internalized, and reduced, by managers and entrepreneurs. Where information is diffuse, or buyers and sellers have similar costs of acquiring information, auction markets are more common.

Economics is not the science that makes highly accurate monthly or quarterly predictions of individual market responses or of aggregates. The distinction between risk and uncertainty, or between permanent and transitory changes in levels and in rates of change, helps to explain why short-term forecasts are subject to errors that often are large relative to the predicted changes. These distinctions seem highly relevant, also, to such frequently discussed issues as the meaning of unemployment, the relation of spot to forward prices, the term structure of interest rates,[15] and the measurement of the social costs of variable economic policies. I have tried, in this chapter to suggest that the distinction is relevant also to price setting, wage setting, and other institutional practices that remain puzzling if we assume that everyone has access to the same information on equal terms.

Notes

1. In Meltzer (1981), I discuss and interpret Keynes's views on expectations more fully.

2. Muth (1960, 1961) showed the conditions under which distributed lags used by Friedman and others gave optimal forecasts.

3. The stochastic process is described in Karl Brunner, Alex Cukierman, and Allan Meltzer (1980) as confusion between persistent and transitory changes. Lucas's (1977) less formal discussion of business cycles relies on this mechanism. A method of estimating the type of change that occurs is developed by Bomhoff (1982).

4. A very similar objection is made by Hirshliefer and Riley (1979), but these authors do not distinguish Knight's (1921) model from Lucas's (1972).

5. Knight also accepted the terms *objective* and *subjective* to refer to the two probabilities, but these terms are now used in different ways, so they are best avoided.

6. Keynes (1979, p. 288) refers to the process of using *equivalent certainties* to make decisions. A modern treatment might reformulate Keynes's *weight* in Bayesian terms and interpret low weight as a diffuse prior.

7. A recent application and extension of this framework by Brunner, Cukierman, and Meltzer (1980) provides a more formal analysis and application of some of the ideas in this section with α constant. Beveridge and Nelson (1981) show that this assumption of constant α cannot be rejected for the United States. It would be interesting to see their method applied elsewhere, for example, in Brazil or Japan.

8. The first difference of equation 1.1 is stationary for constant α, but the level is nonstationary. Equation 1.3 shows that changes in α eventually dominate the forecast of $\Delta \ln X$.

9. The longest expansion during this period, 106 months, is excluded because it includes the Vietnam War.

10. During the Conference on Crises in the Economic and Financial Structure, at New York University, November 1981, I learned that James Ramsey (1980, pp. 17–18) uses a similar argument to explain why some items (oil leases, timber lots, antiques) are sold at auction.

11. Alchian (1969) uses a similar argument to explain the cost of changing prices.

12. If producers learn about new events more quickly than consumers, a Phillips curve relating the rate of inflation to output for given expected output and expected inflation is positively sloped. Producers increase the demand for labor in response to changes in demand before suppliers of labor (consumers) recognize that, at prevailing money wages, real wages will fall as employment increases.

13. The market for automobiles is another market in which prices of final sales are negotiated. The buyer, typically, trades a used car about which he has more information than the seller. Price, net of trade-in, is negotiated. Ramsey (1980, pp. 17–18) gives other examples.

14. Benjamin Friedman (1979) was one of the first to show that gradual learning is not inconsistent with rational expectations.

15. This point is made by Alex Cukierman (1981).

References

Alchian, Armen. 1969. "Information Costs, Pricing, and Resource Unemployment," *Economic Inquiry* 7 (June):109–128. Reprinted as chapter 2 of *Economic Forces at Work*. Indianapolis, 1977.

Arrow, Kenneth. 1978. "The Future and the Present in Economic Life," *Economic Inquiry* 16 (April):157–169.

Beveridge, Stephen and Nelson, Charles R. 1981. "A New Approach to Decomposition of Economic Time Series Into Permanent and Transitory Components with Particular Attention to Measurement of the Business Cycle'." *Journal of Monetary Economics* 7 (March):151–174.

Bomhoff, Eduard J. 1982. "Predicting the Price Level in a World That Changes All The Time." *Carnegie-Rochester Conference Series on Public Policy*. Vol. 17 (Fall):7–56.

Brunner, Karl; Cukierman, Alex, and Meltzer, Allan H. 1980. "Stagflation, Persistent Unemployment, and the Permanence of Economic Shocks," *Journal Monetary Economics* 6 (October):467–492.

Cagan, Phillip. 1965. *Determinants and Effects of Changes in the Stock of Money, 1875-1960*. vol. 13 of Studies in Business Cycles, National Bureau of Economic Research. New York: Columbia University Press.

Cargill, Thomas. 1969. "An Empirical Investigation of the Wage-Lag Hypothesis," *American Economic Review* 59 (December):806–816.

Cukierman, Alex. 1981. "Interest Rates During the Cycle, Inventories and Monetary Policy: A Theoretical Analysis." *Carnegie-Rochester Conference Series on Public Policy*. Vol. 15 (Autumn):87–144.

Dunlop, John T. 1938. "The Movement of Real and Money Wage Rates," *Economic Journal* 48 (September):413–434.

Fischer, Stanley. 1977. "Long-Term Contracts, Rational Expectations, and the Optimal Money Supply Rule," *Journal Political Economy* 85 (February):191–205.

Friedman, Benjamin. 1979. "Optimal Expectations and the Extreme Information Assumptions of 'Rational Expectations' Macromodels," *Journal Monetary Economics* 5 (January):23–42.

Friedman, Milton. 1957. *A Theory of the Consumption Function.* Princeton: Princeton University Press.

Hirshliefer, J. and Riley, John G. 1979. "The Analytics of Uncertainty and Information—An Expository Survey," *Journal of Economic Literature* 17 (December):1375–1421.

Kantor, Brian. 1979. "Rational Expectations and Economic Thought," *Journal Economic Literature* 17 (December)1422–1441.

Kessel, R.A. and Alchian, A.A. 1950. "The Meaning and Validity of the Inflation—Induced Lag of Wages Behind Prices," *American Economic Reveiw* 50 (March):43–66.

Keynes, John Maynard. 1921. *A Treatise on Probability.* London: Macmillan.

———. 1936. *The General Theory of Employment, Interest and Money.* London: Macmillan.

———. 1973. *The General Theory and After. Part 2: Defense and Development.* vol. 14 of *The Collected Writings.* Donald Moggridge, ed. New York: St. Martins Press; for the Royal Economic Society.

———. 1979. *The General Theory and After: A Supplement.* vol. 29 of *The Collected Writings.* Donald Moggridge, ed. Cambridge and New York: Cambridge University Press.

Knight, Frank H. 1921. *Risk, Uncertainty, and Profit.* Boston: No. 16 in Series of Reprints of Scarce Tracts in Economics. London School of Economics (1933).

Lucas, Robert E., Jr. 1972. "Expectations and the Neutrality of Money." *Journal Economic Theory* 4 (April):103–124.

———. 1977. "Understanding Business Cycles," *Carnegie-Rochester Conference Series on Public Policy.* vol. 5:7–19.

———. 1980. "Methods and Problems in Business Cycle Theory," *Journal Money, Credit and Banking* 12 (November, part 2):696–715.

McCallum, Bennett T. 1980. "Rational Expectations and Macroeconomics Stabilization Policy: An Overview," *Journal Money, Credit and Banking* 12 (November, part 2):716–746.

Meltzer, Allan H. 1981. "Keynes's General Theory: A Different Perspective," *Journal of Economic Literature* 19 (March):34–64.

Muth, John F. 1960. "Optimal Properties of Exponentially Weighted Forecasts," *Journal American Statistical Association* 55 (June):229–306.

———. 1961. "Rational Expectations and the Theory of Price Movements," *Econometrica* 23 (July):315–335.

Phelps, Edmund S., et al. 1970. *Microeconomic Foundations of Employment and Inflation Theory.* New York: Norton.

Phelps, Edmund S. and Taylor, John B. 1977. "Stabilizing Properties of Monetary Policy under Rational Expectations," *Journal Political Economics* 84 (February):163–190.

Ramsey, James. 1980. *Bidding and Oil Leases.* Greenwich: JAI Press.

Samuelson, Paul A. 1958. "An Exact Consumption-Loan Model of Interest with or without the Social Contrivance of Money," *Journal Political Economy* 66 (December):467–482.

Tarshis, Lorie. 1939. "Changes in Real and Money Wages," *Economic Journal* 49 (March):150–154.

Tobin, James. 1980. "Are New Classical Models Plausible Enough to Guide Policy," *Journal Money, Credit and Banking* 12 (November, part 2):788–799.

2

Monetary Innovation and Crises in American Economic History

Richard Sylla

The atmosphere of economic and financial crisis that has developed during the past fifteen or so years is one in which old truths have been questioned and discarded but few new truths have been discovered and accepted. This is certainly the case with respect to the subject of money. Two decades ago the dominant Keynesian influences were such that economists and policy-makers did not pay much attention to money. Milton Friedman and his then small group of monetarist followers were viewed as a fringe group who dealt with relatively unimportant questions. This view retreated as the monetarists demonstrated the power of their analyses in explaining historical inflations, deflations, crises, and depressions, as well as in accounting rather well for the renewed outbreak of inflation during and after the Vietnam War. The monetarists' new truth, namely, that the control or eradication of inflation depended upon controlling the money supply, gained widespread acceptance in the academic and financial communities. By October 1979, it appeared finally to have gained acceptance even at the all-important policy-making level of the Federal Reserve System.

Just as monetarism reached its moment of practical triumph, however, there arose a new and rather disturbing question. What is this animal, the money supply, that is to be controlled? Early in 1981 the *Wall Street Journal* published a bar graph indicating that in 1980 M-1A grew 4.2 percent; M-1B, 6.4 percent; the monetary base, 8.2 percent; M-2, 9.6 percent; M-3, 10.1 percent; and currency, 11.6 percent.[1] The *Journal's* caption read, "Will the Real Money Supply Please Stand Up?" (It probably should have read, "Will the *Nominal* Money Supply Please Stand Up?"—which illustrates how confusing these matters can become.) Others have registered similar concerns about the Fed's or any other institution's ability to control

For helpful comments on an earlier version of this chapter I would like to thank Michael Bordo, Martin Bronfenbrenner, Rondo Cameron, John Dutton, Stuart Greenbaum, Thomas Huertas, John James, William Parker, Anna Schwartz, Peter Temin, Paul Wachtel, and participants in seminars or workshops at Chicago, Columbia, North Carolina State, and Northwestern universities, and Research Triangle Park, North Carolina. Financial support from the National Endowment for the Humanities also is gratefully acknowledged. Parts of this chapter appear in a shorter piece, "Monetary Innovation in America," *Journal of Economic History* 42 (March 1982). Albert Gailord Hart, William L. Silber, and Thomas Mayer made valuable comments on the contents of this chapter at the Conference on Crises In the Economic and Financial Structure at New York University. I would like to thank them, too.

the supply of money when no one knows what money is. Nothing contributes more to a continuing atmosphere of crisis than a realization that the accepted solution to a critical problem has turned out to be an illusion.

The simple notion that the problem of inflation can be solved by controlling the money supply has been confounded by monetary innovation, that is, by the creation of new forms of money. Not long ago economists argued whether the correct definition of money was M-1, currency plus checking accounts, or M-2, which consisted of M-1 plus savings or time deposits at commercial banks. Shortly after 1960 the appearance of large negotiable CDs (certificates of deposit) led to a new definition of M-2 that excluded them, but the debate between adherents of M-1 and the revised M-2 continued as before. How quaint that debate now seems. Today a variety of thrift institutions as well as commercial banks offer checking accounts that pay interest, and one also can write checks on margin accounts at brokerage houses, on some CDs, and on money market mutual funds. The debate about what money is has become correspondingly complex. It involves such thorny if not intractable issues as how much of new assets (for example, money market fund shares) should be treated as money, and whether other assets (for example, government debt) ought also to be considered as money. On a higher level, the debate concerns the question of whether money, however defined, can be controlled if—as seems to be the case—many of the new forms of money are not subject to reserve requirements and other regulations of the monetary authority.

Confusing as the current monetary situation seems to be, it is not without precedents. Indeed, monetary innovation has been an ongoing phenomenon in the United States since the days of first settlement. By examining the historical record of monetary innovation we can gain perspective on the problems of our own day, and we can begin to understand the forces that caused new forms of money to appear. Although some of these forces were of a long-term and persistent nature, crises often underscored the limitations of existing moneys and led both to monetary innovation and to attempts to restrict or control it.

A Framework for Analyzing Monetary Innovation

Through the ages up to and including the discovery and settlement of North America by Europeans, money consisted for the most part of the precious metals, gold and silver. Let us suppose that this customary practice had continued to the present, with other economic developments occurring as they did. That is, we shall assume (1) that populations and labor forces grew at their high modern rates, (2) that production of goods and services per person and per worker also grew at the sustained high rates of recent centuries,

(3) that specialization and roundabout production processes increased inter-mediate transactions relative to final goods transactions, (4) that the share of all goods and services sold in markets (that is, market exchange) grew in relation to total production, (5) that the accumulation of wealth increased the asset demand for money, and (6) that the scope of governments and their need for money revenues grew in relation to total production. Under these assumptions there would occur an unprecedented increase in the long-run demand for money as both a means of exchange and a store of wealth.

If at the same time gold and silver had continued to be the only recog-nized and accepted forms of money, we might predict with some confidence that these metals, relatively inelastic in supply compared to other goods and services, would have increased in value in the long run, or, in other words, that there would have been a great deflation of goods and services prices. The great deflation, however, would have been anything but steady and pre-dictable during the series of short runs in which people live and make economic decisions. If history is any guide, the real-sector developments listed above would not have been steady and predictable, nor would discoveries of new sources of the precious metals and new techniques for their production. Our hypothetical world, in short, would have nearly all the forces of economic instability that actually existed in modern history in addition to whatever added instability would have resulted from protracted but (in the short run) unpredictable price deflation. The metallic moneys, moreover, would become increasingly costly over time in terms of the real resources required to produce or pay for additional units.

One supposes that persons interested in maximizing utility would find some way or ways to get around or even abandon the customary regulation that made gold and silver the only acceptable moneys. Adherence to that regulation would increase instability and constrain growth and development to lower levels than would be possible under alternate arrangements. Monetary innovation is the response to this challenge. Its primary purpose is to remove the constraints on real economic development that are implicit in an existing set of monetary arrangements and regulations.[2] In the language of economists, the innovation of new forms of money, like money itself, can increase utility by reducing the costs of exchanging real goods and services in a world of specialization and uncertainty.[3]

Like other types of innovation, however, monetary innovation may have an unpleasant side. Suppose the innovation is overdone and too much money is created after old constraints are removed. The result would be price-level inflation with added economic instabilities and negative exter-nalities as newly created moneys reduced the value of existing stocks. In such circumstances monetary innovation creates a demand for new regula-tions to control its unpleasant side effects. When the new regulations are put in place they become the next generation's constraints; eventually they may lead to more monetary innovation. The story of monetary innovation is therefore one of the interaction of constraints on real development implicit in an existing monetary system and the regulations that society designs to avoid the negative effects of excessive money creation.

The concept of monetary innovation developed here fits rather well into theories of financial innovation developed in recent years by a number of economists. One such theory is that financial innovation is a response to regulation.[4] For example, interest rate ceilings on thrift deposits in an environment where free market interest rates have moved far above the regulated ceilings led to the innovation of the money market mutual fund. But, as William L. Silber has rightly argued, government regulations are only one set of constraints under which financial units operate.[5] There are also, Silber argues, self-imposed constraints and market constraints on financial behavior. Silber's analysis of financial innovation is thus more general than the regulatory theory, but in dealing only with private firms and the constraints they face, Silber's theory is also less general than a theory of monetary innovation has to be. For in history, governments and even whole societies as well as individual firms have been monetary innovators. Thus, a theory of monetary innovation in one sense may be thought of as a subset of existing theories of financial innovation, but in another sense it needs to be broader than those theories.[6] A first step toward such a theory is understanding the historical record of monetary innovation and the role of crises therein.

The American Experience

The Colonial Era

One would be hard pressed to find a place and time in which there was more monetary innovation than in the British North American colonies in the century and a half before the American Revolution. Whatever English money the colonists brought with them or gained in other ways was returned to the mother country almost as quickly as it came in. The colonists therefore turned to an ingenious variety of experiments to provide local media of exchange. These experiments are quite well known to economic historians. One was the adoption of wampum, the token shell money of the native Indians. Commodity moneys—corn, rice, tobacco, and beaver pelts, for example—were also granted monetary status. Precious metallic moneys gained mostly from trade with Spanish America circulated in the colonies, and some attempts were made to provide local coinages from inflows of bullion. Extensive use of so-called book credit has also been documented.

The most notable achievement, however, was the innovation of the first fiat paper moneys in the western world.

Why did all this monetary innovation take place on a periphery far removed from the heart of western civilization? Explanations are varied. A common one is that an unfavorable balance of trade drained specie from the colonies and necessitated a search for money substitutes. British regulations may have compounded the problem, especially when they forbade both the export of specie from Britain and the establishment of mints in the colonies. Nineteenth-and twentieth-century writers of "sound money" persuasions were convinced that the colonial schemes were a means by which some factions in society (debtors) set out to deprive others (creditors) of their property. Still others, beginning in the 1930s, saw the colonial experiments as precursors of Keynesian measures to overcome depressions and stimulate trade. Another hypothesis, of more recent vintage but rooted in eighteenth-century rhetoric, is that an aversion to taxes led to paper currency finance by colonial governments, which also had to finance numerous wars against the French and the Indians.

These explanations carry varying degrees of validity, but it seems to me that they miss the essential point. The British North American colonies in all likelihood had the most rapidly growing economy in the world of the seventeenth and eighteenth centuries. Population growth rates of 3 to 4 percent per year probably set a lower bound to the rate of growth of total production. There may have been some small, premodern gains in product per person or per worker as well. No doubt there was a modest increase both in specialization and in market exchange relative to the growth of total product. And the growing financial requirements of colonial governments in fact were closely connected with monetary innovation. Only one of the previously set forth reasons that would lead us to expect a growing demand for money did not seem to have been present to an extraordinary degree in the colonies, namely, the use of money as an asset to hold, and that may be a mere illusion since silver coin and bullion were routinely converted to plate by colonial silversmiths.[7]

In short, although the colonial North American economy was premodern in the sense that product per capita did not grow at the high rates that characterize modern economies, it was decidedly modern in its overall rate of economic growth. The traditional moneys, gold and silver, were either unavailable or available in insufficient amounts to sustain this growth, and more generally, colonial economic development. The innovation of new forms of money was the solution to a persistent problem of colonial life.

If the demand-induced innovation thesis is correct, one would expect the most rapidly growing colonies to be the most innovative. This seems to have been the case. Massachusetts was the second largest colony in population and perhaps the most developed of all the colonies in a commercial sense. Massachusetts made corn a legal tender in 1631, a practice that other colonies subsequently put into effect for different commodities.[8] Massachusetts also made wampum legal tender in 1643 and was again followed by others. Neither innovation, however, was a satisfactory solution. Debtors would pay with inferior qualities of "eligible" commodities, and an officially rated monetary status for commodities also led to overproduction, in the sense that market prices fell below official ratings. Wampum, moreover, was "counterfeited" with bones and stones. So Massachusetts established a mint in 1652 for the purpose of coining silver; the pine tree shilling was the most famous coin.[9] This solution apparently worked because the colony ended the legal-tender status of wampum in 1661. In 1684, however, regulation reared its ugly head; the crown ordered the mint to be shut down because it violated the royal prerogative of coinage.[10] Six years later, in 1690, Massachusetts came forth with the innovation of bills of credit, which quickly evolved into a fiat paper currency.

The Massachusetts bills of credit of 1690 were born of a genuine political-economic crisis. During King William's War the Bay Colony had sent a military expedition against the French in Quebec and had assumed that it would be both successful and self-financing, the soldiers to be paid out of the captured enemy treasure. Instead the expedition failed and the soldiers returned to Boston empty-handed, demanding to be paid their wages and threatening mutiny if they were not. The colony's treasury was empty and there was no time to levy and collect a tax to pay the wages due the soldiers. So the colony printed bills of credit in small denominations and discharged its obligation to the soldiers. Initially the bills—like most true innovations—were met by skepticism and were sold at a discount. But when future taxes were promised for their redemption and a provision was enacted in 1691 for receiving the bills at a modest premium in payments due the government, they became "better than money."[11] Very soon—and very interestingly—there was little demand for redemption or retirement of the bills. Instead, the Massachusetts bills of credit functioned as money and the colonial authorities discovered that they could go on issuing new bills and rolling over older issues to meet the ordinary expenses of government.

Massachusetts's notable innovation, providing as it did solutions both to the recurring short-run crisis of government finance that plagued colonial governments and to the long-run problem of providing an adequate money supply for a rapidly growing economy, was widely copied. Students of the diffusion of innovations sometimes plot logistic diffusion curves showing the penetration of innovations—their share of the market, so to speak—as a function of time. One can almost visualize such a curve as the Bay Colony's bills were emulated by South Carolina (in 1703), New Hampshire, Connecticut, New York, New Jersey (all in 1709), Rhode Island (1710), North Carolina (1712), Pennsylvania (1723), and Maryland (1733). The remaining three mainland colonies eventually made use of the technique. A closely related innovation was the *loan office* (or *land bank* or *loan bank,* as it is sometimes called). Colonial governments organized these banks to lend bills to individual borrowers with land as security. South Carolina led the way in 1712, followed by Massachusetts (in 1714), Rhode Island (1715), New Hampshire (1717), Pennsylvania and Delaware (1723), New Jersey (1724), North Carolina (1729), Connecticut and Maryland (1733), New York (1737), and Georgia (1755).

Only Virginia did not establish a loan office, and its first bills of credit did not come until 1755. This fact might seem to raise a question about the demand-induced monetary innovation hypothesis, since Virginia was the largest colony in population and perhaps also the wealthiest. Virginia, however, was primarily a plantation economy oriented toward overseas export markets and possibly had less internal commerce than other, smaller colonies. Moreover, Virginia had innovated and perfected its own currency based on tobacco. Tobacco as money had the defects of similar commodity moneys, but many of them eventually were mitigated by the establishment of warehouses that graded the commodity and issued transferable tobacco notes.[12] These served the same purposes in Virginia (and later Maryland) that bills of credit and loan office bills did in other colonies.   .

All in all, the colonial North American experience appears to be a near perfect example of monetary innovation in practice. The results, we know, were sometimes quite inflationary, especially in New England during the 1730s and 1740s. This side effect of monetary innovation is in no way surprising; monetary innovations may have as many unpleasant side effects as other innovations. What is surprising is that the inflationary side effects of colonial monetary innovations have received disproportionate attention from historians. The beneficial effects—the removal of what otherwise would have been most serious constraints on colonial economic growth and development—are often downplayed or ignored. Colonial monetary innovation was a rational, purposive activity motivated by perceived economic opportunities and directed toward utility maximization.

The rationality of colonial monetary innovation was insufficiently appreciated by many contemporary and later observers because the innovations often seemed to be stopgap measures carried out in times of crisis. The century before the American Revolution was marked by numerous wars as the English, the French, and the Spanish contested one another for control of North America. In other words, there were recurrent political crises that necessitated answers to the age-old question of how to pay for the war. The existence of these crises may explain why almost all colonial monetary innovation was carried out by governments rather than by private enterprise. But the political factor cannot provide the whole explanation of public versus private monetary innovation because in the middle colonies of New

York, New Jersey, Pennsylvania, Delaware, and Maryland, as Richard Lester has shown, the colonial governments first issued paper money to combat economic depressions, not to combat foreign enemies.[13] In these activities, Lester demonstrated, the governments of middle colonies were very successful; their paper money issues generated a half-century of relatively noninflationary economic growth before 1776. This experience and the absence of privately issued moneys suggests that in the colonial era governments had a comparative advantage over private enterprise in monetary innovation.

The worst inflationary excesses came in New England and the South, which were the flank regions most exposed to territorial conflicts with the French and the Spanish. During King George's War, for example, Massachusetts bills of credit outstanding increased from £300 thousand in 1744 to £2.1 million in 1748; by 1749 the price of silver measured in bills was double what it had been in 1743.[14] This war-related experience provoked reaction both within New England and in Parliament, and it provided countless later writers with their prime example of the dangers of paper money and the folly of colonial monetary practices. In point of fact, however, the Massachusetts inflation during King George's War was about the same as the later inflations of the Civil War and World Wars I and II, all of which had a similar duration.

In the 1740s, however, such inflationary excesses were new and shocking. The British Parliament reacted by passing the Currency Act of 1751, which placed stringent limitations on fiat paper money issues in New England. In 1764 another Currency Act extended the limitations to the rest of the colonies. The colonists protested against these British interferences with their longtime monetary practices and secured some relaxation of the regulations before the Revolutionary crisis of the 1770s.

During that crisis, the great colonial innovation of fiat paper currency was carried to its illogical conclusion. The Continental Congress, within a week of the battle of Bunker Hill in 1775, authorized an issue of $2 million in Continental bills of credit. From then until the end of 1779, forty more issues amounting in all to $241.6 million of *Continentals* were authorized by the Congress, while at the same time loan certificates and state paper money issues added to the stock of money. By the beginning of 1780, Continental bills had depreciated to one-fortieth of their nominal value in relation to specie; a year later they were worth one-hundredth part of their nominal specie value, and soon thereafter they were essentially worthless.

The Specie Standard and State Banking, 1781-1863

Americans of the Revolutionary era did become suspicious of fiat paper money, but it was not the excesses of the colonial era that turned attitudes. Rather it was the obviously excessive paper issues during the War of Independence. The founding fathers were anxious to prevent the possibility of repetition of this chastening experience, a possibility that became very real in the 1780s as some of the newly independent states began to issue more paper money to alleviate the postwar depression. To do so, they introduced to America a time-honored European custom, the specie standard. The Constitution of 1787 declared that thenceforth gold and silver were the only legal tenders and that no state was ever again to issue fiat paper money. These constitutional provisions, especially the specie standard, were the most important monetary regulations of the United States for well over a century. They were very much in the spirit of the Currency Acts of 1751 and 1764, although made in Philadelphia rather than in London.

The specie standard reintroduced a constraint on development that colonial Americans had largely abandoned. It proved less than onerous, however, because at the same time it was adopted as a U.S. policy Americans also adopted the European innovation of modern commercial banking. Although states could no longer create paper money, they could create banks that in turn created liabilities in the form of notes and deposits serving the same purposes. The innovation of banking diffused itself quite rapidly in the early United States, and it seems everywhere to have followed a pattern that would be predicted by the thesis of demand-induced monetary innovation. That is, it appeared first and developed to its greatest extent in the most rapidly growing and developing state economies—Pennsylvania, New York, and Massachusetts—and then spread to other states.

Despite its popularity in the more progressive states, the banking innovation met with a great deal of resistance. This resistance was based on both principle and interest. Principled Jeffersonian agrarians—John Taylor of Caroline provides a leading example—argued that banks chartered by governments were bastions of privilege that violated the intent of the framers of the Constitution and undermined the ideal of a simple agrarian republic.[15] To an extent—and this is where self-interest enters—the agrarians were correct because existing chartered banks attempted to preserve and increase their monopoly power by attempting to prevent new banks from being chartered and by seeking to stamp out the "unauthorized" competition of unincorporated private bankers and other private issuers of money.

The resistance to banking enjoyed some successes and in the process it provoked a number of crisis and monetary innovations. One such crisis on a national scale occurred during the War of 1812. Just before the War, in 1811, the Bank of the United States—Alexander Hamilton's 1791 brainchild modeled on the Bank of England—went out of existence because the men of principle thought it unconstitutional and the men of interest—the state-chartered bankers—disliked its competition. Without the Bank to provide it with loans and facing a military crisis that threatened the republic, the federal government had little choice but to turn to monetary innovation. Beginning in 1812, it issued short-term (one-year), interest-bearing treasury notes that were made a legal tender currency for all government transactions; as such the treasury notes were an ideal form of bank reserves and by 1816 they amounted to about 75 percent of the monetary base.[16] Outside of New England, the nation's banks suspended specie payments, for which they were roundly blamed even though it was the government's treasury-note innovation that drained the banks of their specie. From 1816 to 1818 the treasury notes were retired in a deliberate attempt to deflate and resume specie payments; that end was accomplished but at the cost of depression and, in 1819, financial panic. An important lesson had been learned: in a crisis the federal government could and would print whatever money it needed, even if it were disguised as treasury-note debt, and the specie standard could and would be abandoned.

Crises of similar nature, albeit on a smaller scale, were faced in the early nineteenth century by those states whose short-sighted laws and regulations had made it difficult or impossible for state-chartered banking facilities to be put into place. Without an adequate supply of money the economic development of these states would have lagged. But private, unsanctioned money issuers filled the void that antibank regulatory zeal tried to create. In state after state unincorporated bankers, who by law were forbidden to issue bank notes, innovated engraved "certificates of deposit," "checks," and "drafts" in round denominations as low as one dollar.[17] Further, acute shortages of small-denomination notes and minor coin were alleviated by numerous varieties of tokens and scrip issued both by county and municipal governments and by private "nonfinancial" enterprises such as transportation companies.[18] The record of monetary innovation by Americans in the early and middle decades of the nineteenth century, though long ignored, is shown by recent research to have been every bit as rich as it was in the colonial period. Around midcentury the adoption by most states of so-called free banking laws (laws that removed earlier restrictions on bank chartering) and the provision by the federal government of an adequate coinage removed the need for these diverse monetary innovations. Today they are being rediscovered and reinterpreted by economic historians. The innovations indicate that individuals and communities, like the federal government itself, would find ways to provide whatever money they needed in spite of specie standards and restrictive banking laws.

The Civil War and National Banking (1860–1914)

The Civil War was the greatest political crisis of U.S. history, and the financial crisis that accompanied it led to extensive monetary innovation. The U.S. notes or *greenbacks* that began to be printed in 1862 are the best-known example. These were an innovation of degree rather than of kind. In the War of 1812 (and again after the Panic of 1837 as well as during the Mexican War) the federal government resorted to issuing treasury notes, which in fact were money (although disguised as short-term debt) and were, for denominational reasons, held mainly by banks as reserves rather than by the public as currency. The greenbacks dispensed with these disguises. They were issued in small denominations and were made legal tender for all private transactions. Repeated issues of greenbacks and other lesser monetary innovations more than doubled the 1860 price level by 1864. The specie standard—then a de facto gold standard—was, of course, suspended from 1862 until 1879.

The second major monetary innovation of the Civil War crisis was the National Banking System with its national bank note currency. This was an attempt to enact free banking on a national scale and to furnish the country with a uniform bank note currency backed (conveniently for purposes of war finance) by U.S. government bonds.

In a practical sense the Civil War innovations of greenbacks and national bank notes ended the gold standard in the United States for good (and not just until "resumption" in 1879). Believers in the mythical powers of the gold standard would dispute this contention, but in point of fact the greenbacks and the national bank notes became part of the U.S. monetary base during the war and they remained there both before and after 1879. Moreover, after these innovations were made, the American public—when it worried about the convertibility of privately produced bank money into real money—did not worry about converting bank deposits into gold but rather into these new forms of paper base money. With one or two brief exceptions the public after the Civil War did not exhibit any strong desire even in the crises surrounding financial panics to convert the new forms of paper currency into gold.

Although the gold standard thus became more a symbol than a reality in the postbellum United States, an almost mythological attachment to it prevented what otherwise might have become positive results of the Civil War paper innovations. This attachment manifested itself in policies that froze the level of greenbacks outstanding and failed to provide adequate incentives for a steady expansion of national bank notes as the U.S. economy grew to industrial maturity in the postbellum decades. The short-run consequences of these policy failures were recurrent financial panics (1873, 1884, 1893, and 1907) resulting from inadequate supplies of base money (paper or gold) into which bank money could be converted. The long-run consequence was price-level deflation from 1864 to 1897.[19]

Solutions to these problems were proposed by the greenback movement, which called for an expansion of U.S. notes, and by the silver forces, who wanted the shiny metal—then abundant in supply—to be freely coined into dollars of the traditional weight even though (or perhaps because) the market price of that weight of silver had fallen well below one dollar. These proposals for adding to the monetary base were dismissed—in a period of deflation—as being inflationary. They represent perhaps the only example from U.S. history in which a widespread and protracted demand for monetary innovation, or at least an extension of it, was largely frustrated. Such was the power of gold a century ago.

A partial solution to the long-run problem of a monetary base that grew too slowly came in 1900 when greater incentives were given to national bank note expansion.[20] A partial solution to the short-run problem of convertibility came in 1908 (in response to the 1907 panic) when the Aldrich Vreeland Act provided for emergency currency issues to be taken out by banks to stem convertibility panics by paying off the panicky depositors.[21] These solutions were adaptive responses to problems caused by the regulatory spirit of the gold standard long after it, riddled by monetary innovation, had ceased in practice to operate. Available evidence indicates that gold did not constitute so much as one-half of the U.S. monetary base at any time between 1863 and 1913, whereas in 1860 gold was all of the base.[22]

Saddled with an inflexible, if not exactly gold, standard, postbellum Americans relied on the further diffusion of the banking innovation to do most of the work in providing the money demanded by real growth and development. Between 1867 and 1913, according to the data of Milton Friedman and Anna Schwartz, the U.S. money stock expanded 11.7-fold, while the monetary base increased only 2.6 times.[23]

The diffusion of banking, remarkable as it was, was hindered in the late nineteenth century by regulation. The National Banking System, a Civil War innovation, was intended to become *the* U.S. banking system, but the new banking laws and regulations put so many production constraints on national banks (and also state banks) that banking development was retarded in large parts of the country. In this atmosphere of regulatory constraints, private, unincorporated banks flourished even more than they did before 1860. And when the states, toward the end of the century, relaxed some of their own regulatory constraints on banks, the state systems surpassed in a number of respects the national system that had been intended to replace them.[24] The result was a dual system made up of thousands of independent banks. Restrictive banking regulation joined with an inflexible monetary standard and rapid real development to produce the secular deflation of the late nineteenth century.

The Federal Reserve Era (1914–present)

What was called the problem of banking reform before 1914 essentially involved the search for a way quickly to expand the monetary base during incipient financial panics to prevent banks and bank money from being destroyed, with deleterious economic consequences. Hardly anyone at the time, despite the alleged gold standard, thought that the solution lay in accumulating large stocks of gold. Paper currency was what panicky bank depositors wanted, and there were various ways in which it could be supplied from the types of paper-treasury issues and national bank notes already in existence. The Aldrich-Vreeland Act represented a variant of this solution, but it was temporary and by the time it could be tried (in the incipient panic at the outbreak of World War I) it had already been superseded by a more permanent solution.[25] This permanent solution, the Federal Reserve System, illustrates the American penchant for monetary innovation: it represented a new institution and a new form of money at a time when existing institutions and forms of money might just as well have been extended to solve the problem of banking panics.

In a sense, the Fed was only an innovation in the U.S. context. Many other countries possessed central banks by 1914, and the theory of central banking had been widely understood since the 1870s. The innovative nature of the Fed was not so much in its being a solution to the short-run problem of panics as in its long-run implications, which were not fully understood in 1914. The Fed's power to create new money with the stroke of a pen meant that in principle the old problem of economic development being constrained by inadequate provision for monetary growth within existing arrangements had been overcome. In practice, as we know, monetary constraints on economic growth have not been the serious problem in the twentieth century that they were in earlier times. Indeed, a lack of restraint on money creation has become a new problem, and to it new solutions such as monetary rules—lineal descendents of the Currency Acts of 1750 and 1764 as well as of the old gold standard—are today proposed.

Monetarist historians are fond of attributing the U.S. inflationary trends of this century to the Fed. Armed with better data than exists for earlier centuries, they make a good case. But from the perspective of monetary innovation I would argue that this is only part of the story. Some of the long-term real forces that historically generated a growing demand for money no longer are as strong as they were in the American past. Population and labor force growth, for example, are not what they once were. The impetus to money demand that came from increased specialization, intermediate transactions, and market exchange is less than before, largely because a developed economy has approached saturation levels on these fronts. Modern technology and business organization may even have reversed some of these trends; business historians, for example, argue that more and more important economic activities that once were coordinated by markets and monetary transactions are now internalized within large corporations. Such developments serve to moderate the growth of demand for money. Perhaps the recently discovered and much lamented decline in productivity growth, if it is a long-term phenomenon, also belongs in this category.

On the other hand, one historical factor that generated increased monetary demand is much greater today than before. This element is the demand coming from government, which seems unable to raise all of the revenue it needs through taxation and thus resorts to deficits financed by money creation. Such a practice need not be inflationary, as is demonstrated by some of the colonial experience with currency finance. In twentieth-century circumstances, however, it has led to inflation.

Although most of the real demand forces that historically induced monetary innovation may have tapered off in our era (which has also witnessed the removal of older supply constraints such as specie standards), monetary innovation nonetheless proceeds. The economic crisis of the Great Depression has played a major role in stimulating monetary innovation to the present day. Although today many would argue that the Federal Reserve failed fundamentally to do its duty, in the 1930s the nation's banks were blamed for causing the Great Depression and all sorts of new regulations were placed on them.[26] A pre-Depression innovation in banking, the multifunction banking firm that ventured into investment and real-estate banking in addition to traditional commercial activities, was stopped in its tracks by new regulations. More rigid controls were placed on bank entry, and more examination and supervision of existing banks by old and new public authorities was introduced. The payment of interest on bank deposits became regulated, and a national system of deposit insurance was put in place. The net impact of these and other Depression-engendered regulations was to reduce the ability of the banking system to innovate and compete in the money and capital markets. As a result nonbank financial institutions gained competitive ground on the banking system by innovating new *near moneys*. (How near to the real thing near money becomes when one can write checks on a variety of thrift accounts, margin accounts at investment brokerage houses, certificates of deposits, and money market funds!) The banks, of course, have not entirely been left behind in the recent wave of monetary innovation.

These more recent forms of monetary innovation have resulted from regulation rather than the demands of real economic development. They are somewhat wasteful—even when they improve an existing situation—because modern regulation itself absorbs substantial resources and causes still more resources to go into the innovative efforts that are made to get around the regulations. In contrast, the demand-induced monetary innovations of past history were innovations that augmented both resources and the efficiency of their use. It is something of a paradox that Americans of this century, who have come so close to making monetary innovation unnecessary for purposes of sustaining their further economic development, should give the innovative process such great and unneeded incentives through regulation. Such regulatory developments, of course, always have been a part of the history of monetary innovations.

Conclusion

Monetary innovation deserves more study. Its historical benefits and costs are as worthy of attention as the benefits and costs of technological changes in the real sector. Monetary innovation also has theoretical and policy implications. Is the money supply determined exogenously? To what extent can money be regulated and controlled by a monetary authority or a monetary standard? The answers to these questions from history remain far from clear.

What history does make clear is that because money provides so much utility in an exchange economy, individuals, business enterprises, governments, and even whole societies will go to very great lengths to provide themselves with adequate supplies of it. In nearly every era of U.S. history the prevailing monetary system—either because of inherent limitations (specie standards) or excessive regulations designed to protect vested interests or to prevent inflation–proved incapable of meeting the demands placed upon it. The result was monetary innovation. Although crises of various kinds—political, economic, financial—often triggered the monetary innovations that one observes in the historical record, the most persistent long-term force behind these innovations has been the unparalleled economic growth of the last two to three centuries. Today we understand the contributions of money to a healthy, growing economy much more than in the past, and our current monetary system is in most respects superior to those that preceded it. Nonetheless, since our current atmosphere of crisis has parallels with the 1690s, the 1780s, the 1860s, and the 1930s, I doubt that we have seen the last chapter in the history of monetary innovation.

Notes

1. *Wall Street Journal,* January 22, 1981, p. 50.

2. In discussion, Albert Gailord Hart expressed reservation about the use of the word *purpose* here. His point is well taken. Perhaps I should have used the word *function* in place of purpose to avoid possible confusion. But I will not plead guilty to Hart's charge that I here am "letting *historical explanation* rear its ugly head." In my view, I was using *purpose* in the same way that Adam Smith used its synonym, *end,* in the celebrated economic theoretical (not historical) passage from the *Wealth of Nations* about the

individual who was "led by an invisible hand to promote an *end* which was no part of his intention" (italics added). That actions often promote ends that were not a part of the actors' purposes is, in fact, a characteristic that economic theory shares with historical interpretation.

3. For analysis of the utility of money, see Karl Brunner and Allan H. Meltzer, "The Uses of Money: Money in the Theory of an Exchange Economy," *American Economic Review* 61 (December 1971):784–805.

4. See S.I. Greenbaum and C.F. Haywood, "Secular Changes in the Financial Services Industry," *Journal of Money, Credit and Banking,* 3 (May 1981), part 2, pp. 555–603.

5. William L. Silber, "Towards a Theory of Financial Innovation," in Silber, ed., *Financial Innovation* (Lexington, Mass: D.C. Heath, Lexington Books, 1975), pp. 53–86.

6. In discussing my work William L. Silber expressed the view that a framework of innovation induced by constraint(s) is broad enough for analysis of monetary innovations provided that we extend it to deal with the questions of when and how innovative actions of a collective nature will be taken. In particular, Silber emphasized that innovation might result when the constraints of existing monetary arrangements generate rising costs that are jointly and simultaneously experienced by the members of a group. Silber raised the question of whether such a group would be private or public (that is, governmental), and suggested that the answer might depend upon the relative costs of forming private or public coalitions to carry out the innovation. These insights are valuable, and Silber's example of the innovation of the clearing house loan certificate by U.S. bankers in the latter decades of the nineteenth century is particularly apt because it was a private-group innovation that subsequently was replaced by governmental innovations (the Aldrich-Vreeland Act's emergeny currency issues and, of course, the Federal Reserve System as a lender of last resort). See my further discussion in note 21.

7. Alice Hanson Jones, in her recent book, *Wealth of a Nation to Be* (New York: Columbia University Press, 1980), ch. 5, shows that financial assets of the colonists circa 1774 were quite small in relation to their real assets and also that "cash," which includes precious metals in monetary forms, was a small part of financial assets. But silversmithing was very common in the colonies, and it has been suggested recently that conversion of silver coin to plate, which could be marked and easily identified, was a method of wealthholding that minimized risks of theft. See James A. Mulholland, *A History of Metals in Colonial America* (University, Ala.: University of Alabama Press, 1981), pp. 86*ff.*

8. Arthur Nussbaum, *A History of the Dollar* (New York: Columbia University Press, 1957), p. 4.

9. Ibid., pp. 6–7.

10. Ibid.

11. Leslie V. Brock, *The Currency of the American Colonies, 1700–1764* (New York: Arno Press, 1975), pp. 21–23.

12. Ibid., pp. 5, 21.

13. Richard A Lester, *Monetary Experiments—Early American and Recent Scandinavian* (Princeton: Princeton University Press, 1939), ch. 3–5.

14. Brock, *Currency of American Colonies,* pp. 33–34.

15. John Taylor, *An Inquiry into the Principles and Policy of the Government of the United States* (London: Routledge and Kegan Paul Limited, 1950; first published in 1814), ch. 5, "Banking," pp. 267–353.

16. See Richard H. Timberlake, Jr., *The Origins of Central Banking in the United States* (Cambridge, Mass: Harvard University Press, 1978), ch. 2.

17. See Richard Sylla, "Forgotten Men of Money: Private Bankers in Early U.S. History," *Journal of Economic History* 36 (March 1976):173–188.

18. See Richard H. Timberlake, Jr., "The Significance of Unaccounted Currencies," *Journal of Economic History* 41 (December 1981):853–866.

19. See Richard Sylla, *The American Capital Market, 1846–1914* (New York: Arno Press, 1975), ch. 2.

20. See Milton Friedman and Anna J. Schwartz, *A Monetary History of the United States, 1867–1960* (Princeton: Princeton University Press, 1963), p. 182.

21. Ibid., pp. 170–172. In November 1860, the financial crisis related to Lincoln's election and the threat of southern-state secession prompted the New York City banks that were members of the New York Clearing House Association (founded in 1853) to introduce the clearing house loan certificate. These certificates were issued to member banks that pledged specified assets as collateral and could then be used by the banks as an emergency reserve asset in settling adverse clearing balances with other member banks. Clearing house loan certificates thereby freed up specie for payment to panicky depositors seeking to convert their deposits to specie. The innovation was adopted and routinely used during panics by the clearing houses of other cities in later years and decades. During the panic of 1907, fifty-one clearing houses issued certificates and in some cases they were issued in low denominations for public, as distinct from interbank, use. Such a privately issued emergency currency posed dangers of abuse, and so the Aldrich-Vreeland Act called for the emergency currency to be issued by the government for circulation through ad hoc National Currency Associations rather than through established clearing houses. This history illustrates well the themes of private innovation and governmental regulatory response developed in the text. I am indebted to William L.

Silber for bringing up the example of the clearing house loan certificate in his discussion of my work (see note 6 above). For a lengthier treatment of the origins and development of the clearing house loan certificate see Fritz Redlich, *The Molding of American Banking* (New York and London: Johnson Reprint Corp., 1968), pt. II, ch. 17.

22. Friedman and Schwartz, *A Monetary History,* table 1, p. 17; table 5, pp. 130–131; table 8, p. 179.

23. Ibid., table A-1, pp. 704–708.

24. See John A. James, *Money and Capital Markets in Post-Bellum America* (Princeton: Princeton University Press, 1978), and Sylla, *The American Capital Market, 1846–1914.*

25. Friedman and Schwartz, *A Monetary History,* p. 172.

26. For an excellent survey of these regulations, see Homer Jones "Banking Reform in the 1930s" and the "Discussion" by Anna Schwartz, both in Gary M. Walton, ed., *Regulatory Change in an Atmosphere of Crisis* (New York: Academic Press, 1979), pp. 79–99.

3

Federal Reserve Policy in the 1973-1975 Recession: A Case Study of Fed Behavior in a Quandary

Thomas Mayer

Our first line of defense against massive failures of depository institutions and a resulting financial collapse consists of the Federal Deposit Insurance Corporation (FDIC) and the Federal Savings and Loan Insurance Corporation (FSLIC). But since our second line is the Federal Reserve it is appropriate in a book on financial crises to consider how the Fed functions. Note that I have said how the Fed functions and not how the Fed *should* function. Much of the literature on monetary policy consists of determining what the Fed should do rather than investigating what the Fed actually does. It is in the rationalistic tradition to assume that once you have convincingly demonstrated what should be done, it will, in fact, be done— because our institutions are run by reasonable and public-spirited people. But even such people do not always function in this way. Institutional arrangements may hinder the choice of the best policy. It is therefore necessary to investigate empirically how government agencies, such as the Fed, behave.

Unfortunately, while we economists are eager to investigate the behavior of households and firms, we often ignore the behavior of government agencies and assume simply that they will behave appropriately. This tendency can be seen clearly in the great monetary policy debate on *rules versus authorities;* Milton Friedman's (Modigliani and Friedman, 1977, p. 18) view that "the real argument for a steady rate of monetary growth is at least as much political as it is economic" has been too much ignored.

This chapter therefore offers a case study of the Federal Reserve in the 1973-1975 recession—the most severe recession since the 1930s and one that was accompanied by a serious threat of financial crisis. It is also the last

I am indebted for useful suggestions to Robert Hetzel, Raymond Lombra, Paul Wachtel, Henry Wallich, and Robert Weintraub, and for thorough research assistance to Marlene Kim. I am also indebted to Steven Axilrod, John Balles, Joseph Bisignanio, Phillip Coldwell, Robert Holland, Bruce MacLaury, Paul Meek, George Mitchell, Charles Partee, James Pierce, and Henry Wallich for answering questions about the Fed's policy. I also wish to thank the Earhart Foundation for financial support.

41

complete cycle phase for which the source material used here, the *Minutes* of the Federal Open Market Committee (FOMC), are available; no *Minutes* are available after 1975. (However, I gather from conversations with Fed officials that not very much has changed since then.)

Primarily what I have done in this chapter is to exploit the FOMC *Minutes* to see what they tell us about the Fed's analysis. In addition, I interviewed a number of former and current governors, Reserve Bank presidents, and staff economists. Since the *Minutes* were not made available until five years after the event, the discussions at FOMC meetings were probably not much inhibited by fear of unfavorable public reaction.[1] Despite this, these *Minutes* have been largely ignored by economists, though they have been used in a few notable studies of monetary policy (Brunner and Meltzer, 1964; Friedman and Schwartz, 1963; Lombra and Moran, 1980; and Wicker, 1966).

Although the *Minutes* are not verbatim transcripts they are remarkably detailed. Hence the quotations given below, while not necessarily the actual words used by a speaker, do represent what he said. (All page numbers given below, unless otherwise indicated, are to the *Minutes*.)

For two reasons, my focus is not on whether the Fed did the right thing but on the sophistication of its analysis. First, while it would be rare for most economists to agree on what the Fed should have done in a given situation, it is much easier to get agreement about the quality of the Fed's analysis. In giving examinations professors sometimes ask students to discuss a certain statement. The students are then graded not on whether they agree or disagree with the statement but on the quality of their reasoning. It is this approach that I have tried to use here. Second, while the Fed's policy is likely to be different from case to case, the quality of its analysis probably changes less.

The Fed's analysis that I am concerned with is not the product of its technical staff. We all know that this analysis is of the highest caliber. Instead, I am dealing with the arguments expressed at FOMC meetings, that is, with the quality of the analysis that goes directly into policymaking.

This analysis is hard to summarize. Since the Committee as a whole did not adopt a particular line of reasoning, it is necessary to look at the statements made by each of the participants. The people who are cited are listed in table 3-1. To give the flavor of this reasoning I have used many quotations. I apologize for the resulting length.[2] Fortunately, individual sections can be read on their own.

The first section summarizes the behavior of some financial magnitudes at the time. Appendix 3A provides a summary of general economic conditions during this recession. Two factors deserve to be highlighted. First, the recession came in two stages—a downturn in November 1973, which many economists attributed to supply factors, and then a second downturn in the

Table 3-1
Federal Open Market Committee Participants Cited

Governors:	Andrew Brimmer,[a] Jeffrey Bucher, Arthur Burns, Phillip Coldwell,[a] Robert Holland, John Sheehan, Henry Wallich[a]
Presidents:	John Balles (San Francisco), Robert Black (Richmond), George Clay (Kansas City), Phillip Coldwell[a] (Dallas), David Eastburn[a] (Philadelphia), Darryl Francis (St. Louis), Alfred Hayes (New York), Monroe Kimbrel (Atlanta), Bruce MacLaury (Minneapolis), Robert Mayo (Chicago), Frank Morris (Boston), Willis Winn[a] (Philadelphia)
First Vice-Presidents:	Richard Debs (New York), Eugene Leonard (St. Louis), Clement Van Nice (Minneapolis), Mark Willes[a] (Philadelphia)
Staff Members:	Stephen Axilrod, Ralph Bryant, Lyle Gramley, Charles Partee, James Pierce
Account Managers:	Alan Holmes, Peter Sternlight

[a]Held this office only during part of period.

fall of 1974. The other factor is that the existence of the recession was not realized until long after the turning point.

The next section deals with the way the FOMC is organized. The following section takes up some external constraints on the Fed. The subsequent two sections deal with the FOMC's attitude towards inflation and its views on monetary theory. The succeeding section deals with the policy the Fed actually followed.

An issue that transcends the question of why the Fed did what it did in the 1973–1975 recession is whether the Fed has the necessary knowledge to operate a successful countercyclical policy. This issue is taken up in the next section of the chapter on the feasibility of stabilization policy. After describing what knowledge is necessary for this I take up the Fed's knowledge of future economic conditions and of the size of the impact of its policy. This discussion is followed by a summary of some general aspects of the FOMC's functioning. Since I have been very critical of the Fed, I then try to provide a defense of the Fed. A final section summarizes the results.

Monetary and Financial Developments

As table 3–2 shows the money growth rate declined sharply in the 1973–1975 recession. This decline we now know started in the second quarter of 1974 for M–1 and M–2 and in the second or third quarter for M–3 on both the new and the old definitions. The contemporaneous data show the decline as starting in the third quarter of 1974. A pickup in the growth rate then

Table 3–2
Growth Rates of Money and Interest Rates, 1973–1975

| Year and Quarter | New Measures | | | | Old Measures | | | | | | Federal Funds Rate | Yield on Long-Term Treasury Bonds |
| | M-1A | M-1B | M-2 | M-3 | Revised Estimates | | | Current Estimates:[a] | | | | |
					M-1	M-2	M-3	M-1	M-2	M-3		
1973 I	8.2	8.4	10.3	14.0	8.5	9.8	10.9	7.0	8.8	10.7	6.54	6.10
II	4.9	4.9	6.9	11.7	5.1	7.7	8.3	7.5	8.7	9.1	7.82	6.23
III	4.4	4.5	6.0	11.2	5.2	7.7	7.4	5.5	7.9	7.2	10.56	6.60
IV	4.8	4.8	5.4	8.0	5.4	9.0	8.2	3.9	8.5	7.3	10.00	6.30
1974 I	6.7	6.7	8.0	10.1	7.3	10.3	9.6	5.5	9.3	8.8	9.32	6.64
II	3.6	3.6	5.2	10.6	4.1	7.0	6.4	7.0	7.9	6.6	11.25	7.05
III	3.1	3.1	4.4	7.7	4.1	6.1	5.2	1.6	4.5	4.0	12.09	7.27
IV	4.9	5.0	5.8	5.4	4.6	6.6	6.4	4.6	7.0	6.9	9.35	6.97
1975 I	2.6	2.9	7.8	7.2	2.0	6.4	8.2	0.6	5.6	7.5	6.30	6.70
II	5.9	5.9	14.9	9.4	5.8	9.5	12.4	7.4	10.2	12.6	5.42	6.97

Sources: Thomas Simpson, "The Redefined Monetary Aggregates," *Federal Reserve Bulletin*, February 1980, pp. 112–14; Board of Governors, Federal Reserve System, *Annual Reports*, 1973, p. 44; 1974, p. 46; 1975, p. 53; *Business Conditions Digest*, November 1980, pp. 98, 100.

Note: All money growth rates are seasonally adjusted percentages at annual rates.

[a]*Current estimates* refers to estimates published toward the middle of the following year in the *Annual Report* of the Board of Governors.

occurred in the second quarter of 1975. Interest rates rose during much of the recession, presumably due to a rising inflation premium. All in all, regardless of whether one follows the monetarists by looking at the money growth rate or the Keynesians by looking at nominal interest rates, the data suggest a highly restrictive policy. Not surprisingly, the Fed had few friends at the time. As Alan Blinder (1979, pp. 179, 189) summarized it:

> By the beginning of 1975 there was an almost universal chorus of condemnation of the Fed for its tight money policies. . . Observers with views as far apart as Paul Samuelson and Milton Friedman were criticizing the Fed sharply—which is hardly unusual. What is unusual is that both men agreed on the direction in which the Fed had erred. . . . Friedman noted the anemic money growth rates between June 1974 and January 1975 and claimed that they "surely contributed to the recent deepening of the recession." . . . Samuelson charged that "if we go into a deep depression, the Fed will surely bear much of the blame." The Fed seemed to have few friends.

In the late spring of 1974 a credit squeeze threatened financial collapse as the market was shaken by the de facto failure of Franklin National, by the collapse of the Herrstatt bank with its resulting losses to U.S. banks, and by the financial difficulties of a large public utility. According to the Board of Governors (1974, pp. 41–42):

> There was widespread concern in financial circles that such evidence of financial difficulty at a few firms might represent the tip of the iceberg. . . Lenders responded . . . by tightening their credit standards. In the squeeze that followed, many lesser-rated borrowers found their access to security markets partially or completely curtailed, and they were forced to fall back on standby lines of credit at banks. Since banks experiencing these unexpected loan demands were also finding it necessary to pay sharply higher costs for . . . funds, they increased their own loan rates . . . Stock prices . . . fell dramatically during the spring and summer period of maximum financial strain. The composite stock index of the New York Stock Exchange . . . at the low was nearly 50 percent below the record high reached in early 1973.

The Fed ameliorated the situation by making massive loans to Franklin National, thus propping it up until it found a merger partner in the following year, as well as by announcing its readiness to serve as a lender of last resort not only for banks but also for others.

Rising interest rates hurt not only financial markets. They also inflicted grave damage on the residential construction industry through disintermediation and the problems created for the Real Estate Investment Trusts (REITs). Residential construction had its most severe decline in thirty years, largely due to the problems of the mortgage market (*Economic Report,* 1975, p. 35).

With this brief survey of the background let us now look at the Fed's policymaking process.

Organization of the FOMC and the Policy Process

Open market operations are controlled by the FOMC, consisting of the seven governors of the Federal Reserve Board plus the presidents (or occasionally the first vice presidents) of five Federal Reserve Banks. However, all the other banks also participate, though without voting, in the Committee's deliberations. Staff members attend the meetings and in 1973-1975, the senior staff member, Charles Partee, was usually invited to participate in the discussion of policy. In 1973-1975 this Committee met once a month, though it sometimes held a telephone conference between meetings.[3]

Though it may ask the FOMCs advice, the Board of Governors on its own decides about reserve requirement changes and discount rates. These decisions appear to be made with relatively little formal discussion so that the board *Minutes* for this period are much less informative than the FOMC *Minutes*.

The FOMC has available to it a *Green Book* that contains forecasts for the economy prepared by the board's staff, a *Red Book* that presents material gathered by the Federal Reserve Banks on local business conditions, and a *Blue Book*. The latter discusses conditions and developments in the financial markets and presents financial forecasts. It also provides (usually three) alternative policies, composed of what the staff believes are compatible ranges for the aggregates and for the federal funds rate, usually for two-months' periods and for two quarters. Parts of these periods were usually already past by the time of the meeting.

In the period covered in this chapter the FOMC meetings usually lasted one day but sometimes ran a day and a half. Reports were given by senior staff members on international finance, on domestic economic conditions, on the Desk's money market operations, and on financial markets. These reports were discussed by the Committee before it turned to a discussion of the Directive to be given to the Desk in New York. The discussions about the Directive were oriented around the alternatives the staff had presented in the *Blue Book;* participants would either state a preference for one of these alternatives or suggest a modified version of one of them. What went on, and still goes on, at FOMC meetings is not really a *discussion* in the full sense of the term. Instead, each participant asks questions of the staff and makes statements about his view of economic developments and appropriate policy. There was, at least during the period covered here, almost no give-and-take; only rarely did someone say that he agreed, or disagreed, with a previous speaker.[4] Different views were not challenged or probed, nor were different chains of reasoning brought out into the open.[5] If the purpose of having policy made by a committee rather than by a single person is to average out extreme views, then the FOMC's procedures are effective. But if the purpose is to improve thinking through a clash of ideas, then they are not.

As several former and present participants explained to me, the reason for the absence of give-and-take discussions is that, including the staff people who spoke out on policy, there were more than nineteen people who had their say. Each of the participants had only a few chances to make statements and this made it impossible to have "bilateral duels."[6]

Constraints on Fed Policymaking

In making policy the Fed has to—or more accurately, believes it has to—take account of a number of constraints. These are political pressures, international factors, potential reactions of market expectations, and the dangers of a financial collapse.

The general impression one gets from reading the *Minutes* is that the Fed was not seriously constrained by political pressures, in part because its own preferences did not depart so much from those of the White House and Congress. (It is also possible, however, that some policies the Committee thought desirable, but politically unfeasible, simply were not being discussed.)[7]

Thus at a time of great financial strain, Burns was able to say the Fed had strong support in Congress, "he had been receiving almost no critical mail from that source" (June 1974, p. 62). And subsequently when some participants raised the political issue, Burns responded: "it would be a tragic mistake to yield to political pressures; the political pressures of today would not necessarily be those of tomorrow. The Congress had established the System as an independent entity and the Committee ought to live up to the responsibility imposed by that independence" (Feb. 1975, pp. 61–62).

On the other hand, MacLaury stated that "the Committee had been concerned last winter about possible reactions in the Congress if interest rates had been allowed to rise rapidly at that time. It seemed to him that there would be even greater grounds for concern about reactions if the Committee should fail to evidence in some way its recognition of the change in the economic outlook" (Dec. 1973, p. 81).

And Bucher in discussing the inflation-unemployment trade-off remarked that "it was important also to consider the trade-off which the Congress might consider appropriate. Although many people now regarded a rate of unemployment in excess of 4 percent as acceptable, he was not convinced that Congress as a whole was prepared to accept a rate as high as 5 percent; certainly, it would not find a 6 percent rate acceptable" (Feb. 1974, p. 59).[8]

Apart from this, several participants argued that if the Fed's restrictive policy generated extensive unemployment, Congress would adopt too expansionary fiscal measures. But, *on the whole,* it does not seem that political pressures created a *great* problem for the Fed. Admittedly, this conclusion may be an illusion created because the Committee avoided discussion of political pressures. As one insider informed me, "it is absolutely incorrect to infer that the FOMC was not subject to political pressures because of an absence of statements to this effect. It was considered extremely bad manners to suggest that politics were important."[9]

Balance of payments considerations too, were not a major constraint on Fed actions. However, they were certainly not ignored entirely. Early in the recession some participants who advocated more expansionary policies argued that since other countries were adopting restrictive policies the United States had to adopt an expansionary policy to reduce the danger of a world recession. (Dec. 1973, pp. 57–58; Feb. 1974, pp. 6–9, 57–58.) However, others used international considerations to argue for the opposite policy. Burns warned that a substantial reduction in interest rates "would have highly disturbing consequences for foreign exchange rates" (Dec. 1974, p. 71) and Hayes, Holland, and Kimbrel expressed similar views (Dec. 1974, pp. 87, 98, 107).

Later in the recession international factors played a role again when Burns argued that allowing short rates to fall would cause a decline in the exchange rate that would reduce confidence and raise the inflation rate. Beyond this "every weakening of the dollar in the foreign exchange markets did something to reduce the strength of the country's international political position. . . . The Committee . . . should keep in mind to at least some minor degree the performance of the dollar in the foreign exchange markets" (Jan. 1975, pp. 80–81).

Several other participants supported this position. Although Wallich argued that "international considerations should not be permitted to determine domestic monetary policy; priority had to be given to domestic considerations," he too opposed a cut in the discount rate because of its effect on the exchange rate (March 1975, pp. 99–100). And several other participants also opposed a cut in the discount rate for this reason (Feb. 1975, pp. 69–70). But, all in all, international considerations were far from dominating.

Apart from political pressures and balance of payments considerations, another potential constraint arose from market expectations. At times many participants were afraid that a policy that was the appropriate one on objective grounds would lead to unfavorable—and damaging—market reactions. This fear appeared to be a substantial constraint. As Sheehan stated, "The System found it difficult to make policy changes because of the market's great sensitivity to System actions. It would be better if the market were both more uncertain about and less sensitive to actions of the System, so that policy changes could be taken in small rather than giant steps'' (Aug. 1974, pp. 68–69).

Hayes argued that "the Committee continued to be up against the old danger that moderate slackening of monetary restraint might be overinterpreted by the market and might lead to an unwanted acceleration of inflationary expectations" (Oct. 1974, p. 64). He also gave as one of the reasons why he opposed easing: "the market was all too likely to seize upon any modest easing move as the beginning of a major policy change" (Sept. 1974, p. 58). Similarly, Wallich declared that "it was critical to avoid a decline in the Federal funds rate to an extent that would give a false signal" (Sept. 1974, p. 69). Burns agreed, stating, "it was extremely important to avoid giving a false signal, and for that reason, he would prefer a funds rate range of 10½ to 12 percent to one of 10 to 12 percent" (Sept. 1974, p. 69). MacLaury "shared the common view that the Committee should be careful to avoid giving a false signal to the financial market and therefore, he would be content with a funds rate of 10 to 12 percent" (Sept. 1974, p. 80).

Mitchell observed that "the Committee had one problem with respect to its public image and credibility and another problem with respect to the effects of monetary policy on real economic activity" (Nov. 1974, p. 50). While arguing for lower rates, he admitted that "the operation would be a tricky one because efforts to achieve somewhat lower rates could give rise to expectations of further reductions which would defeat the purpose" (Dec. 1974, p. 110). And similar statements of others could be cited.

But not all the participants took this position. Thus Morris did not think that errors in the market's interpretation would last long, and "in any case, for years the System had given too much weight to the fear of excessive market reaction to its actions. The Committee should take the actions that the members thought were desirable, and if market professionals made misjudgments they would have to pay the price" (Sept. 1974, p. 84). Roughly similar views were expressed by Gramley and Bucher (Sept. 1974, pp. 67, 76).

So much for the FOMC's concern about market expectations. The Board of Governors too was very concerned. In numerous cases when it turned down requests for discount rate changes by various Federal Reserve Banks, fear of unfavorable market reactions was *the* reason, or one of the major reasons, it gave.

How about the monetarist solution of announcing policy in advance? This was suggested by Wallich who wanted the Committee to state that it would seek higher money growth rates for the next six-to-nine months and then bring the growth rate down again[10] (Dec. 1974, p. 96). But this suggestion was not accepted.

A related constraint on the Committee—or more accurately something the Committee perceived as a constraint—was the need to limit interest rate fluctuations. This constraint did not get much discussion, perhaps because something generally agreed upon need not be mentioned. However, Eastburn did remark that "the basic issue was a reluctance . . . to allow movements in the Federal funds rate of the sort necessary for achievement of the goals for the monetary aggregates" (Oct. 1974, p. 50).

Wallich complained that the range set for the funds rate was too narrow: "The System ought to educate the market about its willingness to tolerate larger fluctuations in rates" (Oct. 1974, p. 52). However, he added that this was not the time to do it.

Black, too, argued that "the real problem . . . was that the market was not yet ready to accept large fluctuations in interest rates. Such acceptance would need to develop before the System could stabilize rates of growth in the monetary aggregates" (Oct. 1974, p. 51). But, like Wallich, he too wanted to postpone the education of the market. The extent to which the wish to stabilize interest rates actually caused the Committee to miss its money targets will be discussed below.

A closely related constraint was the fear that fragile financial markets would collapse, a fear that is hardly surprising, given the conditions described previously. The May 1974 meeting was dominated by this fear. Partee reported:

> Market conditions were more sensitive than they had been in a long time. . . . Paper that was not of prime grade was just not selling . . . Questions were being raised in the market not only about the paper of nonbank issuers but also about the paper of some bank holding companies. Some concern was being expressed about the soundness of some banks and large investors appear to be backing away from CDs of banks outside the major money centers. . . . The REITs were having a difficult time not only in the commercial paper market but also in holding their bank lines of credit together and generally in keeping their heads above water. . . . If the situation went out of control and some serious financial constrictions developed, there was a possibility that economic conditions could change materially for the worse. While the staff was not predicting such a development, it nevertheless was a distinct possibility . . . He would recommend that the Committee focus . . . on the stabilization of money market conditions, and that it formulate its directive in money market terms. . . . That was a course which he had not often suggested to the Committee (May 1974, pp. 42–43).

This situation divided the participants into two groups. The substantial majority argued that the Fed should abandon its policy of putting pressure on the money market to control the aggregates. Instead, it should focus on stabilizing the money market and preventing further sharp increases in interest rates. For example, Burns argued that "interest rates had moved up sharply and financial markets might be described as bordering on disorder. . . . It was necessary to pause, and allow the markets to absorb what had already occurred. . . . It would be dangerous not to pause" (May 1974, pp. 48–49).

Similarly, Black remarked that "as far as the financial markets were concerned, a critical stage may well have been reached. . . . The System's function as lender of last resort could very well override any policy decision arrived at today" (May 1974, p. 53). Many others also expressed concern about financial fragility.

A minority of participants, however, argued that the Committee should persist in its restrictive policies. Willes, for instance, argued that "it was in extraordinary times that it was most important to maintain the focus on the longer run targets for monetary growth" (May 1974, p. 46), and Kimbrel argued, out of a concern about inflation, that the Fed should allow the funds rate to be set at the level needed to control the aggregates (May 1974, pp. 50–51).

At the June 1974 meeting the staff's report on economic conditions called the prospect of "serious trouble" in the financial markets "somewhat more remote than a month ago, at least domestically, as markets have tended to be quiet" (June 1974, p. 16). However, Holmes's report on financial conditions still talked about "trouble spots that contribute to a substantial feeling of unrest in the markets. Rumors abound about various possible failures or the inability of some lesser known names to find financing at any price" (June 1974, p. 30).

The Committee was very much concerned about this financial fragility, and a number of participants were afraid that financial markets could not tolerate additional tightness. For example, Morris thought that "the economy's ability to adapt to much more monetary restraint was rather limited" (June 1974, p. 70). And Coldwell stated that "in light of the problem of inflation he had advocated gradual increases in monetary restraint over recent months. Now, however, he would favor holding steady; conditions in financial markets, and perhaps other considerations . . . argued against adding to the existing degree of restraint" (June 1974, p. 49).

M–1 had grown much faster than desired. It is likely that the Committee would have adopted a sharply restrictive policy at this meeting if it were not for both the fear of financial collapse and the mounting recession.

Concern with financial fragility continued at the July meeting. The *Blue Book* stated that "the possibility of a credit crunch . . . cannot be ignored. . . . Such a development could be triggered by a series of failures . . . here or abroad" (*Blue Book,* July 1974, p. 11), and Holmes stated in his report:

> There was a sharp deterioration in financial market conditions, both domestic and international, over the period since the Committee last met.

> An excess of investor caution virtually dried up the capital markets and a further move towards selectivity played havoc with the money market. The viability of individual banks was called into question by many observers, a few large industrial firms dropped CDs completely from their investment portfolios, and most investors became still more reluctant to purchase CDs issued by any but the top banks. There was also some evidence of a deposit shift from regional to money market banks.
>
> REITs and utility firms found it increasingly difficult to borrow in the commerical paper market and some bank holding companies found themselves in the same unenviable position (July 1974, pp. 37–38).

Even those participants who were hawks on inflation wanted to temper the wind to the shorn lamb. Hayes remarked that "the principle change in recent weeks seemed to him to have been an increase in the degree of unease in domestic and international financial markets. Obviously, the strained state of those markets and the possibility of further failures posed very real risks at this point" (July 1974, p. 55). And Black talked about "the possibility of imminent and dangerous financial disruptions" (July 1974, pp. 46, 64–65, 68).

But this does not mean that the participants were ready to ease policy sharply. They generally believed that some risk had to be taken; as Holmes pointed out, "It had been apparent all along that a monetary policy capable of bringing . . . [the fight against inflation] to a successful conclusion would entail risks. . . . It would be necessary to live with those risks for some time to come" (July 1974, p. 55).

After July concern about a financial crisis diminished sharply, though at the September meeting some participants were still worried about the fragility of financial markets and the depressed stock market. (Sept. 1974, pp. 65, 74, 77). At the October meeting Partee was still concerned that particular banks known to have made a large volume of unsound loans "could well experience liquidity problems," and Burns stated that "security markets were not functioning as well as desired" (Oct. 1974, pp. 44, 62).[11]

All in all, the Committee was clearly constrained by financial fragility in May and June and perhaps—though this is more questionable—also in July, but not at other times.

What does this episode tell us? On the surface it seems to say that when the financial system is obviously in a weak condition the Fed will modify its policy accordingly. But is this correct? By July the Fed seemed to have restored a considerable part of its emphasis on inflation. I can well imagine a situation in the future in which the Fed, having been again and again frustrated in its fight against inflation, reaches a state in which the *threat* of financial collapse no longer carries much weight. It would allow the collapse actually to occur before changing policy.[12]

Rather surprisingly, one factor that has frequently been thought of as a major constraint on monetary policy, the wish to protect the residential construction industry, did not play such a large role in this recession. It did receive some attention when Brimmer said that one of the goals of monetary policy "recently . . . had been to assure an availability of funds consistent with a structure of interest rates over the rest of the year that would bring about a revival in the housing sector" and went on to say that this was inconsistent with a much further rise in interest rates (March 1974, p. 111). But several participants replied that the specialized housing agencies could take care of this situation (March 1974, pp. 88–89, 124).[13] However, towards the end of the recession Morris called the establishment of conditions that "would permit a strong revival of the mortgage market" the main task of policy (Jan. 1975, pp. 67–68) and previously the problem had been discussed a bit at the October 1974 meeting.

To summarize, to the extent that one can tell from the *Minutes*, neither international considerations nor political pressures seem to have been a serious constraint on the Fed, while the fear of upsetting market expectations and the perceived need to stabilize interest rates were much more serious constraints.[14] Fragile markets were important in May and June, and to a lesser extent in July of 1974, while the protection of the residential construction industry played a surprisingly small role. But all of this is subject to a caveat. Whether something is an important constraint or not depends on the desired policy. For example, suppose that the Fed had wanted to carry out a rigid policy of stabilizing the price level in the face of the oil shock. This would have required a much sharper rise in interest rates than the policy the Fed actually adopted. And such a sharp rise in interest rates might perhaps have transformed Congressional pressures, international considerations, or the fate of the residential construction industry into much more serious constraints.

The Fed's Policy Attitude toward Inflation

Before looking at the Committee's actual decisions it is useful to look at its underlying views. As background keep in mind that the Nixon administration started to look at inflation as the top problem in mid-1973, and the Ford administration did so beginning in September 1974. Burns stated his strong opposition to inflation:

> The country at present was on the threshold of a two-digit inflation. If headway were not made this year in dealing with the problem, the country would be experiencing a Latin-American type of inflation, and the American people would not tolerate that for long. One way or another highly restrictive policies would become inevitable and the nation might have to go through a long and serious contraction. By leaning on the side of caution

now, the Committee might be able to make some contribution to preventing such an unfortunate development (Sept. 1974, p. 82).

He therefore opposed accommodating the Treasury:

> [W]hile the Federal Reserve always would accommodate the Treasury up to a point, the charge could be made . . . that the System had accommodated the Treasury to an excessive degree. Although he was not a monetarist, he found a basic and inescapable truth in the monetarist position that inflation could not have persisted over a long period of time without a highly accommodative monetary policy. . . . Governments were weak in all of the democratic countries of Europe. . . . Because weak governments could not cope with the problem of inflation the task had become the inevitable responsibility of central banks. . . . Because the System had substantial independence . . . it could resist political pressure to pursue inflationary policies, and it should do so. . . . There was no question in his mind . . . that inflation was the major economic problem facing the nation as well as the world[15] (March 1974, pp. 111–113, 139.)

Early in the recession when the problem was mainly a supply shock, the Committee was willing to accept some more inflation rather than further unemployment. Thus, although the staff's forecast pointed out that even a moderately expansionary policy might "add more to inflationary pressure than to real output" (Dec. 1973, p. 48), nearly all participants seemed willing to take this risk. Several explicitly argued that the rise in oil prices should be accommodated and real balances not be allowed to shrink. But this attitude did not persist. By June 1974 Governor Holland surmised that "virtually everyone around the table would agree that monetary policy had to stay tight in the interest of contributing what it could to slow the present inflation" (June 1974, p. 51). Even a liberal (by which I mean in this context someone who tends to favor expansionary policies) like MacLaury stated at that meeting:

> The Committee was being forced by circumstances to choose between recession . . . and a totally unacceptable rate of inflation, which could lead to collapse. . . . Given such a choice, he was prepared to maintain prevailing money market conditions, even though he recognized that such a course probably would make a recession—on his definition, at least likely and perhaps unavoidable (June 1974, p. 64).

Subsequently another liberal, Sheehan, hoped "that economic activity would remain near the current reduced level—or, ideally, decline another 1 percent—until about the middle of next year, and then turn up and expand at a rate not above 2 percent for an indefinite period" (Sept. 1974, p. 69).

Still another leading liberal, Morris, declared that "the most desirable course of economic activity—if policy could be find-tuned—would be one that moved the unemployment rate up to 6 percent [it had been 5.5 percent the previous month] and held it there for the next two years. The American people now would be willing to accept a 6 percent rate as a cost of combating inflation" (Sept. 1974, p. 83).

Many others expressed more or less similar views. Burns did "not wish to see a prompt recovery" because he was afraid of an acceleration in the inflation rate (Sept. 1974, p. 65); Wallich wanted to maintain real per-capita gross national product (GNP) more or less constant and tolerate some rise in unemployment (Sept. 1974, p. 68); Holland wanted a firm policy to continue to dampen aggregate demand "for another month or two" (Sept. 1974, p. 72); and Clay wanted "economic activity to remain close to the current level" (Sept. 1974, p. 84). Mayo argued that "over the six-to-nine months period it would be better if economic activity remained near the current level" (Sept. 1974, p. 60). Coldwell wished the economy "to remain near its current level for about three months . . . and then to start on a course of real improvement. Inflation was still the biggest problem" (Sept. 1974, p. 61). And both Winn and Hayes also pointed to inflation as the foremost problem (Sept. 1974, pp. 57, 85).

Thus in a month in which the unemployment rate reached 5.9 percent, compared to 5.3 percent in the 1970–1973 period, and just two months before the recession would turn into the worst postwar recession, the Committee was too worried about inflation to take expansionary action. Its opposition to inflation was not just idle talk.

What were the factors underlying these positions? One aspect was the staff's estimate of future inflation as shown in table 3–3. Another one was the slope of the Phillips curve. Thus, at the July 1974 meeting, the staff reported that if the M–1 growth rate were raised to 7.5 percent, real GNP would rise by one percent, unemployment would fall by 0.3 percent and the fixed weight GNP deflator (which is the index the Committee focused on) "might be about two-tenths of a point higher" (July 1974, pp. 22–23). And previously, at the April 1974 meeting, Partee had also stated that the choice among the three alternative money growth rates suggested in the *Blue Book* would have relatively little effect on the inflation rate.

But this analysis was challenged by several participants on two grounds. First, both Coldwell and Clay argued, along modern rational expectations lines, that expectational effects would increase the response of prices to the money growth rate (April 1974, pp. 78–80). Second, Partee's price forecast applied only to a period of about six months.

Some participants argued that, with inflation being largely due to cost-push, little relief could be gained by increasing the slack. But on the other side of the debate Balles argued that there was no permanent trade off, that any reduction in unemployment obtained by tolerating more inflation would be only temporary (Feb. 1974, p. 76). Hayes and Wallich believed

Table 3-3
Actual and Predicted Changes in Gross National Product

Year and Quarter	GNP Estimate Available in:			Federal Reserve Forecast		
	May 1981	July 1974	December 1974	November 1973	May 1974	November 1974
Nominal GNP in Billions of Dollars						
1973 IV	39.0	33.0	35.1	31.6	n.a.	—
1974 I	11.0	14.7	14.8	29.7	n.a.	—
1974 II	36.1	23.1	25.0	26.3	28.2	—
1974 III	27.8	—	31.6	24.1	32.0	—
1974 IV	22.2	—	—	26.3	36.0	20.9
1975 I	6.0	—	—	—	30.0	21.0
Real GNP (percentage change at annual rate)						
1973 IV	3.3	1.6	2.3	3.8	—	—
1974 I	− 3.8	− 6.3	− 7.0	3.0	—	—
1974 II	0.5	− 0.8	− 1.6	2.5	− 0.4	—
1974 III	− 2.4	—	− 2.1	2.0	2.4	—
1974 IV	− 5.1	—	—	2.0	3.0	− 5.5
1975 I	− 8.2	—	—	—	2.3	− 2.5
Gross Private Product, Fixed Weight Price Index (percentage change at annual rate)						
1973 IV	7.6[a]	8.6	9.1	5.8	—	—
1974 I	11.2[a]	13.5	14.1	6.2	—	—
1974 II	9.8[a]	9.0	12.3	5.4	9.3	—
1974 III	12.9[a]	—	13.8	5.0	7.0	—
1974 IV	12.8[a]	—	—	5.0	6.7	12.7
1975 I	8.0[a]	—	—	—	5.8	9.7

Sources: U.S. Department of Commerce, *Business Conditions Digest,* May 1981, pp. 98ff; Board of Governors, Federal Reserve System, *Green Books,* November 1973; May, August, December 1974, pp. 1-6.
—Not available or not applicable.
[a]Index for Gross Business Product.

that the current unemployment rate was not much above the natural rate, a view that Brimmer rejected (Feb. 1974, p. 56; March 1974, pp. 134, 145).

These discussions of inflation versus unemployment were therefore conducted in fairly general and common-sense terms. Little use was made of sophisticated economic or econometric analysis, and the arguments presented were essentially the same as those used in public discussions and newspapers, except that at least several participants realized that the long-run Phillips curve is vertical and that expectational effects may speed up the response of prices.

The FOMCs Framework for Monetary Theory

Not surprisingly the FOMC did not set out its theoretical framework systematically, and the theoretical presuppositions of its participants became apparent only occasionally.

In its approach to forecasting income the FOMC was more or less Keynesian. The staff's forecast came in part from a mainly Keynesian econometric model and in part from judgmental forecasts that were in the Keynesian tradition of building up forecasts of GNP by looking at aggregate demand in various sectors—rather than in the monetarist tradition of relating changes in income to previous changes in the money stock. While the money-income nexus was stressed by Francis this was definitely a minority position.

But when it came to forecasting the effect of its actions the Committee's approach was not really Keynesian. To be sure, it paid a lot of attention to the short-term interest rate, but it did so mainly in an un-Keynesian way. This rate played three roles in its thinking. First, it was to be set to induce the public to demand a certain quantity of money that the banks would then create. While using the interest rate as an instrument to achieve a particular money supply is not inconsistent with Keynesian theory, there is nothing in Keynesian economics that suggests doing so. The second role of the short-term interest rate target was to prevent excessive damage to the residential construction industry. This use of an interest rate to influence investment is certainly Keynesian. The third role of the interest rate target was to avoid substantial interest rate fluctuations. This emphasis on preventing money market disturbances is certainly not Keynesian. Keynesian theory tells us to choose that interest-rate target that optimizes the income level even if this means substantial variations in the interest rate.

Moreover, while the short-term rate is certainly relevant for residential construction and perhaps for inventory investment, Keynesian theory has traditionally stressed the long-term interest rate as the main transmitter of the effects of monetary policy. If the Committee had been Keynesian it would surely have looked beyond the short-term rate and set a target for the long-term rate. To be sure, eventually, changes in short rates are transmitted to long rates, but the term structure linkage is not so tight that the Committee could simply set a short rate and let nature take its course.

By and large, the Committee showed surprisingly little concern about the long-term rate, despite Wallich's warning that "the interest rate which figures most prominently in the discussion—the funds rate—was not really the most relevant; . . . long-term bond and mortgage rate were the relevant rates" (March 1974, p. 133).

In early 1975 the Committee, or at least several participants, wanted a steeply upward sloping yield curve to give banks an incentive to make longer term loans. But the Committee did not seem willing to do much about this. Thus when Eastburn asked the manager (Sternlight) "whether one could assume that the Desk would also have objectives with respect to longer term interest rates in mind in deciding whether to lean towards purchases of coupon issues," Sternlight replied "that that would be one of the factors taken into consideration. There also would be other factors" (March 1973, p. 54). All in all, this does not sound very Keynesian.

At the same time the Committee heard some statements that sounded monetarist. The staff stated in December 1974 that "fiscal policy as well as monetary policy can raise the inflation rate . . . but that the expansionary effects of fiscal policy on *real* activity" would rather quickly run out of steam "because of crowding out" (Dec. 1974, pp. 18, 21–22). And it warned the Committee that "previous declines in the real money stock during the postwar period usually were followed by recessions" (Dec. 1974, p. 7). Pierce stated that "ultimately the rate of inflation depended on the long-run course of monetary policy. Thus while the level of prices might inevitably be raised by an exogenous increase in the price of oil or other commodities, the subsequent rate of inflation could be eventually controlled" (Dec. 1974, pp. 23–24).

However, on the other hand, Mitchell stated that "monetary policy by itself could not turn the economy around, some contribution from fiscal policy would be desirable" (Dec. 1974, p. 110). Admittedly, this *may* reflect not doubt about the potential role of changes in the money stock but, instead, doubts about how much change it would be politically feasible to bring about. However, Mitchell also argued that the fall in real balances did not portend a decline in income but, rather, a weaker demand for money (Dec. 1974, p. 109). "He could think of no time when the monetary aggregates were less useful for policy purposes than they were now" (Dec. 1974, p. 109).

Not surprisingly, Burns too was critical of a monetarist approach. He felt that

> income velocity was a far more important variable than the rate of growth of the money stock. . . . He had an uneasy feeling that too much emphasis tended to be placed on the behavior of the money stock and too little on the income velocity of money—which, as he had observed earlier, was subject to tremendous fluctuations. Fundamentally, velocity depended on confidence in economic prospects. When confidence was weak, a large addition to the money stock might lie idle, but when confidence strengthened, the existing stock of money could finance an enormous expansion in economic activity (Dec. 1974, pp. 83, 103–4).

In discussing velocity Burns stated:

> [T]he willingness to use money—that is, the rate at which money turned over, or its velocity—underwent tremendous fluctuations; velocity was a much more dynamic variable than the stock of money, and when no account was taken of it, any judgment about the growth rate of M-1 was likely to be highly incomplete. . . . In the fourth quarter of 1970 income velocity of M-1 declined at an annual rate of about 4 percent but in the very next quarter it rose at a rate of about 8 percent. While that was a short-run movement, the data also indicated that there were enormous cyclical changes (Dec. 1974, pp. 78-80).

When Partee pointed out that "in the staff's view, changes in velocity were largely a function of interest rates (Dec. 1974, p. 80) Burns responded "that he would seriously question the linking of income velocity to interest rates exclusively" since the level of economic activity is also relevant (Dec. 1974, p. 82). But this ignored the fact that the staff had previously mentioned the level of activity as a determinant. Wallich added:

> [C]hanges in monetary velocity were important and that interest rates were a main determinant of them. He noted, however, that while income velocity was customarily measured in terms of current levels for both income and money, monetary effects were ordinarily viewed as occurring with a lag of six months or so. He thought it would be useful to take account of that lag by relating the current level of GNP to the level of the money stock six months earlier (Dec. 1974, p. 81).

Bucher pointed out that the growth of long term CDs with substantial withdrawal penalties was probably reducing the velocities of M-2 and M-3 (Dec. 1974, p. 81). MacLaury then drew a distinction between secular and cyclical changes: "Cyclical changes in velocity might well be determined primarily by interest rates. His own concern, and evidently that of Mr. Bucher also, was with secular changes. The latter might well require changes in the definitions of the monetary aggregates" (Dec. 1974, p. 81).

In addition, Black referred to "the probable decline in the income velocity of money as economic activity declined further" (Dec. 1974, p. 93), while Mitchell referred to a "secular uptrend in the turnover of money" as the explanation of the decline of real balances (Dec. 1974, p. 109).

At the May 1974 meeting when Wallich questioned the staff's implicit projection of an unusual rise in velocity, Partee responded that the staff had "recently found some evidence of a secular rise in velocity" (May 1974, p. 39). But even by January 1975 the staff considered the evidence for a shift in the money demand function to be far from conclusive (Jan. 1975, p. 41). Apart from some discussion in connection with the choice between M-1 and

M–2 and M–3 this comprised virtually all of the Committee's discussion of velocity, a concept central to monetary policy.

Although it did bring out the fact that velocity is dependent on the interest rate and income, this discussion was still remarkably unaffected by the work on velocity in the professional literature. By then, the distinction between measured and permanent income, distributed adjustment lags, and the use of nonhuman wealth in addition to, or instead of, income, had all become well-established elements in the debate about velocity. Laidler's comprehensive survey of this debate (Laidler 1969) had been out for five years. Yet none of this had made any impact on the Committee's discussion of the strength of its policy.

A basic quantity theory proposition is that while the central bank determines the *nominal* money stock, the public determines the *real* money stock. It is therefore useful to look at the Committee's discussion about whether it should use the nominal money stock or the real money stock as its target.

Early in the recession several participants suggested that the Fed should accommodate the oil shock.[16] But this issue did not receive extended discussion until August 1974. Then the staff report noted that real balances had declined despite a rise in nominal balances. Eastburn responded by pointing to the dangers of using the real money stock as a target. While the real money stock "could be useful in studying the past and in explaining financial pressures, there were some dangers in using it as a policy target. Specifically, an effort to correct what might appear as an unduly low real money stock might simply reinforce the upward price spiral (Aug. 1974, p. 26).

Winn, too, was concerned that too much emphasis on real balances could be inflationary (Aug. 1974, p. 29). Wallich argued that the concept of the real money supply "was meaningful, but the central bank could not determine the real money stock; attempting to do so would be a serious mistake" (Aug. 1974, p. 33). Subsequently, Burns pointed out that the real money stock is a "slippery and dangerous" concept because as more money is printed the inflation rate increases so that the real money stock falls again. There is then an outcry to repeat this process until hyperinflation is reached (Feb. 1975, p. 56).

On the other side, Partee agreed that a constant real money stock might be consistent with hyperinflation, and that "the concept of the real money stock had to be used with caution," but felt that "the money stock had something in common with all measures that were in terms of current prices, and it had been found necessary to deflate, for example, retail sales" (Aug. 1974, p. 26). Gramley supported this by arguing that in the postwar period protracted declines in the real money stock were always followed by a recession and that real GNP was more closely correlated with the real money stock than with the nominal money stock. Given the cost-push nature of the current inflation, "it would be erroneous to conclude that monetary policy had been expansive over the past year because the money stock had grown 6 percent" (Aug. 1974, pp. 27-28). And Holland stated that the staff was not suggesting that the real money stock be used as a target but merely was suggesting an additional way of examining the issue and helping the Committee to avoid overemphasizing the nominal money stock (Aug. 1974, p. 35).

This discussion illustrated a major weakness of the Committee's procedures. It never resolved the issue but left it dangling. Those participants who were not familiar with it, and some were not economists, could conclude that some economists believed that the real money stock was a useful measure and target, while others believed that it was not. It is simple to show that if a constant real money stock is used as a target when the inflation is due to an excess supply of nominal money, the inflation will tend to explode. If the inflation is cost-push, then using a real constant money stock target will tend to accommodate and support the inflation, and is a desirable target, if and only if prevention of inflation is not a significant goal. A thorough discussion of the real money stock issue would not only have clarified the question but would have confronted the Committee forcefully with the issue of whether the inflation was entirely cost-push and whether it wanted to accommodate it fully. As it was, these issues were left unresolved.

In connection with the Committee's choice between the real and the nominal money stock it may be useful to discuss briefly the Committee's choice among the various measures of money. Although the Directive set ranges for the instrumental variable, reserves against private deposits (RPDs), and for M-1, M-2, and M-3, most of the discussion focused on M-1. RPDs got almost no attention and M-2 and M-3 got only a little. Occasionally a participant would say that the Committee should not focus entirely on M-1—that M-2 and M-3 were also "significant magnitudes" (Holland, June 1974, p. 51)—or that the Committee should "take greater account" of M-2 and M-3 "rather than focusing entirely on M-1" (Winn, July 1974, p. 54). Burns, in particular, was skeptical about M-1, saying:

> If, as he suspected, time deposits increasingly were taking on the characteristics of demand deposits, the Committee should be paying progressively more attention to M-2. The Committee has shown a tendency . . . of emphasizing M-1 heavily—sometimes it seemed almost to the exclusion of the other aggregates. It should be recognized, however, that the world was not standing still. . . . The Committee tended to focus unduly on the narrowly defined measure of money (Dec. 1974, pp. 82-83; Jan. 1975, p. 50).

At one time he suggested focusing on M-5 (which includes all bank and thrift deposits) but there was no explicit support for this in the Committee.

In summary then, the Committee was neither Keynesian nor monetarist but was eclectic. Eclecticism can be justified on two grounds. First, if there are several competing theories it is reasonable to minimize risk by selecting a policy that according to none of the theories would lead to a large loss, even though it is not the preferred policy according to any of the theories. Second, when a decision is made by a group, different members may adhere to different theories, and the policy selected may be a compromise.

But it is doubtful that either of these justifications are applicable here. There is no evidence at all in the *Minutes* that the Committee followed a conscious minimax strategy or that it had a clear idea about the theories between which it was striking a compromise. Second, the individual participants did not seem to advocate clearcut theories which were then combined or compromised to reach a consensus. Raymond Lombra and Michael Moran's (1980, p. 42) criticism of the Committee's eclecticism is therefore as applicable to 1974 as it is to the 1970–1973 period they studied.

The Policy Actually Followed

As discussed above the Fed was torn between concern about inflation and concern about recession; it did not have a clear conceptual framework, and it paid excessive attention to interest rate stabilization. Can such ingredients be transformed into efficient policy? Occasionally this might occur, but in the 1973–1975 recession such a miracle did not happen.

Table 3–4 shows the Fed's longer run targets and the operating ranges for M–1 (old definition) as well as the estimated achieved growth rate. Anyone interpreting the Fed's policy on the basis of its longer run targets would be surprised to learn that the Fed was criticized for being sharply deflationary by monetarists as well as by Keynesians. In fact, these longer run targets did not differ much from the growth rates recommended by the monetarist Shadow Open Market Committee.[17] Similarly, the midpoint of the tolerance range did not represent a sharply restrictive policy.

But these targets and ranges had little effect on what actually happened. The money growth rate dropped sharply and was even negative for a month.

Why did this happen? The usual interpretation is that the Committee's ranges for the funds rate and for money growth were inconsistent, and that the Committee, or the Manager, resolved the inconsistency by abandoning the money growth target. (Indeed, under the procedures then prevailing, only the funds-rate target had operational significance for the Manager.) Such an inconsistency is hardly surprising because as Lombra and Moran (1980, p. 44) have shown for the 1970–1973 period, the ranges adopted by the Committee were frequently not those recommended as consistent ranges by the staff. Instead of using one of the staff's alternatives for the Directive,

Table 3-4
Targeted and Achieved M-1 Growth Rates and Interest Rates

Month and Year	M-1				Funds Rate	
	Six-Months' Target	Two-Months' Tolerance Range[a]	Midpoint of Range	Estimated Achieved Rate[b]	Two-Months' Tolerance Range[a]	Mean for Statement Weeks Given[b]
	(in percent)					
November 1973	5.00	4.50–6.50	5.50	6.4	9.00–10.50	10.10
December 1973	5.25	3.00–6.00	4.50	4.9	8.75–10.00	9.76
January 1974	5.75	3.00–6.00	4.50	4.0	8.75–10.00	8.93
February 1974	5.75	6.50–9.50	8.00	11.8	8.25–9.50	9.03
March 1974	5.25	5.50–8.50	7.00	9.2	9.00–10.25	10.02
April 1974	5.50	3.00–7.00	5.00	6.5	9.75–11.25	11.46
May 1974	5.50	3.00–7.00	5.00	6.7	11.00–11.75	11.60
June 1974	5.25	3.50–7.50	5.50	8.3	11.25–12.25	13.34
July 1974	5.25	2.00–6.00	4.00	3.2[c]	11.50–13.00	12.02
August 1974	5.25	4.75–6.25	5.75	2.6	11.50–12.50	11.64
September 1974	5.75	3.00–6.00	4.50	1.7	10.25–12.00	10.43
October 1974	5.75	4.75–7.25	6.00	5.6	9.00–10.50	9.37
November 1974	5.75	6.50–9.50	8.00	6.4	8.50–10.00	8.86
December 1974	6.00	5.00–7.00	6.00	1.1	7.50– 9.00	7.76
January 1975	6.00	3.50–6.50	5.00	–2.3	6.50–7.25	6.72
February 1975	6.00[d]	5.50–7.50	6.50	7.0	5.25–6.25	5.94

Sources: Federal Open Market Committee, *Minutes* and *Blue Books.*
Note: M-1 is measured by old definition of currency plus demand deposits in commercial banks.
[a]Includes changes made between meetings.
[b]Given at next meeting of Federal Open Market Committee.
[c]Series revised.
[d]December 1974 to September 1975.

various participants would select from them as from a Chinese menu, saying, for example, I like the money growth rate of alternative *A* but the funds rate of alternative *B*. [18] In the period covered here, as in the period examined by Lombra and Moran, the Committee often chose its target ranges in such a fashion. [19]

One way of interpreting this procedure is to say that the participants were, in effect, sabotaging the process of monetary policy selection by indulging in wishful thinking and posturing. However, another interpretation is probably more correct. The numerical ranges transmitted to the Desk were not hard-and-fast instructions. The Manager attended the meetings and, from long practice, distilled an interpretation of the Committee's wishes. He then tried, to the extent feasible, to meet them. Hence, it was legitimate for someone to state the funds rate and money growth rate he wanted even if these two might be in conflict. The Manager could then use this information to bring about conditions that provided the best trade-off between these conflicting wishes. In practice, however, it usually meant that the Desk stayed within its funds rate range, and let the money growth rate get out of its range.

In any case, since the failure to reach the money targets was known to the Committee, it must take responsibility for the highly restrictive policy actually followed during the sharpest postwar recession.

How did it react to these shortfalls? Whether one says that the shortfalls received much or little attention depends on whether one calls the glass half-full or half-empty. While they were discussed extensively at the April and October 1974 meetings, they were not discussed much at other meetings. Mitchell stated that because of the previous shortfall ''it was essential to raise the rate of growth in M-1. While he was not particularly concerned about the rate of monetary growth the public was'' (Oct. 1974, p. 67). And Mayo made a similar point:

> [T]he importance of the shortfall had been overemphasized in terms of the System's ability to achieve its longer run objectives, but he recognized that the Committee had to pay more attention to short-term fluctuations in monetary growth than he would like, because of press interpretations of their significance. . . . He was not overly concerned because of the probabilities that the rate of growth would pick up over the next few months, thereby compensating for the recent shortfall (Oct. 1974, pp. 70, 53).

But Morris complained:

> The Committee had not achieved its objectives for monetary growth in the second half of 1974 and . . . as a result it had produced a more restrictive financial climate than it had sought. It seemed unlikely, in retrospect, that any member of the Committee would have advocated the 3.5 percent annual growth rate in M-1 that would be recorded for that period (Dec. 1974, p. 89).

Francis was worried that regardless of which of the three alternatives the Committee chose for its objective, the results were likely to be similar to the most expansionary alternative (March 1974, p. 141).

Given some concern about the shortfall why did the Committee not eliminate it by changing its Directive? One explanation suggested to me by James Pierce is that the Committee really wanted a very tight policy. It was, as shown above, deeply worried about inflation. But it was afraid to cut the money growth rate sharply earlier in the recession when interest rates were high and rising because of fear of political reprisals. Then, when interest rates started to decline in the fall of 1974, it could follow a sharply restrictive policy, since the public was as usual looking at interest rates and did not realize that the Fed was being so restrictive. This interpretation is supported by something Robert Weintraub told me. At a reception after the September 1974 White House meeting on inflation Burns told him that we are going to make money so tight that even you monetarists will complain about it.[20] Since President Ford strongly favored an antiinflation policy and since the Fed's policy does follow the wishes of the President (Weintraub, 1978), this statement by Burns is hardly surprising.

A second explanation is that the shortfall was an illusion or was only temporary. Thus Clay stated that the shortfalls "at least in part were a lagged response to the high levels of short-term interest rates prevailing in the spring. The rate of monetary growth was likely to pick up, and committee members should be concerned about the possibility of provoking a rate of growth that was too rapid" (Oct. 1974, p. 80). With greater generality, Clay cited Ogden Nash on ketchup bottles: "You shake and shake and shake the bottle, at first none will come, and then a lottel." (Feb. 1975, pp. 62–63).

Eastburn and Burns made similar points, while Winn suggested that the meaning of M-1 may be changing. Burns also believed that the shortfall was not so important because there had been previous overshoots that compensated for it (Oct. 1974, p. 74). In December 1974 he stated: "Taking a somewhat longer period, one could argue that there had been an overshoot rather than a shortfall. A policy geared to compensating for every shortfall would be too mechanical" (Dec. 1974, p. 104). But Morris responded that the shortfall was even greater if one reckoned it starting in June rather than in August 1974 (Dec. 1974, p. 68).

The discussion left matters too vague. Gerald Corrigan (1973) in a paper published in the *Review* of the New York Federal Reserve Bank had used the MIT-Penn-SSRC (MPS) model to determine how long and how large a shortfall had to be to have a serious effect on income, and Pierce and Thompson (1972) in a paper published by the Boston Fed had also done this using the St. Louis model. Surely, at least some of the participants had read these papers, but they were not mentioned in the discussion.[21]

A third explanation is something already discussed: the Committee while realizing that there was a serious shortfall was afraid to lower the funds rate. As Morris pointed out "there was a systematic propensity to avoid moving the funds rate—in either direction—to the extent necessary to control the aggregates, and as a result "the Committee had recently lost ground in its pursuit of its objectives for the aggregates" (Oct. 1974, p. 49). Sheehan too stated that "two or three times during the past year . . . the Desk had not acted briskly enough because of its excessive sensitivity to market conditions" (Oct. 1974, p. 50). A major reason why the Committee was so reluctant to move the funds rate was fear about the effect on market expectations, a point already discussed.

While Burns and Hayes did once refer to the impact of falling interest rates on the exchange rate (Dec. 1974, pp. 71, 87) this did not play a major role. However, this issue might have come up more frequently and more forcefully had the Committee seriously considered cutting the funds rate.

One other reason for tolerating a shortfall is a much more subtle one and one that academic critics of the Fed generally have missed: if the funds rate is reduced sharply and the money growth rate raised substantially to compensate for the shortfall, then it will be necessary to raise the funds rate and lower the money growth rate again in the future. And this may be difficult.[22] For example, MacLaury, who nonetheless was in favor of lowering rates, remarked:

> [T]he main reason some Committee members were not ready to adopt a policy that would assure moderate growth in the aggregates . . . was the fear that the Committee would not be able—or would not be prepared—to let interest rates turn back up once expansion in economic activity began. He believed that reasons could be found for that fear, even in the Committee's own past history (Jan. 1975, pp. 74–75).

Burns explained the difficulty of raising rates again later on by saying that "the economy might still not be in recovery, or the recovery might appear to be so delicate, fragile, and uncertain that it would be hard to face up to a course that would bring about rising interest rates at that time" (March 1975, p. 69).

Similarly, Kimbrel said that if the Committee adopted a too expansionary policy at that time this might "force the Committee to face the difficult decision to raise rates later on . . . when the unemployment rate was still undesirably high" (Dec. 1974, p. 98). Partee too, stated that "it probably would not be feasible" to lower the money stock target at a time of high unemployment (Dec. 1974, p. 31).

Objectively, there may not have been much of a problem here; if the funds rate, after having been reduced, were raised again to its previous level, the current expansion need not necessarily be significantly weaker than it would have been had the rate not been reduced at all. This is all very well, but the psychological strain and political problems involved in raising the funds rate at such a time *may* be more than Fed officials could bear. This *may* point to a weakness in the elegant control theory solutions to monetary policy.

Turning to those times when the money growth rate was above rather than below target (so that a rise in the funds rate was called for) a fear of hurting residential construction was cited as a reason for not raising the funds rate. In the May–June 1974 period another reason was the prevailing financial fragility.[23]

The Feasibility of Stabilization Policy

The Fed's thinking and behavior in the 1973–1975 recession is of interest not so much for its own sake as for the light it throws on the Fed's ability to operate a successful countercyclical policy. Along the lines of Friedman's (1953) classic analysis of stabilization policy, to do so the Fed must estimate with sufficient accuracy nominal income in the absence of its stabilization policy, the size of its impact on income, and the lag in the effect of its policy. Let us see whether the Fed had such information in the 1973–1975 recession.

Forecasting GNP

The Board forecasts GNP by combining the predictions of its econometric model with the judgmental forecasts of staff members. As explained by Partee: "The staff was not bound by the econometric model. The staff presented a judgmental projection, which of necessity followed a middle course, taking into account the behavior of the model, other kinds of evidence, and the judgments of various senior staff members (Oct. 1974, pp. 29–30). In general, the judgmental projections seemed to play a larger role than the model. Various Federal Reserve Banks make their own forecasts, some of them using econometric models.

Table 3–3 shows a comparison of the staff's forecasts with the actual changes in nominal GNP, real GNP, and the fixed weight gross private product deflator. Since the *actual* GNP figures are really not actuals but are *ex post* estimates, the table shows three different estimates: the latest available one, as well as two estimates made in 1974.

For nominal GNP the staff's forecasts were fairly good except for 1975 I, particularly if one compares them to the GNP estimates made in 1974 rather than to the 1981 revised estimates. Like other forecasters at the time the Fed made serious errors in decomposing nominal GNP changes between changes in output and in prices. Its real GNP forecast was quite poor, and this was true for prices too. This performance was in line with that of private forecasters. Lombra and Moran (1980, p. 25) show a comparison of the Fed's forecasts and the median of selected private forecasts for 1973 III–1974 III. The Fed does better for nominal GNP and for the price deflator but a bit worse for real GNP.

It may be useful to try an exercise with the Fed's real GNP forecast. Assume that the Fed had a definite target for real GNP growth and had adopted a policy to eliminate a certain proportion of the gap between this target and the predicted real GNP growth rate. Assume further—though this is, of course, quite unrealistic—that the Fed knew exactly the magnitude of the effect on real GNP of a given change in the money growth rate or the federal funds rate and assume also that it knew the relevant lags. If so, the only source of error is the prediction of real GNP in the absence of the policy change.

Table 3–5 shows to what extent, under these hypothetical circumstances, the Fed would have succeeded in stabilizing real GNP. To calculate this one must make an assumption about the specific real GNP growth rate the Fed was aiming at. Accordingly, I used four hypothetical GNP growth-rate targets: 0 percent, 1 percent, 2 percent, and 3 percent. The first column shows the gap between these hypothetical target rates and the actual growth rate. The other columns show the percent of this gap between the desired and actual growth rate that would be eliminated if the Fed had used its real GNP forecast to set policy. In doing so the Fed would have had to decide how much of the predicted gap to offset. Accordingly, table 3–5 shows the results for four different policies that try to offset 100 percent, 50 percent, 25 percent, and 10 percent of the gap. The figures shown in these columns are the percentages of the gap, after using the policy, as a percent of the initial gap. They include overshoots as well as undershoots. For example, assume that the Fed aimed at a 2-percent growth rate, and the actual growth rate in the absence of policy was 1 percent, while if stabilization policy is undertaken based on the inaccurate GNP projection, the resulting real GNP growth rate is 3 percent. This is counted as a 100-percent error.

Would any of these four policies have succeeded in closing the GNP gap substantially? As table 3–5 shows the Fed's errors in predicting GNP were large enough to limit severely the efficacy of stabilization policy.[24] Hence, quite apart from the errors in predicting the size—and lags—of the effects of its policy, the Fed would not have been able to make much progress toward a particular real GNP growth target because of its errors in predicting real GNP.[25]

Table 3–5
Effects of Errors in Real Gross National Product Forecasts on Efficacy of Stabilization Policy

Year and Quarter	Gap between Actual and Targeted Real GNP Growth Rates as Percent of GNP[a]	Policy That Tries to Offset Following Percent of Gap: Gap after Use of Policy as Percentage of the Gap without the Policy			
		100%	50%	25%	10%
Assumed Target Growth Rate = 0					
1974 II	.5	400	140	20	60
1974 III	− 2.4	154	125	112	104
1974 IV	− 5.1	159	129	116	106
1975 I	− 8.2	80	90	95	98
1975 II	4.9	139	120	110	104
1975 III	9.3	45	72	86	95
Assumed Target Growth Rate = 1%					
1974 II	− .5	200	60	20	60
1974 III	− 3.4	79	76	74	71
1974 IV	− 6.1	116	100	92	87
1975 I	− 9.2	61	75	83	86
1975 II	3.9	200	162	144	133
1975 III	8.3	63	88	100	107
Assumed Target Growth Rate = 2%					
1974 II	− 1.5	0	20	27	33
1974 III	− 4.4	39	45	50	52
1974 IV	− 7.1	86	79	75	73
1975 I	− 10.2	45	63	72	76
1975 II	2.9	303	238	203	183
1975 III	7.3	85	105	116	123
Assumed Target Growth Rate = 3%					
1974 II	− 2.5	40	28	24	20
1974 III	− 5.5	13	29	36	40
1974 IV	− 8.1	63	63	63	63
1975 I	− 11.1	32	53	62	69
1975 II	1.9	516	384	321	284
1975 III	6.3	114	132	140	144

Sources: Based on U.S. Department of Commerce, *Business Conditions Digest,* May 1981, p. 98; Board of Governors, Federal Reserve System, *Green Book.*
[a]Negative sign means that actual Gross National Product was below assumed target.

The Strength and Lags of Monetary Policy

Little need be said about the Committee's view of the strength of monetary policy. The Committee's discussion of how money affects income has already been taken up. The reader should recall that this discussion was entirely in vague qualitative terms, terms that would, for example, not allow the Committee to conclude that a 2-percent increase in the money growth rate would raise nominal income by, say, 1 percent or 2 percent or more during the period considered.

To be an effective stabilizer the Fed had to know, not only the magnitude of its impact on the economy, but also the timing of the impact. There was no systematic discussion of this in the period covered here, but at various meetings participants made a number of statements about the lag. As usual, it is not possible to go beyond individual statements. But as far as one can judge from them the lag seems to have been thought of as six months or more.[26]

At the December 1974 meeting when the economy was in a deep recession that was projected to end in six months the problem of the lag in the effect of monetary policy on the economy was particularly acute. The staff report stated that an expansionary policy, "beginning now, would produce a markedly more robust economic upturn after mid-1975" (Dec. 1974, p. 19). Wallich, too, stated that the lag is "ordinarily viewed as six months or so" (Dec. 1974, p. 81). Bucher believed that "monetary policy could no longer have much effect on economic activity in the first-half of next year," while Mayo went further, and argued that to advocate an expansionary policy was to exaggerate the effect of monetary policy "in the next six to twelve months" (Dec. 1974, pp. 86, 90). To give some examples from other meetings, Brimmer implied a lag of six months or more for the main effect of monetary policy (June 1974, p. 59). Mitchell referred to the lag as "at least" three months, "probably" six months, and "perhaps" nine months (Sept. 1974, p. 87). Many participants pointed out that the lag would be longer for prices than for output.

This focus on "six months or so" is surprising because in March 1973 the staff had pointed out that the lags were much longer. Thus Partee then told the Committee "the lags in monetary policy are such that far and away the major economic impact from a shift in posture now would come in 1974, aside from the effects on public psychology" (March 1973, p. 8). And Pierce stated "there is substantial evidence that the real sectors of the economy do not even begin to respond significantly . . . for six to nine months unless expectations change drastically" (March 1973, p. 13).

There are several problems with the Committee's discussion of the lag. First, while some participants talked in terms of a single figure for the lag and others talked about the time needed for the main effect, none seemed to have a clear idea of the distributed lag. Second, the six-months-or-so figure cited by many participants may well have been wrong. While a number of specific studies of the monetary policy lag had come up with a similar conclusion, others found considerably longer lags (See Mayer, 1968, p. 188, and Uselton, 1974, ch. 2). Moreover, econometric models, which unlike *some* of the specific studies take account of multiplier and accelerator effects, have usually found much longer lags. Thus Carl Christ in his survey of eight models shows one as reaching its peak effect in the eighth quarter, with the others having still longer lags (Christ, 1975, pp. 68–69). Moreover, the Board's own MPS model shows a substantial lag, with the peak effect on nominal GNP coming in the eighth quarter (Modigliani, 1971).[27] What is disturbing is that not once in the discussion of lags did any Committee member mention the lag estimate of the Board's own model.[28]

To sum up, the Fed's forecast of real GNP was not very good and its information about the strength and lags of its policies was quite primitive. None of this suggests that stabilization policy is actually stabilizing.

Some General Aspects of the FOMC's Discussion

As the above quotations from the *Minutes* show, despite the fact that the majority of its members were professional economists, the Committee's discussions were not technical. The fact that it used technical terms only infrequently is, of course, irrelevant, but what is more serious is that the overall level of the discussion made so little use of current economic research.[29] As already discussed, the Committee's treatment of velocity, real balances, and the lag in monetary policy did not come to grips with the issue in the way in which most economists, or at least academic economists, would like. This unwillingness to make use of modern techniques and ways of thought is illustrated by the role the MPS model played in the Committee's discussion. While it was, of course, used in making the staff forecasts and in preparing the alternatives for the Directive, the Committee used model simulations only rarely to determine the effects of various policy options. To be sure, the model was referred to fairly frequently, but these were mainly passing references.[30]

A second characteristic of the FOMC meetings is that basic issues were generally not discussed.[31] The main reason for this is that the FOMC meetings are businesslike meetings that had to come up with a particular Directive. Hence, the focus was on "current events" and on "what do we do now?" rather than on how the economy works. Other reasons cited by some people interviewed were that several of the participants were not economists and that the governors could, and did, discuss theoretical issues with the Board's staff, while the presidents had access to their own staffs.[32] However, this argument is not convincing. As was shown, when theoretical discussions did occur, they were not very sophisticated.

One thing that is clear in the *Minutes* is that the absence of debates on many fundamental issues did not mean that everyone was satisfied with the way the Fed functioned. Thus Francis, a firm monetarist, remarked that the current downturn "was one of the few declines, if not the only one, to have developed without having been preceded by the stabilization policy actions that brought it about" (Dec. 1974, p. 99). And Partee, who is no monetarist, pointed out:

> [A] pattern typical of past business cycles was for the money supply to grow more slowly, or even decline, in the last stage of the boom and the beginning of the recession, and to grow rapidly after the recovery began. According to his recollection, the recovery phase of all postwar cycles had been marked by rapid monetary growth. . . . Presumably, the Committee, which was now paying increased attention to growth rates in the monetary aggregates, would resist a sharp acceleration in money growth [in the coming expansion] (Dec. 1974, p. 73).

A third characteristic of the FOMC was that it focused on the short run. Most of the discussion of the Directive dealt with the ranges to be set for a two-months' period (two or three weeks of which were already over at the time), and even the longer run targets were usually only six months' targets. (Fortunately, the Humphrey-Hawkins Act has now forced the Fed to adopt a longer time frame.) A major reason for this focus was that the Committee had very little faith in longer run forecasts. It realized that, since at least some of the effect of its actions showed up only in the longer run, it should plan for the longer run. But it lacked the information to do so. Everyone I posed this problem to was aware of this dilemma.

Since the painful results of a restrictive policy occur much sooner than the painful effects of an expansionary policy the Committee's short-run focus generated a bias towards inflation. This was well recognized by a number of participants.

Willes stated that in the three meetings he had attended in the past three years the inflationary situation had:

> made it desirable to reduce the rate of growth in the monetary aggregates. But, every time, there seemed to be some special factor . . . that cautioned against doing so. He had the uneasy feeling that the frequency of such occasions explained the somewhat excessive rate of monetary growth over the past three years and contributed to the rate of inflation. . . . It was in extraordinary times that it was most important to maintain the focus on the longer run targets for monetary growth and to endeavor, even at some risk, to avoid allowing temporary pressures to distract the Committee from those targets (May 1974, p. 46).

Not surprisingly, Francis supported him in this (May 1974, p. 47). Eastburn stated that despite the risk of financial brinksmanship it was necessary to take strong action. The excessive growth rate of M-1:

had come about because the Committee had been unwilling to adhere to its long run growth targets in the face of short run developments in credit markets. . . . The excessive rate of growth in the monetary aggregates . . . had also contributed to the precarious state of financial markets. There had been a tendency to keep financial conditions from deteriorating by means that added to prevailing inflationary pressures—a course that could be self-defeating (June 1974, p. 45).

And Clay complained that the "Committee has been overshooting its targets . . . over a long period, and it had been responding by raising the target" (June 1974, pp. 47–48). Morris pointed out since the effects on employment come earlier than the effects on inflation this makes an expansionary policy look unduly good (July 1974, pp. 23, 25). To the request that the staff should therefore provide longer run forecasts, Partee replied: "The staff's ability to develop reliable projections even for short periods ahead seemed to decrease. Of necessity projections several years ahead would be econometric rather than judgmental in nature and he would have no great confidence in such forecasts under circumstances such as those now prevailing (July 1974, p. 25).

All in all, the way the FOMC is organized is not beyond criticism. It would probably be useful to have longer meetings with more back-and-forth discussion, and greater focus on theoretical issues and less on current events.[33] In general, the Committee seems to be flooded by disconnected facts and such facts are often the enemy of the truth. Thus, in discussing why the Japanese achieved surprise in their attack on Pearl Harbor, Roberta Wohlstetter (1962, pp. 386–87) wrote: "our decision makers had in hand an impressive amount of information. . . . We failed to anticipate Pearl Harbor not for want of the relevant materials, but because of a plethora of irrelevant ones." The way it is now organized the Committee functions well below the average quality of its members. (Any academic who doubts that this could happen should think back on his or her last department meeting.)

Moreover, if the Committee does not believe that it can rely on longer run forecasts it should try to avoid myopia in some other way. For example, it could start with a strong prior in favor of a stable monetary growth rate set with an eye to noninflationary secular growth.

In recent years much effort, both by the Fed's own staff and by academic economists, has been devoted to applying control theory to monetary policy. Judging by the way the FOMC functioned in the 1973–1975 recession this work is far removed from the way in which policy is actually made. For example, any attempt to apply control theory would come up against the Fed's reluctance to move to a restrictive policy early in the upswing when unemployment is still high.

More generally, the above evidence rejects the belief that, with its large and highly competent staff, the Fed is able to analyze problems and make decisions in a state-of-the-art fashion. The Fed's research appears to have only limited influence on the actual making of policy. It reminds one of Stephen Goldfeld's statement about his experience as a member of the Council of Economic Advisers. Goldfeld observed that when he had been merely a staff member, he "never got a view of how weirdly decisions are made at the top" (Rattner, 1980).

The FOMC's inability to fully digest available economic information and analysis has an implication for the question of whether the Fed should use a single target, such as the money stock, or "look at everything." Benjamin Friedman (1977) has shown that, in principle, using a single target is inefficient. But if I am right, the FOMC's capacity to manipulate information effectively is quite limited. If so, a rule of thumb, such as a money stock target, is likely to make for better policy than is the formally more correct, but overly ambitious, principle of looking at everything.

All this has an obvious bearing on the issue of discretionary monetary policy versus a stable growth-rate rule. The case for discretionary policy is intuitively appealing because it seems as though highly competent policy-makers should be able to do better than a mechanical rule. While the above evidence is obviously insufficient to disconfirm this definitively, it should at least serve to make it less plausible. Admittedly, it relates only to 1973–1975, but from talking to various FOMC members I get the impression that not very much has changed since then.

In Defense of the Fed

Having criticized the Fed it is only fair to see whether there is also a reasonable case for the defense. Such a case could be made in three ways; first by arguing that, regardless of any lack of sophistication in its analysis, it did adopt the right policies. Second, one should judge the Fed's sophistication not by any abstract standard but by comparison with the sophistication of the policy advice of others. Third, one could argue that using greater technical sophistication would have been useless because sophisticated analysis is still inadequate to contribute much to monetary policymaking.

Rober Craine, Arthur Havenner, and James Berry (1978) used simulations of the MPS model to compare several monetary policies, including the Fed's actual policy, in the period 1973 III–1975 II. In this comparison the Fed's actual policy performed best. This study may seem to make my complaints about the quality of the Fed's analysis irrelevant, but this is not so. To start with, the study assumes that the MPS model is a correct representation of the economy, which may or may not be the case. Second, the Fed's performance is not really so good because just toward the end of the period covered the inflation rate appears to take off.[34] Third, even an unsound policy will sometimes give good results; errors in predicting GNP may largely offset errors in predicting the impact of policy. Sometimes two wrongs *do* make a right.

It is difficult to compare the sophistication of the FOMC with that of others. One obvious group for comparison are academic economists testifying before Congress on current monetary policy. On the whole, their testimony impresses me as more sophisticated, or at least as more focused on the evidence that is available on basic issues. One might object that this comparison is misleading; that the weakness of the Committee certainly does not arise from any lack of ability of its members but from its format, particularly the current events focus of the discussion. This point is true, but it merely shifts the blame from the individual members to the way the Fed is organized.

Another possible comparison is with the Shadow Open Market Committee. I have the impression that the Shadow's discussion compared favorably with that of the substance; but then I am hardly an impartial judge since during this time I was one of the shadows.[35]

A third possible comparison is with other government agencies. Here too, it is hard to make a comparison because so little information is available. But Daniel Moynihan (1981, p. 103) reports that "I have served in the Cabinet or sub-Cabinet of four Presidents. I do not believe I have ever heard at a Cabinet meeting a serious discussion of political ideas . . . The lesser coin of economics drives all else out of circulation save only foreign policy."

Conclusion

This chapter has examined the thinking behind monetary policy in the 1973–1975 recession. It has shown that the Fed was seriously concerned about both inflation and unemployment. International considerations and probably political considerations did not seem to be as serious constraints on Fed policy as concern about market expectations and about interest-rate variability were. For at least two months the Fed was also seriously constrained by the prevailing financial fragility. The Fed lacked the knowledge needed to run an efficient stabilization policy. Its forecasts of real GNP and inflation were, like most others, poor, and its discussion of the strength and lags of monetary policy were disappointing.

What lessons can one draw? First, as far as financial panics are concerned, the 1974 episode shows the Fed as being aware of the problem and knowing what to do about it. However, it is *possible* that if the Fed is again and again frustrated in its attempt to bring the money growth rate down, it might eventually become willing to run the risk of a financial panic and hence allow one to develop. If Wojnilower (1980, p. 291n) is right that in stopping a boom "there is no kill except overkill" then the Fed might once go too far.

For stabilization policy in general the message of this chapter is pessimistic. What makes countercyclical policy seem so attractive is that it is easy to believe that with all our elaborate mathematical and econometric models we know enough to do better than blind market forces. But insofar as the FOMC still operates now as it did in 1973–1975 (which is probably the case) this sophisticated knowledge has little bearing on how policy is made. As Lombra and Moran (1980, p. 43) point out with respect to an earlier period, its policymaking operates by seat-of-the-pants judgments.[36]

None of this denies that some slow progress has been made. However much one may want to criticize the Fed's type of analysis in 1973–1975 it still was a great improvement over the analysis unearthed by Brunner and Meltzer in 1964. Progress *has* occurred. In fact, one might argue that what should be faulted is not the Fed's sophistication—which is probably superior to that of most other government agencies—but the sophistication of those who hold an idealized view of government and expect the Fed to operate in a state-of-the-art fashion rather than on the basis of casual thinking.

Would we be better off shifting from ad hoc discretionary policy to a control theory approach? This is a problem I hope to discuss in a subsequent paper. But if the FOMC still functions now as it did in the 1973–1975 recession, as is probably the case, a stable monetary growth-rate rule with its pessimistic view about what policy actually does achieve does not look bad by comparison.

Appendix 3A
Economic Conditions

In the first three quarters of 1973 the U.S. economy was in a strong upswing, having reached its output ceiling early in the year (*Economic Report,* 1974, p. 47). But in the last quarter of the year the oil embargo caused widespread disruptions, particularly for the automobile industry. At the same time there occurred a serious downturn in residential construction. The National Bureau of Economic Research (NBER) locates the upper turning point in November 1973, with the subsequent trough in March 1975. However, this interpretation is disputed. Norman Bowsher (1975) has cogently argued that there were in effect two distinct recessions. In one, from November 1973 to early fall 1974, the decline in output was due mainly to supply constraints and distortions caused by the oil shock.[1] The second contraction starting in the fall of 1974 was, Bowsher argues, the more usual type of recession occasioned by a decline in aggregate demand that resulted from a marked decline in the money growth rate. Regardless of whether one views 1973–1975 as a single recession or as two consecutive downturns, the overall decline during what Otto Eckstein (1978) called the "Great Recession," was the most severe since the 1930s.

Although, according to Alan Blinder (1979, p. 37), "there were plenty of warning signals," these signals were disregarded. By late 1973 the consensus forecast was that "business will drag" and *perhaps* slide into a recession in the first half of 1974, but that there will be a recovery in the second half (*Business Week,* Dec. 22, 1973, p. 49).

A failure of forecasts is not unusual. What is more surprising is that the recession was not recognized for so long after it had started. Thus in September 1974—ten months after the NBER turning point—*Business Week* (Sept. 21, 1974, p. 28) warned its readers that the odds have risen for a recession in the first half of 1975. According to Poole (1975, pp. 126–127):

> The consensus forecast in early 1974 was for a flat economy. Pessimists argued that a couple of quarters of declining real gross national product were likely and optimists thought a recession would be avoided. No one foresaw either a deep recession or a boom. By June the forecasts became, if anything, a bit more optimistic . . . From what is known now, the business cycle peak may be tentatively placed at November 1973. However, after a significant decline in the early months of 1974, the economy remained basically on a plateau until autumn. As the year continued, the consensus forecast was revised downward, but this plateau led most forecasters to believe that any further contraction would be relatively mild.

The recession, whether acknowledged or not, was certainly not the only problem facing the Federal Reserve. In 1973 the Consumer Price Index (CPI) had risen by 8.8 percent, a faster rate than any year since the Korean War, and in 1974 it rose by a further 12.2 percent. Real wages fell in 1974. This led to the fear that nominal wages would rise very rapidly in 1975 as unions would try to catch up. While Keynesians attribute the inflation primarily to supply shocks and to the elimination of price controls, monetarists attribute it in large part—though not entirely—to excessive growth in the money stock.

Chapter Notes

1. Occasionally, the FOMC would hold dinner meetings prior to the formal sessions. However, these did not involve significant policy discussions off the record.

2. For scholars an even more-detailed chronological summary of the FOMC discussions is available upon request.

3. For a further discussion see Pierce (1974).

4. While later speakers would, of course, modify their statements in light of what had gone before, only once in the seventeen months covered here did Burns ask, toward the end of the policy discussion, whether anyone wanted to modify his position as a result of what was said subsequently.

5. However, the governors did have plenty of chances to discuss policy among themselves.

6. Admittedly, there are frequently more than nineteen people at university faculty meetings and a back-and-forth discussion does take place. But at a faculty meeting not everyone, is required to speak. At FOMC meetings all nineteen persons were expected to participate.

7. In addition, it is possible that some informal discussions of political constraints did not find their way into the *Minutes.*

8. Bucher stated elsewhere Congress, as the reflection of public opinion, limits the amount of unemployment that is feasible. "Thus, things which we might be able to do in a vacuum, and which would probably make the most economic sense cannot be fully implemented because of possible Congressional reaction" (U.S. Cong. 1974, p. 43).

9. Moreover, William Poole (1980, p. 276) has remarked: "My distinct impression from following the monetary policy over a period of years is that Federal Reserve officials do feel constrained to follow policies that 'look right' to the public and the Congress."

10. Winn and Clay too suggested—again without effect—that the Fed announce what it is doing (January 1975, pp. 99, 101).

11. In response to the problems experienced in the summer, banks

subsequently followed a conservative policy for several months. They improved their capital/assets ratios by reducing their lending and security purchases, and, in anticipation of possible future needs, they reduced their borrowing at the discount window. As the Committee subsequently discussed, these actions complicated its attempt to ease credit.

12. As Robert Weintraub (private communication) pointed out, money growth was reduced cumulatively during the Franklin crisis and also declined in 1970 during the Penn Central crisis.

13. Joseph Bisignanio (private communication) suggested that the existence of specialized housing agencies was an important factor in what otherwise would seem to be a deemphasis on the plight of the housing industry. He also pointed to a temporary recovery of construction in the spring of 1974.

14. In his interviews with Federal Reserve officials (U.S. Cong., 1974, pp. 5–76), Weintraub also found great emphasis on the need to stabilize interest rates.

15. In March 1975, in the course of a long disquisition on his view of postwar long cycles, Burns pointed out that a recession is a necessary corrective that restores balance and prepares the economy for another upswing (p. 27).

16. Robert Weintraub's survey of the views of governors and presidents shows them as mostly having an essentially middle-of-the-road view of accommodation (U.S. Cong., 1974, pp. 7–8, 14, 25, 44–46, 61, 87–89, 118).

17. The Shadow Open Market Committee recommended the following M–1 growth rates: March 1974, 5 to 5½ percent; September 1974, 5½ percent; March 1975, 5½ percent plus a one-time increase to make up for the previous shortfall.

18. While some participants may have selected what they believed to be consistent ranges based on work by their staff, this apparently was not usual.

19. However, the Committee's ranges were in many cases not *necessarily* inconsistent with the staff's estimates. For example, for the month ending in April 1974, the *Blue Book's* alternative B ranges were 6½ to 8½ percent for M–1, 9½ to 10¾ percent for the funds range. The Committee's ranges were 5½ to 8½ percent for M–1 and 9 to 10½ percent for the funds rate. Due to the overlap it is not easy to tell whether the implicit underlying relationships are compatible.

20. This story has been corroborated by a witness.

21. At a Congressional hearing Hayes implicitly referred to the results reached by these studies (U.S. Cong., 1974, p. 363).

22. For a discussion of this subject by an academic—who is a former Fed staff economist—see Poole (1979, p. 477).

23. In their discussion of the FOMC during 1970–1973 Lombra and Moran (1980, pp. 48–50) suggest three factors for the Committee's concern about short rates. They are the unreliability of the money data, a tendency for some participants to harken back to the old operating procedures, and a fear that a rise in interest rates would lead to the extension of price controls to cover interest rates. The first two may also have been important in the period covered here.

24. The actual GNP growth rate already includes the effects of the policy the Fed actually did follow, and this is a weakness of my procedure. I also ignored rational expectations effects.

25. But before blaming the Fed for this error one should remember that private forecasters also did badly for this period.

26. Francis thought of the lag as variable and as preventing monetary policy from being a very useful device for offsetting short run fluctuations, while Balles believed that though we do not know much about the lag, it is important (U.S. Cong., 1974, pp. 68, 71–72, 98).

27. Since the MPS model is continually being changed, its lag estimate may have been different in 1974 from the one cited here, but the difference is not likely to be large.

28. Lombra and Moran (1980, pp. 49–51) argue that despite the Committee's realization that monetary policy operates with a lag, the Committee, in practice, tended to ignore the lag and focus on current conditions. This is supported by a statement made by Clay that "prompt action would be taken to stem an actual, but not a prospective, decline" (September 1974, p. 84).

29. The only citation of an article in a professional journal was a self-citation by Brimmer.

30. There were also a few references to the Fed's money market models, the San Francisco Federal Reserve Bank model, and the Wharton model. At a Congressional Hearing (U.S. Cong., 1974, p. 326) Burns stated his belief that "the forces affecting economic activity and prices . . . are far too complex to be described by a simple mathematical equation or by a large number of them."

31. Currently, because of the Humphrey-Hawkins Act the FOMC has to discuss its policy trade-offs more than it did in 1973–1975.

32. Moreover, some participants may have preferred to make a current events argument rather than a theoretical one because they believed that the former would be more effective since it is hard to change people's minds on basic issues.

33. In this view of one insider, the Committee thought that the more detailed its discussion of current events the more sophisticated it was.

34. I am indebted for this point to Arthur Havenner.

35. Moreover, it is hard to compare the two committees for several reasons. First, the Shadow Committee more or less agreed on an underlying

view of the economy; in fact, unlike the real thing, its members had been selected precisely for this. Second, while its meetings were open, no minutes were kept, and hence I had to rely on its position papers and on my memory. Third, it met only twice a year, so that it naturally tended to focus on longer run and, hence, more on fundamental issues.

36. In another piece (Mayer, forthcoming) I have looked at the Board of Governor's decision-making process when it lowered the Regulation Q ceiling in 1966. This too showed a disappointing picture; the longer run effects of this action received almost no attention.

Appendix Note

1. William Poole (1974, p. 243), too, attributed the fall in real GNP in the first quarter of 1974 to a supply shock rather than to a traditional recession.

References

Blinder, Alan. 1979. *Economic Policy and the Great Stagflation.* New York: Academic Press.

Bowsher, Norman. 1975. "Two Stages to the Current Recession," Federal Reserve Bank of St. Louis, *Monthly Review* (June):2-8.

Brunner, Karl and Allan Meltzer. 1964. *Some General Features of the Federal Reserve's Approach to Policy,* U.S. Cong. House, Committee on Banking and Currency, Subcommittee on Domestic Finance, 88th Cong. 2nd sess.

Christ, Carl. 1975. "Judging the Performance of Econometric Models of the U.S. Economy," *International Economic Review* 16 (February): 54-77.

Corrigan, Gerald. 1973. "Income Stabilization and Short-Run Variability in Money," Federal Reserve Bank of New York *Monthly Review* (April):87-98.

Craine, Roger, Arthur Havenner, and James Berry. 1978. "Fixed Rules versus Activism in the Conduct of Monetary Policy," *American Economic Review* 68 (December):769-783.

Eckstein, Otto. 1978. *The Great Recession,* New York: North Holland.

Federal Open Market Committee. 1973-1975. *Memoranda of Discussion* (*Minutes*).

Friedman, Benjamin. 1977. "The Inefficiency of Short-Run Monetary Targets for Monetary Policy," *Brookings Papers on Economic Activity* 2: 293-335.

Friedman, Milton. 1953. "The Effects of a Full Employment Policy on Economic Stabilization: A Formal Analysis," in *Essays on Positive Economics*. Chicago: University of Chicago Press, pp. 117–132.

Friedman, Milton, and Anna Schwartz. 1963. *A Monetary History of the United States*. Princeton: Princeton University Press.

Laidler, David. 1969. *The Demand for Money*. New York: Dunn-Donnelly.

Lombra, Raymond, and Michael Moran. 1980. "Policy Advice and Policy-making at the Federal Reserve," in Karl Brunner and Allan Meltzer (eds.), *Carnegie-Rochester Conference on Public Policy* 13 (Autumn): 9–68. (Supplement to *Journal of Monetary Economics*.)

Mayer, Thomas. 1968. *Monetary Policy in the United States*. New York: Random House.

———. Forthcoming. "Regulation Q in 1966: A Case Study of Federal Reserve Policymaking," *Journal of Monetary Economics*.

Modigliani, Franco. 1971. "Monetary Policy, and Consumption," in Federal Reserve Bank of Boston, *Consumer Spending and Monetary Policy: the Linkages,* Boston: Federal Reserve Bank of Boston, pp. 9–84.

Modigliani, Franco, and Milton Friedman. 1977. "The Monetarist Controversy: A Seminar Discussion," Federal Reserve Bank of San Francisco, *Economic Review* (Spring) *Supplement*.

Moynihan, Daniel P. 1981. Review of K. Galbraith, "A Life in Our Times," *New Yorker*. August 10, pp. 91–106.

Pierce, James. 1974. "Quantitative Analysis for Decisions at the Federal Reserve," *Annals of Economic and Social Measurement* 3 (January): 11–19.

Pierce, James, and Thomas Thompson. 1972. "Controlling the Stock of Money," in Federal Reserve Bank of Boston, *Controlling the Monetary Aggregates II*. Boston: Federal Reserve Bank of Boston, pp. 115–136.

Poole, William. 1974. "Reflections on U.S. Macroeconomic Policy," *Brookings Papers on Economic Activity* 1:233–246.

———. 1975. "Monetary Policy during the Recession," *Brookings Papers on Economic Activity* 1:123–140.

———. 1979. "Burnsian Monetary Policy: Eight Years of Progress?" *Journal of Finance* 34 (May):473–484.

———. 1980. "Macroeconomic Policy, 1971–1975: An Appraisal," in Stanley Fisher (ed.), *Rational Expectations and Economic Policy*. Chicago: University of Chicago Press, pp. 269–279.

Rattner, Sidney. 1980. "Economist Sans Politics," *New York Times* September 21.

Simpson, Thomas. 1980. "The Redefined Monetary Aggregates," *Federal Reserve Bulletin* 66 (February):97–114.

U.S. Board of Governors, Federal Reserve System. 1974, 1975. *Annual Reports*. Washington, D.C.

———. 1973–1975. "Blue Books" (unpublished).

———. 1973–1975. "Excerpts from the Minutes of the Meetings of the Board" (unpublished).

———. 1973–1975 "Green Books" (unpublished).

U.S. Congress, House, Committee on Banking and Currency. 1974. *Federal Reserve Policy and Inflation and High Interest Rates Hearings,* 93rd. Cong., 2nd sess. (July–August).

U.S. Executive Office of the President. 1974, 1975. *Economic Report of the President.* Washington, D.C.

Uselton, Gene. 1974. *Lags in the Effects of Monetary Policy.* New York: Marcel Dekker.

Weintraub, Robert. 1978. "Congressional Supervision of Monetary Policy," *Journal of Monetary Economics* 4 (April):341–361.

Wholstetter, Roberta. 1962. *Pearl Harbor, Warning and Decision.* Stanford: Stanford University Press.

Wicker, Elmus. 1966. *Federal Reserve Monetary Policy 1917–1933.* New York: Random House.

Wojnilower, Albert. 1980. "The Central Role of Credit Crunches in Recent Financial History," *Brookings Papers on Economic Activity* 2:277–326.

Discussion

William L. Silber

My role as discussant in part I of this book is straightforward. It is to pick and choose individual points made by Sylla (ch. 2) and Meltzer (ch. 1) in an effort to integrate some of their ideas. Let me begin by developing Sylla's main thesis and then focusing on a particular related point raised by Meltzer.

Sylla's basic notion is that the innovation of new monetary standards and the uses of new forms of money respond to the constraints that are implicit in existing monetary arrangements and regulations. Very often, Sylla notes, these innovations respond to crises in the monetary system. The examples given include the revolutionary war and the crisis over paper money; the Civil War and the innovation of the National Banking System; the Panic of 1907 and the creation of the Federal Reserve System; and the Great Depression—which produced a host of new monetary regulations and institutions.

In looking for a framework to analyze such innovations, Sylla references some earlier work on constraint-induced innovation by firms and points out that such a perspective is too narrow to explain the government's role in monetary innovation. Now, that might, in fact, be the case, but I think it is useful to view Sylla's story of monetary innovation in a somewhat amended constraint-induced framework. Sylla is really trying to isolate the incentives for *collective* action by groups of firms or groups of individuals who are trying to remove the burdensome monetary constraints that impinge jointly on their individual behavior. The key, it turns out, is *jointness* in experiencing the constraint.

One of the best examples of such joint innovative behavior in response to collective experience of distress is cited by Om. W. Sprague in his 1910 classic, *History of Crises under the National Banking System* (Washington, D.C.: National Monetary Commission). Commercial bank clearinghouse associations innovated loan certificates to substitute for normal reserves in just about every financial crisis from 1873 through 1970—even during the oft-ignored Panic of May 1884. These are obviously classic examples of collective action by private groups that responded to jointly experienced constraints imposed by financial crises.

I think it is useful, therefore, to restate somewhat more generally Sylla's basic hypothesis: innovations of moneys and monetary systems respond to the rising cost of constraints generated by the existing monetary arrangement—where the rising cost is felt by a number of individuals or firms simultaneously. The collective action that results can be either joint innovation by private groups or by formal government action.

The interesting thing about a collective decision is that it is, by its nature, *more* difficult to accomplish than individual action. This difficulty is the standard academic problem with public goods—each individual has an incentive to shirk his responsibility. This tendency for inaction in collective matters explains the role of crises in stimulating innovation in monetary standards. The crisis causes separate interest groups to coalesce to generate a joint product. Thus, not only is government innovation stimulated under these circumstances but so is private trade-association behavior elicited as well.

This discussion of collective action brings me, rather surprisingly, to one of the points raised by Meltzer, in his provocative view of risk, uncertainty, and market responses. I have always thought that market information, such as prices and trading opportunities, had many of the characteristics of a public good. Like the classic case of the bridge, price information has zero marginal cost in use once it is produced. It surprised me, therefore, that so few clear examples of collective innovation to disseminate price information could be cited. In financial markets, perhaps, the innovation of the National Association of Securities Dealers' Automated Quotation System is the most notable example.

But Meltzer's discussion of the individual firm's incentive to internalize the cost of gathering and disclosing price information is most helpful in this context. Firms are offering a joint product—whatever it is they produce plus market price information. The necessity for collective action is reduced because firms internalize the costs of collecting and disseminating price information, therefore, it is not unreasonable to see relatively little forced disclosure of price information.

Let me conclude by noting that the stimulus to joint action (by private interest groups as well as by individual firms) is often underestimated by advocates of government intervention. In point of fact, there is often some form of joint action that is in place before government recognizes the problem. I would say, therefore, that in formulating a further refinement or in superimposing equity on efficiency, government responses should work within the framework established by private-sector behavior.

Discussion

Albert G. Hart

Chapter 1, by Allan H. Meltzer, may well represent a turning point in the formulation of models of rational expectations, registering the need for models that incorporate uncertainty and gradual learning. Meltzer's proposals for such models, though exploratory rather than definitive, are rich in useful suggestions. I would praise in particular his reflections on the need to consider differences in interpreting experience on the part of participants in different countries and at different times.

To get the full benefit of Meltzer's proposals, we would do well to adopt a semantic twist I learned from a colleague at Columbia University, Lucas Papedemos: where the literature uses the term *rational expectations,* it is clarifying to substitute the term *model-consistent expectations.* It is worth knowing about any model how it will work if market participants believe in it. But participants can scarcely believe simultaneously in all the models offered (and may not have been operating for the last twenty years as if they believed the model a theorist was inspired to formulate last week). There is need to consider the voluminous evidence offered by *ex ante* data as to how decision makers actually frame expectations.

I agree with Meltzer that the tendency to wed rational expectations to general equilibrium analysis, is very useful. The question of under what conditions expectations will turn out self-fulfilling or self-defeating (which needs a great deal more work now that the problematics have been better clarified) is an important example of a problem where interactions across the whole economy need to be considered. To allow for expectational aspects of the Phillips curve analysis is a similar problem. Yet preoccupation with *equilibrium* has its drawbacks. Actual expectation-framing and decision go on in the midst of dynamic processes that carry the economy from one *disequilibrium* position to another; that do not pause for any length of time in an equilibrium position; and that, in fact, may follow a path that never gets close to an equilibrium position. Simulation of such models (which strikes me as much more promising than algebraic analysis) requires rules that purport to tell us how expectations are formed. But, to base these rules on the notion that dynamic processes will converge upon an equilibrium is rash.[1]

Meltzer seems to me to overrate the usefulness of the Knight/Keynes view that probabilistic thinking fits *risk* but not *uncertainty.* Real-life decision makers probably hold views about the domain of applicability of probability that would make philosophers turn in their graves. Secondary-school training in business arithmetic and university training in elementary statistics persuade multitudes of people that they know probability applies to most situations. Besides, there is a quasi-automatic selection process to put in the position of decision makers people who can convince themselves they can sort out uncertain futures: there is no use trying to set up shop as a man of action if you let yourself be paralyzed by uncertainty.[2] I would point out, besides, that even meticulous intellectuals can operate with the notion of a *fair bet*. Take such an uncertain "unique event" as the election of 1984. While there may remain a range of doubt at this writing (1982), anybody would be willing (though perhaps with some sense of shame over taking a fool's money) to agree to pay one dollar if the Republicans again win the presidency against payment of one hundred dollars from the betting partner if the Republicans do not do so—or equally, to pay one dollar if the Democrats win against (say) twenty if they lose. Or if asked for estimates about a company's sales in 1983, any of us (with a reasonable amount of study of the record and market environment) would be willing to frame estimates corresponding to Shackle's focus-gain and focus-loss, lying at upper and lower bounds of a reasonably likely range.[3] And we would expect people with fuller knowledge of the company's position and more experience in sizing up markets to be able to make similar estimates with a narrower range.

I would urge that in trying to meet Meltzer's challenge for the development of models that recognize uncertainty, we should pay careful attention to the presumption that with uncertainty a rational decision maker will *keep options open*. Meltzer remarks rather casually that "as the event approaches, more information may become available." (For *may*, I would have written *probably will*.) The *value of information*, about which a few years ago economists were so much concerned, will drop to zero if the decision has been frozen before the information arrives; on the other hand, the value of information will drop to zero also if appropriate preparatory steps have been neglected.

Rather than think only about whether and how far uncertainty is a deterrent to investment, we would do well to analyze the effect of uncertainty on the character of investment. Suppose a firm we are observing is about to make a commitment for a new facility and has just learned that the producer of a competing product has become pessimistic about the market and has dropped a project for extending its capacity. We may suppose our firm sticks to its estimates as to the expectation value of sales over the period of usefulness of the new facility; but now the dispersion of sales prospects is wider because our firm may capture orders the competitor would have received—or the competitor may be right and the market may weaken seriously. Should plans for the new facility be revised? Why, yes! To be able to benefit from additional orders in the optimistic case, our firm needs a larger capacity than previously planned. But to be able to reduce aggregate costs in case the market turns out to be weak, our firm needs to reduce capital intensity so as to abate costs that will not vary with output. Whether capital expenditures should be raised or lowered will depend on whether the scale-of-capacity effect outweighs the lower capital-intensity effect.[4]

It must be admitted that the available data archives about the forecasts and plans of decision makers consist almost entirely of survey statements that are *single valued* so that we have to rely upon side evidence for measures of the degree of uncertainty. But plainly uncertainty within a single decision maker's mind is an analogue of a difference of opinions among different people's minds. In fact, a decision maker is most often actually a committee under present-day business and consumption standards, and if we had full access to discussions underlying decisions we would find some diversity of views expressed. Using this analogue, we can probably do fairly well with uncertainty indicators that take the form of dispersion-indexes as among stated views of those who offer public forecasts or as among pieces of evidence (such as *leading indicators*) that are widely used as inputs into forecasting.

In putting together the series of chapters that comprise part I, the editor has made a good choice in including the work of Richard Sylla (ch. 2)—who in turn has shown good taste by starting with a framework for analyzing monetary innovation that calls for thinking like an economist about history. But it worries me somewhat to find Sylla letting *historical explanation* rear its ugly head in the midst of his framework-formulation. We find as the "purpose" of monetary innovation "to remove the constraints on real economic development that are implicit in an existing set of monetary arrangements and regulations." As applied to governmental innovations, the fostering of development has some place; though the chapter demonstrates that most governmental innovations were designed to obviate inflationary effects of private innovations. And surely the purpose of private innovations has been private gain for the innovators—incidentally offering gains to their customers so as to induce them to adopt the practices the innovator finds advantageous. These private gains constitute elements of social gain insofar as the innovations release man-hours for nonfinancial productive activity or for leisure. There may be favorable externalities insofar as the changes liberate Schumpeterian innovators who were boxed in by credit restrictions or obviate damaging deflations. But as Sylla points out, private innovations (or government innovations that constitute ill-judged steps toward deregulation) can also have major unfavorable externalities when they foment inflation by coming on top of otherwise sufficient monetary expansion. The redistribution of command over resources that results is all too likely to be in favor of financial manipulators rather than production managers; the unit of account is distorted so as to render cost calculations misleading; saving is discouraged; economic horizons are shortened and long-term investment disadvantaged. We should beware of letting general complacency about the usefulness of financial innovations to obviate metallic-money deflation, blind us to the heavy social costs of the inflationary overload created by the innovations of the 1970s and 1980s.

Reservations should be expressed also about Sylla's stress on *constraint* as the mother of financial innovation. There can be no doubt, of course, that financiers are aware of chafing restraints and look for ways to escape them. But in large part, financial innovations are adaptations to changes in technology and management outside the financial field. In the nineteenth century, a potent force for financial change was the acceleration of transport and communication. I would instance a curious episode just over a century ago when the powerful upswing of 1879 seems to have been triggered by a *deflationary* event—resumption of gold payments and appreciation of the dollar. The explanation I offer is that fixing exchange rates generated a change in banking practice that liberated a great deal of lending power: bankers could now take advantage of rapid ocean shipping and cable communication to use their London funds as effective excess reserves and cease holding excess reserves at home.

The recent and continuing wave of financial innovation seems to hinge on exploitation of the availability and network linkage of computers. These forces could probably not have been *repressed:* nobody knows how to disinvent the computer. But they could have been much better utilized. Mismanagement at the level of Fed strategy and congressional legislation has let these forces push us into a situation where the money stock of the United States is *open-ended.* By this I mean that vast amounts of financial assets representing long-term accumulation are now in forms that permit monetization at the option of the holder, without subjecting the banks to reserve pressure.

Thomas Mayer's chapter (ch.3) is a handsome specimen of the case-study approach to the understanding of policy. Mayer has been extraordinarily successful, it seems to me, in introducing illuminating comments as he goes along, without clouding our image (derived from his quotations) of what FOMC members were saying at stated dates on stated questions.

While, of course, Mayer is able to give us only a selection of stated views, it seems unlikely that he would have missed any strong tendency in FOMC opinions that was explicitly stated. If we dare draw inferences from behavior of a Sherlock-Holmesian "dog that didn't bark," we should be impressed by the silence of FOMC on many matters. Notably, the whole literature of central banking indicates that the Fed can tighten or relax its pressure on financial markets not only by open-market operations but by changes in the level and structure of reserve requirements. Particularly since during the period in question there was no noticeable enthusiasm about the possibility of modulating the influence of open-market dealings by varying the composition of dealings (principally between long-term and short-term securities), it would seem logical that the possibility of more discriminating influence by way of changes in the classification of deposits for reserve purposes and for the relative height of required percentages against different classes of reservable deposits called for exploration. Yet we never find indications that the FOMC considered whether the goals of policy could be better achieved by using the reserve-requirement tool instead of the open-market tool, or by using the reserve-requirement tool to focus the results of open-market operations.

Oddly enough, the period studied was one when financial innovation was introducing a variety of new types of effective money (actually used for payment or immediately available for transformation to make payments to "third parties or others"). With the sufferance and even the active cooperation of the Fed authorities, banks and other financial institutions were able to develop new effective moneys that were chiefly *nonreservable liabilities*. Some data on the main types of *other-visible-transactions balances* appear in table 3–6, which is drawn from my study for the Joint Economic Committee. From the end of 1971, when the process began to pick up momentum to the end of 1978, M–1 (old series) rose from $233.5 to $365.3 billion, or by 56.4 percent, while other-visible-transactions balances rose from $5.8 to $81.3 billion, or by 32.3 percent of the end-1971 level of M–1. (During the year 1974, on which Mayer focuses, the relative contribution of the other-visible-transactions balances was smaller than for the 1970s as a whole, but still substantial.) In addition, there was a great expansion of *invisible* forms of effective money, including consumer lines of credit under bank credit cards and *privilege checking accounts* (which nullified the traditional U.S. rule against overdrafts). Corporations greatly enlarged contractual lines of credit against which they could withdraw with only a notice (not a request for credit) to the bank. And rules against checking upon savings accounts were nullified by providing automatic transfer or transfer by telephone instructions or the punching of simple entries into a cash machine.[5]

The rate of expansion of the effective money stock was much faster than the FOMC was recognizing. And the question should surely have been raised whether these developments were not deforming into uselessness the fulcrum of reserve requirements on which the FOMC's level of open-market operations was supposed to work.[6] Admitting that the authority of the FOMC is narrower than that of the Board of Governors, to ignore these questions was to accept increasingly meaningless terms of reference for FOMC action.

As Mayer points out, it is disappointing to the economist to find the

Table 3-6
Composition of Total Visible Transactions Balances, 1964-1978
(billions of current dollars at year's end)

Year	EMONE	Other Visible Transactions Balances						Total Visible Transactions Balances
		RPFF	BACI	OTHCHE	MMMF	MSBS	Total	
1964	$163.4	0.0					0.0	163.4
1965	170.6	0.4					0.4	171.0
1966	175.5	0.3					0.3	175.8
1967	186.7	1.0					1.0	187.7
1968	201.0	1.1					1.1	202.1
1969	208.8	5.3					5.3	214.1
1970	218.8	3.6	0.0				3.6	222.4
1971	233.5	5.4	0.4				5.8	239.3
1972	252.9	9.3	0.6	0.0			9.9	262.8
1973	268.5	16.8	1.2	0.3	0.0	0.0	18.3	286.7
1974	282.7	18.4	1.2	0.4	2.2	0.2	22.4	305.1
1975	295.1	16.6	2.6	0.6	5.8	2.3	27.9	323.0
1976	312.2	26.7	4.5	1.3	5.9	11.5	49.9	362.1
1977	336.8	35.2	7.4	2.1	5.8	15.8	66.3	403.1
1978	365.3	38.8	11.7	3.1	11.7	16.0	81.3	446.6

Source: Albert G. Hart, "Regaining Control over an Open-ended Money Supply," in Joint Economic Committee, *Special Study on Economic Change*, vol. 4, *Stagflation: The Causes, Effects and Solutions*, Washington 1980, pp. 85–142.
Notes: *EMONE*: Old Federal Reserve Board series for M–1, not including NOW, ATS, and such. *RPFF*: Nonreservable liabilities (net) of U.S. banks under repurchase agreements and federal funds. *BACI*: Claims of "United States other than parent bank" on U.S.-bank branches purporting to be in Bahamas and Cayman Islands. *OTHCHE*: Other checking accounts: NOW accounts at savings institutions plus NOW and ATS accounts at commercial banks. *MMMF*: Shares outstanding at money market mutual funds. *MSBS*: Savings accounts at commercial banks of municipalities and corporations.

FOMC talking monetary policy as if monetary economics (not only the work of academics but also that of the Federal Reserve's own staff) had no bearing. I find particularly disconcerting the sloppy and casual treatment of monetary lags reported by Mayer and the FOMC's apparent lack of concern about systematic explanation of changes in velocity of circulation.[7] If it had seriously asked itself about monetary lags and about the repeatedly demonstrated incompatibility between its monetary growth targets and its interest targets, the FOMC would have had to reconsider its optimism about the possibility of steering the economy by monetary actions. Time was, of course, when economists argued that monetary policy should stand in the first line in the struggle for economic stabilization because the effects of monetary policy shifts would come in rapidly and policy could feel its way without undue reliance on forecasting. When we recognize long, *distributed,* and variable lags in the effects of monetary measures, we have to recognize also that it is absurd to assign primary responsibility for economic stabilization to monetary policy alone. Perhaps to be candid about this fact would conflict with the role of the Fed; the Fed is supposed to stand fire like a good soldier, never complaining that it has been left needlessly exposed by the failures of others. The FOMC, with its rather narrowly defined responsibilities, is not in as good a position as the Board of Governors or its chairman to publicize the extent to which apparent monetary policy failures are in fact the results of defaults and errors in other branches of economic policy. But has the FOMC an obligation to help cover up for other branches of policy by faulty diagnosis within its own domain?

There is no escape from Mayer's finding that the FOMC during the period scrutinized was an underperformer relative to the caliber of its individual members. Like the Federal Reserve as a whole, the FOMC was long on tactics but short on strategy. Since that time, the FOMC has pushed its horizon up to a year and expresses concern as to whether its short-term targets are on the track of its longer term objectives. Both in 1974 and in 1981, the FOMC has shown enough courage to face explicitly acknowledged risks—and even to face the risk of unpopularity. Yet it has allowed the effectiveness of open-market policy to be undermined by monetary innovations that leave uncontrolled many forms of money-creation and that have grown up with tolerance and even active help from Fed authorities. The Fed remains overloaded with responsibilities at the same time that the reaction pattern for open-market actions becomes more flabby.

Notes

1. I offer a definition that has drawbacks as well as virtues but offers a useful antidote to common misunderstandings: an equilibrium situation is

one that can exist and persist *even though* expected. Most actual situations are possible only because participants in the process expected something different.

If I understand Meltzer's point on this topic, he feels the advantages of an equilibrium approach can be scored without the drawbacks by thinking in terms of equilibrium for individual economic units (firms and households) and in an extremely short-run sense. That is, we can cling to the idea that choice is exercised to select the best of a set of alternatives. Fine; but we cannot afford to forget that much of what we do is *involuntary* in the sense that we are constrained to deal with things we would never intentionally have gotten into. (True, I didn't have to give the mugger my wallet. I did this in preference to the alternative of telling him to go ahead with his knife.) In the analysis of dynamic processes, we need to be free to use such notions as involuntary inventory accumulation, involuntary decline of a unit's liquidity, employer preference for a price boost rather than a strike. And we need to be free to admit that there is involuntary unemployment and to apply at the level of the firm the Keynesian notion of insufficient demand for products.

2. Meltzer's quotations from Keynes (1973, pp. 13–14) make clear the following: After saying "We simply do not know" to the statement that "the necessity for action and decision compels us," Keynes continued to behave as if uncertainty does not bar probabilistic thinking.

3. See G.L.S. Shackle, *Expectations in Economics* (Cambridge at the University Press, 1949).

4. James Albrecht and I are in process of revising an article that deals with these two offsetting effects. It appears that there is no way to prove (what the received *deterrent effect view* would require) that the scale effect will always be the smaller. But how does one demonstrate such a negative finding? Our view will have to be supported by working out "reasonable" special cases in which the scale effect predominates.

5. Such arrangements are presumably what Meltzer had in mind in one of his comments. He said he had little patience with the idea that there had been a sudden downward jump in the public's demand for money. He saw rather the provision of new assets that could satisfy part of the demand for money.

6. The only sign of attention to these developments in the FOMC record as spread out by Mayer is a casual remark at the December 1974 meeting by Chairman Arthur F. Burns to the effect that "if, as he suspected, time deposits increasingly were taking on the characteristics of demand deposits, the Committee should be paying progressively more attention to M-2." This remark (foreshadowing later behavior of the FOMC) was of course a nonsequitur. For (a) only a few small elements of time deposits were significant for transactions purposes during the 1970s

and (b) the most important nonconventional forms of money were items included *neither* in M-1 nor in M-2.

7. I agree heartily with a remark of Meltzer's to the effect that rather than accept the idea of abrupt changes in the monetary demand function, we should consider the rise of new means of payment that compete with what was previously regarded as money in filling that demand. Of course both Meltzer and I speak with the benefit of a good deal of hindsight that was not possible in the period Mayer is analyzing.

Part II
Bankruptcy Issues

4

The Insolvency of Financial Institutions: Assessment and Regulatory Disposition

Jack Guttentag and
Richard Herring

The development of deposit insurance has eliminated the possibility of runs at most financial institutions, and converted potential runs into *walks* at others. This innovation has largely transformed the bankruptcy decision from a market-driven process to a deliberate, administrative process. In this chapter we explore a number of issues connected to this process: the requisites for maintaining a credible deposit insurance system that will continue to prevent runs; the basic rationale for supervisory intervention when market pressures to intervene do not arise; the traditional methods of determining solvency and their shortcomings, especially in a world of volatile interest rates; the special problems of thrift institutions and how application of the traditional solvency criteria leads to errors in solvency determination by the insuring agencies and dysfunctional behavior by thrift institutions; the disposition decision after an insolvency determination has been made, as to whether the institution should be liquidated, merged, or continued with financial assistance under the insuring agency's control; and the need for a new type of *capital assistance* for thrift institutions that are solvent but threatened by a walk because they are perceived as insolvent by the market.

A Schematic Overview of Definitions, Concepts, and Problems

It may be useful to define some of the terms used in this chapter, at the same time indicating how the problems we are investigating fit into a broader complex of issues. The shaded boxes in figure 4–1 show the problem areas covered in this chapter.

The term *problem bank* will be used here to mean a financial institution that is subject to regulatory or supervisory intervention because of an administrative decision that it is already insolvent or that without intervention it might become insolvent. (For convenience we shall refer to all such financial institutions as banks although the analysis applies as well to thrift

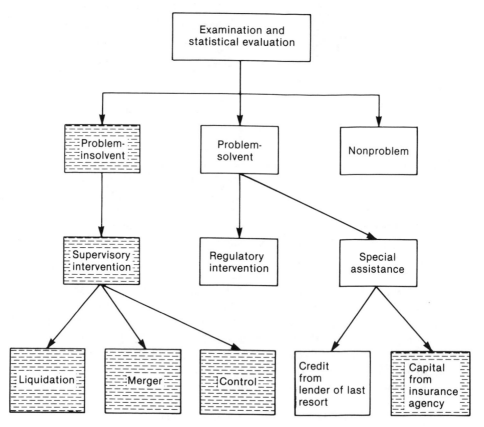

Figure 4-1. Schematic Overview of Regulatory Assessment and Disposition

institutions that issue deposit liabilities.) An insolvent bank is one with an economic net worth of zero or less or one that is expected to have a non-positive net worth within a short time. The question of how to identify problem banks has been studied at some length[1] and will not be considered in this chapter. Our major concern is with the identification of insolvent banks and with their subsequent disposition, issues that have been largely neglected in the literature.

The term *regulatory intervention* refers to actions taken by a bank regulator (which may or may not be the insuring agency) to affect the behavior of a problem bank. Such actions may range from *suggestions* to *cease-and-desist* orders to suspension of insurance or removal of management. Regulatory intervention problems will not be considered in this chapter.[2]

The term *supervisory intervention* will be used to mean actions taken by insuring agencies in dealing with insolvent banks. All such actions involve some sort of financial outlays or commitments by the agency. Decisions about supervisory intervention must be worked out jointly between the lender of last resort (which will want to recover any funds it may have lent the problem bank), the bank's chartering agency (which has the legal responsibility for declaring the bank insolvent), and the insuring agency (which in the end must bear the financial burdens involved in the disposition).

Supervisory intervention usually involves termination of the bank as a separate legal entity, either through liquidation or (more commonly) through merger into another bank. But supervisory intervention also includes continuance of the bank with financial assistance under insurance agency control, usually (but not always) combined with replacement of the existing management. In general, management is replaced when there is an indication that malfeasance or incompetence has contributed to the bank's problem status.

If solvent problem banks are misperceived as insolvent by the market, they may require special assistance of a type that does not involve any significant cost to the agency providing it. The traditional credit assistance provided by lenders of last resort (LLRs) falls in this category. We will argue that currently there is an analogous need for a special type of capital assistance to thrift institutions by their insuring agencies.

Private-Market Identification and Disposition of Problem Banks

Before the development of lender of last-resort facilities and deposit insurance, the identification and disposition of problem banks was largely a market decision. The suspicion that a bank was illiquid or insolvent would precipitate a run by depositors, and if the bank was unable to replace its reserves by liquidating assets or borrowing from other banks , it would be unable to meet these demands and was forced to close.

Banks have been peculiarly vulnerable to runs because they have been heavily dependent on maintaining the confidence of their creditors. Since a large part of bank liabilities are very short term, creditors have the opportunity to run whenever insolvency is suspected. Creditor confidence is inherently fragile since it depends on expectations regarding the quality of a bank's loans and securities. These expectations are often shallowly held and subject to abrupt revisions, since they are based on information that is difficult to obtain and verify. Moreover, since banks are highly leveraged, there is always the possibility that a major, unanticipated shock may have wiped out the bank's capital. Banks are also subject to contagion, in that a weakening of creditor confidence in one bank may easily give rise to suspicions about others, especially when there are substantial interbank transactions.

The private-market process for identifying and disposing of insolvent banks was subject to manifest inefficiencies. The run that caused a bank to close might or might not be well founded in terms of the bank's true condition. The bank's closure under pressure, furthermore, generally involved loss of a major part of the bank's going-concern value, which a less precipitate demise (as through merger with a strong bank) could have preserved.

Because of the peculiar vulnerability of banks to runs, and because of the social costs of banking crises,[3] most societies have developed arrangements to reduce or eliminate the vulnerability of banks to run. The earliest was the evolution or creation of LLRs, which are charged with responsibility for providing credit to banks under conditions of stress. An effective LLR prevents solvent banks from being closed by a run. But LLRs have their limitations. Their reach may be limited to only a subset of vulnerable institutions—as was the case in the United States until very recently. By tradition, and law, moreover, LLRs have made only collateral loans, which under some circumstances limits their ability to aid solvent banks and in other circumstances may encourage them to aid insolvent banks at the expense of other creditors.[4] Finally, LLRs have not had the legal powers required to dispose of insolvent banks.

While LLRs attempt to prevent sound banks from being overwhelmed by runs, deposit insurance aims at preventing runs altogether by making the soundness of banks irrelevant to depositors. This device performs the dual function of insuring individual depositors against loss and protecting the banking system against crises. In addition, because deposit insuring agencies can consolidate the claims of creditors they are strategically positioned to dispose of insolvent banks in the most advantageous way. Hence, the insuring agencies play the key role in making solvency determinations and in disposing of insolvent banks.

Deposit Insurance

Insuring Agency Solvency

As a theoretical simplification one might depict the insuring agency as an intermediary between the bank and depositors, as in the set of balance sheets shown in table 4–1.[5] A_i is the market value of the *i-th* bank's loans and securities, D_i is the market value of the *i-th* bank's deposit liabilities, ENW_i is the market value of the *i-th* bank's economic net worth, ΣR_i is the

Table 4–1
Balance Sheets of Bank, Insurer, and Depositors

Bank$_i$		Insurer		Depositors	
A_i	D_i	$\sum_i D_i$	$\sum_i G_i$	G_i	Net worth
	ENW_i	$\sum_i R_i$	Net worth		

reserves of the insurer and $\sum G_i$ is the market value of depositors' claims on the insurer. So long as there is confidence in the insurer, depositors will consider their deposits (G_i) default free and, therefore, $G_i \geq D_i$. Any difference between G_i and D_i would be due to the risk that bank i might default on its deposit obligations.

Assume that banks are ordered in terms of the difference between the default-free market value of their deposit liabilities and the market value of their assets: $G_i - A_i$. For some set of banks $1, \ldots, J$, this difference will be positive. Since the insurer is liable for the difference $G_i - A_i$ when it is positive, the condition of insurer solvency is:

$$\sum_{i=1}^{J} G_i - \sum_{i=1}^{J} A_i < \sum_{i=1}^{N} R_i$$

The difference between the default-free value of deposits issued by all insolvent banks and the market value of assets held by all insolvent banks must be less than the insurer's reserves.

While it is conceivable that in a stationary world

$$\sum_{i=1}^{N} R_i \text{ might exceed } \sum_{i=1}^{N} G_i$$

and thereby sustain confidence in the insurer regardless of the size of the shocks to which banks are exposed, in a growing economy this is hardly possible. The resistance of banks to payment of insurance premiums also constrains the accumulation of reserves. (In the United States, a portion of premiums are rebated when reserves exceed a specified percentage of insured deposits.)

Insuring agencies, however, may have access to other sources of funds in an emergency. They may have the right to borrow from the United States Treasury or Central Bank or to assess solvent banks. They may even obtain a special appropriation from the federal government. Indeed, since there is always some shock to the banking system that would exhaust the insuring agency's reserves, complete credibility is not possible without one of these other sources as a fallback when needed.

Insurance agencies in the United States have only small credit lines with the U.S. Treasury, do not have the right to impose additional levies on solvent banks, and have no explicit legal right to more moneys from the federal government. Although most observers believe that Congress would appropriate additional funds to meet an emergency situation, this cannot be known with any degree of certainty. The situation is ambiguous.

Assuring Credibility

In our view the three policies that might be followed with regard to the federal government's ultimate liability should the insurance reserve prove insufficient (in order of their desirability) are:

1. An explicit and unconditional assumption of full liability[6]
2. An explicit declaration of no liability
3. Ambiguity—the current situation

We believe that the federal government should explicitly assume full liability for deposit insurance commitments because this is the only way to make the insurance system fully credible when potential claims against the agencies' reserves loom large. The Federal Savings and Loan Insurance Corporation (FSLIC), the insurance agency for the savings and loan industry, is rapidly approaching this situation today. If the insurance agencies' promises are not accepted without reservation, depositors will not be dissuaded from running under pressure, and the system will at some point fail.

A second reason for assumption of full liability is that the failure of the government to meet all the insurance agencies' commitments would be morally, and perhaps legally, indefensible. Deposit insurance in the United States has never been marketed or publicized as if the government's liability was limited. On the contrary, it has always been implied that the insurance agencies were a part of the U.S. government. In corporate law, the doctrine of estoppel holds that if Corporation A owns Corporation B and if creditors of B were led to believe that lending to B was tantamount to lending to A, then in the event of B's failure A cannot hide behind a claim of limited liability.[7] The federal government should not be held to a lower standard than private business.

A third reason the federal government's commitment should be made explicit is that, if the worst did happen, political pressures would ultimately force the government to assume full liability. The delay in accepting the commitment, however, would impose heavy and unnecessary costs. In the worst scenario, significant depletion of the insurance reserves would lead to a loss of confidence by insured creditors in the deposit insurance system, to runs on many institutions, and to a volume of closings beyond the capacity of the insuring agencies to make orderly dispositions. Because of limitations on their human resources, there is a limit on the number of terminations the agencies can effectively handle at one time. If they are swamped, the result would be a destruction of going concern values that would otherwise cut their losses, and the ultimate costs to the government and society would be well above what it should have been. In a less severe variant, the insuring agencies might attempt to protect the reserve funds by carrying banks that should be terminated. In such cases continuance could lead to a further dissipation of the banks' capital and higher losses to the agencies and society in the future (see the discussion below of the hazards of keeping non-viable institutions alive).[8]

Absent an explicit assumption of responsibility by the federal government, an explicit disavowal may be better than ambiguity. This would encourage depositors to exercise greater care and surveillance. To permit meaningful private adaptation and avoid setting off a panic, it is important that such an announcement be made at a time when the insurer's reserves are clearly adequate. Ironically, it is just such a time when the issue is least likely to be addressed.

Converting Runs into Walks

Deposit insurance, even with 100 percent credibility, would not completely eliminate the possibility of runs unless insurance covered all bank liabilities. It seldom does. In the United States the portion of a deposit above some specified level (currently $100,000) is not insured and nondeposit liabilities are not insured at all. These exclusions from coverage can be rationalized on the grounds that creditors of substantial means can afford to protect themselves, and their efforts to do so by monitoring bank-risk exposure help the regulators to constrain tendencies to assume excessive risk.

To be sure, deposit insurance systems may indirectly protect bank liabilities that are not explicitly insured. The lender of last resort, in assisting the insuring agency to make an orderly disposition of an insolvent bank, may provide liquidity for a period long enough that uninsured creditors can be paid off before the bank is closed. Moreover, whenever possible, the insurer tries to avoid liquidating a bank, preferring instead to merge it with another bank that assumes its liabilities. De facto insurance, however, is not operationally equivalent to de jure insurance. So long as there is some probability that the authorities will liquidate an unsound bank, uninsured depositors have an incentive to withdraw their accounts if the solvency of the institution becomes suspect, as they did with Franklin National Bank and more recently with First Pennsylvania.

Thus, deposit insurance eliminates the possibility of runs only for banks that have mainly insured deposits. In the United States that category includes the great majority of small and medium-sized banks and thrift institutions. Larger firms typically have larger proportions of uninsured liabilities that will be withdrawn if doubts arise concerning the solvency of the bank. But withdrawals by large creditors do not have the precipitate and lemming-like quality of runs by the general public. They tend to occur gradually over time as deposits mature and one-after-another large creditor decides to bank elsewhere. The process is perhaps better described as a walk than a run. This being the case, and assuming the cooperation of the LLR that will have to replace some of the liabilities that have walked, the insuring agency has time to make a considered decision regarding the future of the bank.

Market-Imposed Decisions versus Administrative Decisions

Before deposit insurance most closings were forced by the market. The Federal Reserve after 1913 attempted to prevent panicky reactions from depositors from terminating the existence of a sound member bank, but the Fed would not carry a bank indefinitely and usually required collateral to protect itself, while nonmember banks and thrift institutions had only uncertain access to private LLRs when they got into trouble.

Today in contrast, largely because of deposit insurance, administrative decisions predominate. This is clearly the case with small institutions having largely insured deposits, where the insuring agency can delay taking action indefinitely. In the case of large institutions subject to a walk by uninsured creditors the insuring agency is forced to take *some* action but ordinarily it has wide latitude regarding what action to take—including the option of continuance.[9] This raises important questions regarding the basis for both the primary decision to intervene, and the secondary decision regarding disposition.

There is a presumption that the process of solvency determination and subsequent disposition is more efficient under the deposit insurance system. First, bank runs before deposit insurance were often capricious and the contagious effect that sometimes accompanied them often caught up solvent banks even when the earliest target of the run was well selected. And while the Federal Reserve and the de facto LLRs often saved such solvent firms, no doubt many with inadequate collateral perished. Second, prior to the insurance reserve system no adequate machinery existed for the preservation of going-concern values of insolvent banks. This function can be performed only by an institution that can consolidate all the creditor claims against a failed bank.[10]

On the other hand, administrative procedures used by government agencies may have their own problems. Before examining these problems, however, we shall investigate why there should be supervisory intervention in the instances where the market does not compel the authorities to intervene.

The Rationale for Supervisory Intervention

A principal rationale for supervisory intervention in an insolvent bank is that once a bank's capital has been depleted there is no longer a buffer to protect uninsured creditors from additional losses. If the supervisory agency knows that the bank is insolvent, but some uninsured creditors do not, the supervisory agency would be morally if not legally culpable if such creditors lend the insolvent bank money and suffer loss as a result.

But not only is a bank's capital a buffer against loss to the bank's creditors, it also constrains the owners of the bank to act in the best interest of the bank's creditors and society. We believe that this is the more important role of bank capital.[11] When a bank's capital declines relative to potential claims against it (or, what amounts to the same thing, potential claims rise while capital does not), the potential arises for moral hazard to the bank's creditors. The hazard is that the bank will act in such a way as to increase the probability of both large profits and large losses.[12] To the degree that the losses exceed remaining capital they will be borne by creditors and/or by the insuring agency. A bank's capital position is like a deductible clause in an insurance contract: the smaller the deductible the greater the risk of moral hazard.

If the bank still has a significant amount of capital so that the risk of moral hazard is not severe, regulatory intervention may suffice to protect creditors and the insuring agency. But if the bank's capital is completely depleted all risk is borne by a bank's creditors while all returns (in excess of the contractual payments to the bank's creditors) accrue to the bank's shareholders. Under these circumstances, the managers have a strong incentive to "go for broke," that is, to select investment and loan options with the highest possible returns even if the *expected* return is substantially lower than for less risky options.

For example, suppose a bank has liabilities to creditors totaling one billion dollars, it can choose between two operating strategies that yield different end-of-period asset positions, and there are two possible future states of the world that carry probabilities of .9 and .1 (see table 4–2). Strategy *A* will yield an end-of-period asset position of one billion dollars in both states of the world, which is just enough to cover the bank's obligation to its creditors but with nothing left over for the shareholders. Strategy *B* will yield a very low end-of-period asset position (one million dollars) if the first state of the world occurs. But if the second state of the world occurs Strategy *B* will yield an end-of-period asset position of two billion dollars. While Strategy *B* has a lower expected value, the bank's management may adopt it nonetheless since there is one chance in ten that the bank's shareholders will earn one billion dollars and they cannot be worse off than under Strategy *A*. The bank's creditors and society, however, are much worse off under Strategy *B*.

Moreover, when a bank's capital position has been (or is about to be) depleted, incentives increase for self-dealing transactions and fraud. When continuance of the bank is in doubt, the bank's managers face greater temptations to take the money and run.

Financial penalties for excessive risk-taking imposed on the firm, as under a system of variable premium deposit insurance, do not necessarily induce the managers of a problem bank to adopt conservative policies. Viewed *ex ante,* such policies do shift risk-return relationships in favor of more conservative policies. But the actual payments required of problem banks weaken their financial position and this tends to shift them in the opposite direction.[13] To reduce the risk of moral hazard unequivocally, financial penalties for excessive risk-taking must be imposed on the management, not on the firm.

Thus the case for supervisory intervention when a bank's capital has been or will be severely depleted is that losses are likely to accelerate. When the bank's capital has been depleted, the bank's managers will have strong incentives to conduct the bank's business in a socially inefficient manner and the standard regulatory constraints are likely to prove ineffective.

Solvency Determinations

We turn next to the methods the insuring agencies use to determine solvency, and their deficiencies.

The Traditional Method. The criteria used in solvency determinations by the two major deposit insurance agencies in the United States (the FDIC and FSLIC) are quite straightforward.[14] A bank is considered insolvent when its adjusted book net worth falls to zero or less. Adjustments consist mainly of asset value writedowns associated with actual and probable defaults. (A variety of procedures are used to do this.) Assets used for trad-

Table 4–2
Alternative Bank Operating Strategies

	State 1 (Probability = .9)	State 2 (Probability = .1)	Expected Values of Assets
Strategy A	$1 billion	$1 billion	$1 billion
Strategy B	$1 million	$2 billion	$.2 billion

ing may also be *marked to market*. Given its most recent net worth benchmark, reports on current operating income are used to project future book net worth. If the benchmark is already low (say less than 2 percent of assets) and current deficits would erode the remaining net worth within a relatively short period, the bank is marked for supervisory intervention.

This approach probably differs little from that used by national and state bank examiners in the nineteenth century. However, since intervention decisions today are much less likely to be forced by pressures of a run, they are more subject to legal challenge. When the Centennial Bank of Philadelphia, Pennsylvania was shut by the banking commissioner of the state in 1976, with the approval of FDIC, the bank was quite liquid, virtually all its deposits were insured, and there is little question that the bank could have survived indefinitely. Subsequently, the stockholders of the bank sued the commissioner and the state for depriving them of their property. The commissioner claimed that the bank was insolvent but the stockholders denied this and alleged that the commisioner had not properly appraised its financial condition. Similar cases have arisen in connection with termination of thrift institutions, a recent example being Washington Federal Savings and Loan, which is suing FSLIC for wrongfully shutting it down.

Legal challenges to termination decisions to date have been based on judgmental or procedural grounds. The supervisory agency, for example, is alleged to have erred in classifying loans as loss, which were in fact good, or it imposed an unreasonable constraint on the firm that prevented it from meeting its commitments. Since regulators are human beings and are bound to make mistakes occasionally, such challenges are to be expected. But we have found no cases where the basic criteria used by the agencies in terminating institutions has been challenged. These criteria will now be examined.

Book Net Worth versus Economic Net Worth. In principle, solvency determinations should be made on the basis of economic net worth (*ENW*) rather than book net worth (*bnw*). Assume that the bank has the following balance sheet:

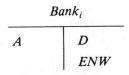

A is the present value of *all* the bank's assets. This measure of the bank's assets is comprehensive. It includes not only the tangible assets and financial instruments that appear on standard accounting balance sheets but also the present value of options such as lines of credit, acceptances, and forward contracts as well as the present value of intangible assets such as the bank's charter, customer relationships that the bank has established, and the expertise of the bank's management. These assets are expected to yield a stream of cash flows $(\tilde{R}_1, \tilde{R}_2, \ldots, \tilde{R}_N)$.

It is useful to disaggregate A into three components:

1. A^s, the present value of the bank's tangible assets and financial instruments that appear on standard balance sheets
2. A^f, the present value of the bank's commitments and assumptions of liability including forward contracts, lines of credit, acceptances, and such
3. A^g, the present value of the bank as a going concern

The bank has issued a mix of deposits on which it promises to make a stream of payments $(E_1, E_2, \ldots, E_N)$ that has a present value of D. Since we assume that all the deposits are insured, the stream of payments is discounted at a risk-free rate.[15]

ENW is the economic net worth of the bank. It represents the present value of the risky stream of net income $(\tilde{R}_1 - E_1, \tilde{R}_2 - E_2, \ldots, \tilde{R}_N - E_N)$ to the bank. The balance sheet constraint implies that ENW also can be expressed as $ENW = A - D$. An intervention decision is appropriate when $ENW \leq 0$.

Now consider how book net worth, denoted *bnw*, differs from economic net worth. The book value of assets, A, will generally reflect the original cost of tangible assets and the original cost or face value of financial claims. Few, if any, assets will be recorded at current market value. The value of options will not appear on the balance sheet and the value of the bank as a going concern will not appear at all. Thus the book value of assets equals:

$$a = A - A^f - A^g - \bar{\Delta} A^s$$

where $\bar{\Delta} A^s$ is the change in the market value of the bank's tangible and financial assets between the acquisition date and the current period. On the right-hand side of the balance sheet, the book value of deposits, D, will be the sum of the principal amount due each depositor. Assuming that deposits were originally entered in the bank's balance sheet at market value, the book value of deposits will equal:

$$d = d - \bar{\Delta} D$$

where $\bar{\Delta} D$ is the change in the market value of the bank's deposits between the date they were acquired and the current period. The bank's book net worth can be expressed simply as:

$$bnw = a - d$$

The difference between economic net worth and book net worth is thus:

$$ENW - bnw = (A - D) - (a - d) = A^f + A^g + \bar{\Delta} A^s - \bar{\Delta} D$$

Bias in Using bnw**.** The extent to which these differences bias solvency determinations depends both on their magnitude and on the ability of supervisory agencies to assess them. The agencies are not unaware that bnw may be misleading. A major objective of the examination process is to ferret out certain disparities between bnw and ENW.

1. A major portion of bank examination effort is directed toward that part of $\bar{\Delta} A^s$ associated with losses on defaults or impending defaults that have not yet been recorded as loss. Obviously this component of $\bar{\Delta} A^s$ is always negative.

2. Examiners also seek to identify negative components of A^f—they are less interested in positive components—and banks are often asked to report such information. Since commitment-generating activities are often easy to conceal, they may be overlooked. But this is an information disclosure problem rather than a problem inherent in the criteria.

3. A^g is nowhere reported nor is it sought by examiners. However, A^g will be reflected in the bank's income stream and income ordinarily is taken into account in solvency determination. As noted earlier, a solvency determination is based on current and *near-term expected bnw*. The future change in bnw is estimated from current income statements. This approach without doubt overemphasizes near-term cash flows, which to some degree may be due to the fact that the solvency criteria applied does not explicitly identify A^g. This omission is probably not a major source of error in solvency determination, however, because of the great difficulty in estimating A^g even if it were identified.

4. Changes in A and D from changes in market interest rates affect ENW but they are not reflected in bnw unless the assets or liabilities affected

are cashed at market values. Assets can be converted through sale at the discretion of the bank and *bnw* will be adjusted by the difference between book value and market value at that time. No attempt is made by the supervisory agency to adjust other assets, which would violate generally accepted accounting principles (GAAP). Deposits can be cashed only by their holder but since banks seldom repurchase their liabilities at a price other than face value plus accrued interest, changes in the market value of liabilities are not reflected in *bnw*—except indirectly over time as they affect the income statement.

Changes in A and D resulting from changes in market interest rates have always been a source of difference between ENW and *bnw*. When interest rates were stable, it did not matter much, but when, as now, interest rates are volatile it can matter a great deal. While a change in rates affects A and D in offsetting directions, the positive and negative components will be the same only if the duration of the banks assets is exactly the same as the duration of its liabilities. If asset duration is longer (shorter), a rise (decline) in interest rates will reduce (increase) ENW.

Thus, in a world of volatile interest rates, a major discrepancy may arise between *bnw* and *ENW,* the direction and extent of the discrepancy depending on the size of the rate change and on the asset and liability composition of the specific firm. In such a world, *bnw* (or projected *bnw*) becomes a treacherous criteria for determining solvency. It may cause some banks to be terminated that should be continued and some banks to be continued that should be terminated.[16]

The Case of Thrift Institutions

Errors in Solvency Determinations. Thrift institutions in the United States (savings and loan associations and mutual savings banks) circa 1981 are a particularly striking example of the problem created by volatile interest rates. Because their asset portfolios have been of very substantially longer duration than their liabilities, the upward ratcheting of interest rates in years prior to 1981 reduced the market value of their liabilities by substantially less than that of their assets. As a result ENW declined abruptly for the industry as a whole, and the correlation between *bnw* and ENW dropped sharply. There is thus a very strong presumption that solvency determinations by the insuring agencies are subject to serious error.

In a recent set of studies Frederick Balderston (1981) valued the mortgage portfolio of each of 2183 savings and loan associations, and compared the resulting *revised net worth* to book net worth. The coefficient of determination (R^2) between the revised and book net worth was .44 for all mutual associations, and for the twelve Federal Home Loan Bank districts the R^2s ranged from .14 to .71. For stock associations, in contrast, the R^2 was .88. Balderston made no attempt to value other assets or liabilities but the presumption is at least as strong that a more comprehensive set of net worth adjustments would reduce the R^2s as that it would raise them. These results confirm that solvency determinations based on book net worth are highly unreliable for mutual associations.

In reading examination reports on terminated institutions at FSLIC, Guttentag came across a particularly striking illustration of a questionable solvency determination. Because their solvency is evaluated by *bnw,* thrift institutions cannot sell mortgages that have declined in market value without writing down their net worth, and therefore their portfolios of low rate mortgages have been largely frozen.[17] One institution, however, thought it had a way to circumvent this difficulty.

This particular association sold mortgages on a participation basis, where it is the custom to sell at par and adjust the contract rate to the current market yield by supplementing the interest payment out of the seller's own resources. (For example, if a 10 percent mortgage is sold to yield 11 percent, instead of discounting the mortgage the seller adds 1 percent of the balance to the payment every month.) In fact, GAAP requires that when the yield to the buyer exceeds the rate on the mortgage the seller must book a capital loss equal to the full present value of the supplementary interest payment committed to the buyer, but the association's president did not understand this requirement and did not book the loss. (His view was that since he reinvested the proceeds of the sale at a yield above the yield paid the buyer, he was making a profit rather than a loss.) When the examiner pointed out the error in his thinking and showed him the magnitude of the book loss that would be charged against his net worth, the president asked for an opportunity to reverse the sale transactions. Alas, the examiner was forced to explain that reversal would constitute a new transaction and could not erase the loss. The conversion of book value into market value was irreversible and fatal. Soon thereafter the association was terminated through a supervisory merger.

Dysfunctional Behavior. The association in the illustration above was atypical. Most thrift institutions know that they must protect their *bnw* at all costs, and if *bnw* is under pressure they may engage in dysfunctional behavior; they may increase *bnw* at the expense of *ENW*.[18] The change in *ENW* is:

$$\Delta ENW_t = R_t - E_t + \Delta A_t - \Delta D_t$$

In contrast, the change in the *bnw* is:

$$\Delta bnw_t = R_t - E_t + \bar{\Delta} A_t^{sr}$$

where $\bar{\Delta} A_t^{sr}$ is the portion of the change in the market value of the bank's assets between the acquisition date and $t + 1$ that are realized during the accounting period from t to $t + 1$. If the initial value of bnw was so low that it attracted regulatory attention or if the bank's managers expect that Δbnw_t will reduce $bnw_{t + 1}$ to zero, they will have a powerful incentive to make Δbnw_t as large as possible to avoid supervisory intervention. They can increase operating revenue, or they can increase realized capital gains while deferring capital losses. Such actions are simply harmless balance sheet cosmetics so long as they merely involve trading future revenues for current revenues at market rates; however, such behavior becomes dysfunctional when increases in book net worth are achieved at the expense of decreases in economic net worth.

Some indication of the range of methods available to increase bnw, even at the expense of ENW, is suggested by the following examples of thrift institution behavior in 1980–1981:

1. An institution that customarily retains a ¼ percent servicing fee on mortgages it sells reduced the servicing fee to ⅛ percent to obtain a higher price.
2. An institution, 97 percent of whose portfolio was being carried above market value, sold the 3 percent that was being carried below market value, recording the capital gain as income in the current period.
3. An institution failed to realize capital losses on its portfolio that could have reduced its tax liabilities to zero.
4. An institution provided a developer with mortgage commitments below the going market rate in exchange for an equity participation, taking its share of profits on property sales in the current year.
5. An institution sold its banking offices to a real estate company and leased them back to realize a capital gain in the current period.
6. An institution with an opportunity to acquire assets in its local market above market rates passed up the opportunity because to obtain the necessary funds it would have been obliged to sell assets at a book loss.

All of these practices have in common that they shifted recorded income from the future to the present. They are dysfunctional when the trade-off rate between current and future income exceeds the market rate, which must occur frequently if an entire industry is under pressure to make such trade-offs. Examiners are aware of most of these devices and when they find them they may recalculate income before making net worth projections, but in many cases they do not find them.

Adoption of an economic net worth standard would go a long way toward eliminating dysfunctional behavior. For example, if a firm with one hundred dollar book value of mortgage loans can sell them at seventy-three dollars to yield 15 percent and reinvest the proceeds in 16 percent loans in its local market, the present value of the new loans (discounted at 15 percent) would be seventy-seven dollars. This transaction would increase *ENW* by four dollars, but it would cause *bnw* to fall by twenty-seven dollars. The option would be attractive if an *ENW* standard were used, but not if a *bnw* standard is used.

In short, intervention decisions based on the book value of net worth are inefficient. The *bnw* standard leads to errors in identifying which banks should be continued and which should be closed. Moreover, the criterion gives rise to dysfunctional behavior by problem banks.

Assessing *ENW* in a World of Volatile Interest Rates. One implication of adopting an *ENW* yardstick for assessing solvency in a world of volatile interest rates is that the stochastic element which is always present in solvency determinations, looms much larger than in the past.

When insolvency determinations are based largely on asset defaults, the stochastic element is relatively small. A portion of the substandard assets that examiners force a bank to write off will in fact be recovered later, and this portion will be larger if business conditions in the future are favorable. But the differences are small and it is unlikely that many serious misjudgments of solvency arise because of this. When an insolvency determination is based on past changes in market interest rates, the supervisor is tempted to consider that future changes in market interest rates could just as readily reverse the judgment.

Our view, however, is that this temptation to forbear in the hope that rates will move in the right direction should be resisted. Assuming that valuations have been properly determined, the possibility that unexpected, future changes in market interest rates could convert an insolvent firm into a solvent one should not in fact enter the supervisory decision.[19] Policymakers should view the probability of a future rise in rates as identical to the probability of a future decline, so that the expected present value of changes in *ENW* from future changes in rates is zero. (On the other hand, as noted below, if a decision is made to continue an insolvent firm under the insurer's control, the possibility of a reversal in market interest rates makes the firm's existing management more trustworthy.)

Yet adoption of an *ENW* yardstick for assessing solvency does not imply that portfolios should be valued every second, or every day, or even every month. There would be no point in having recorded *ENW* bounce around in response to market noise. Developing a manageable market valuation system in a world of volatile interest rates is not a trivial undertaking.

An insolvency arising from changes in market rates does have a special significance under some circumstances. If it has been government policy not to allow firms to protect themselves against interest rate risk, which was the case until very recently for thrift institutions in the United States, then this type of insolvency does not carry the implication of managerial incompetence, nor does it imply that going-concern value, A^g, would be less than that of a solvent firm. Insolvencies from credit losses and related causes often do carry these implications. If going-concern values of insolvent firms are relatively large, and especially if the number of such firms is also large (which is the case today) great importance attaches to the disposition decision.

The Disposition Decision

Once the insolvency decision has been made, under what circumstances should a bank be liquidated and under what circumstances should it be continued? And if a bank is to be continued, under what circumstances should it be merged and under what circumstances should it be continued with aid from the insurer? These are the questions to which we now turn.

Liquidation versus Continuance. When the bank is liquidated it will have a value L where:

$$L = A - D - A^g = ENW - A^g$$

The difference between the liquidation value of the bank and the net economic value of the bank is its value as a going concern, A^g. When a bank is liquidated, its value as a going concern is lost. Conceptually A^g is the present value of the net income the bank would be expected to earn on new business if it were to retain only its offices, employees, and customers. A^g depends on the bank's authorized powers including power to do business within specified areas, the market structure in these areas, the expertise of the bank's employees, and the customer relationships it has developed.

Appropriate intervention and continuance decisions depend on the relationship between L and A^g, as illustrated in figure 4–2. The dashed line indicates all combinations of L and A^g that sum to a zero ENW. Supervisory intervention is appropriate at all points on and to the southwest of that line. In this area ENW is zero or less and the interest of the bank's shareholders and managers diverge from those of the bank's creditors, insurers, and society.

Given intervention, liquidation is the appropriate disposition if A^g is negative. If A^g is positive losses can be reduced by continuing the bank.

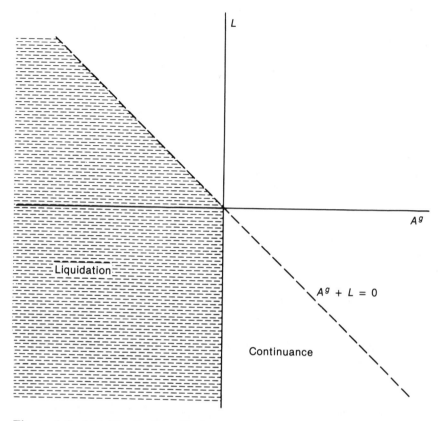

Figure 4-2. Net Worth, Liquidation Value, and Going-Concern Value

Negative liquidation value L is irrelevant to the disposition decision because it is a sunk loss to the insurer; regardless of disposition the loss cannot be avoided. Thus, A^g is the principal determinant of the appropriate disposition of an insolvent bank.[20]

Liquidation involves a much larger immediate cash drain on the insurer than continuance even when A^g is negative. This should not, but under existing institutional arrangements might well, influence the agency against liquidation. It is not difficult to envision a scenario where potential claims on the funds from past and impending interventions are so large that the insuring agency opts to continue a firm with negative A^g, or perhaps to avoid any intervention at all if the market permits it. This would constitute dysfunctional behavior analogous to that of thrift institutions that pay an exorbitant price to shift recorded income into the current accounting period.

Loss to the Insurer and Loss to Society. The intervention and disposition criteria formulated above assume that by minimizing financial loss to itself the insuring agency also minimizes the loss to society. This may or may not be the case.

A^g can be disaggregated into two components:

$$A^g = A^e + A^c$$

A^e is the present value of the expertise of the bank's employees and the present value of its stock of customer relationships. A^c is the present value of the bank's charter, the right to perform banking functions in its present offices. (In principle the charter is a marketable asset, but in practice its marketability is severely restricted by the chartering agency.) To the extent that A^c represents monopoly power or barriers to entry in a particular market, its social value may be nil. This fact would suggest that positive A^e rather than A^g should be the criteria for continuance. On the other hand, the bank's monopoly power might be construed as a result of a careful trade-off, presumed to be socially optimal, between the competitiveness of markets and the risk of bank failure. The importance of this issue is illustrated by the recently adopted practice of the FSLIC of entertaining merger bids from out-of-state associations that are willing to pay significant premiums to enter attractive markets from which they are otherwise barred. The presumption underlying this policy is that existing restrictions on entry are not optimal, and we concur.

A question also arises regarding the extent to which the loss of the bank's expertise and customer relationships is a social loss. Some of this value of an insolvent bank may be transferable to other banks as individuals find jobs with other banks. Both of these questions deserve more careful examination.

Mergers versus Control with Financial Assistance. If continuance is warranted, the insurer may choose to merge the bank with another institution or it may choose to assist the bank while imposing conditions that restrict the capacity of the existing management to run up additional losses. The conditions are the quid pro quo for financial assistance.

In general the insurer will prefer to merge the problem institution if there is a qualified bidder who is willing to pay for the going-concern value of the problem institution (A^g). The insurer must, however, consider the impact of the proposed merger on bank competitiveness in the market in question. In some instances the value of the charter of the problem institution may be very high to one bidder largely because it increases the bidding institution's monopoly power. Insuring agencies in the United States are required to consider the impact of a merger on market structure.

Because of legal or regulatory limitations on branching across state lines, and on mergers between banks and thrift institutions, the agencies may be faced with the problem that the only available merger partners are the strongest firms within the insolvent bank's own market area. These rules were recently relaxed for savings and loan associations as noted above, and pending legislation would extend the exception to bank-thrift institution mergers across state lines.

When no qualified bidder is willing to pay a sufficient amount for the insolvent institution's going-concern value, the insurer should continue the problem institution under the insurer's control with financial assistance. Such control requires first that the insurer have confidence in the firm's management. There is usually a presumption that the management of a bank with negative net worth has behaved badly, but if the firm's plight can be attributed to exogenous forces outside of management's control, this presumption may be unwarranted. As noted earlier, the current plight of the thrift industry is largely attributable to the effects of rising interest rates on unbalanced portfolios, and since these institutions were prevented as a matter of public policy from protecting themselves, the typical firm's problems do not necessarily carry an implication of management incompetence and culpability. The management of thrift institutions that have become insolvent because of rising interest rates, furthermore, may be less inclined to adopt go-for-broke policies because their situation is inherently reversible if interest rates decline. (Historically, most financial institutions have become insolvent because of credit losses, which are generally *not* reversible). The possibility of a general market reversal may appear more promising than a gamble in the markets.

The insurer's judgment regarding the management should take account not only of the usual factors that examiners look for (competence, absence of self-dealing transactions, and such) but also compensation arrangements that can have an important bearing on management behavior. Bonus plans tied to current income, for example, should be viewed with suspicion because in a firm with negative L they create an incentive to adopt go-for-broke portfolio strategies and to make dysfunctional shifts of income from the future to the present.

Control measures can take a variety of forms, including placing persons of the insurer's own choice on the board of directors, requiring the submission of regular operating plans and reports, limiting the volume or size of some types of borrowing, specifying "unusual" transactions that require the insurer's approval, and prohibiting or severely restricting interest rate futures transactions.

The last restriction could severely hamper the firm but is hard to avoid. The development of the Government National Mortgage Association (GNMA) pass through securities futures market provided all thrift institution managers with an opportunity to play go-for-broke through a prima facie legitimate market tool. So long as operations in this market cannot be fully monitored and controlled, all managers of problem institutions are "less trustworthy," in the sense that a hungry boy faced with an unlocked candy jar is less trustworthy than one who is not hungry.

Variable insurance premiums would be even less effective in controlling the risk exposure of an insolvent firm under insurer control than they would be in influencing a problem firm before insolvency (see above). The ultimate deterrent for management misbehavior of an insurer-controlled firm is replacement of the management.

A possible approach toward controlling the risk exposure of an insolvent bank without reducing the effectiveness of management in operating the bank is to divide the bank into liquidating and going-concern components. The separation would be for accounting rather than organizational purposes, although some organizational changes might be appropriate. (Complete organizational separation would prevent cost sharing and therefore be very inefficient). The performance of the management would be assessed mainly in terms of the going-concern component where go-for-broke incentives would not exist. Monitoring would focus on the liquidating component (the insuring agency could even take it over) while management would be free to develop the going-concern component without crippling constraints.

Making this separation between a liquidating component and a going-concern component would not be difficult in principle. All assets, liabilities, and commitments on a base date would be *tagged* and thenceforth separate accounts would be maintained for them. Cash flows on the assets would be used to retire liabilities, and new liabilities would be issued only as needed to replace maturing liabilities. New assets, liabilities, and commitments would belong to a going-concern component for which separate accounting records would be maintained. The major problem would be cost allocation but acceptable conventions could be developed for that purpose.

The Need for Capital Assistance

It can be expected that the supervisory agencies, becoming aware of the deficiencies in the *bnw* criteria for determining solvency, will move gradually toward an *ENW* criteria. In specific cases they are trying already to do this. Market perceptions, however, may continue to be based on *bnw,* if only because the market has even less factual basis than the agencies for estimating *ENW*. The accounting profession, furthermore, has been reluctant to adjust GAAP to meet the problems addressed in this chapter, so that financial statements offered the public are likely to follow the traditional formats and may differ significantly from those used by the supervisory agencies.

This raises the possibility that a firm with positive ENW but negative bnw, which is viewed by the insuring agency as solvent, will be perceived by the market as insolvent, which could lead to a walk by uninsured creditors. This possibility creates a need for a type of capital assistance analogous to the credit assistance traditionally offered by LLRs. In both cases the assisted firm is solvent but suspected of insolvency by the market, and in neither case is there a need nor intention to provide a subsidy. While in principle a solvent firm with negative bnw could be saved by an LLR alone, the LLR would be obliged to replace all the uninsured liabilities of the firm for an indefinite period, and this runs counter to the short-run nature of LLR assistance. Such firms require longer term assistance.

The simplest way to provide this longer-term assistance is for the firm to sell noninterest bearing subordinated debentures to the insuring agency in exchange for noninterest bearing notes of the agency. No cash would change hands. If note sales were allowed in amounts equal to current losses when bnw reached some base level (say 2 percent), then bnw would never fall below that base level.

The sale of subordinated debentures to the insuring agencies would calm uninsured creditors for two reasons. First, the erosion of bnw would be halted. Second, in the event of liquidation the subordinated debt increases the insuring agency's loss and correspondingly reduces that of uninsured creditors.[21]

It is an important point that even though no cash changes hands between the thrift institution and the insuring agency, the subordinated debt provides a real benefit to uninsured creditors. From their standpoint, the debt represents *capital* in the sense of a buffer against loss.[32] While the insuring agency's potential risk exposure is increased, the agency will not lose anything if its judgment regarding the firm's solvency is correct. Even if the agency errs in this judgment its loss will not increase unless the firm ultimately is liquidated and the uninsured creditors lay claim to the agency's notes. If the insuring agency knows that a specific firm would never be liquidated because its A^g is positive, capital assistance is riskless.

The above proposal was developed and circulated at FSLIC in June 1981. In September 1981 FSLIC adopted a modified version, which at this writing has been applied to two cases and a number of others are in the offing. The modification is that both the FSLIC notes and the firm's subordinated debentures pay interest, the first on a current basis, the second on a cumulative deferred basis awaiting a return to profitability. (The note rate is tied to short-term market rates while the debenture rate is tied to a longer term market rate.) Thus, the modified plan involves much more of a subsidy element than our proposal and has the unfortunate effect of muddying the distinction between the treatment of solvent and insolvent firms. Evidently the only operational distinction that will be made is that solvent firms will be subjected to fewer, and perhaps no, insurer controls.

A potential problem that may arise out of failure to distinguish solvent and insolvent firms receiving assistance from the insuring agency pertains to mergers between assisted firms. The insurer is in a position to dictate such a merger without having to negotiate compensation to the surviving bank for absorbing the losses of the other bank. If both banks are insolvent, this is appropriate. If one bank is solvent, on the other hand, the temptation to minimize cash outlays by refusing compensation should be resisted, since it may jeopardize the bank's solvency, creating a control problem that would not otherwise exist.

Implementation of Improved Solvency Criteria

An interesting aspect of the proposed criterion for evaluating troubled institutions is that the insuring agencies in the United States now come close to an estimate of both A^g and L in considering the most appropriate disposition of a firm already marked for intervention. In other words, they assemble the basic information that should be used to determine whether a bank is solvent *after* a decision of insolvency has been made.

The law requires that any disposition of a firm that involves insuring agency assistance be less costly to the agency than liquidation. Hence, the liquidation cost to the agency is calculated for every disposition and this differs from L only by the amount of the loss that would be borne by uninsured creditors, which is easily broken out.

The agencies do not attempt to measure A^g as such but the procedures used in putting a firm up for bids have the effect of isolating A^g. In a purchase and assumption, which is the clearest case, the agency takes over the assets, and the bidders offer a *premium* to take over the existing offices and liabilities. (In a straight merger the bidders retain the assets under a reimbursement to cover losses.) This premium reflects the value of the existing and future deposit base of the defunct bank, as well as any value attaching to the right to do a lending business in the areas serviced by the bank's existing offices with the staff of the defunct bank that the bidder hopes to retain. If the conditions for a perfect auction were met,[23] the winning premium would be the firm's A^g. Because these conditions are not met, the winning premium is likely to be less than A^g, by an amount which no doubt varies from case to case. While the insuring agencies cannot place a bank up for bids merely to determine its A^g, it could use the same procedure now used by bidders in calculating how large a premium they are prepared to pay. Indeed, the insuring agencies should be able to improve on the procedure since unlike the typical bidder they would perform such evaluations on a systematic rather than an ad hoc basis. As an additional bonus, when a bank did come up for intervention, the insuring agency would be in a much stronger position to negotiate if it had its own estimate of the firm's A^g.

We are aware that a proposal for the insuring agencies to change their evaluation methods cannot properly be viewed as a short-run strategy. Implementation would require changes in data collection formats and information systems, and probably organizational changes within the agencies as well. Unfortunately, the need to change the evaluation system has become acute at the same time as the agencies (especially FSLIC) are swamped with work. Still, no progress can be made without knowing where one should go.

Notes

1. See Mark Flannery and Jack Guttentag (1980) and the sources cited there.

2. For a recent study of regulatory intervention by three federal agencies, see Comptroller General of the United States (1977).

3. See Jack Guttentag and Richard Herring (1981b).

4. See Jack Guttentag and Richard Herring (1981b) for a discussion of the limitations of collateral lending.

5. William Sharpe (1978) follows this convention.

6. The simple way to make such a commitment is to eliminate the insurance reserve accounts, transferring their assets to the U.S. Treasury, and make all future obligations of the insuring agencies unconditional obligations of the treasury. The agencies' credit lines would be redundant. This change would have no bearing on the size or structure of insurance premiums, on cash flows between the (consolidated) government and the public, or on the functions of the insurance agencies.

7. See Richard Posner (1976).

8. The agencies' tendency to protect the reserve funds may be reinforced by political considerations. Several years ago the financial operations of the agencies were placed within the federal budget, since it was always a surplus item. The possibility that it may now become a deficit item is a source of serious concern to the current administration.

9. The need to take action to deal with a problem bank from which large creditors are taking a walk is a double-edged sword. If the pressures are very great there may be insufficient time to explore available options. On the other hand, if there are no pressures at all the agency may delay too long before it does anything. Such delay may be costly for reasons indicated below. Given bureaucratic inertia, in the continuum between walk and run there is in principle an optimum speed of liability depletion.

10. In the coalition models of bankruptcy developed by Jeremy Bulow and John Shoven (1978) and Michelle White (1980, 1981), suboptimal results are often achieved—in the sense that firms that should be liquidated are continued and firms that are continued should be liquidated—because of the conflicting interests of different creditor groups. Under some institutional arrangements, for example, equity holders are able to bargain for continuance with bank creditors by appropriating the share of bond creditors.

11. Walter Bagehot (1921, p. 230–232) emphasized this role of bank capital, noting that capital was needed "not to work the business but to guarantee the business . . . (T)he capital is wanted to assure the public and to induce it to trust the concern." Bank capital was ". . . only wanted as a 'moral influence' . . . " An implication of this view of the role of bank capital is that subordinated debt should not be counted as capital for regulatory purposes. While subordinated debt serves as buffer against loss to creditors holding superior claims, it does nothing to counter moral hazard, which should be the main concern of regulators.

12. For a formal analysis of the impact of moral hazard on lending decisions, see Jack Guttentag and Richard Herring (1981a).

13. Joseph Stiglitz and Andrew Weiss (1981) make a similar point.

14. This description of solvency criteria is based on Guttentag's reading of examiner and other reports of FSLIC and informal enquiries at the FDIC.

15. In the case of demand deposits, the stream of payments includes the costs of providing transactions services.

16. In Michelle White's terminology (1980, p. 552), the *bnw* criterion leads to ex post inefficiency (pareto nonoptimality) in continuance and liquidation decisions.

17. In a study for the Federal Home Loan Bank Board, Jack Guttentag (1980) proposed several accounting conventions that would have the effect of allowing institutions to write off book losses on mortgage sales over a period of time. In September 1981 the board adopted such a rule for regulatory purposes though it has not been accepted into GAAP.

18. In Michelle White's terminology (1980, p. 552), the *bnw* criterion leads to ex ante inefficiency in that the bank's managers make decisions that are not socially efficient.

19. Interest rate changes that are expected by the market will be reflected in the existing term structure. If future cash flows are discounted at market rates on securities of the same duration as the flow, current valuations will automatically take account of rate changes anticipated by the market.

20. An interesting question pertains to firms to the left of the vertical axis but above the zero net worth line—banks with negative going-concern

value but positive economic net worth. Should such banks also be subject to intervention to prevent erosion of economic net worth? In these circumstances the shareholders will have strong incentives to liquidate the banks or replace the management and until ENW falls to zero, the shareholders bear the costs of inaction. If shareholders can be depended on to pursue their interests, supervisory intervention would not be necessary. If the firm is a mutual institution, however, there may be no adequate mechanism to prevent an erosion of net worth, and supervisory intervention may be appropriate.

21. Every dollar of debentures sold the insurer would shift loss from uninsured creditors to the insurer by one dollar times the ratio of uninsured liabilities to total liabilities (excluding subordinated debentures). Indeed if subordinated debentures came to equal the difference between the institution's total liabilities and the liquidation value of assets, the liquidation loss to uninsured creditors would be zero.

$$
\begin{aligned}
\text{Let: } G &= \text{Insured deposits} \\
S &= \text{Subordinated debentures} \\
A &= \text{Liquidation value of assets} \\
U &= \text{Uninsured liabilities} \\
Q &= \text{Total loss} = G + U - A \\
Q_g &= \text{Insurer's loss} = (G + U - A)G/(G + U) \\
&\quad + S(U(G + U)) \\
&= G + (SU - AG)/(G + U) \\
Q_u &= \text{Uninsured creditors' loss} = Q - Q_g \\
&= U - (A + S)U/(G + U).
\end{aligned}
$$

If $S = G + U - A$, then $Q_u = 0$. Of course, uninsured creditors would not be able to calculate Q_u without information on A, which is not now available.

22. As we noted earlier, however, subordinated debt should not be regarded as part of the bank's capital for regulatory purposes.

23. These conditions would require that every financial institution could bid, that the agency could assemble all the relevant information required by potential bidders, and that there would be ample time for potential bidders to assess the value of the firm to them.

References

Bagehot, Walter. 1873. *Lombard Street,* New York: E.P. Dutton, reprinted in 1921.

Balderston, F. 1981a. "S and L Mortgage Portfolios: Estimating the Discount from Book Value," Working Paper No. 81-36, Center for Real Estate and Urban Economics, University of California at Berkeley.

―――. 1981b. "Regression Tests of the Relationship Between Book Net Worth and Revised Net Worth of S and Ls," Working Paper No. 81-38, Center for Real Estate and Urban Economics, University of California at Berkeley.

Bulow, J., and J. Shoven. 1978. "The Bankruptcy Decision," *Bell Journal of Economics* (Autumn):437-456.

Comptroller General of the United States, 1977. *Federal Supervision of State and National Banks* Washington, DC.

Flannery, M., and J. Guttentag. 1980. "Problem Banks: Examination, Identification, and Supervision," in *State and Federal Regulation of Commercial Banks,* Federal Deposit Insurance Corporation.

Guttentag, J. 1980. "The Conventional Passthrough Market: Trickle or Flood?" in *Savings and Loan Asset Management Under Deregulation,* Proceedings of the Sixth Annual Conference of the Federal Home Bank of San Francisco, December.

Guttentag, J., and R. Herring. 1981a. "A Framework for the Analysis of Financial Disorder," Working Paper, No. 7-81, Rodney L. White Center for Financial Research.

―――. 1981b. "The Lender of Last Resort Function in an International Context," Working Paper No. 9-81, Rodney L. White Center for Financial Research.

Posner, R.A. 1976. "The Rights of Creditors of Affiliated Corporations," *University of Chicago Law Review* 43, no. 3 (Spring):499-526.

Sharpe, W.F. 1978. "Bank Capital Adequacy, Deposit Insurance, and Security Values," *Journal of Financial and Quantitative Analysis* (November):701-718.

Stiglitz, J., and A. Weiss. 1981. "Credit Rationing in Markets with Imperfect Information," *American Economic Review* (June):393-410.

White, M.J. 1980. "Public Policy Toward Bankruptcy: Me-First and Other Priority Rules," *Bell Journal of Economics* (Autumn):550-564.

White, M.J. 1981. "Economics of Bankruptcy: Liquidation and Reorganization" Working Paper No. 239, Salomon Brothers Center for the Study of Financial Institutions, New York University (August).

5 Government Loan Guarantees for the Relief of Financial Distress

Thomas Ho and
Ronald F. Singer

The U.S. Congress has enacted legislation providing for federal-government guarantees of private loans to a number of entities on the verge of financial distress. Lockheed, New York City, and most recently, the Chrysler Corporation have been recipients of such government assistance. In these cases, the government guarantees the payment to a new debt issue. This guarantee permits restructuring of the firm's capital structure with the apparent intent to avoid bankruptcy. In addition the government requires modification to the structure of the claims on, and operations of, the firm.

The reaction to intervention of this type has been a general criticism of government intervention in the market place. However, there is a lack of systematic investigation into the possible economic benefits resulting from such intervention. The purpose of this chapter is to investigate a rationale for loan-guarantee programs to relieve financial distress. With particular reference to the Chrysler experience, the distributional and allocative effects of the loan-guarantee program are examined. The relevant variables to be considered in devising a program of this type are identified, and policy implications are considered.

It is argued that government guarantees of loans enable the government to intervene in a possible bankruptcy to further a public interest goal. Bankruptcy procedures are designed to resolve the conflict of interest among the claimants to the firm. Most bankruptcies have an insignificant effect on other parties so that there is no need to consider a broader perspective. However, when a bankruptcy results in significant economic effects that go beyond the direct parties of the bankruptcy, the bankruptcy procedure is ill-equipped to consider the public interest. The intent of government guarantees is to circumvent the bankruptcy procedure and resolve the conflict among interested parties while furthering a specific public interest objective. This intent contrasts with other views of the rationale of guaranteed loans. One such view is that it avoids bankruptcy. From the standpoint of general economic welfare, the avoidance of bankruptcy through government intervention is not a desirable goal in itself. Proponents of this view

127

fail to identify the underlying economic rationale for government assistance to avoid a bankruptcy. Another view is that government guarantees are offered to stimulate investment in forms of economic activity deemed to be especially desirable by federal legislators.[1] The intent is similar to loan guarantees offered to stimulate housing, agriculture, and steel production. In this view, the guaranteed loans are simply a form of subsidy to a specific economic activity and not the consequence of economic distress.

In the specific case discussed here, it is argued that a Chrysler bankruptcy would result in significant unemployment concentrated in a small geographic region. This unemployed labor would not be readily absorbed into a productive segment of the economy for some time, leading to a decrease in national output. To avoid this, a loan-guarantee program has been devised to reduce the rate at which labor becomes unemployed. This action permits an orderly transition of labor from Chrysler to more productive segments, avoiding the loss in output that would result from a sudden increase in unemployed labor. The cost of this program is the retention of labor in less-productive activity during the transition period. Thus an optimal program entails a trade-off between the present value of output foregone by supporting unproductive activity versus the gain in the present value of output by avoiding or delaying the unemployment that would result from a bankruptcy. The magnitude of these costs and benefits depends on the effect of the loan-guarantee progam on the timing and probability of bankruptcy, the level and duration of unemployment that would result from a bankruptcy, and the productivity of the labor retained in the unproductive activity relative to the rest of the economy. This chapter derives a model that is amenable to quantification of this trade-off and permits analysis of a specific loan-guarantee program.

In the following section the institutional setting surrounding the Chrysler case is examined; following that an overview is presented. The features of a government loan-guarantee program are then modeled and subsequently, the analysis and policy implications of this model are presented. Finally, the results are summarized.

The Chrysler Case

On December 21, 1979, the U.S. Congress passed the Chrysler Corporation Loan Guarantee Act[2] in response to Chrysler's rapidly deteriorating financial position. As a consequence of a general decline in automobile sales and a shift in consumer preferences toward small cars, Chrysler sales declined by 7 percent by the end of the third quarter of 1979, compared to sales through the first nine months of 1978. Its share of the domestic automobile market deteriorated from over 12 percent to 10.7 percent. This decline led to record losses of $207.1 million and $460.6 million in the second and third quarters of 1979, respectively, and to a predicted annual loss of over $1 billion. The financial consequences of Chrysler's economic position were immediate. Working capital declined to $356 million, $244 million less than the $600 million required by creditors. Furthermore, use of short-term credit had doubled to $550 million of its $750 million credit line.

In an attempt to avert technical default, Chrysler sought to extend its credit line for another year. Negotiations among a consortium of Chrysler's largest creditors began as early as August 1979. Unfortunately negotiations were hindered by the large number of creditors necessary to reach an agreement.[3] In August 1979, a consortium of Chrysler's largest creditors failed to reach an immediate resolution of the problem. Some consortium members refused to extend further credit without similar commitments from the more than two-hundred-and-fifty smaller banks. The smaller banks resisted expanding their own commitments waiting for the consortium members to take on the additional burden. Intensive negotiations continued for two-and-one-half months. Finally an agreement was reached that fell short of the credit extensions hoped for when negotiations began.

Chrysler's experience highlights the problems confronting corporations and the general public when a major entity suffers financial distress. Given a complex capital structure consisting of a large number of creditors, negotiations become exceedingly difficult and costly. It is rational for each creditor to attempt to shift the burden of additional commitments to others. If successful, the creditor benefits from improved security while avoiding additional exposure. Third-party intervention is necessary to resolve this conflict. However, a court-administered solution may have external effects that are inconsistent with more general economic objectives. Thus legislative intervention may be desirable to resolve the conflict along lines consistent with these objectives.

In the Chrysler case, the loan-guarantee program was designed to withdraw reorganization from court administration and place it in the hands of the legislature. This act would permit a reorganization in line with minimizing the economic impact of a Chrysler bankruptcy. The interested parties—management, creditors, and labor—were induced to provide concessions by the promise of government guarantees. The important terms of the agreement were:

1. *The Government:* Provided guarantees for up to $1.5 billion in new loans over a ten year period.
2. *Management:* Sell $300 million in assets, raise $50 million in new equity, and distribute $762.5 million in equity to labor. In addition the Loan Guarantee Board obtained veto power over investment and operating plans.

3. *Creditors:* Concede $100 million in existing obligations and provide at least $5.5 million in new credit.
4. *Labor:* Concede $587.5 million in wages and salaries.

The new injection of funds and the wage concessions would make it possible for Chrysler to revitalize and operate plants that may have been liquidated in a court-administered plan. These funds, together with concessions from labor, and government control over operating and investment decisions, could have the effect of reducing the rate at which Chrysler's labor force would decline. The result would be a reduced impact of Chrysler's difficulties on employment and a more orderly transition of labor and other resources from Chrysler to more productive sectors of the economy.

General Overview

It has been argued that a program of loan guarantees by the government may be looked upon as a means of reorganizing a firm outside of the normal bankruptcy procedure. This procedure may be justified when the normal bankruptcy procedure would lead to significant externalities. A loan-guarantee program could resolve the conflicts associated with a bankruptcy while adverse external effects are minimized. The remainder of this chapter provides a framework for the analysis of this issue. The study identifies the costs and benefits of a guarantee program and highlights the policy implications of relevant economic factors.

Typically, a firm finds itself in financial distress as a result of a sudden decrease in demand for its product. The natural reaction is to attempt to reduce its scale of operation by liquidating the least productive assets. However, both labor and creditor agreements may limit the ability of management to freely liquidate assets. The next step is to negotiate with labor and creditors to reduce the firm's commitments. If this step is unsuccessful a court-administered reorganization or liquidation may be necessary.

Under a court-administered procedure, a reorganization or liquidation plan is negotiated to resolve the claims among creditors. In the process, preservation of firm value usually requires the partial or total liquidation of the firm's assets and a significant reduction in employment. The court supervises this procedure to facilitate negotiation among the creditors and to assure that the interests of the involved parties are preserved. For most firms, this procedure is satisfactory. However, the liquidation or reorganization of a large firm may have economic consequences beyond the narrow scope of the parties to the litigation. In these cases, the court procedure is not designed to consider this broader economic impact of a bankruptcy.

Thus government intervention to withdraw the bankruptcy procedure from the courts may be justified in the interest of furthering a broad economic objective.

In the case of Chrysler, it was felt that a court-administered plan would lead to wide-scale liquidation of its old Detroit plants. This decision would cause significant unemployment concentrated in a relatively small geographic area. The guarantee program was designed to continue the operation of at least some of these plants and reduce the rate at which Chrysler's labor force was reduced.

Essentially, the government program was to have the effect of retaining labor in a less productive sector through an implicit subsidy. If labor markets were frictionless this would make no economic sense. However, when labor markets are congested (that is, when unemployed labor can be expected to remain unemployed for some time) there is a justification, on allocative grounds, to reduce the rate at which labor becomes unemployed. The government, by inducing the firm to retain more labor than it otherwise would, has the effect of retaining labor in a less productive sector. The alternative, however, is unemployment for some time. While idle, this labor would produce nothing. Thus, there is a trade-off between the loss associated with retaining labor in less productive sectors for some time and the loss associated with labor idled for a period of time until it is absorbed into the more productive sector.

In the following section, economic and financial models are presented that incorporate the essential features of a congested labor market and a government loan-guarantee program. The existence of agency and renegotiation costs provide a link between the financial and economic models. The characteristics of the loan-guarantee program determine the ultimate probability and timing of default and the extent of the redistribution of wealth among bondholders, stockholders, and the taxpayer. Once these effects are determined, the effect of alternative programs on the present value of national output are investigated. Finally the factors to be considered and the policy implications of a loan-guarantee program are identified.

The Model

This section models a government loan-guarantee program and describes the assumed economic and financial environment. The assumptions characterize the three entities associated with the government guarantee program: the firm, the labor market, and the government guarantee.

First, the characteristics of the firm are:

1. The firm's market value is expected to grow at a constant rate subject

to a single source of uncertainty. Specifically, this value is represented by an Ito process: $dV/V = adt + \sigma dz,$ where V is the market value of the firm, a is the expected (instantaneous) growth rate of the firm's value, σ is the instantaneous standard deviation, and z is the standardized Wiener process.

2. The firm's capital structure, prior to any government guarantee, consists of equity and a single debt instrument with a single promised payment, F, at maturity, T.

3. The firm is prohibited by the credit arrangement to sell any real assets without the consent of bondholders.[4]

4. Renegotiation of the credit arrangement is prohibitively costly.

5. Bankruptcy occurs if the firm is unable to pay the promised payment at maturity. In bankruptcy, control of the firm (costlessly) passes to the bondholders, and equityholders lose all claims on the firm.

The labor market can be characterized as:

6. The firm's labor force is hired in accordance with an existing labor contract enforcing a given wage rate, w.

7. Renegotiation of the labor contract is prohibitively costly.

8. Labor is less than perfectly mobile, so that unemployed labor is not instantaneously absorbed in alternative pursuits.

The characteristics of the government loan-guarantee program are:

9. A loan with a government guarantee is a new discount debt issue, the proceeds of which are utilized to redeem the firm's existing debt at par,[5] $F_e^{-c\tau}$, where c is the initial yield to maturity of the firm's outstanding debt and τ is the time to maturity of the debt from the time of the issuance of the loan with a government guarantee.

10. The firm is obligated to make the promised payment of the loan with the guarantee at maturity. Bankruptcy occurs if the firm is unable to make this payment. In bankruptcy, bondholders take over all assets in the firm and the government pays bondholders the difference between the market value of the firm's assets and the promised payment.

These assumptions are formulated to be as simple as possible while retaining the essential features of a government loan-guarantee program. Assumptions (1) to (5) permit the debt to be valued as an option on the value of the firm. The value of this debt is given by Robert Merton (1974) as:

$$D = VN(z - \sigma\sqrt{T}) + Fe^{-rT}N(-z) \qquad (5.1)$$

where r = the known instantaneous rate of return on the riskless asset

$$z = \frac{\ln(F/V) - (r - \frac{1}{2}\sigma^2)T}{\sigma\sqrt{T}}$$

N = the cumulative standard normal density function.

Equation 5.1 gives the value of the debt as the present value of the possible payments to debtholders. The first term represents the present value of these payments in bankruptcy, while the second term represents the present value of the payments if the firm does not default.

The labor-market assumptions characterize "congested labor markets" as presented by Donald Parsons (1978). Labor, once unemployed is absorbed slowly into alternative pursuits. The rate at which labor is reemployed is assumed to be proportional to the level of unemployment in the economy. This is characterized by the following labor transfer function:

$$\frac{dL}{dt} = \alpha U \tag{5.2}$$

where L = the total level of employment, outside of the firm

α = the instantaneous rate at which unemployed labor is absorbed into the economy

U = the level of unemployment.

The loan with the government guarantee is riskless to the bondholders by virtue of assumptions (9) and (10). Thus, the promised payment of that issue is:

$$G = (Fe^{-cT})e^{r\tau} \tag{5.3}$$

Given G and the dynamics of the value of the firm, Merton (1977) values the present value of the cost to the taxpayer as:

$$C(\tau) = Ge^{-r\tau}N(\xi) - VN(\xi - \sigma\sqrt{\tau})$$
$$= Fe^{-cT}N(\xi) - VN(\xi - \sigma\sqrt{\tau}), \tag{5.4}$$

where

$$\xi = \frac{\ln(G/V) - (r - \frac{1}{2}\sigma^2)\tau}{\sigma\sqrt{\tau}}$$

This model constitutes a synthesis of recent literature in capital structure, agency theory, and labor markets. The impact of government intervention on financial markets alone has been considered by Robert Merton (1974) and Howard Sosin (1980). The impact on labor markets has been considered by Donald Parsons (1980) and Harvey Lapan (1976). Assumptions (3) and (4) characterize the agency costs of this model. Because of these assumptions, the two markets are interdependent. The event of a bankruptcy will affect the real decisions of the firm and thus unemployment. As a result, government intervention in financial markets (by providing government loan guarantees) affects the probability and timing of a bankruptcy and, in turn, affects the level of unemployment and ultimately the present value of national output. Thus a rationale can exist for government provision of loan guarantees on the basis of maximizing the present value of national output.

Analysis and Implications

This section considers the economic and financial impact of a government loan-guarantee program on three areas of concern:

1. The probability and timing of default of the firm
2. The bondholders' and the shareholders' wealth
3. The labor market and the present value of national output

In light of these analyses, some policy implications are discussed.

The Impact of a Government Loan-Guarantee Program on the Probability and Timing of Default of the Firm

A loan guaranteed by the government substitutes a new debt issue for the firm's existing debt. This affects the probability of default in two ways:

The leverage effect. Since the government absorbs the default risk that would have been borne by holders of the guaranteed loan, it will be priced to return the riskless rate of interest. Furthermore, if the guaranteed loan matures at the same time as the initial loan and, since the initial debt is redeemed at par, the firm's quasi-leverage ratio[6] declines from Fe^{-rt}/V to Fe^{-ct}/V. (Note that $c > r$.) The decline in quasi-leverage reduces the probability of default.

The maturity effect. The guaranteed issue, in general, changes the maturity of the debt. For a given quasi-leverage ratio, a change in maturity can affect the probability of default (Merton, 1974).

It follows that the net impact of the guaranteed loan on the probability of default depends on the par value of the redeemed debt, the time to maturity of the guaranteed debt relative to the existing debt, and the value, risk, and expected return of the firm's assets. Given these parameters, the change in the probability of default can be determined analytically.

By assumption (1), the value of the firm possesses a lognormal probability distribution at some time, t. Bankruptcy occurs when the value of the firm is less than the promised payment, so that the probability of default with and without a government guarantee of loans can be written as p_1 and p_2 respectively, where:

$$p_1 = N[(ln\{F/V\} - \mu T)/\sigma\sqrt{T}] \quad = N(q_1) \qquad (5.5a)$$

$$p_2 = N[(ln(G/V) - \mu\tau)/\sigma\sqrt{\tau}] \quad = N(q_2) \qquad (5.5b)$$

and, $\mu = a - \frac{1}{2}\sigma^2$, the expected growth rate of the firm's value over a finite period. N is the standard normal probability distribution.

Then the change in the probability of default can be calculated directly as:

$$p_2 - p_1 = N(q_2) - N(q_1) \qquad (5.5c)$$

and its direction of change will have the sign of:

$$\psi = q_2 - q_1 \qquad (5.6)$$

Simplifying, ψ can be written as:

$$\psi = \frac{(\{1/\sqrt{\ell}\} - 1)\, ln(F/V) - cT/\sqrt{\ell} + [r\sqrt{\ell} + (1 - \sqrt{\ell})\mu]\, T}{\sigma\sqrt{T}} \qquad (5.7)$$

where, $\ell = \tau/T$.

The effect of the loan guarantee will depend on the characteristics of the firm (its value, V, expected growth rate, μ, and risk, σ) the characteristics of the existing debt (its discount rate, c, and time to maturity, T), and the time to maturity of the guaranteed loan, τ. Note that different loan guarantee programs can be characterized by the relative maturity of the guaranteed loan, ℓ. In the simple case, when the term to maturity of the existing debt equals the term to maturity of the guaranteed loan ($\ell = 1$), ψ simplifies to:

$$\psi = \frac{-(c - r)T}{\sigma\sqrt{T}}$$

In this case, ψ is unambiguously negative; that is, the probability of default declines by virtue of the loan guarantee because the firm's quasi-leverage ratio declines while there is no maturity effect—leading to an unabiguous reduction in the probability of default. As the term to maturity of the guaranteed loan gets large (ℓ goes to infinity), ψ goes to minus infinity. In fact the probability of default goes to zero. This is because the promised payment to the debt will grow, as maturity increases, at a rate that is less than the rate that would exist without the guarantee, since the government absorbs the risk of default. That is, the firm's market debt ratio declines to zero. However, for some finite values of the maturity of the guaranteed loan, it is possible for the probability of default to increase. This will depend on the firm's initial leverage and the relative maturity of the government guaranteed loan.

Figure 5–1 describes the effect of a government loan guarantee on the probability of default as a function of the ratio of the promised payment, F, to its current value, V, and the relative maturity of the loan with the government guarantee, ℓ. In this figure, the shaded areas represent an increase in the probability of default as a result of the guaranteed loan. The figure can be conveniently partitioned into three regions:

Region A: $ln(F/V) < [r - \sqrt{(\mu - r)(c - r)}]2T$
In this region, when the maturity of the guaranteed loan is less than the maturity of the existing debt the probability of default declines. However, when the guaranteed debt has a longer time to maturity than the existing debt, the actual probability of default may increase or decrease, depending on the initial leverage ratio and the relative maturity of the guaranteed debt.

Refinancing the debt at par will tend to decrease leverage and thus decrease the probability of default. As the maturity of the guaranteed loan increases the increased risk associated with increased maturity will dominate, leading to an increase in the probability of default. However, if the maturity of the guaranteed debt is sufficiently long, the leverage reduction resulting from the artificially low yield on the guaranteed debt will dominate, again causing the probability of default to decline.

Region B: $[r - \sqrt{(\mu - r)(c - r)}]\,2T \le ln(F/V)$
$\le [r + \sqrt{(\mu - r)(c - r)}]\,2T$
In this region, the firm's quasi-leverage ratio is moderate. Under these conditions the effect of maturity is minimal so that the leverage effect dominates, reducing the probability of default.

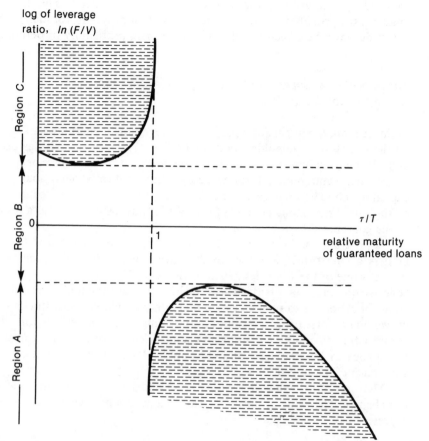

Figure 5–1. The Effect of Government-Guaranteed Loans on the
Probability of Default

Region C: $ln(F/V) > [r + \sqrt{(\mu - r)(c - r)}] \, 2T$

In this region the quasi-leverage ratio is relatively high (exceeding
unity). Thus, shortening maturity tends to increase the probability of
default. As a result, the net effect of a guaranteed loan may be to increase the probability of default when the guaranteed loan has a shorter
maturity than the existing debt, and decrease it when the guaranteed
loan has a longer maturity.

It is interesting to note that programs for loan guarantees are generally
characterized by points located in the northeast quadrant of figure 5–1.
That is, programs of the type discussed here are aimed at firms with high
quasi-leverage ratios. Furthermore, the debt restructuring entails a length-

ening of the maturity of the debt by use of a guaranteed loan. In this quadrant the probability of default declines so that programs for loan guarantees do have the effect of reducing the ultimate probability of default.

The Impact of a Government Loan-Guarantee Program on the Distribution of Wealth

In this section, the impact of a program for government guarantees of loans on the wealth of bondholders and stockholders is considered. It has been argued that government guaranteed loans are used as an inducement for stockholders and bondholders to reorganize the firm's operations and capital structure without the force of law present in a judicial procedure. To do this, all of the claimants to the firm's assets must be better off as a result of the guaranteed loan program.

A program for loan guarantees shifts some of the risk borne by the holders of the firm's securities to the government. This raises the total market value of the securities issued by the firm. However, it is possible to conceive of a program that transfers wealth from (or to) bondholders to (or from) stockholders to such an extent that either bondholders or stockholders would be worse off as a result of the government guarantee program. To consider this possibility a contingent claims-pricing model is used to value the change in bondholders' and stockholders' wealth as a result of the government guaranteed loan.

Merton (1974), values a discount bond under the assumptions used in this chapter. The value of the debt, prior to a government guarantee can be expressed as:

$$D(V; F, T) = VN(Z - \sigma\sqrt{T}) + Fe^{-rt}N(-Z)$$

where $$Z = [\ln(F/V) - (r - \tfrac{1}{2}\sigma^2)T]/\sigma\sqrt{T} \qquad (5.8)$$

Equation 5.8 represents the market value of the debt as the present value of the payment to bondholders if the firm defaults, plus the present value of the promised payment if the firm does not default. As a result of the redemption of the debt at par, bondholders receive Fe^{-ct}, so that the wealth transfer to bondholders is equal to:

$$\Delta B = Fe^{-ct} - D(V;F,T) \qquad (5.9)$$

Clearly, if the market value of the debt were greater than its par value, this would be negative. However, under those circumstances stockholders would have been willing to call the debt without the aid of the government.

It is therefore reasonable to assume that the wealth transfer to bondholders would be positive.

In guaranteeing the new debt issue, the government contracts to pay bondholders the difference between the promised payment of this issue and the value of the firm in default. Thus, the government is committed to pay $Max\,(G - V, 0)$ at, τ, the time to maturity of the government issue. Robert Merton (1977) values this commitment as a European put, so that the present value of the guarantee can be expressed as:

$$C(\tau) + Ge^{-r\tau}N(\xi) - VN(\xi - \sigma\sqrt{\tau}) \qquad (5.10)$$

where
$$\xi = [\ln(G/V) - (r - \tfrac{1}{2}\sigma^2)\tau]/\sigma\sqrt{\tau}$$

$C(\tau)$ represents the present value of the cost to the taxpayer as well as the increase in the total market value of the securities issued by the firm. $C(\tau)$ increases with the firm's leverage and time to maturity of the guaranteed loan.

Equation 5.10 may be written as:

$$C(\tau) = Fe^{-ct} - [VN(\tau - \sigma\sqrt{\tau}) + Ge^{-r\tau}N(-\xi)]$$
$$= Fe^{-ct} - B(\tau) \qquad (5.11)$$

where $B(\tau)$ represent the market value of a bond with promised payment, G, and time to maturity, τ. Thus, $B(\tau)$ represent the value of a bond identical to the debt guaranteed by the government but without the guarantee. That is, equation 5.11 says that the present value of the cost to the government of the guarantee is simply the difference between the market value of the debt with the guarantee and the worth of the debt if it were not guaranteed.

Now the change in stockholders' wealth (ΔS) is equal to the change in the total market value of the firm's securities less the wealth transfer to bondholders. That is:

$$\Delta S = C(\tau) - \Delta B$$
$$= Fe^{-ct} - B(\tau) - [Fe^{-ct} - D(T)]$$
$$= D(T) - B(\tau), \qquad (5.12)$$

the difference between the market value of the redeemed debt and the value that the market would place on the debt with a government guarantee if it did not have a guarantee. The value of $B(\tau)$ relative to $D(T)$ can be determined by the quasi-leverage ratio and time to maturity of each issue. Recall that the quasi-leverage ratio of the loan with a guarantee is less than the quasi-leverage ratio of the redeemed debt. If the loan with a guarantee has the same time to maturity as the redeemed debt ($\ell = 1$), this is equivalent to a reduction in promised payment so that $D(T)$ exceeds $B(\tau)$ and stockholders' wealth increases. Furthermore, for a given quasi-leverage ratio, an increase in maturity decreases the market value of the debt. Thus, the program for government guarantees of loans increases stockholders' wealth as long as the guaranteed loan increases the time to maturity of the debt payment. Typically programs for loan guarantees increase the time to maturity of the debt. Thus, stockholders' wealth will increase in general. However, it is possible for a loan with a government guarantee to have a maturity date sufficiently short so that stockholders' wealth declines. Clearly, under these conditions, stockholders would have to be forced to involuntarily accept the guarantees.

Government-Guaranteed Loans and the Present Value of National Output

Up to this point, the analysis has dealt only with the financial aspects of loan guarantees. In perfectly competitive real and financial markets these effects would have no impact on output. The present value of the cost to taxpayers would be exactly offset by an increase in wealth to security holders—a pure distribution problem that is Pareto neutral.[7] However, the presence of imperfect labor markets, and the existence of agency costs can lead to changes in the firm's output decisions as a result of changes in the probability and timing of default. It is the intent of this section to consider the implications of these imperfections on the decision to provide loans which are guaranteed by the government.

In addition to the assumptions already imposed, it is also assumed that:

1. The economy is composed of two sectors—the firm in question (firm X) and the rest of the economy.
2. The economy as a whole is in competitive, full employment equilibrium. The value of the marginal product of labor v is equal to the economy wide wage rate w, and the total labor force is L_T.
3. For simplicity, it is assumed that the total labor force and total national output are expected to remain constant over time.

Suppose that firm X's financial crisis is precipitated by a sudden, unexpected decrease in demand for its goods. By the assumptions outlined in the previous sections, restrictive bond covenants and costly renegotiation stop the firm from liquidating unprofitable assets.[8] Therefore, the value of the marginal product of labor employed by X declines to $P_x F'(N_x)$, where P_x

is the new price of X's product, $F'(N_x)$ is the marginal product of labor in X. Furthermore:

$$P_x F'(N_x) < v \qquad (5.13)$$

In the absence of constraints on the firms operating and investment decision, management would liquidate its unprofitable plants and reduce employment until the value of the marginal product of labor is again equal to the wage rate. Suppose that this would lead to a reduction in the labor force, λ, employed by X. Then the total labor force, at any instant in time, t, can be represented by $L_T = L(t) + (N_x - \lambda) + U(t)$, where $L(t)$ is employment oustide of X at time t and $U(t)$ is unemployment at time t. Given the labor transfer function (equation 5.2) the level of employed labor in the rest of the economy can be expressed as:

$$L(t) = L_T - (N_x - \lambda) - \frac{1}{\alpha} \frac{dL(t)}{dt} \qquad (5.14)$$

That is, at any time, t, employment in the rest of the economy can be represented by the total labor force, less employment in X less unemployment at that time. This unemployment is determined by equation 5.2, and determines the movement of unemployed labor to employment in the rest of the economy.

Given the constraints on the firm's operating decision, the firm will not be able to significantly reduce employment, except in the event of bankruptcy. Thus, loans that are guaranteed by the government, in delaying or avoiding bankruptcy, affect the level of unemployment and the allocation of labor between the two sectors. As a result, the guaranteed loan affects the present value of national output, $PV(Q)$. It is now possible to evaluate the role of government guarantees of loans in achieving this objective.[9]

First, in the absence of default, the present value of national output can be written as:

$$PV(Q \,|\, \text{No Default}) = \int_0^\infty \left\{ vL + P_x F(N_x) \right\} e^{-\rho t} dt$$

$$= [vL + P_x F(N_x)]/\rho$$

where ρ is the appropriate discount rate for national output and $F(N_x)$ is firm X's production function. Now, if no guarantee were granted, there would be a possibility of default at T, the maturity date of the firm's existing bonds. By assumption, default would lead to the firm reducing employment by λ, so that the present value of national output conditional on the firm defaulting at T is:

$$PV_1(Q|\text{Default}) = \int_0^T \left\{ vL + P_x F(N_x) \right\} e^{-\rho t} \, dt$$

$$+ \int_T^\infty \{vL + P_x F(N_x - \lambda)\} e^{-\rho t} dt$$

$$= (vL + P_x F(N_x)) \frac{(1 - e^{-\rho T})}{\rho} + P_x F(N_x - \lambda) \frac{e^{-\rho T}}{\rho}$$

$$+ \int_T^\infty vL e^{-\rho t} dt$$

The change in the present value of output as a result of default can be expressed as:

$$PV_1(Q|\text{Default}) - PV(Q|\text{No Default})$$

$$= \frac{e^{-\rho T}}{\rho} \left\{ \frac{v\lambda}{(1 + \rho/\alpha)} - P_x[F(N_x) - F(N_x - \lambda)] \right\} \quad (5.15)$$

The impact of a default at T is equal to present value of the output resulting from an increase in labor in the rest of the economy less the value of the output foregone in sector X. If the government guarantees a new debt issue of maturity τ, then the occurrence of bankruptcy at τ will result in:

$$PV_2(Q|\text{Default}) - PV(Q|\text{No Default})$$

$$= \frac{e^{-\rho T}}{\rho} \left\{ \frac{v\lambda}{(1 + \rho/\alpha)} - P_x[F(N_x) - F(N_x - \lambda)] \right\} \quad (5.16)$$

The probability of default with and without government guarantees are equal to p_2 and p_1 respectively, as given by equations 5.5a and 5.5b. Thus, the present value of national output with and without government guarantees respectively is:

$$PV_2(Q) = p_2 PV_2(Q|\text{Default}) + (1 - p_2)PV_2(Q|\text{No Default})$$

$$PV_1(Q) = p_1 PV_1(Q|\text{Default}) + (1 - p_1)PV_1(Q|\text{No Default})$$

Letting:

$\Omega = PV_2(Q) - PV_1(Q)$, and simplifying yields:

$$\Omega = -(p_2 e^{-\rho t} - p_1 e^{-\rho T})\phi/\rho, \tag{5.17}$$

where

$$\phi = P_x F(N_x) - F(N_x - \lambda) - \frac{v\lambda}{(1 + \rho/\alpha)} \tag{5.18}$$

Ω gives the impact of a loan guaranteed by the government on the present value of national output. A government policy of maximizing the present value of national output leads to the conclusion that loans with government guarantees are desirable as long as there exists a guarantee program that yields a positive Ω.

At this point it is desirable to summarize the important features of this model. It is assumed that negotiation costs, agency costs, and congested labor markets would lead to a significant increase in unemployment as a result of a default of the firm in question. Given this assumption, a loan with a government guarantee can be utilized to reduce and/or delay the probability of default and therefore affect the magnitude and timing of unemployment. Under these conditions it may be optimal for a government to implement a loan guarantee program to increase the present value of national output.

Some Policy Implications

It has been established that a government program, such as loan guarantees in order to avoid financial distress, can be desirable if the government objective is to maximize the present value of national output. By delaying and/or reducing the probability of default, the government is fostering employment in a less productive sector. However, the alternative would be to permit the default to occur, resulting in unemployment and reduced production during this time. Thus the government is confronted with the trade-off between less productive employment (and slower absorption into the more productive sector) versus unemployment for some time period.

The intent of this analysis is to identify the factors that determine the nature of this trade-off. If we limit consideration to programs in the northeast quadrant of figure 5–1 (that is, programs that lengthen the maturity of the firm's debt and are offered to firms suffering from relatively high leverage ratios), the government guarantee is desirable as long as equation

5.18 is positive. The first term on the right hand side of 5.18 represents the value of additional production of good X as a result of the guarantee. The second term is the value of production in the rest of the economy resulting from the eventual absorption of unemployed labor into the rest of the economy. It is the opportunity cost (in present value terms) of employment in X. Notice that if the labor absorption rate, α, is infinite then unemployed labor is instantaneously absorbed into the rest of the economy. The second term becomes $v\lambda$, the output of the labor released from firm X when employed in the rest of the economy. Thus as long as employment in X is less productive than in the rest of the economy, government guaranteed loans would reduce national output. On the other hand, for α close to zero, the second term approaches zero as well. By retaining labor in X the present value of output foregone from the rest of the economy is small since unemployed labor would be absorbed very slowly. Thus, a government policy to retain labor in X would increase the present value of national output as long as the excess labor produces some positive output.

Similarly, if ρ is very large, future income is much less valuable than current income. The opportunity cost of labor in X is small in present value terms. Thus it could be desirable to support current production, even in a less productive sector rather than wait for labor to be absorbed into the more productive sector. Notice that *ceteris paribus*, given less than perfect labor mobility, an economy that is characterized by a high degree of uncertainty about future output (that is, ρ large), implies that government guarantees are more likely to be desirable. That is, when the economic environment is uncertain, current production is more likely to be desirable relative to some uncertain future output.

Furthermore, when the unemployment rate for the economy as a whole is relatively high, or if unemployment is concentrated in specific geographic areas, the absorption rate will be low. Again government intervention is more likely to be desirable in this case. It is interesting to note that what is important is the rate of labor absorption relative to the discount rate. That is, the rate at which labor is absorbed over time has little economic consequence in itself. It has economic meaning only with respect to the time value of output.

Summary and Conclusion

This chapter develops a model to analyze the possible benefits resulting from federal-government guarantees of loans with specific reference to Chrysler, it has been shown that the presence of monitoring and negotiation costs results in a public interest concern toward bankruptcy. The government objective of maximizing the present value of national outuput may be furthered through federal loan guarantees. The effectiveness of the loan guarantee program depends on the firm's bond convenants, the characteristics of the labor market, and the specific characteristics of the guaranteed loan. Furthermore, the model permits consideration of alternative loan programs to determine the optimal program in a specific economic and financial environment.

The thrust of the argument is that a default can cause significant externalities that are not normally treated in the standard judicial process. Thus the program for guarantees of loans removes resolution of the crisis from the judicial system so that the government can take into account these externalities.

It should be noted that this chapter concentrates on the possible benefits of loan guarantees while ignoring the possible costs. A government loan guarantee program is no doubt associated with costly monitoring and administrative costs. Furthermore, the danger of a moral hazard problem developing as a result of expectations of loan guarantees to other firms approaching bankruptcy should be an important consideration. An additional factor ignored here, which may loom heavy in offsetting the beneficial effects of loan guarantees, is the traditional role bankruptcy has played in the allocation of managerial talent. Faced with imperfect markets for managerial skills, it is possible that bankruptcy plays a major role in disciplining inefficient management. The costs of eliminating this allocative role of bankruptcy may be high indeed.

Although the model has been framed to reflect the important elements of the Chrysler case, they may be relevant to future bankruptcies. The basic elements justifying intervention in a Chrysler bankruptcy are present in many large corporations. Specifically, complex capital structures and organizations make monitoring and negotiation among interested parties costly. Thus one can expect an increased reliance on third parties to resolve conflicts of interest. Furthermore, the increasing size of industrial corporations makes it more likely that an individual bankruptcy will have a significant impact on regional labor markets and national output. Thus, the desirability for government intervention to further the public interest during instances of financial distress is likely to remain an important issue in the future.

Notes

1. Merton (1977) considers the cost and distributional impact of third-party deposit insurance. This analysis is expanded by Jones and Mason (1980) to include government guarantees of callable and convertible debt

issues. Sosin (1980) considers the allocative impact of loan guarantees intended to affect the allocation of resources to specific economic activity.

2. See Hector (1981) and Moritz and Seaman (1981) for detailed discussion of the economic and financial environment surrounding Chrysler loan guarantees.

3. When there is a large number of parties involved, the *public good* nature of an agreement and the danger of *free riders* can make negotiations between creditors and management especially difficult.

4. The assumption that bonds are secured is consistent with Chrysler's capital structure and can result from high monitoring costs.

5. In practice, most corporate bonds are callable near par.

6. Merton (1974) defines quasi-leverage as the ratio of the present value of the promised payment, discounted at the riskless rate, to the current value of the firm.

7. It should be cautioned here that possible real costs of the guarantee are ignored.

8. There may also be other reasons for the firm not selling assets prior to bankruptcy. Labor-union pressure to protect labor security may lead to this result.

9. This objective may be achieved by alternative means such as a direct wage subsidy. This chapter does not consider these alternatives.

References

Black, F., and M. Scholes. 1973. "The Pricing of Options and Corporate Liabilities," *Journal of Political Economy,* May/June, pp. 637–659.

Hector, G. 1981. The *Chrysler Saga.* New York: The American Banker, March 30, p. 1.

Jensen, M., and W. Meckling. 1976. "The Theory of the Firm: Managerial Behavior, Agency Costs, and Ownership Control," *Journal of Financial Economics,* October, pp. 305–360.

Jones, P. and S. Mason. 1980. "Valuation of Loan Guarantees," *Journal of Banking and Finance.* March, pp. 89–107.

Lapan, H. 1976. "International Trade, Factor Market Distortions and the Optimal Dynamic Subsidy," *American Economic Review.* June, pp. 335–346.

Merton, R. 1977. "An Analytical Derivation of the Cost of Deposit Insurance and Loan Guarantees: An Application of Modern Option Pricing Theory," *Journal of Banking and Finance.* June, pp. 3–12.

———. 1974. "On the Pricing of Corporate Debt: The Risk Structure of Interest Rates," *Journal of Finance,* May, pp. 449–470.

Moritz, M., and B. Seaman. 1981. *Going for Broke: The Chrysler Story*. New York: Doubleday.

Parsons, D., 1980. "Unemployment, the Allocation of Labor, and Optimal Government Intervention," *American Economic Review*. September, pp. 626–635.

Sosin, H. 1980. "On the Valuation of Federal Loan Guarantees to Corporations," *Journal of Finance* December, pp. 1209–1221.

Discussion

Peter Crawford

Thomas Ho and Ronald Singer (ch. 5) seem to imply that loan guarantees are more appropriate for large firms—where shutting down would eliminate tens of thousands of jobs—than for small companies, which would disgorge only a few dozen or a few hundred workers. If this distinction were to become public policy, government would bestow a rent to the shareholders of those large firms. Employees, seeking employment guarantees, would accept lower wages at large firms than at small firms. Physical capital and credit would be available at lower cost to these sheltered, large companies. Thus government would provide a new economy of scale, unrelated to economic efficiency, which could both distort resource allocation and unnecessarily limit competition.

A second problem with the Ho and Singer framework is that it seems to neglect some of the options open to society. For example, it might be more economic to subsidize migration of employees—including geographical migration and functional migration through retraining—than to inject loan guarantees to limit labor displacement per unit of time. Subsidized migration would encourage speedy movement of labor to areas of higher marginal product.

Without question, the Jack Guttentag and Richard Herring (ch. 4) represents a major contribution. I find two themes especially appealing. The first is its persistent rejection of subterfuge and ambiguity, especially its suggestion that we replace the present arbitrary system of *book value accounting* with a full-fledged system of *economic value,* or *market value, accounting.*

The second theme is its persistent stress on questions of social benefit. In all regulated industries, questions of efficiency and public welfare tend to become subordinated to regulators' concerns about fair treatment of existing firms—their stockholders, employees, and customers. In transportation, regulatory bodies tend to divide up the market under a vague concept of *fair share*—so much for railroads, so much for truckers, so much for barge carriers. Exactly the same thing has occurred historically in the financial sector. Twenty years ago, these burdens were painful enough. But they have mounted dramatically in recent years as interest rates have climbed and as technological changes have accelerated.

My admiration for this chapter is tempered only by a concern that present-day regulatory conventions would tend to corrupt and subvert the benefits of the Guttentag and Herring reforms. I also wonder about both the economic wisdom and the political wisdom of their suggestion that regulatory agencies should assume—in applying economic value accounting—that tomorrow's interest rates will be equal to today's rates.

But before turning to these issues, it is appropriate to ask whether the universal popularity and acceptance of book value accounting imply an intrinsic merit in today's accounting conventions. Guttentag and Herring suggest that a bank or a thrift would be regarded by its regulator as insolvent—hence subject to liquidation or shotgun merger—only if economic net worth is determined to be negative or if the regulators foresee an imminent collision with zero economic net worth. Now, their arguments for economic value accounting are so persuasive that one can't help asking: Why does anyone pay any attention whatsoever to the fictions embodied in conventional book value accounting? In the case of commercial banks and stock-issuing, publicly owned savings and loan associations, the stock market presumably already is looking at economic net worth. And, as Guttentag and Herring point out, the regulatory agencies must focus on economic valuation when they step in to serve as a marriage broker. All that Guttentag and Herring propose is that the FSLIC and the FDIC undertake this function on a more systematic basis.

I was struck recently by a couple of newspaper items. The *New York Times* ran an extensive analysis of the New York City savings banks—distinguishing between the mildly ill and the seriously stricken. The arithmetic and the discussion were entirely in terms of book value. *The American Banker* published a thoughtful piece on the thrift problem by Sanford Rose, almost entirely focused on book value accounting. Now, the *Times* is a reputable newspaper, and Rose is one of the best financial journalists in the business. He's certainly aware of the vast difference between market and book value. Why then, does everyone pretend that the emperor is clothed?

A possible hypothesis is that everyone knows that the market value of thrifts' assets is much less than the market value of their liabilities, but no one wants to shout "fire" in a crowded theater for fear that the thrifts will be forced under by massive runs by depositors. So everyone continues to pretend. But that's difficult to believe. The thrifts' problems are big news today. There is always a premium on bad news, and thus there are special rewards today for the journalist who shouts that the federal agencies have been engaging in a cover-up conspiracy to pretend that insolvent thrifts are solvent.

The simplest and probably the most attractive hypothesis to explain the popular focus on book value is that the public is principally interested in thrifts near the brink of extinction—those whom the federal agencies will terminate, either through outright liquidation or through a shotgun wedding, plus those thrifts and banks that might otherwise survive a little longer but who, seeing the handwriting on the wall, arrange their own extinction through merger, spurning the brokerage services of the FSLIC or the FDIC. Since the federal agencies make the rules, and since life or death for a troubled thrift is determined by these rules, the public and the press naturally focus on book value statements, even though everyone knows that they are fairy tales.

There is another hypothesis, however, that might explain why people focus on book value. This hypothesis is that book value may happen to roughly coincide with economic value. At first glance, this might seem to be ridiculous. After all, the mortgages and bonds owned by a thrift have a market value today that is typically 70 to 80 percent of book value. Throwing in the higher ratios for liquid assets and marking up the understated value of real estate owned by thrifts would still leave the economic value of many thrifts' total assets some 10 to 20 percent below book value. The economic value of thrifts' liabilities are also less than book value. But the overstatement in book value of liabilities typically is much smaller than the overstatement in book value of real and financial assets. That's mainly because the average maturity of thrift liabilities typically is much less than the average maturity of thrift assets, so the rollover of liabilities keeps the average interest cost on liabilities fairly close to market.

Because the market value of a thrift's tangible assets today typically seems to be less than 90 percent of the market value of its liabilities, and since book value of net worth typically is only 5 percent or so of book assets, it is easy to see why many people have concluded that a large number of thrifts have negative economic net worth. But as Guttentag and Herring point out, one must also take into account the going-concern value of the thrift. At Citicorp, we have followed the stocks of a couple of dozen savings and loan associations. We note that going-concern value most often seems to run in the neighborhood of 10 to 15 percent of total assets. In other words, some associations with poor earnings records in the past two years and with extremely low ratios of book value net worth to book value assets nevertheless are valued in the stock market as having significant economic net worth.

Moreover, there seems to be a crude but pervasive correlation for stock savings and loan associations (S&Ls) between economic net worth as a ratio to assets and book net worth as a ratio to assets. To a considerable extent, the associations with the highest book net worth ratios are also the S&Ls with the highest economic net worth ratios. And the associations with the lowest book net worth ratios tend to be the S&Ls with the lowest economic net worth ratios. So there may be a rough justification for the popular focus on book net worth.

However, we have noticed that many of the stock S&Ls at the bottom of the distribution—those with the poorest economic performance—seem to have a surprisingly high market value or economic net worth. This fact raises some nettlesome questions for the Guttentag and Herring proposals—especially under present-day regulatory treatment of weak thrifts.

At the present time, the FSLIC and the FDIC seem to be willing to liquidate a failing thrift if it is comparatively small. Even so, outright liquidations are rare. In the case of a large thrift, the agencies go to considerable lengths to prop up the troubled institution. Examples include large loans to S&Ls at below-market rates, guarantees to acquiring thrifts in a merger that any losses will be offset by the insurer, and takeover by the insurer of unwanted assets. The sweeteners and subsidies to National Steel in the West Side Federal merger are an illustration of the lengths to which regulators will go to achieve a takeover.

Under these circumstances, the going-concern value of a thrift or a bank can be immensely inflated by the willingness of the regulators to underwrite its mistakes. Even in untroubled times, a thrift or a bank owes a large portion of its going-concern value to its charter—that is, to the quasi-guarantee of limited competition. For example, the quarter-point differential between Regulation Q rate ceilings for thrifts and banks is an ingredient in a thrift's franchise. And both thrifts and banks are protected to an extent from the entry of others into the transaction-deposit market.

The rents embodied in these franchises muddy economic value accounting. For one thing, every actual or impending change in the regulatory environment will alter the going-concern value of each thrift and bank. Moreover, the impact of any change in the regulatory infrastructure will be different for each individual bank and thrift, depending on its individual economic environment. That fact would impose a heavy burden on the federal accountants, responsible under the Guttentag and Herring proposal for tracking economic net worth—since every change in regulation would send the accountants back to their ledgers. But much more troublesome is the notion that the regulatory agencies would be simultaneously responsible for altering regulations and for certifying the impact of those changes on the net worth of each bank and thrift. Would this burden corrupt the accountants—lead them to shade their assessments of economic value? Equally troublesome, would economic value accounting intimidate those responsible for changing the rules? Most regulatory changes would improve the economic net worth of some banks and thrifts while impairing the net worth of others. The necessity of hanging these changes up on a billboard might deter federal agencies from socially desirable regulatory reforms.

But the problems mount in the present environment of a huge, unanticipated rise in interest rates in 1980–1981 and sharply reduced economic net worth for all banks and thrifts. Because the regulators have a profound bias against bankruptcy of a large bank or thrift—that is, because they are unwilling to liquidate—they are willing to provide a very large subsidy to effect a merger. The present value of that potential subsidy is an element in the going-concern component of a thrift's assets and thus in its economic net worth. Accurate application of economic value accounting today would require writing up the assets and net worth of large banks and thrifts proportionately more than those of smaller institutions. Since the present value of potential future subsidies is directly related to the probability of receipt of those subsidies, accurate accounting would require writing up assets and net worth of weak institutions with a long history of mistakes much more than the assets and net worth of strong, successful institutions.

It's apparent that the result might be to inhibit change and reward inefficiency. Now that need not be the case if the clear light of accurate economic value accounting would serve to restrain those subsidies. But as a practical matter, one might fear that the accountants would take refuge in inaccuracy—concealing the potential subsidy element—or that they would ascribe the going-concern value of potential subsidies to other factors—potential market growth, for example. Such subterfuges would be most likely if the accountants were employed by the regulatory agencies themselves.

Guttentag and Herring suggest that regulatory accountants should assume that interest rates in the future will be equal to today's rates. It's obvious that in the absence of this rule, regulators may be disposed to assume that rates will decline. This bias would justify propping up troubled thrifts on grounds that lower rates soon will improve both earnings and economic net worth. But the Guttentag and Herring proposal seems unnecessarily strict. The thrifts are most vulnerable near cyclical rate peaks. At such times, an anticipation of declining rates usually is incorporated in a negative yield curve. Why shouldn't the regulators share those expectations and assume that declining rates in the future will reduce or reverse the pressures on the thrifts?

The propensity of regulators to project declining interest rates ought to be especially keen in 1981—not only in view of the historically high real interest rates today, so vulnerable to decline, but also in light of the Reagan administration's determination to cut inflation and thus interest rates over the next few years. For the FDIC and the FSLIC to assume no change in future interest rates would seem almost unpatriotic. There are limits on the ability of a government agency to ignore government policies.

Discussion

Michelle J. White

Two interesting chapters have been presented in part II, both arguing in favor of government intervention in the affairs of failing firms. However, the two chapters support very different policies. The Jack Guttentag and Richard Herring chapter (ch. 4) argues that the government ought to intervene to facilitate the orderly liquidation or merger of failing banks. The Thomas Ho and Ronald Singer chapter (ch. 5), on the other hand, argues in favor of government intervention to prevent the bankruptcy of large failing firms. An obvious question raised by each is why we should favor a public policy that closes down some failing firms but rescues others.

What I would like to do here is, first, to restate some of the arguments made in favor of government intervention in potential bankruptcies, second, to say something about these arguments, and, third, to address the question posed above of whether it is in the public interest for the government simultaneously to rescue some failing firms while administering the coupe de grace to others.

The Ho and Singer chapter in effect poses a *bigness* argument concerning bankruptcy. They argue that the adverse effect of one large firm going bankrupt exceeds that of one-hundred small firms going bankrupt, when each of the small firms is one-hundredth the size of the large firm.

Why might this be the case? Ho and Singer focus on labor market effects—one large firm failure causes concentrated unemployment in a few geographical areas, while one-hundred small firms failing spread their unemployment impact over a wide area, so less unemployment occurs in any one place. Now suppose that all unemployed workers take, on average, 120 days to find a new job. In that case it doesn't matter how concentrated the unemployment is, since the cost of lost output is the same regardless of whether one big firm or one-hundred small firms go bankrupt. One the other hand, suppose in a local labor market with a particularly high rate of unemployment, the average worker takes 180 days, rather than 120, to find a new job. Then the cost of lost output may be higher in the case of the one large firm going bankrupt than in the case of the one-hundred small firms. The bigness argument thus depends on congestion effects; that is, the notion that the average time required to find a new job rises with the level of unemployment in the local labor market.

Similar congestion arguments can be made in the context of credit markets or supplier markets. Thus if one large firm fails, there may be relatively large losses and secondary failures among its banks and suppliers. But if one-hundred small firms fail, then losses to banks and suppliers are widely dispersed and are likely to be less disruptive.

Guttentag and Herring's argument in favor of public intervention in bankruptcies is that the government should try to prevent runs or walks on banks to maintain public confidence in the banking system. But they suggest that once the government becomes an insurer of banks' deposits, then it has an incentive to intervene early in failing banks' affairs to protect its own assets because larger losses to depositors result in larger losses to the FDIC or the FSLIC.

A third argument supporting government intervention in potential bankruptcies emerges from timing issues—failing firms in general do not shut down when it is economically most efficient for them to do so. A government intervention policy could therefore be used to prevent them from shutting down too early or from going on too long.

An example is useful here. Suppose the hula hoop or the gas guzzler fad is over, demand for these produces has fallen and many producers will leave the industry. Now suppose producing hula hoops takes specialized machinery. Economic theory says that hula hoop producers should continue to operate as long as revenues cover variable costs (at least until the specialized capital wears out), even if revenues do not cover total (or fixed plus variable) costs. But some type of bankruptcy procedure is necessary to accomplish this, since the firm continues to operate while not paying all its debts. However if the capital used to produce hula hoops can easily be transformed to produce some other good (garden hoses), then the firm should close down as soon as revenues fall short of total costs, thus enabling its capital to be quickly transferred to the more valuable use.

U.S. bankruptcy procedures pose a problem in this regard, however, since they are not structured to encourage economically efficient behavior. For example, if the firm's assets are specialized, we would like it to continue operating and to continue paying its variable cost creditors (trade creditors who supply raw materials), while defaulting on claims of fixed cost creditors (bondholders, mortgage holders, or fixed capital suppliers). However the bankruptcy system actually encourages default on trade creditors' claims, while encouraging payment of fixed cost creditors' claims, except those of bondholders. The reason is that fixed cost creditors generally are secured by liens on physical assets, which they can foreclose on if the firm defaults. Trade creditors, on the other hand, are typically unsecured. Thus failing firms may tend to close down too quickly when secured creditors foreclose on assets that are crucial to the firm's operation or when trade creditors stop delivering supplies.

The opposite can also happen, however, and failing firms may go on too long. For example, suppose the firm has outstanding bonds that are publicly traded and are unsecured. In the past the proceeds of the bond issue were used to finance equipment purchases. But the failing firm later uses the equipment to secure new loans to finance variable costs. By the time the firm finally shuts down, it has no free assets left to pay anything at all to its bondholders. This shifting of claims across creditors' classes allows the firm to continue operating while it consumes its free assets. But this is inefficient if its assets are *not* specialized and would be more valuable shifted to some other use.

Thus the bankruptcy system encourages some failing firms to continue operating too long, especially if their assets are not specialized, while simultaneously causing others with specialized assets to shut down too quickly. This fact suggests that there may be efficiency gains from a policy of government intervention in bankruptcies, but that government intervention would have to be a very carefully structured policy.[1]

I turn now to some comments on the arguments just stated favoring government intervention in bankruptcies. One problem that I have with the Ho and Singer labor market argument is that they make too strong a distinction between the effects of bankruptcy and solvency; that is, they seem to assume that bankruptcy would cause all the firm's workers to become unemployed while solvency would allow them all to remain employed. Reality is not so cut and dried. In the Chrysler case, for example, what has been termed *bankruptcy* would presumably have consisted of a *reorganization* under Chapter XI of the old Bankruptcy Act rather than outright *liquidation*. Under a reorganization, if a majority of creditors agrees to a cutback in their claims, the rest can be compelled to agree to a similar cutback. Secured creditors in a reorganization are also prevented from foreclosing on their lien assets if these assets are deemed essential to the firm's continued operation. If the firm wants to shut down part of its operation, then the affected assets are returned to the creditors holding liens on them.

Thus in a bankruptcy reorganization the firm usually continues to operate but at a reduced scale. Some workers retain their jobs, while others are thrown out of work. However, what has happened to Chrysler under government intervention is quite similar—even though Chrysler has remained out of bankruptcy. Creditors have agreed to a reduction in their claims and the firm is continuing to operate but at a sharply reduced scale. Presumably part of the reason for creditors agreeing to a cutback is that they are aware of the fact that Chrysler could have always filed under Chapter XI, proposed such an agreement, and compelled all creditors to accept it as long as a majority of creditors went along.

In fact, Chrysler's employment level did drop substantially, despite the fact that it remained out of bankruptcy and received substantial government support. For the period 1978–1980, Chrysler's labor force dropped by 45 percent, compared to a drop of 15 to 18 percent for General Motors and

Ford during the same period. My feeling is that the drop in employment levels probably would not have been much greater had Chrysler failed to get the government loan guarantees and instead filed for a bankruptcy reorganization. If the government's goal in intervening to prevent a Chrysler bankruptcy was to preserve jobs, then the intervention was probably not very successful. It caused a group of unsecured creditors whose claims came under the loan guarantees to walk away with 100 percent payoff of their claims, while in a Chapter XI proceeding they would have received much less. But it probably preserved very few jobs.

Turning to the Guttentag and Herring argument in favor of government intervention to close down failing banks, I find their argument plausible within the framework discussed above. In particular, banks would appear to fall into the category of firms that have few specialized assets. Their capital—office buildings, retail space, computers, and white collar workers—are easily transferred to other uses and their retail space in particular often may be more valuable if put to some other use. Further, banks fall into the category of failing firms that have free assets—depositors' cash—that can be used to finance continued operation. Thus failing banks probably have a tendency to go on too long. By the time they shut down in the absence of outside intervention, there is probably substantial erosion of assets available to pay unsecured creditors and depositors.

On the other hand, government intervention often leads to merger of failing banks with solvent ones, rather than to actual shutdown. While this solution is attractive to the FDIC or FSLIC since it reduces their costs, merger amounts to a subsidy from the U.S. Treasury, since the solvent bank absorbs the failing bank's net operating losses and can deduct them from its taxable profits. Thus merger saves money for the insurer but not for the government as a whole. For many failing banks, liquidation would seem to be a more economically rational alternative, particularly in light of recent deregulatory trends in banking that have decreased the monopoly value of banking charters.

Finally, to return to the question posed at the beginning, is it reasonable for the government to save large failing firms such as Chrysler but to allow and even encourage failing banks and small failing firms to go under? The arguments presented here would seem to justify such a policy only if Chrysler had undepreciated, specialized assets not useful elsewhere in the economy. This conclusion seems somewhat doubtful for Chrysler, since substantial investment in modernizing its plants has occurred since the rescue.

My feeling is that in rescuing Chrysler, and Lockheed, Congress was mainly interested in protecting U.S. industry and the U.S. balance of payments from a flood of Japanese and European cars and aircraft. Questions of economic efficiency seemed to have little or no effect on the decision-making process.

Note

1. See M.J. White, "Public Policy Toward Bankruptcy: Me-First and Other Priority Rules," *Bell Journal of Economics,* Autumn 1980, and M.J. White, "Economics of Bankruptcy: Liquidation and Reorganization," Salomon Brothers Center for the Study of Financial Institutions, Working Paper No. 239, August 1981, for discussion of these issues.

Part III
International Crises

6

What If We Lose the Persian Gulf?

Knut Anton Mork

Among the many crises that may hit the U.S. economy in the near future, the possibility of a major disruption in the world supply of oil seems to rank high among the most likely candidates. No less than two such major disruptions occurred in the last decade: the oil embargo and quadrupling of world oil prices in 1973–1974 and the loss of the Iranian supply as a result of the revolution in that country.

If we are lucky, a new disruption of oil supplies can be absorbed by the current glut in the world oil market. This was apparently what happened when Iraqi supplies were reduced as a result of the Iran-Iraq war. However, even in today's market, the sudden loss of Saudi Arabian production or the entire Persian Gulf area would have much more serious consequences. Furthermore, the current glut can hardly be expected to last very long, so the prospects for absorbing a disruption seem much dimmer a few years ahead.

When the supply of oil goes down, its price goes up. This simple implication of the laws of supply and demand seems confirmed amply by the evidence of the last decade. With higher oil prices, real income is transferred from oil-importing to oil-exporting nations. However, the increase in the oil-import bill, while substantial enough, seems only part of the total economic cost of a major supply disruption. Equally important are the costs in terms of lost jobs and below-capacity production levels as world economies scramble to adjust to the new environment of higher energy prices.

If an oil-supply disruption occurs, it is likely to be one of many symptoms of a tense and confused international situation, economically as well as politically. Thus, a major problem for economic agents will be how to react rationally to uncertain and confusing signals. This environment of uncertainty and confusion also makes it difficult to analyze oil-supply disruptions meaningfully. Nevertheless, it seems possible to tell a reason-

Part of the analysis underlying this chapter was carried out at the M.I.T. Energy Laboratory. It was sponsored by ICF, Inc. under a contract with the U.S. Department of Energy. Neither the U.S. Department of Energy, nor M.I.T., nor ICF Inc., nor any of their employees assume any legal liability or responsibility for the accuracy or usefulness of any information. Any views expressed in this chapter are solely those of the author and do not necessarily coincide with the official views of M.I.T., ICF, Inc. or the U.S. government.

able story about the economic costs of a disruption, based on the evidence of the last decade combined with the methods of modern macroeconomics.

The present chapter makes an attempt to use these insights in a study of the possible effects of a hypothetical disruption of all oil supplies from the Persian Gulf Area. The result presented are derived from simulation of a model, which was constructed for the special purpose of analyzing oil-supply disruptions and oil-price shocks. The model was originally developed at the Massachusetts Institute of Technology Energy Laboratory by Robert E. Hall and this author. It has previously been used successfully in studies of the effects of the oil-price shocks of 1973–1974 and 1979–1980 (see Mork and Hall, 1980a, 1980b, 1981).

The model is based on an analytical framework presented elsewhere by this author (Mork, 1982a). It follows a classical approach in that it emphasizes the role of relative prices (oil prices, wages) rather than income streams and spending propensities. A Keynesian approach would emphasize the latter. It has been used for the analysis of oil-supply disruptions by Robert Solow (1980) and Robert Pindyck (1980) and in analyses based on large econometric models, such as Otto Eckstein (1978). A third line of thinking has emphasized the foreign-trade linkages, such as in Ronald Findlay and Carlo A. Rodriguez (1977), Michael Schmid (1976), Horst Herberg (1976), and in the simulation study by Michael Bruno and Jeffrey Sachs (1981).

It is hardly necessary to emphasize that no single approach can fully explain all the complexities of a major oil-supply disruption. The following pages represent an attempt to cover those aspects that to the author seem the most essential. In the continuing debate about these problems, other views and alternative policy solutions are likely to be proposed.

For the hypothetical case of a complete, temporary loss of oil supplies from the Persian Gulf, the results of the model used here suggest that the consequences for the U.S. economy would be quite dramatic, in terms of inflation as well as unemployment and loss of real output. Capital formation would particularly suffer. On the other hand, the estimates do not indicate that the economy would come to a complete standstill; and after the shock is over, life is predicted to go on, although with a somewhat reduced level of productive capacity.

The organization of the chapter is as follows. The section immediately following discusses the main building blocks of the model and reviews the various components of the economic costs of an oil-supply disruption. The subsequent section presents the simulation results produced by the model for an oil-supply disruption equivalent to the loss of all supplies from the Persian Gulf. The chapter then turns to the discussion of a particular issue, which may be quantitatively important: since oil-exporting nations accumulate claims on the U.S. economy, changes in our interest payments on these claims are potentially an important part of the costs of an oil-supply disruption. This issue assumes significance because the model predicts a substantial rise in real interest rates in the longer run as a result of the disruption. A latter section discusses this issue and some possible related policy implications. The final section offers some conclusions.

Modeling Oil-Supply Disruptions

The losses associated with oil-supply disruptions can conveniently be divided into losses of aggregate supply and losses of aggregate demand. Aggregate-supply losses are associated with the transfer of income from oil-importing to oil-exporting nations occurring as oil prices are driven up by the supply disruption. Demand-side losses occur as resources are left unemployed while the economy is adjusting to the new regime of higher oil prices.

The rise in oil prices, as we witnessed it in 1973–1974 and again in 1979, has been compared to a tax on oil with the proceeds going to the oil-exporting nations. This comparison is a way of putting the fact that an increase in the price of oil entails a transfer of real income from oil-importing to oil-exporting nations. This loss would occur even if the government were successful in maintaining employment and real economic activity during and after the disruption. It represents a loss of potential real income and may thus be classified as a supply-side loss.

Unfortunately, the supply-side losses do not seem to represent the full effect of an oil-supply disruption. Typically, the accompanying oil-price shock tends to make aggregate demand fall below the new, lower level of aggregate supply, so that production falls below its potential. Investment activity in particular suffers, and unemployment rises. In short, the economy enters a recession, as we saw it in 1974–1975 and again in 1980. And as if this were not enough, oil-induced recessions tend to occur at the same times as the economy is plagued by oil-induced inflation.

The model employed in this chapter was constructed with the intention of capturing the effects outlined above. The following paragraphs contain a verbal presentation of the model. The equations of the model are listed in appendix 6A.

The aggregate-supply structure of the model is built around the framework of a neoclassical growth model of the U.S. economy. The model assumes that energy is used in combination with labor and capital in the production of goods and services. The production possibility constraint is represented in dual form as a cost function, with a flexible functional form and with an approximate putty-clay formulation. The supply of labor is assumed to be inelastic and to grow at a constant rate over time. Capital accumulated as saving allows new investment (via a physical lag) to add to the existing capital stock. The supply of savings comes from consumers, whose behavior is modeled according to the life cycle/permanent income hypothesis under rational expectations.

The supply part of the model also includes domestic and international energy markets. The representation of the domestic supply of energy is derived from the economic theory for extraction of nonrenewable natural resources. The excess of domestic energy demand over domestic supply is assumed to be satisfied by oil imports. In the long run, the real price of oil in the world market is assumed to grow at a constant rate until it reaches a backstop price determined by some renewable energy substitute. For the short run, the model computes the world price according to an OPEC (Organization of Petroleum Exporting Countries) price reaction function similar to the one used by Chao and Manne (forthcoming). However, in contrast to their model, the demand for oil imports by the United States and other non-OPEC countries is assumed to depend on actual rather than full-employment production levels. The recession induced by the hypothetical supply disruption is assumed by the model to have the same relative magnitude in other countries as in the United States.[1] This feature considerably softens the oil price increase in the model as caused by a given oil-supply disruption.

A specification of foreign trade in nonenergy goods closes the supply part of the model. The trade balance in the model is allowed to be in deficit in the short run after an oil-supply disruption, reflecting the observed accumulation by oil-exporting nations of claims on the U.S. economy. Specifically, net exports of nonenergy goods are assumed to grow smoothly at the economy's natural rate of growth. However, trade is balanced in a long-run sense by the requirement that the discounted value of net exports of nonenergy goods equals the discounted value of present and future oil imports. This requirement fixes the level of the growth path for nonenergy net exports.

Given this outline of the representation of aggregate supply, it is relatively easy to discuss those features of the model that allow for a discrepancy between aggregate demand and aggregate supply, or between potential and actual levels of output. An external shock, like an oil-supply disruption, changes the market-clearing levels of wages and prices in the economy. However, reflecting a wide range of empirical evidence, the model assumes the adjustment to the new wage and price levels to take place slowly and over time. Thus, wages are assumed to be rigid in nominal terms, with a partial adjustment for cost-of-living wage increases, and to approach their new market-clearing levels slowly and over time. Similarly, the overall price level is modeled as a fixed markup over wages in the short run, whereas in the long run the markup adjusts to correspond to the market return to capital.

The model defines the overall price level as the money price of goods. Money supply is assumed to be unaffected by an oil-supply disruption. Money demand is assumed to be unit elastic in nominal spending and to have a negative elasticity with respect to the nominal interest rate. The difference between the nominal interest rate and the real return to new capital in the model is made up by rationally expected inflation.

Some of the recent additions to the model are still in an experimental stage and may be in need of improvement. This is the case for the representation of foreign and domestic energy markets and for the trade balance. These extensions have, however, added considerable realism to the model and have made it a more flexible instrument for analysis.

The flow chart in figure 6-1 illustrates how an oil-supply disruption works itself through the model. The disruption is entered in the representation of the world oil market as a leftward shift on the OPEC price reaction curve, resulting in a price increase for oil. This increase immediately leads to a loss of real GNP in the form of a transfer of real income to oil-exporting nations. This loss reduces potential GNP and can thus be characterized as a supply-side loss.

At this point, the conventions of measurement in the model differ slightly from the conventions of the National Income and Product Accounts (NIPA). This difference results in a somewhat larger GNP decline in the model than NIPA would record for a similar case. It occurs because of a difference in the method of deflating the nominal figures to get real GNP. Nominal GNP can be defined as:

$$GNP^N = PA - P_E M \qquad (6.1)$$

where P_E is the nominal price of oil, M is the real quantity of oil imports, and PA denotes the nominal values of the remaining GNP components. The model now deflates this whole expression by the money price (P) of finished goods in the model. Real GNP in the model is then:

$$GNP^R = A - (P_E/P)M \qquad (6.2)$$

In contrast, NIPA uses separate deflators for each component. In particular, imported oil is evaluated at its 1972 price (P_E^0) in the computation of real GNP. Ignoring differences for the other components, real GNP according to the NIPA definition can be written as:

$$GNP'^R = A - P_E^0 M \qquad (6.3)$$

An oil-supply disruption typically leads to a sharp increase in P_E^0/P, the real price of oil. From equation 6.2, this increase is easily seen to have a substantial direct effect on real GNP in the model. This direct effect is the

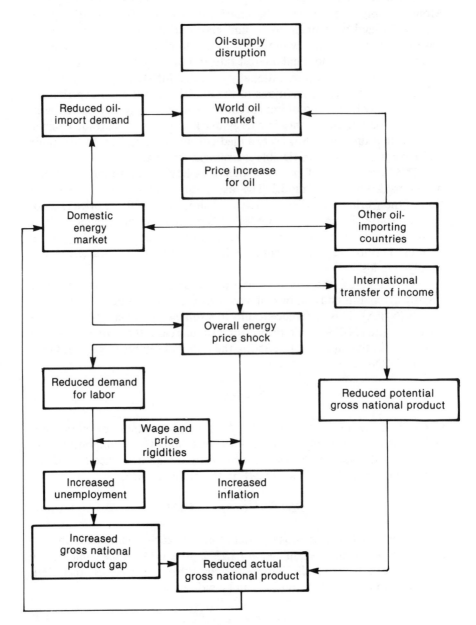

Figure 6-1. Flow Chart Illustrating the Effects of an Oil-Supply Disruption

transfer of real income referred to above: As an oil-importing nation, we have to transfer more of our wealth to foreign countries as payment for our external purchases. As 6.3 shows, this effect is absent from the official NIPA figures, because of the different convention of deflation. It does, however, represent a real loss because larger amounts of other goods have to be given up in exchange for foreign oil.

In our experience so far, this transfer of income has to a considerable extent taken place in financial terms; that is oil exporters have stored a large part of their new wealth in various financial assets in the United States and in other oil-importing countries. Sooner or later, however, the oil exporters must be expected to claim payments in real terms by directly or indirectly buying U.S. goods and services. Thus, more of domestic U.S. production will have to go to exports, so that the real supply of goods and services for domestic use is reduced.

Returning to the chart in figure 6–1, we see that the price increase for oil combines with sympathetic (although usually more modest) increases in other fuel prices so as to result in an overall energy-price shock. This shock in turn leads to a one-shot increase in inflation as well as to increased unemployment.

The inflationary surge is relatively easy to explain. As the price of imported oil goes up, so do the prices of domestic oil and other fuels, such as coal and natural gas. The increased cost of crude oil and other primary fuels is passed on almost immediately to the prices of gasoline, heating oil, electricity, and other forms of energy used directly by consumers. Indirectly, the prices of other goods and services rise also because increased energy prices drive up the costs of production. Had wage rates declined markedly in response to the increase in energy prices, or had the cost increase been absorbed as reduced profits, then the overall price level need not have gone up in response to an oil-price shock. For some reason, however, this does not seem to happen. As a result, the overall price level increases substantially in a round of one-shot inflation.

The increase in unemployment is a result of a decline in the demand for labor brought about by the oil price increase. If full employment is to be maintained, real wages must decline in response to the reduction in labor demand. The decline in the market-clearing real wage is a reflection of the decline in real income—the supply-side effect—discussed above. The decline in income is likely to take the form of a reduction in market-clearing wages as well as in the return to capital.[2] However, since wages seem to respond slowly to this and other unexpected changes in the economic environment, actual wage rates are likely to remain above their market-clearing levels for some time, so unemployment increases above normal levels. The economy enters a recession.

The recession amounts to shortfall of GNP below its potential level. As figure 6-1 indicates, this shortfall combines with the decline in potential GNP to give the total GNP decline.

The decline in GNP is an important outcome of the model. It is also a link in an important feedback loop that is illustrated in figure 6-1. As economic activity declines, so does the demand for energy and, in the case of the United States, the demand for foreign oil. This decline in energy demand comes on top of any direct effect of prices on U.S. energy demand and supply and is probably larger. A similar decline must be expected to take place in other countries' demand for imported oil. As a result, the world oil market will not be quite as tight as a result of a disruption as it would have been if economic activity had been kept at its normal level everywhere. Even so, as the next section will show, the potential losses are large.

Two important issues are not covered in figure 6-1. First, a disruption may affect the rates of return that oil exporters can extract from their investment of oil revenues in claims on the U.S. economy. This issue will be further discussed.

Second, oil-supply disruptions raise serious problems in terms of the domestic distribution of income and wealth. In an unregulated market, a supply disruption raises oil prices substantially without affecting production cost for domestic oil production. As a result, huge windfall profits may be accumulated by domestic oil producers. These windfalls are paid for by the rest of the economy. If a disruption raises the price of crude oil by thirty-five dollars per barrel as an annual average, the accumulation of windfall profits in the oil industry may amount to an income transfer of more than one-hundred-ten billion. Adding similar, although smaller, windfalls for coal and natural gas brings us to a figure in the neighborhood of 5 percent of GNP. This large potential transfer is of obvious social concern.

Another equity problem arises in the unequal distribution of the direct hardships of higher oil prices. The poor, the elderly, those living in extreme climates, and all those who in any sense depend more on oil than others are the ones that feel the burden the most.

A further discussion of these equity issues lies beyond the scope of the present chapter. It is important to realize, however, that any successful policy for managing oil-supply disruptions must somehow come to grips with these problems.

Estimates of Economywide Effects of a Major Oil Disruption

This section takes a closer look at the effects on the U.S. economy of a "worst-case" oil-supply disruption: the loss of the supplies of the entire

Persian Gulf area. Specifically, we consider a reduction in OPEC productive capacity of eighteen million barrels per day (mmbd). This dramatic disruption is thought of as occurring unexpectedly in 1985. After a year of disrupted supplies, oil production capacity is assumed to be restored gradually to its previous level over the three following years.

The analysis is carried out with the help of the model described in the previous section. The model is first run to give a baseline projection under the assumption of no disruption of world oil supply. Next, the model is run under the same assumptions, except that an eighteen mmbd disruption is assumed to occur as described above. The difference in results between the two model runs are used as estimates of the effects of the disruption.

The baseline projection is presented in table 6-1. It should be emphasized that this projection is not a forecast; its only purpose is to serve as a basis for comparison. The projected rate of inflation is based on assumptions that simply imply a continuation of current trends. No attempt was made in the projection to incorporate the potential long-run effects of recent attempts by the Federal Reserve to curb monetary growth.

As discussed in the previous section, the model does not use double deflation in the computation of real GNP. Because of this, and because real oil prices are considerably higher now than in 1972, the projected figures for real GNP may be somewhat lower than expected from the reading of current data.

The projected values of real variables may be low for another reason as well. The model was calibrated to actual 1980 data in nominal terms. Furthermore, consistently with the use of a single price index, the overall price level of the model was calibrated to the 1980 Consumer Price Index (CPI). Since the CPI is higher than the GNP deflator not only because of the inclusion of import prices, but for other reasons as well, this convention yields somewhat lower real values than the National Income and Product Accounts.

Table 6-1
Baseline Projection of Key Economic Variables for the United States with No Oil-Supply Disruption, 1985-1988

Item	1985	1986	1987	1988
Inflation (percent per year)	9.3	9.3	9.3	9.2
GNP (1972 billion dollars)	1,540.6	1,585.8	1,634.2	1,684.7
Investment (1972 billion dollars)	353.8	383.1	416.4	452.7
Consumption (1972 billion dollars)	937.2	955.9	975.1	994.6
Unemployment (percent)	6.0	6.0	6.0	6.0
Price of oil (1980 dollars per barrel)	38.71	39.82	40.94	42.04
Energy demand (1972 billion dollars)	39.7	40.9	42.1	43.4
Oil imports (million barrels per day)	14.0	15.1	16.3	17.8

The model assumes no productivity growth[3] and 2 percent annual growth in the labor force. The higher stable growth rate for GNP (around 3 percent) is due to the projected real increase in energy prices over time. The expectation of rising energy prices provides an incentive in the model to save now for worse times ahead.

The projections of oil imports and overall energy demand may to some extent reflect the experimental character of the recent extensions of the model. The lagged effects of the oil price increases in the 1970s on domestic energy supply and demand seem to be understated, so the projected oil import levels may be unreasonably high. Even apart from this phenomenon, the decline rate for domestic energy production may be too high.

It might be argued that reduced U.S. import levels for oil by 1985 might soften the impact of a supply disruption, so that the estimates shown below represent an overstatement. This would be true for the supply-side effects, since the income transfer can be shown to be proportional to the level of oil imports. For the demand side, it could be argued that a lower level of oil imports could lead to a slacker world market for oil, so the price shock would be smaller. The argument would be that a disruption could more easily be absorbed in a slack oil market, without large price increases, than it would in an already tight market. The ability of the oil market to absorb the recent reduction in oil supply resulting from the Iran-Iraq war could be taken as evidence in support of this view. However, over a period of several years, a general contraction of world oil demand may equally well lead to a contraction of readily available productive capacity. Thus, relative to the new capacity levels, the oil market may be tighter, or at least as tight in 1985 as it is today.

Table 6–2 shows the estimated effects of an oil supply disruption of eighteen mmbd occurring unexpectedly in 1985. The table shows the changes in the variables compared to the baseline projection. The disruption is projected to double world oil prices in real terms in the first year, to raise it by more than 40 percent in the second year, and to raise it by 10 percent in the third year. By the fourth year, when world oil capacity is assumed almost restored to predisruption levels, the reduced level of economic activity causes the price of oil to drop slightly below the baseline projection. The first-year jump in oil prices is even higher in nominal terms, because of the increase in the overall price level (see below). Even so, the numbers for oil price increases may seem somewhat low considering the magnitude of the disruption. The low numbers are obtained because of the softening effect of the projected worldwide recession. Also, the projections are for annual averages, so the price reactions over the first few months of the disruption may very well be much more violent.

The doubling of oil prices in real terms is projected to raise the inflation rate in 1985 by 13 percentage points. Even at the recent high inflation rates

Table 6-2
Projected Effects of an Eighteen Million Barrel Per Day Oil-Supply Disruption, Occurring Unexpectedly in 1985 (Deviations from Baseline Projection)

Item	1985	1986	1987	1988
Inflation Rate				
Change in percentage points	12.9	−0.2	−0.9	−0.8
GNP				
Change in 1972 billion dollars	−239.0	−126.5	−89.3	−82.1
Percentage change	−15.5	−8.0	−5.5	−4.9
Investment				
Change in 1972 billion dollars	−205.9	−112.4	−84.3	−80.1
Percentage change	−58.2	−29.3	−20.2	−17.7
Consumption				
Change in 1972 billion dollars	−30.6	−31.3	−31.9	−32.5
Percentage change	−3.4	−3.4	−3.4	−3.4
Unemployment				
Change in percentage points	5.9	1.4	0.3	0.3
Price of oil				
Percentage change	97.5	43.2	10.5	−5.0
Energy demand				
Percentage change	−17.4	−15.6	−11.2	−7.4
Oil imports				
Change in million barrels per day	−6.0	−5.4	−3.9	−2.3

this number is extremely high and could bring the inflation rate above 20 percent. The projected decline in energy prices from the first year of the disruption to the next combines with the slowing of the economy to reduce the inflation rate slightly in 1986, and a similar effect is projected for the next two years. However, in spite of the substantial decline in energy prices and the deep recession, this effect is hardly noticeable. The reason is simply that fewer goods are now being chased by the same amount of money.

In 1974, a quadrupling of world oil prices added only a few percentage points to the inflation rate. The larger projected effect for doubling of oil prices in 1985 follows from the fact that the economy starts from a much higher level of all energy prices than in 1974. Since the value share of energy in total cost is much larger, the price-level effect of a given percentage oil-price increase is larger as well.

The real effects of the disruption are, if possible, even more dramatic. Real GNP is reduced by almost two hundred and forty billion (1972) dollars in the first year of the simulated disruption, or over 15 percent. The loss in GNP tapers off somewhat thereafter as the economy adjusts to the shock and OPEC capacity is gradually restored. However, a substantial loss remains permanently because the recession leads to a permanent loss of productive capacity. This loss is vividly illustrated by the decline in real investment. In the first year, investment activity is cut down to one-third of its predisruption level.

The decline in real economic activity, although painful, also serves the purpose of reducing energy demand to levels compatible with the disrupted supply without astronomic price increases. Although domestic energy production (not shown) is not expected to change very much in response to the sudden, temporary price increase, energy demand reacts sufficiently to reduce the level of oil imports by six mmbd. In this sense, the United States is projected to carry a third of the total burden of the eighteen mmbd disruption. Only a small part of the demand reduction is a substitution effect; most of it is accomplished by the decline in real output.

Employment is projected to decline substantially in the first disruption year—the unemployment rate increases by no less than six percentage points. However, since the disruption is assumed to be temporary, the unemployment rate is projected to get back to normal after two years. The increased activity in the domestic energy sector, although small, contributes to this recovery.

The model assumes that consumption follows a path determined by consumer's permanent income. Under this and some further assumptions used by the model,[4] the shift in the consumption path can be used as an indicator of the net welfare cost of a disruption. It is a more reliable measure than GNP because it summarizes the effects on future as well as current economic conditions. The decline in consumption is only 15 percent of the decline in real GNP in the first year. Still, a 3.4 percent loss of permanent income is substantial.

The total economic cost of this hypothetical disruption for the United States can be measured as the present value of the permanent (current and future) decline in consumption.[5] In 1972 dollars, the model puts this figure at $516 billion, corresponding to $1,017 billion in 1980 dollars.[6] The latter figure is not less than $4,624 per person living in the United States, or almost $18,500 per household of four.

Although the projected losses are very large, this model also seems to suggest that the U.S. economy is quite resilient to shocks of this magnitude. Although a deep recession is projected—indeed, it might be called a depression—it is expected to be relatively short-lived.

Paradoxically, this resilience is partly due to the rigidities of the economy, particularly in regard to investment. Since a large portion of new investment projects have been decided upon, or even started, well ahead of the time an unexpected oil-supply disruption occurs, it may be very costly to change all investment activity on short notice. This costliness is reflected in the model and contributes to the dampening of the overall effects of the disruption.

The Burden of the Debt to Oil-Exporting Countries

This section analyzes in some detail one particular component of the projected losses under the disruption scenario described above. As indicated earlier, the model allows for a temporaty accumulation of a trade deficit as a result of oil imports, so that foreign trade balances only in a present value sense.

This feature of the model reflects the observed phenomenon of reinvestment of oil revenues by oil-exporting countries in claims on the U.S. economy. From 1973 to 1981, OPEC as a whole accumulated net foreign assets surpluses of $380 billion. Of this, $157 billion was accumulated by Saudi Arabia alone.[7] It seems reasonable to assume that a major part of these investments took the form of claims on the U.S. economy.

In general, the recipients of these funds are not the same people as those who actually import the oil. Still, from the point of view of the country as a whole, we may think of this process as the United States buying oil on credit. The return on oil exporters' investments may then be thought of as the interest charge we as a country have to pay on this debt. Clearly, if an oil supply disruption results in an increase in the rate of interest on this debt, this increase is a part of the total cost of the disruption.

In the model, this relationship is formulated as follows. Let X_t denote real net exports of nonenergy goods, p_t the real price of imported oil, M_t the quantity of oil imports, and r_t the real rate of interest, all in year t. Furthermore, let T denote the year after which the backstop technology becomes available (and profitable) in the model. The balancing of trade in the present-value sense may then be written as:

$$X_1 + \sum_{t=2}^{\infty} \prod_{\tau=2}^{t} \left(\frac{1}{1+r_\tau}\right) X_t - p_1 M_1 - \sum_{t=2}^{T} \prod_{\tau=2}^{t} \left(\frac{1}{1+r_\tau}\right) p_t M_t = 0$$

The model assumes net exports of nonenergy goods, X_t, to grow at a constant trend. Ignoring this trend for simplicity, we may assume:

$$X_1 = X_2 = \ldots = X$$

and rewrite the condition as:

$$X = V/R \tag{6.4}$$

where

$$V = p_1 M_1 + \sum_{t=2}^{T} \prod_{\tau=2}^{t} \left(\frac{1}{1+r_\tau}\right) p_t M_t$$

and

$$R = 1 + \sum_{t=2}^{\infty} \prod_{\tau=2}^{t} \left(\frac{1}{1 + r_\tau}\right)$$

It may be noted that the model ignores the interest burden on any past net foreign investment. In the model, all foreign debt is accumulated by purchasing oil on credit in 1985 and beyond. The debt is accumulated whether or not a disruption occurs; but the burden of the debt may be affected by a disruption. In particular, an increase in expected future interest rates will reduce R and thus require higher amounts of net exports of nonenergy goods as installment payments for the same amounts of oil imports.

In the real world, the rates of return on oil exporters' investments are affected by many factors, most of which cannot be dealt with here. It seems reasonable to expect, however, that these returns will follow the same long-run trends as other interest rates in the U.S. economy. The model used here assumes the return on oil exporters' claims to be the same as the real return to new capital in production. It then makes an interesting prediction: since investment is hit especially hard by the projected oil-induced recession, the stock of capital left for the future will be significantly reduced. As the reduced capital stock is allocated to users in competitive markets, the increased scarcity will lead to higher rental prices for capital. In other words, real interest rates will increase after the oil-induced recession and stay high for a long time afterwards.[8] This effect occurs in spite of a prediction of lower interest rates *during* the recession. As a result, the model predicts a substantial net increase in interest payments on our debt to oil exporters. According to the model, these payments contribute sixteen billion dollars (1972) to the reduction in aggregate consumption in 1985.

This number is rather large; in fact, it suggests that half of the real welfare loss of the disruption (as measured by the level of consumption) comes from this source. It may thus be instructive to consider in a little more detail how this effect is obtained.

For this purpose, it may be useful to develop a simple model, which may serve as a pedagogic device for understanding the larger, computerized model. Consider an economy that uses capital (K), labor (L), and oil (E) each period in the production of output (Y), according to the production function:

$$Y_t = F(L_t, K_t, E_t) \tag{6.5}$$

For simplicity, I assume no productivity growth in production and no growth in the labor force. Also, I ignore any differences between oil and other fuels and treat them all as equivalent to oil.

In the first period, this simple economy produces some oil domestically ($\bar{E}_D$) with a zero supply elasticity, using a fixed amount of goods ($\bar{Z}$) as its input in oil production. The remaining demand for oil ($M = E_1 - \bar{E}_D$) is imported at price p. This price may fluctuate unexpectedly if world supply is disrupted. In the second and all the following periods, a perfect substitute for oil is produced domestically according to a backstop technology. This backstop technology has a constant marginal cost $\bar{p}$, which is below or equal to the world price of oil, so that no oil is imported.

Using these assumptions, we may write the distribution of output as:

$$Y_1 = C_1 + X_1 + I_1 + \bar{Z} \tag{6.6a}$$

$$Y_t = C_t + X_t + I_t + \bar{p}E_t, \qquad t \geq 2, \tag{6.6b}$$

where C is aggregate consumption, I investment, and X net exports of goods other than oil.

Assume now that aggregate consumption is determined according to the life cycle/permanent income hypothesis with rational expectations. Coupling this hypothesis with the additional assumption of a zero elasticity of intertemporal substitution in consumption implies the constraint:

$$C_1 = C_2 = \ldots = C \tag{6.7}$$

We also assume that imported oil is paid for in real terms with equal installments so that:

$$X_1 = X_2 = \ldots = X \tag{6.8}$$

Capital stock accumulates according to the formula

$$K_t = I_{t-1} + (1 - \delta)K_{t-1} \tag{6.9}$$

and K_1 is given by history. Following the argument by Solow (1974), we find that under the assumption of a zero elasticity of intertemporal substitution in consumption, the economy must attain a steady state in period 2. Consequently:

$$I_2 = \delta K_2 \tag{6.10}$$

Furthermore, since the model repeats itself from period 2 on, we need only analyze the first two periods.

Because of the latter property, and since oil is imported only in the first period, the present-value constraint on the trade balance may now be written as:

$$\left[1 + \sum_{t=2}^{\infty} \left(\frac{1}{1 + r_2}\right)^t\right] X = p(E_1 - \bar{E}_D)$$

Summing the geometric series and rearranging, this gives:

$$X = \left(\frac{r_2}{1 + r_2}\right) p(E_1 - \bar{E}_D) \tag{6.11}$$

We are now ready to use this model to find the cost of an oil supply disruption, expressed as the present value of the partial derivative of the uniform level of consumption with respect to the first-period oil price. First, use 6.6b and 6.10 to find:

$$\frac{\partial(C + X)}{\partial p} = \frac{\partial Y_2}{\partial p} - \delta \frac{\partial K_2}{\partial p} - p \frac{\partial E_2}{\partial p}$$

Since no shock is assumed to occur in the second (and later) periods, we may assume employment in the second period to be unaffected by the oil price shock in period 1. Furthermore, assuming firms maximize profits, we obtain:

$$\frac{\partial Y_2}{\partial p} = (r_2 + \delta) \frac{\partial K_2}{\partial p} + \bar{p} \frac{\partial E_2}{\partial p}$$

where $r_2 + \delta$ is the real rental price (equal to the marginal productivity) of capital in the second period. Substituting this in the preceeding formula, we get:

$$\frac{\partial(C + X)}{\partial p} = r_2 \frac{\partial K_2}{\partial p}$$

Next use 6.6 through 6.10 to obtain:

$$K_2 - K_1 = \left(\frac{1}{1 - \delta}\right)[Y_1 - (Y_2 - \bar{p}E_2) - \bar{Z}]$$

Thus:

$$\frac{\partial K_2}{\partial p} = \left(\frac{1}{1 - \delta}\right)\left[\frac{\partial Y_1}{\partial p} - \left(\frac{\partial Y_2}{\partial p} - \bar{p} \frac{\partial E_2}{\partial p}\right)\right]$$

With some rigidities in the first period, which need not be specified here, first-period employment is likely to be affected by the oil price shock.[9] On the other hand, the capital stock in the first period is given by history. Thus:

$$\frac{\partial Y_1}{\partial p} = w_1 \frac{\partial L_1}{\partial p} + p \frac{\partial E_1}{\partial p}$$

where w_1 is the real wage rate in the first period.
From the above derivation, we get:

$$\frac{\partial Y_2}{\partial p} - \bar{p} \frac{\partial E_2}{\partial p} = (r_2 + \delta) \frac{\partial K_2}{\partial p}$$

We can now then express the change in the capital stock as

$$\frac{\partial K_2}{\partial p} = \left(\frac{1}{1 - \delta} \right) \left[w_1 \frac{\partial L_1}{\partial p} + p \frac{\partial E_1}{\partial p} - (r_2 + \delta) \frac{\partial K_2}{\partial p} \right]$$

or:

$$\frac{\partial K_2}{\partial p} = \left(\frac{1}{1 + r_2} \right) \left(w_1 \frac{\partial L_1}{\partial p} + p \frac{\partial E_1}{\partial p} \right) \tag{6.12}$$

so that:

$$\frac{\partial (C + X)}{\partial p} = \left(\frac{r_2}{1 + r_2} \right) \left(w_1 \frac{\partial L_1}{\partial p} + p \frac{\partial E_1}{\partial p} \right) \tag{6.13}$$

Next, consider the change in X. From 6.11, we get:

$$\frac{\partial X}{\partial p} = p(E_1 - \bar{E}_D) \frac{\partial \left(\frac{r_2}{1 + r_2} \right)}{\partial p} + \left(\frac{r_2}{1 + r_2} \right) \left(E_1 - \bar{E}_D + p \frac{\partial E_1}{\partial p} \right) \tag{6.14}$$

$$= pM \frac{\partial \left(\frac{r_2}{1 + r_2} \right)}{\partial p} + \left(\frac{r_2}{1 + r_2} \right) \left(M + p \frac{\partial E_1}{\partial p} \right)$$

where $M = E_1 - \bar{E}_D$ denotes oil imports in the first period. Combining 6.13 and 6.14, we now obtain the present value of the change in the uniform level of consumption as:

$$\left(\frac{1 + r_2}{r_2}\right)\frac{\partial C}{\partial p} = w_1\frac{\partial L_1}{\partial p} - M - pM\left(\frac{1 + r_2}{r_2}\right)\frac{\partial\left(\dfrac{r_2}{1 + r_2}\right)}{\partial p} \qquad (6.15)$$

This formula gives the cost of an oil-supply disruption in this model. It may be viewed as a sum of three components. The first component is associated with the decline in employment during the oil-induced recession. The second component represent the transfer of real income to oil-exporting countries. It is easy to show that these two cost components would have been incurred whether or not oil were bought on credit. The third component is, however, a direct result of the recycling of oil revenues into the U.S. economy. In this simplified model, it corresponds to a decrease in R in 6.4. Since the country's oil debt is paid in equal installments indefinitely, with the first installment (X_1) paid before interest starts accumulating, the principal of the debt will stay equal to:

$$pM - X = pM - \left(\frac{r_2}{1 + r_2}\right)pM = pM/(1 + r_2)$$

indefinitely. Thus, interest payments change each period by the amount:

$$pM\frac{\partial\left(\dfrac{r_2}{1 + r_2}\right)}{\partial p}$$

This change adds to the cost of a disruption if $\partial r_2/\partial p$ is positive.

Too see that the latter condition holds, notice first from 6.12 that an oil price shock unambiguously leads to a decline in K_2 since employment as well as oil consumption is reduced in the first period. Second, from the profit-maximizing conditions:

$$F_E(L_2, K_2, E_2) = \bar{p}$$
$$F_K(L_2, K_2, E_2) = r_2 + \delta,$$

where the subscripts E and K denote partial derivatives, we may derive:

$$\frac{\partial r_2}{\partial p} = (F_{KK} - F_{EK}^2/F_{EE})\frac{\partial K_2}{\partial p}$$

Under constant returns to scale:

$$F_{KK} - F_{EK}^2 / F_{EE} < 0$$

as a consequence of the convexity of the technology. Thus, future interest rates are indeed increased by an oil price shock, and this increase adds to the total cost of the shock.[10]

As indicated above, the model suggests that the increased burden on our debt to oil-exporting countries will be a major component of the total cost of an oil supply disruption. This result depends on a number of implicit and explicit assumptions, all of which are subject to some uncertainty. The assumption that the return to foreigners' investment in the United States is always equal to the marginal productivity of new capital may be somewhat extreme. And even if competitive markets force the two rates of return to be equal, they may both be influenced by the returns on investment elsewhere in the world.[11] However, it seems a reasonable assumption that the economies of other industrialized countries react to oil supply disruptions in a similar fashion as the U.S. economy. If this is the case, this influence would not change the results very much.

As seen from 6.4 and 6.15, the effect of higher interest rates is an increasing function of the amount of oil imports and of the number of years that oil can be expected to be imported to the United States. As the comments on table 6–1 indicated, the model may overstate the amounts of future oil import levels. On the other hand, it predicts imported oil to be completely replaced by a renewable domestic substitute in 1995, which seems a rather early date. On balance, these two features may contribute to an overstatement of the interest cost, but the magnitude of the overstatement seems uncertain.

As indicated above, the model ignores completely the stock of oil exporters' claims on the U.S. economy in existence in 1985. Considering the figures cited at the beginning of this section, this omission may lead to a substantial understatement of the interest-rate effect: If higher interest is to be paid on foreign claims, it must be paid on old as well as new debt. On the other hand, the model also ignores all capital flows that are unrelated to oil. In particular, it ignores the return on oil-unrelated U.S. claims on foreign countries. To the extent that the return on these claims is increased by an oil supply disruption, this omission leads to an overstatement of the interest-rate effect.

Finally, the model assumes that oil-exporters' behavior in terms of their purchases of U.S. goods is unaffected by a disruption of oil supplies from the Persian Gulf.[12] This assumption may seem implausible, since in such a situation most of U.S. oil imports would come from the so-called high absorbers among the oil-exporting nations. Thus, it might seem reasonable to expect a larger share of oil exporters' revenues to be spent—directly or indirectly—on goods produced in the United States.

However, it is important to realize (as indeed 6.4 indicates) that the real payments in terms of exports of nonenergy goods in the model are related to oil imports in all future periods, not just the disruption years. After the disrupted production capacity has been restored, the model assumes the supplies from the Persian Gulf to come back on line. Thus, there may be a substantial period after the disruption during which oil is purchased on credit from low-absorbing exporters. Higher interest rates on this future credit will give the results in the model.

A more serious question is whether the current low-absorbing countries will continue to be low absorbers after a disruption. In particular, if the disruption should be associated with a change in government in Saudi Arabia, the new government might well wish to spend a larger portion of the country's oil revenues on real imports. The answer to this type of question is not attempted by the model.

Whatever the bias of the estimate presented here may be, the magnitude of the estimated figure seems large enough to indicate that this phenomenon deserves serious attention. For example, it seems a good justification for monetary or other policies to drive down real interest rates. Moreover, this cost component has the flavor of an externality: since the people who pay the return on foreign investment are not the same people as those who import the oil, oil importers do not take the risk of higher interest payments into account as part of their expected total cost of importing oil. Since this effect depends on the level of oil imports, it seems to provide an argument for a tariff, over and above any argument that might exist from the point of view of U.S. monopsony power in the world oil market.[13] However, like most other arguments for tariffs, this argument should be considered with some caution. For example, it is possible to argue (see Mork, 1982b) that, in the absence of supply disruptions, the reinvestment of oil-exporter revenues in U.S. assets produces an external benefit of oil imports, which would provide an argument against a tariff. Definite policy recommendations do not seem possible without more definite research results.

Conclusion

A major disruption in the world oil supply seems likely to cause great harm to the U.S. economy. This chapter considers the worst possible case: the loss of supplies from the entire Persian Gulf area. Although the chapter assumes these supplies to be restored after four years, the impact on the U.S. economy is projected to be very substantial. Based on a computer simulation model, the chapter estimates that such a disruption would add 13 percentage points to the U.S. inflation rate in the first year. The real effects are, if anything, even more disturbing. Real GNP is projected to fall 15 percent below normal because of the disruption, and investment activity is expected to be reduced to one-third of its normal level. As a consequence, unemployment is estimated to approach levels reminiscent of the Great Depression, although only for a year.

Since investment suffers so badly, the stock of capital left for future production is projected to decline significantly relative to normal. As a result, the market for capital is expected to tighten and to produce higher real interest rates in the long run. A consequence of this interest-rate increase seems to be that we, as a country, will have to pay a higher return to oil-exporting countries on that part of their revenues that is reinvested in U.S. assets. This mechanism may potentially result in an important drain on the U.S. economy. According to the model, this drain makes up half of the long-term cost to the United States of a major oil supply disruption. The total cost is estimated by the model as the present value of current and future losses. For the disruption considered here, the cost is estimated in 1980 dollars as $1,017 billion.

In the midst of this gloomy scenario, it is nevertheless comforting to see that the U.S. economy is not at all predicted to come to an end, or anything like an end, even if such a large disturbance should occur. Although the damage is substantial and the scars will remain, life will go on and go on pretty well, once the traumatic experience is over. In spite of its many weaknesses, the U.S. economy seems too strong to be broken by the loss of oil supplies from the Persian Gulf.

Appendix 6A
Equations of Energy—
Macro Model

List of Variables

C_t	Aggregate consumption
d_t	Investment tax credit
E_t	Domestic demand for energy
G_t	Government demand for goods and services
GNP_t	Real Gross National Product
H_t	Money supply
i_t	Real return on oil exporters' claims on the U.S. economy
$\bar{I}_t$	Level of investment for categories of capital whose levels are determined before the shock
$\hat{I}_t$	Level of investment for categories of capital whose levels are determined after the shock
$\bar{K}_t$	Level of capital stock for categories of capital whose levels are determined before the shock
$\hat{K}_t$	Level of capital stock for categories of capital whose levels are determined after the shock
k_t	OPEC capacity
L_t	Actual employment
$\hat{L}_t$	Employment at normal levels of unemployment
$\bar{L}_t$	Employment corresponding to predetermined component of wages (w_t^*)
M_t	U.S. oil-import demand
M_t^F	Oil-import demand for non-U.S., non-OPEC countries
P_t	Overall price level (money price of goods)
$\bar{P}_t$	Expected overall price level in the absence of a shock
p_t	Real domestic price of energy
$\bar{p}_t$	Expected real domestic price of energy in the absence of a shock
$\bar{p}$	Backstop price of energy
p_t^0	Domestic price of oil
Q_t	Demand for OPEC oil by non-OPEC countries

185

R_t	U.S. domestic energy supply
R_t^F	Domestic energy supply for non-U.S., non-OPEC countries
r_t	Nominal interest rate
S_t	U.S. domestic energy resource stock
t	Time
T	Date after which backstop energy technology is used in the model
u_t	Unemployment rate
v_t^*	Real rental price (shadow price) for categories of capital whose levels are determined before the shock
$\hat{v}_t$	Real rental price for categories of capital whose levels are determined after the shock
v_t	Aggregate real rental price of capital
$\bar{v}_t$	Expected real rental price of capital in the absence of a shock
$\bar{w}_t$	Predetermined nominal wage rate
w_t^*	Predetermined nominal wage rate adjusted for cost-of-living increases
w_t	Aggregate nominal wage rate
X_t	Net U.S. exports of nonenergy goods
Y_t	Gross output of goods and services in the nonenergy sector of the U.S. economy
Y_t^F	Gross output of goods and services in non-U.S., non-OPEC countries
Z_t	Total real cost of U.S. energy production
ϵ_t	Oil supply disruption in percent of OPEC capacity
τ_{ft}	U.S. tariff on oil
τ_g	Rate of sales tax for goods and services in the United States
τ_{pt}	Tax on U.S. energy production
θ	Tax rate on capital in production

List of Equations

1. *Nonenergy sector of the U.S. economy*

1.1 *Production possibility constraint*

Long-run unit cost function (translog):

$$\ln \hat{\phi} = a_0 + a_L \ln(w_t/P_t) + a_K \ln v_t + a_E \ln p_t$$
$$+ (\tfrac{1}{2}) b_{LL}[\ln(w_t/P_t)]^2 + b_{LK}[\ln(w_t/P_t)](\ln v_t)$$
$$+ b_{LE}[\ln(w_t/P_t)](\ln p_t) + (\tfrac{1}{2}) b_{KK}(\ln v_t)^2$$
$$+ b_{KE}(\ln v_t)(\ln p_t) + (\tfrac{1}{2}) b_{EE}(\ln p_t)^2 \qquad (6A.1)$$

a_0	$= -0.7750$		b_{LK}	$= 0.0000$
a_L	$= 0.5590$		b_{LE}	$= -0.0351$
a_K	$= 0.4047$		b_{KK}	$= 0.0315$
a_E	$= 0.0363$		b_{KE}	$= -0.0315$
b_{LL}	$= 0.0351$		b_{EE}	$= 0.0666$

Cost shares and demand elasticities are variable. Using variable values for 1985 for the base case, factor shares and long-run demand-and-substitution elasticities can be computed as:

s_L	$= 0.579$		ϵ_{LE}	$= 0.054$		ϵ_{EK}	$= 0.032$
s_K	$= 0.306$		ϵ_{KL}	$= 0.579$		ϵ_{EE}	$= -0.306$
s_E	$= 0.115$		ϵ_{KK}	$= -0.591$		σ_{LK}	$= 1.000$
ϵ_{LL}	$= -0.360$		ϵ_{KE}	$= 0.012$		σ_{LE}	$= 0.473$
ϵ_{LK}	$= 0.306$		ϵ_{EL}	$= 0.274$		σ_{KE}	$= 0.105$

Short-run cost function, approximating putty-clay:

$$\bar{\phi}(w_t/P_t, v_t, p_t) = \gamma_{0t}[a_t v_t + (1 - a_t)p_t]^{1-\alpha_t}(w_t/P_t)^{\alpha_t} \quad (6A.2)$$

$\gamma_{0t}, a_t, \alpha_t$ are computed from prices and input combinations as predicted by the model in the absence of a shock, so that, at base-case prices, factor demands derived from $\hat{\phi}$ and $\bar{\phi}$ are identical.

Combined cost function:

$$\phi(w_t/P_t, v_t, p_t) = [\hat{\phi}(w_t/P_t, v_t, p_t)]^{g_t} \qquad (6A.3)$$
$$[\bar{\phi}(w_t/P_t, v_t, p_t)]^{1 - g_t}$$

g_t rises from $1/6$ in the year of the shock to 1 after six years.

1.2 Labor market

Cost-of-living escalation of predetermined wages:

$$w_t^* = [1 + \gamma_t(P_t - \bar{P}_t)/\bar{P}_t]\, \bar{w}_t \tag{6A.4}$$

γ_ϵ equals 0.25 in the year of the shock and 0.5 thereafter.

Wage rigidity:

$$w_t^0 = \hat{w}_t^{f_t}\, w_t^{*(1 - f_t)} \tag{6A.5}$$

f_t rises from 1/6 in the year of the shock to 1 after six years

Correction for cyclical variation in labor productivity:

$$w_t = w_t^0(w_t^*/\hat{w}_t)^{h(1 - f_t)} \tag{6A.6}$$

Employment:

$$L_t = f_t \hat{L}_t + (1 - f_t)\bar{L}_t \tag{6A.7}$$

$$\hat{L}_t = (w_t/\hat{w}_t)\phi_{w/P}(w_t/P_t, v_t, p_t)\, Y_t \tag{6A.8}$$

$$\bar{L}_t = (w_t/w_t^*)\phi_{w/P}(w_t/P_t, v_t, p_t)\, Y_t \tag{6A.9}$$

Subscripts for ϕ denote partial derivatives.

Supply of labor:

$$\hat{L}_t = L_0 e^{nt} \qquad n = \ln(1.02) \tag{6A.10}$$

Unemployment rate:

$$u_t = 6 + 73\,(\hat{L}_t - L_t)/\hat{L}_t \tag{6A.11}$$

1.3   Capital market

Dual formulation of investment lag:

$$v_t = \hat{v}_t^{b_t} v_t^{*1-b_t} \qquad (6A.12)$$

b_t rises from ¼ in the year of the shock to 1 after four years.

Demand for capital:

$$\hat{K}_t = (v_t/\hat{v}_t)\phi_v(w_t/P_t, v_t, p_t) Y_t \qquad (6A.13)$$

$$\bar{K}_t = (v_t/v_t^*)\phi_v(w_t/P_t, v_t, p_t) Y_t \qquad (6A.14)$$

Capital accumulation:

$$\hat{K}_t = \hat{I}_t + (1-\delta)\{(b_{t-1}/b_t)\hat{K}_{t-1} + [(b_t - b_{t-1})/b_t]\bar{K}_{t-1}\} \qquad (6A.15)$$

$$\bar{K}_t = \bar{I}_t + (1-\delta)\bar{K}_{t-1} \qquad \delta = 0.09 \qquad (6A.16)$$

1.4 Demand for energy:

$$E_t = \phi_p(w_t/P_t, v_t, p_t) Y_t \qquad (6A.17)$$

1.5 Market for goods and services

Investment demand derived from the capital market.

Consumer behavior:

$$C_t = c_0 \hat{L}_t \qquad (6A.18)$$

c_0 determined by the model as the maximum sustainable per-capita consumption level.

Trade balance:

$$X_t = X_0 e^{nt} \qquad (6A.19)$$

$$X_0 = \left[1 + \sum_{t=2}^{\infty} e^{nt} \prod_{\tau=2}^{t} \left(\frac{1}{1+i_\tau}\right)\right]^{-1} \qquad (6A.20)$$

$$\times \left[(p_1^0 - \tau_{f1})M_1 + \sum_{t=2}^{T} \prod_{\tau=2}^{t} \left(\frac{1}{1+i_\tau}\right)(p_t^0 - \tau_{ft})M_t\right]$$

$$i_t = \hat{v}_t/(1 - d_t) - \delta \tag{6A.21}$$

Distribution of output:

$$Y_t = C_t + b_t\hat{I}_t + (1 - b_t)\bar{I}_t + X_t + G_t + Z_t \tag{6A.22}$$

$G_t = G_0 e^{nt}$ unless otherwise specified.

Definition of real GNP:

$$GNP_t = Y_t - (p_t^0 - \tau_{ft})M_t - Z_t \tag{6A.23}$$

Price equation:

$$(1 - \tau_g)P_t = [\phi(w_t^0, P_t v_t, P_t p_t)]^{a_t}[\bar{\phi}(w_t^0, P_t \bar{v}_t, P_t p_t)]^{1 - a_t}$$

$$\tau_g = 0.0648 \tag{6A.24}$$

a_t rises from ¼ in the year of the shock to 1 after four years.

1.6. *Money market*

Money market equilibrium:

$$ln(P_t Y_t/H_t) + (1 - \lambda) ln(1 - p_t E_t/Y_t) \tag{6A.25}$$

$$= \psi_o + \psi_1 r_t + \mu_2 t$$

$\lambda = 1$ unless otherwise specified

$\psi_0 = 2.0315$ $\qquad$ $\psi_1 = 2.0$ $\qquad$ $\mu_2 = ln(1.095)$

$H_t = H_0 e^{mt},$ $\qquad$ $m = ln(1.05)$ unless otherwise specified.

Relationship between nominal interest rate and real return to new capital:

$$r_t = \hat{v}_t/(1 - d_t) - \delta + \theta + ln[(1 - d_{t+1})P_{t+1}] \tag{6A.26}$$

$$- ln[(1 - d_t)P_t]$$

$\theta = 0.13, d_t = 0.036$ unless otherwise specified.

2. *Domestic energy supply*

Marginal cost of extraction:

$$c(R_t, S_t, t; v_t) = c_1^{v_t} R_t^{v_t} e^{\mu_4 t} + c_2 e^{-\rho S_t} \tag{6A.27}$$

v_t declines from 25 in the year of the shock to 4 after six years.

$$c_1 = 0.0479 \qquad c_2 = 10^{12}$$

$$\mu_4 = 0.077 \qquad \rho = 0.007$$

Total cost of domestic energy supply:

$$Z_t = \left(\frac{1}{1+v_t}\right) c_1^{v_t} R_t^{v_t + 1} e^{\mu_4 t} + c_2 R_t e^{-\rho S_t}, \quad p_t < \bar{p} \tag{6A.28}$$

Arbitrage condition for domestic energy supply:

$$(\hat{v}_t - \delta) [p_t - \tau_{pt} - c(R_t, S_t, t; v_t)] \tag{6A.29}$$

$$= p_{t+1} - \tau_{p,t+1} - p_t + \tau_{pt} - \frac{\partial c}{\partial R_t}(R_t, S_t, t; v_t)(R_{t+1} - R_t)$$

$$- \frac{\partial c}{\partial v_t}(R_t, S_t, t; v_t)(v_{t+1} - v_t) - \frac{\partial c}{\partial t}(R_t, S_t, t; v_t)$$

Depletion of resource stock:

$$S_t = S_{t-1} - R_t \tag{6A.30}$$

Initial resource stock (marginal extraction cost at zero extraction cost is β times initial resource price, p_0):

$$S_0 = (1/\rho) \ln [c_2/(\beta p_0)] \tag{6A.31}$$

For 1980, $\beta = 1/8$, p_0 corresponds to $35/bbl for crude oil.

Terminal resource stock (zero rent at backstop price):

$$\bar{S} = (1/\rho)\, ln\, (c_2/\bar{p})$$ (6A.32)

Resource stock constraint on resource extraction:

$$\sum_{t=1}^{\infty} R_t = S_0 - \bar{S} = (1/\rho)\, ln\, [\bar{p}/(\beta p_0)]$$ (6A.33)

3.   World oil market

U.S. demand for imported oil:

$$M_t = E_t - R_t \quad \text{if} \quad p_t < \bar{p}$$ (6A.34a)

$M_t = 0$ if $p_t \geq \bar{p}$ (except when $p_t > \bar{p}$ as the result of a disruption or a temporary policy).

Aggregate production function for the nonenergy sectors of non-U.S., non-OPEC countries:

$$Y_t^F = [(\eta_t A_t)^{1-1/\sigma t} + B_t^{1-1/\sigma t}(R_t^F + M_t^F)^{1-1/\sigma t}]^{\frac{1}{1-1/\sigma t}}$$ (6A.35)

σ_t rises from 0.04 in the year of the shock to 0.4 after six years.

A_t, B_t are calibrated to actual output and energy input levels for 1980 (as functions of τ_t), with $\eta_t = 1$. A_t approximates inputs of labor and capital. η_t is adjusted by the model to parallel variations in U.S. labor and capital input resulting from oil-supply disruptions.
  Foreign demand for energy (profit maximization):

$$p_t^0 - \tau_{ft} = B_t^{1-1/\sigma_t} [Y_t^F/(R_t^F + M_t^F)]^{1/\sigma_t}$$ (6A.36)

Domestic energy supply in non-U.S., non-OPEC countries:

$$R_t^F = \bar{R}^F$$ (6A.37)

$\bar{R}^F = 39.5$ in units of millions of barrels per day.

Total world demand for OPEC oil exports:

$$Q_t = M_t + M_t^F$$ (6A.38)

OPEC price reaction function (used in the model for the first five years after the shock):

$$p_t^0 - \tau_{ft} = d_1 + \frac{(1 - \epsilon_t)d_2}{(1 - \epsilon_t)k_t - Q_t}$$ (6A.39)

$$d_1 = 28.5715 \qquad d_2 = 38.571$$

$$k_t = 34.9, \text{ all } t$$

The elasticity of the price reaction function is variable. At the base-case price for 1985, the marginal cost of oil (including monopsony premium) for non-OPEC countries is 3.4 times the market price, corresponding to an elasticity of 0.29.

Translation from domestic price of oil to overall domestic price of energy:

$$p_t - \bar{p}_t = 0.8 \, (p_t^0 - \bar{p}_t)$$ (6A.40)

Price of oil after six years:

$$p_t = \bar{p}_t = p_0 e^{\mu_3 t}, \qquad p_t \leq \bar{p}$$ (6A.41)

$$\mu_3 = ln \, (1.02)$$

Notes

1. This assumption applies to the activity levels of the nonenergy sectors of the vaious countries. Thus, it is compatible with the direct increase in real income of oil-exporting nations (such as the United Kingdom and Norway) because of the oil price increase.

2. If labor substitutes much more easily for energy than does capital, the demand for labor may actually increase, so the shortfall in income may fall entirely on capital. If so, an oil supply disruption would tighten the labor market and thus add even more inflationary pressure to the economy. The evidence of the last decade suggests strongly, however, that this has not been the case.

3. This assumption seems consistent with recent observations on productivity growth. Furthermore, the model assumes a zero elasticity of intertemporal substitution in consumption. Under this assumption, the absence of productivity growth allows the model to attain a steady state, see Solow

(1974). Apart from this technical aspect, the zero rate has no substantial consequences for the results of the model.

4. Specifically, the model assumes a zero elasticity of intertemporal substitution in consumption, so that, except for the effect of population growth, consumers insist on the same level of consumption each year. This level is revised upon the advent of new information, such as an oil-supply disruption, so as to be the highest possible level that can be sustained by the model economy.

5. The discounting is made at a geometric average of interest rates in the base case and in the disruption case. Using base-case interest rates would result in an even higher cost figure.

6. Inflated by the Consumer Price Index.

7. See Bankers Trust Company (1981).

8. In a model used here, real interest rates are predicted to stay high permanently once they have increased. This effect occurs because the model assumes a rigid mini-max criterion for allocation of consumption over time, so that the steady-state capital stock is path dependent (see Solow, 1974). If a differentiable intertemporal utility function had been used, the real interest rate would eventually return to its "normal," steady-state level, equal to the rate of time preference, but it might stay high for a very long time.

9. Such rigidities need not contradict the assumption of profit maximization. For example, wage rigidity may lead to unemployment even if firms maximize their profits.

10. This result does not contradict a temporary decline in the real interest rate during the disruption-induced recession. In particular:

$$\frac{\partial r_1}{\partial p} = F_{KL}\,\frac{\partial L_1}{\partial p} + F_{KE}\frac{\partial E_1}{\partial p}$$

If F_{KL}, F_{KE} are positive, as seems reasonable, this expression is negative.

11. Olivier Blanchard reminded me of this point.

12. The following remarks are in response to a comment by the discussant, Roger Kubarych.

13. See, for example, William Nordhaus (1980) and Stephen Peck and James Plummer (1982). For an interesting additional argument made on the basis of a three-country model (OPEC, the United States, and the other OECD (Organization for Economic Cooperation and Development) countries), see Paul Krugman (1981).

References

Bankers Trust Company. 1981. *OPEC Surplus,* New York.
Bruno, Michael, and Jeffrey Sachs. 1981. "Supply Versus Demand

Approaches to the Problem of Stagflation," in H. Giersch, ed., *Macroeconomic Policies for Growth and Stability*. Tübingen: J.C.B. Mohr.

Chao, Hung-Po, and Alan S. Manne. Forthcoming. "Oil Stockpiles and Import Reductions: A Dynamic Programming Approach," *Operations Research*.

Eckstein, Otto. 1978. *The Great Recession. With a Postscript on Stagflation*. New York: North Holland.

Findlay, Ronald, and Carlo Alfredo Rodriguez. 1977. "Intermediate Imports and Macroeconomic Policy Under Flexible Exchange Rates," *Canadian Journal of Economics* 10 (May):208–217.

Herberg, Horst. 1976. "On Imported Inflation," *Zeitschrift fur die Gesamte Staatswissenschaft* 132, no. 4 (Oct.):609–632.

Krugman, Paul. 1981. "Real Exchange Rate Adjustment and the Welfare Effects of Oil Price Decontrol," M.I.T. Energy Laboratory Working Paper No. MIT-EL81-025WP (May).

Mork, Knut Anton. 1982a. "Energy Price Shocks and Economic Activity," mimeographed, University of Arizona (Feb.).

———. 1982b. "Monopsy Power, Revenue Recycling, and the Optimal Level of Oil Imports," mimeographed, University of Arizona (July).

Mork, Knut Anton, and Robert E. Hall. 1980(a). "Energy Prices and the U.S. Economy in 1979–1981," *The Energy Journal* 1, no. 2 (Apr.): 41–53.

———. 1980(b). "Energy Prices, Inflation, and Recession, 1974–1975," *The Energy Journal* 1, no. 3 (July):31–63.

———. 1981. "Macroeconomic Policy Responses to Energy Price Shocks. An Integrated Approach," in K.A. Mork, ed., *Energy Prices Inflation, and Economic Activity*. Cambridge, Mass: Ballinger.

Nordhaus, William D. 1980. "The Energy Crisis and Macroeconomic Policy," *The Energy Journal* 1, no. 1 (Jan.):11–19.

Peck, Stephen C., and James L. Plummer. 1982. "Intermediate Term Oil Import Reduction Policies," in J. Plummer, ed., *Energy Vulnerability*. Cambridge, Mass.: Ballinger.

Pindyck, Robert S. 1980. "Energy Price Increases and Macroeconomic Policy," *The Energy Journal* 1, no. 4 (Oct.):1–20.

Schmid, Michael. 1976. "A Model of Trade in Money, Goods, and Factors," *Journal of International Economics* 6, no. 4 (Nov.):347–361.

Solow, Robert M. 1974. "Intergenerational Equity and Exhaustible Resources," *Review of Economic Studies* (July):29–45.

———. 1980. "What to do (Macroeconomically) when OPEC comes," in S. Fischer ed., *Rational Expectations and Economic Policy*. Chicago: University of Chicago Press (for the National Bureau of Economic Research).

7

LDC Debt in the 1980s: Risk and Reforms

Jeffrey Sachs

The private capital markets of the advanced industrial economies reopened on a large scale to less-developed-country (LDC) borrowers in the past decade, after a hiatus of nearly forty years. Private lending to LDC sovereign borrowers grew sharply in the early 1970s and then soared in the aftermath of the first OPEC oil shock in 1973 (see table 7-1). This momentous change reflected shifts in banking practices within an existing regulatory environment, rather than new official policy governing international capital flows. The International Monetary Fund (IMF) and central banks did not create the new environment and have had to work quickly to adapt their own policies to it. Broadly speaking, this chapter takes the regulator's perspective, by asking what guidelines should govern the oversight and control of private international capital flows to the LDCs. My focus will be on the issue of LDC creditworthiness and the prospects for defaults in international loans. I do not consider an equally important aspect of the debt problem, the vulnerability of the international banks to a major default.

The salutary effects of high international capital mobility on the world economy in the past decade cannot be overstressed. Most importantly, widespread access to foreign capital allowed the middle-income developing countries to sustain very high growth rates in the 1970s, in spite of the OPEC shocks and the sluggish growth of the developed economies. These countries experienced real GNP growth of 5.6 percent per annum during 1970–1980, little reduced from the 6.2 percent rate of the previous decade, in large part because of high domestic investment rates sustained by foreign borrowing.

On the other hand, serious economic and political stresses emerged in a number of countries and in the world financial markets, as some borrowers became seriously overextended in indebtedness. Overall, the non-OPEC LDCs increased their net debt from $57 billion in 1970, or 13.7 percent of GNP, to $221 billion in 1979, approximately 17.7 percent of GNP (see Sachs 1981a, table 1). No less than eleven countries have been required to reschedule debt to official and private creditors since 1975, and in most of those reschedulings, countries have been required by creditors to commit themselves to sharply contractionary policies to restrict new international borrowing. While we shall see that many of these austerity programs have

Table 7-1
Oil-Importing Developing Countries' Current Account Deficit and Finance Sources, 1970–1980
(billions of 1978 dollars)

| | Oil Importers | | | | | | | | | |
| | Low-Income | | | | | Middle-Income | | | | |
Item	1970	1973	1975	1978	1980	1970	1973	1975	1978	1980
Current account deficit[a]	3.6	4.9	7.0	5.1	9.1	14.9	6.7	42.8	20.4	48.9
Financed by:										
Net-capital flows										
Official development assistance	3.4	4.1	6.6	5.1	5.7	3.3	5.3	5.3	6.5	7.9
Private direct investment	0.3	0.2	0.4	0.2	0.2	3.4	5.1	3.8	4.6	4.5
Commercial loans	0.5	0.6	0.8	0.9	0.7	8.9	13.7	21.0	29.4	27.1
Changes in reserves and short-term borrowing[b]	-0.5	-1.1	-0.7	-1.1	2.4	-0.8	-11.7	12.7	-20.1	9.5
Memorandum item:										
Current account deficit as percentage of GNP	1.9	2.4	3.9	2.6	4.5	2.6	1.0	5.5	2.3	5.0

Source: World Bank, *World Development Report 1981*, p. 49.
[a]Excludes net official transfers (grants), which are included in capital flows.
[b]A minus sign (−) indicates an increase in reserves.

been successful in alleviating debt difficulties, their costs in terms of reduced employment and income in the debtor countries have often been very large.

The dangers of the growing international indebtedness are many-sided, with major risks borne both by creditors and debtors. Most directly, the creditors both official and private, bear the risk of an outright repudiation or default of outstanding international debt. The long history of international capital flows in the nineteenth and early twentieth century underscores such default risk, for there is an impressive 150-year record of international defaults by sovereign borrowers, including repeated defaults by Latin-American governments, Turkey, Egypt, Portugal, Russia, and others, as well as defaults by no less than seventeen U.S. states on bonds floated in Europe in the nineteenth century. Of course, the most recent episode of widespread international defaults occurred in 1931 and 1932, during the Great Depression, and was the cause of the collapse of international borrowing for the succeeding forty years. It is a story to which I shall return.

Until the cataclysm of the Great Depression, the cycle of defaults was considered a part of the normal working of the international financial system, and certainly not a threat to the stability of the overall economic order. Creditors received substantial risk premia on foreign loans to compensate for default or *sovereign risk,* and the governments of creditors were typically content to allow their nationals to suffer defaults without significant public intervention on their behalf (however, experiences varied, as we will see below).

With the onset of the worldwide, synchronized defaults of the early 1930s, official attitudes changed, regarding both the merits of free private capital movements and the ramifications of default. Banks, governments, and multilateral institutions have gone to great lengths in recent years to avoid sovereign default, both through positive incentives (for example, concessionary loans in return for debtor adjustment policies) and concerted threats of strong retaliation for debt repudiation. Measured by default frequency, the set of policies has thus far been remarkably successful: there have been almost no cases of outright repudiation of debt since 1945, (examples include North Korea and Ghana, and the repudiation by Ghana was converted to a rescheduling of debt obligations after subsequent multilateral negotiations). Moreover, there is no doubt that recent events in many debtor economies would have led to default under pre-World War II rules of the game but have instead resulted in IMF-supervised adjustment policies and debt reschedulings. Many threats remain, however. Debt reschedulings have become increasingly common, and arrears in interest due have been rising steadily, now topping $5 billion. Moreover, there have been calls in recent years, such as by the *Group of 77* LDCs in 1977, for a moratorium on LDC debt payments. Most large LDC borrowers have rejected this approach though.

One reason for the plethora of pre-1930 defaults versus post-1945 rescheduling is that the early period was characterized by *noncooperative* strategies of creditors and debtors, while the post-1945 period is characterized by extensive bargaining and *cooperative* strategies of banks and the LDCs. Formal models of the costs and benefits of default show that there is often a prisoners' dilemma aspect to loan agreements. The payoff matrix for creditors and debtors might look like table 7-2 (the first entry in each cell is the creditor payoff).

Here, the debtor prefers to default no matter what the strategy pursued by the creditor, and the creditor wants to call in loans no matter what action the debtor takes. The resulting noncooperative solution yields $(-2,1)$, which is clearly dominated by a policy of increased loans and demand restraint, yielding $(0,2)$, which a IMF-supervised debt-rescheduling package might achieve. In situations where the IMF cannot intervene, such as Poland (which is not an IMF member) the risk of default rises accordingly.

A second reason for the reduction in defaults is most likely a shift in bargaining strength between debtors and creditors. After most defaults in the nineteenth and early twentieth century, private bondholder committees fended for themselves in negotiations with debtor countries, and their options for retaliation were rather limited. They could not rely on steady support from the central government nor even necessarily from other financial institutions (for example, banking houses) or foreign bond markets. Since World War II, governments themselves have become large creditors, and also have intervened more aggressively in financial market oversight, in part through the IMF. The potential scope and strength of retaliation to defaults has been considerably enhanced.

Of course, if defaults are prevented by threats of very strong creditor retaliation, there is a risk of another sort imposed on LDC borrowers. The default option can be a way for LDC borrowers to transfer economic risks to their better diversified creditors, and thus may be part of an efficient debt structure. In the past, when a large investment project failed, or a country's terms of trade shifted adversely, a default often resulted. Now, the borrowing country is forced instead to restrain consumption and growth for a number of years to satisfy its debt commitments. It is quite possible that the *ex ante* expected utility of both borrowers and lenders is raised by a debt package that includes a default option with a compensating risk premium.

Aside from the direct risks of default, there is another set of concerns about LDC debt that might be termed *systemic risks*. A major default or series of defaults could lead to bank failures in the advanced economies perhaps with cascading effects through the world financial system. As Charles Kindleberger (1978) has persuasively argued, such risks are inten-

Table 7-2
Debtor and Creditor Strategies

	Debtor Strategy	
Creditor Strategy	Restrain Demand	Default
Reduce loans	2, − 1	− 2, 1
Maintain loans	1, 0	− 5, 2
Increase loan	0, 2	− 10, 3

sified in the international banking community because of the absence of a clear international lender of last resort. There is no settled responsibility of domestic central banks vis-á-vis the foreign subsidiaries of domestic institutions, and the IMF has abjured from a formal role as lender of last resort. Thus, the types of bank bailout operations that forestall domestic financial panics might not be forthcoming in the international setting. Unfortunately, I will be unable to pursue this theme in the current chapter.

There is a similar, though less recognized, risk of cascading default originating in the supply side of the credit markets. In the event of an isolated default or failure of an international loan, there might arise a strong movement among creditor institutions to reduce exposure on LDC debt across the board. The costs of new loans or debt rollovers could rise sharply, thereby pushing a number of additional economies into default. I will suggest later that such a market reaction helps to explain the widespread defaults of 1931 and 1932 and that a similar paralysis almost gripped the international banks in 1974. The possibility of a self-fulfilling prophecy of widespread default may remain the greatest danger posed by the LDC debt today.

There is a growing and very fine literature detailing various empirical aspects of LDC borrowing, so that I may be brief in describing the recent history of international capital movements. Thus, in the first section, I outline a few stylized facts to characterize the international financial market as a basis for the subsequent analysis. Next, I present a simple theoretical model of the international capital markets under risk of sovereign default. Various points are brought out in the model: (1) rationing will be a standard device in credit allocation to sovereign borrowers; (2) rationed borrowers will have an incentive to pursue particular current account goals and to stimulate domestic investment; (3) a cooperative solution between banks and sovereign borrowers will tend to dominate a noncooperative solution in loan negotiations; (4) country risk rises with overall indebtedness of the country and falls with increasing investment rates in the country; (5) defaults, in general, provide a useful, but imperfect, form of insurance to debtor countries, so that an international capital market with no defaults is not necessarily our best policy target. In the third section, I briefly review the history of sovereign default, to document the major shifts in market organization between the pre-World War II and post-World War II international capital markets. Finally, in the last section of the chapter, I analyze some aspects of borrowing in the 1970s in light of the theoretical analysis of the previous section.

LDC Indebtedness in the 1970s

As the description of LDC indebtedness and its growth is well known and is widely available elsewhere, I will merely summarize the key characteristics of the debt for later discussion.[1]

Current account deficits as a percentage of GNP rose sharply for the LDCs in the 1970s, as did the debt/GNP ratio. Table 7–3 shows the current account position of the LDCs, the developed countries, and the major oil exporters throughout the 1970s. The raw numbers must be adjusted for inflation, since debtor countries enjoy capital gains due to inflation on their ourstanding debts (that is, reductions in the real value of their indebtedness) that reduce the effective current account deficits in any year.[2] Thus, in 1978, for example, real LDC deficits were only about half of the official magnitude, while OPEC was really in *deficit* in the sense that the capital losses on its outstanding assets exceeded in value the year's accumulation of financial claims.

Current account deficits can be financed through a variety of financial arrangements, including bank or bond debt, foreign direct investment, equity investment, and so forth. While *all* types of financing reflect a claim by the rest of the world on the future income of the deficit country, only certain types of assets are typically counted as debt. These are the fixed-income claims on the debtor country and its citizens, in the form of bank and bond indebtedness. Most data refer to gross debt, but a more meaningful measure is *net debt,* in which LDC claims on the rest of the world (for example, foreign reserves of the central bank) are subtracted. In many cases, the distinction of debt and other liabilities is important, since equity claims offer yields that are contingent on economic performance, while bonds do not; so that risks are different with alternative mixes of debt and foreign ownership of domestic capital. Often, however, the distinction is misleading, particularly for evaluating total foreign claims on the domestic output stream in future years. In the case of no uncertainty, there is no legitimate distinction between the various liabilities.

Unfortunately, only data for indebtedness in itself are readily available. Some of these data are shown in tables 7–3 and 7–4. Note first that there was a sharp rise in the ratio of debt to GNP for the LDCs as a whole during

Table 7-3
Nominal and Inflation-Adjusted Current Accounts, Major Regions, 1968–1979

	1968	1969	1970	1971	1972	1973	1974	1975	1976	1977	1978	1979
Nominal current account (billions of U.S. dollars)[b]												
Developed countries[a]	3.4	4.0	6.8	11.2	8.6	10.9	−25.1	4.9	−13.7	−19.5	13.5	−28.4
Nonoil LDCs	−6.0	−4.7	−8.8	−12.2	−6.3	−7.3	−25.6	−35.0	−25.2	−19.9	−24.8	−34.3
OPEC	0.8	−1.3	−0.6	1.2	0.4	5.4	54.9	23.5	26.6	20.1	−1.5	39.7
Inflation-adjusted current account (billions of U.S. dollars)[c]												
Developed countries	2.1	2.5	5.2	9.5	7.1	8.6	−26.6	5.1	−13.3	−18.4	14.5	−27.5
Nonoil LDCs	−4.3	−2.5	−6.4	−9.6	−3.9	−3.1	−18.1	−27.3	−19.4	−11.0	−10.0	−17.7
OPEC	−0.9	−1.4	−0.6	1.1	0.2	5.0	51.4	17.9	22.0	12.7	−12.8	27.3
Inflation-adjusted current account (billions of U.S. dollars)												
Developed countries	3.3	3.6	7.1	12.4	8.9	10.2	−29.0	5.1	−12.6	−16.5	12.1	−21.2
Nonoil LDCs	−6.6	−3.6	−8.8	−12.6	−4.9	−3.7	−19.8	−27.3	−18.4	−9.8	−8.3	−13.6
OPEC	−1.4	−2.0	−0.8	1.5	0.3	5.9	56.2	17.9	20.9	11.4	−10.7	21.1

Sources: Nominal current account—International Monetary Fund, *Balance of Payments Yearbook*, various issues; inflation-adjusted current account—calculations by the author. Reproduced from Jeffrey D. Sachs, "The Current Account and Macroeconomic Adjustment in the 1970s," *Brookings Papers on Economic Activity*, 1:1981, Washington, D.C.: Brookings Institution, pp. 201–268. Reprinted with permission.
[a]Developed countries refers to all industrial countries.
[b]The conversion from special drawing rights (SDRs) to dollars was done at the annual average dollar/SDR rate of exchange.
[c]Calculated by adding the capital gains and losses on the net external position in interest-bearing assets to the nominal current account, conventionally measured.

the 1970s. Second, it is important to point out that the vast majority (over 75 percent of total indebtedness is publicly guaranteed by the government of the borrowing country. Even borrowing by private corporations is typically under the aegis of the central government. Third, there has been an enormous rise in the share of government-guaranteed debt extended by private creditors, though both official and private creditors played an important role in LDC financing in recent years.

The aggregate figures hide enormous variations in the borrowing behavior of individual LDCs. The distribution of indebtedness is highly skewed, and this is particularly true for indebtedness to private creditors. Mexico and Brazil alone account for about 40 percent of LDC net bank liabilities, and about 25 percent of total LDC gross debt. The large borrowers, who are principally major exporters of manufacturers, rely heavily on loans from private creditors while the poor countries, with less access to Euromarket loans, have a much higher fraction of financing through official bilateral or multilateral credits. (See table 7–5).

International private sector credits are almost entirely in the form of rollover syndicated loans, with maturities of five to ten years. These are variable interest rate liabilities with quarterly or semiannual interest charges fixed at a predetermined margin (spread) over LIBOR (London Interbank Offered Rate). Official credits have much longer maturities (on average in excess of twenty years) and are usually at fixed and concessional interest rates.

Importantly, there is very little participation of the LDCs in the long-term international bond markets. In contrast to the period before the Great Depression when dozens of countries and the political subdivisions made extensive use of the bond markets in London, Paris, and New York, now there is almost no LDC participation. As shown in table 7–1, net borrowing of nonoil LDCs in the bond market has been a small fraction of total private credits arranged in the 1970s.

Nineteenth century international debt was risky, and the market acknowledged it as such, requiring very large risk premia on LDC loans. A striking aspect of LDC bank debt in the 1970s has been the remarkably small spreads charged by banks, as seen in table 7–6. The difference in interest charges on loans to the industrial versus developing countries is very small and, remarkably, there has been very little tendency for spreads to the LDCs to widen as indebtedness grew. The banks certainly act as if the prospects of default are small; perhaps we will see why in the analysis that follows.

A Model of International Borrowing and Default

To understand the risks of sovereign lending and the role of debt reschedulings, we must first characterize the nature of equilibrium in the interna-

Table 7-4
Medium-Term and Long-Term Debt of Ninety-four Developing Countries, 1972-1979

Item	1972	1973	1974	1975	1976	1977	1978	1979[a]	Average Rate of Change
									(percent)
Debt outstanding (end of period)									
Public debt[b]	72.0	88.3	107.6	130.5	158.0	197.4	250.1	287.9	21.9
Official creditors	47.4	55.5	65.2	75.6	87.7	103.9	122.7	134.0	16.0
Private creditors	24.6	32.8	42.4	54.9	70.3	93.5	127.4	153.9	29.9
Nonguaranteed debt	19.1	23.0	27.1	36.0	44.2	46.8	59.6	71.6	20.8
Total	91.1	111.3	134.7	166.5	202.2	244.2	309.7	359.5	21.7
Debt service									
Public debt[b]	8.2	11.3	13.8	15.3	17.7	23.5	34.1	45.7	27.8
Official creditors	3.6	4.4	5.0	5.8	6.4	7.8	9.4	12.0	18.8
Private creditors	4.6	6.9	8.8	9.5	11.3	15.7	24.7	33.7	32.9
Nonguaranteed debt	3.8	4.1	6.0	8.3	11.4	12.7	14.9	17.0	23.9
Total	12.0	15.4	19.8	23.6	29.1	36.2	49.0	62.7	26.6

Sources: World Bank, *World Debt Tables*; OECD, Development Assistance Committee; and Fund staff estimates. Reproduced in International Monetary Fund, "External Indebtedness of Developing Countries," 1981a, p. 5.
[a]Preliminary.
[b]Public and guaranteed debt.

Table 7-5
Nonoil Developing Countries: Distribution of Debt by Class of Creditor, End of Year, 1973–1981
(percent)

Item	1973	1974	1975	1976	1977	1978	1979	1980	1981
Total outstanding debt of nonoil developing countries[a]	100.0	100.0	100.0	100.0	100.0	100.0	100.0	100.0	100.0
To official creditors	50.4	49.2	47.1	46.4	45.1	43.2	41.8	42.1	42.3
Governments	32.9	36.6	34.2	33.5	31.8	29.9	28.5	28.7	28.5
International institutions	12.5	12.6	12.7	12.9	13.3	13.3	13.2	13.4	13.7
To private creditors	49.6	50.8	52.9	53.8	54.9	56.8	58.2	57.9	57.8
Financial institutions	35.5	39.6	42.0	43.7	45.0	46.0	48.6	48.9	48.7
Other private creditors	14.2	11.3	10.9	10.0	9.7	10.8	9.6	9.0	9.1
Net oil exporters									
Total outstanding debt	100.0	100.0	100.0	100.0	100.0	100.0	100.0	100.0	100.0
Total official creditors	39.6	36.0	34.9	33.6	35.0	35.1	35.0	34.2	33.1
To private financial institutions	41.7	52.8	53.9	56.4	54.2	54.6	55.9	57.1	58.3
To other private creditors	18.7	11.2	11.2	10.0	10.8	10.3	9.1	8.7	8.6

Net oil importers									
Major exporters of manufactures									
Total outstanding debt	100.0	100.0	100.0	100.0	100.0	100.0	100.0	100.0	100.0
To official creditors	27.4	26.4	25.4	26.1	25.4	23.5	21.9	22.7	23.3
To private financial institutions	54.4	58.4	59.9	61.4	62.7	61.6	64.5	64.2	63.6
To other private creditors	18.2	15.2	14.7	12.5	11.9	14.9	13.6	13.1	13.1
Low-income countries									
Total outstanding debt	100.0	100.0	100.0	100.0	100.0	100.0	100.0	100.0	100.0
To official creditors	88.0	86.9	87.0	87.1	86.7	86.1	85.3	84.3	84.2
To private financial institutions	6.2	7.4	7.3	7.3	8.1	9.0	10.3	12.0	11.0
To other private creditors	5.8	5.7	5.7	5.6	5.2	4.9	4.4	3.7	4.8
Other net oil importers									
Total outstanding debt	100.0	100.0	100.0	100.0	100.0	100.0	100.0	100.0	100.0
To official creditors	88.6	87.3	87.3	87.6	54.7	54.5	51.8	51.2	51.4
To private financial institutions	5.4	6.7	6.9	6.9	35.7	36.9	41.1	42.4	42.5
To other private creditors	6.1	5.9	5.8	5.5	9.6	8.6	7.1	6.4	6.1

Source: From International Monetary Fund, "World Economic Outlook," Occasional Paper #4, June 1981, p. 134.
[a]Excludes data for the People's Republic of China prior to 1977. For classification of countries in groups shown here, see the source.

Table 7-6
Average Spreads of External Borrowing Costs over London Interbank Offered Rate, LIBOR 1974-1979
(percent)

Item	1974	1975	1976	1977	1978	1979
All LDCs	1.13	1.68	1.72	1.55	1.20	0.87
Typical industrial country (France)	0.58	1.42	1.09	0.92	0.63	0.36
Difference	0.55	0.27	0.63	0.63	0.57	0.51
LIBOR rate (percent per year)	11.32	7.74	6.26	6.54	9.48	12.12
Addendum						
Brazil[a]	1.1	1.8	2.0	2.0	1.7	0.9

Source: All data except for that on Brazil are from World Bank, *World Development Report, 1980,* table 3.5, p. 27. The Brazilian data are cited in Albert Fishlow, "Latin American External Debt: Problem or Solution?" paper presented at the International Seminar on External Financial Relations and Their Impact on the Latin American Economies (Santiago, Chile, March 1981), table 2, p. 10.
[a]The 1980 value is 1.75.

tional loan markets. What determines a country's desired level of indebtedness or current account deficits? What indicators suggest that an economy is on an *unsustainable* path of foreign borrowing, so that it requires some form of policy intervention? Finally, in what sense, if any, should sovereign borrowers pursue current account targets as a matter of macroeconomic policy? To highlight the role of default risk, I will just briefly take up these questions in a model without defaults, and then turn to the more realistic model in the following part. (See also the extended analysis by Sachs and Cohen [1982].)

Borrowing in a Model without Default Risk

Ignoring issues of default, the essence of sustainability of international borrowing lies in the nations' intertemporal budget constraint. Consider a world of certainty, in which lenders extend credit to agents in an economy at interest rate r. If Q is national output, C is private consumption, I is investment, G is government spending, and D is the level of international indebtedness, we have:

$$D_{t+1} - D_t = (C_t + I_t + G_t) - (Q_t - rD_t) \tag{7.1}$$

Of course, Q is GDP and $Q - rD$ is GNP, so that $D_{t+1} - D_t$, which equals the current account deficit, is the difference GNP and total absorption.

Defining national savings as GNP net of private plus public consumption expenditure, $S_t = (Q_t - rD_t) - (C_t + G_t)$, we have the identity $CA_t = D_{t+1} - D_t = I_t - S_t$, where CA_t signifies the current account balance. We say that a country obeys its intertemporal budget constraint if the *present value* of its debt, $(1 + r)^{-t}D_t$, goes to zero as t approaches infinity. In this case, no creditors is left "holding the bag" over time, with a borrower who is merely borrowing more and more to repay interest due. Using this limiting condition 7.1 implies:

$$\sum_{i=0}^{\infty} (1 + r)^{-i}(C + G + I)_i = \sum_{i=0}^{\infty} (1 + r)^{-i}Q_i - (1 + r)D(O) \quad (7.2)$$

or

$$\sum_{i=0}^{\infty} (1 + r)^{-i}[Q_i - (C + I + G)_i] = \sum_{i=0}^{\infty} (1 + r)^{-i}(TB)_i$$
$$= (1 + r)D(O), \quad (7.3)$$

where *TB* signifies the trade balance, $Q - C - I - G$.

These expressions, then, describe the conditions for sustainable domestic spending. According to 7.2, the discounted present value of total future expenditures must equal the discounted present value of national output, less initial international indebtedness. Equation 7.3 puts this constraint in a slightly different perspective by recording that the discounted sum of future trade surpluses must equal the initial indebtedness of the economy. In other words, trade surpluses and deficits must balance over time; the question for an economy is not *whether* to run deficits but, rather, *when* to run them.

The optimal timing of deficits is in general a complex function of current and future economic variables and characteristics of the economy. Speaking broadly, three considerations dominate. First, households (or governments on their behalf) seek to smooth consumption over time. A *temporary* drop in real income, say because of a crop failure or an adverse shift in the terms of trade, will result in a smaller fall in consumption, with the more steady level of consumption being supported by foreign borrowing. Second, if the market rate of interest exceeds the social rate of time preference, the country will tend to save today (that is, run trade surpluses) to enjoy higher consumption expenditures in the future. Finally, if there are favorable investment opportunities given the world cost of capital, countries will tend to run deficits today to finance the investment expenditure. There will be a tendency to equalize the marginal product of capital and the world interest rate.

When a country's trade deficit rises because of a fall in current income or a drop in the world interest rate, the rise in indebtedness signals a fall in future consumption levels, as the debt must eventually be serviced. But when a deficit emerges because of an investment boom, no future consumption sacrifice is implied. The economy is merely trading one asset, the debt instrument, for another, the claim to physical capital. Assuming that the latter asset has a yield at least as high as the former (which is presumably the motive for the investment expenditure), future consumption possibilities are enhanced, not diminished. For this obvious reason, measures of debt in themselves tell us little about the burdens of future debt service. We must focus separately on national savings and investment rates to determine the sustainable future paths of consumption.

If default is absolutely precluded, bank lending to the economy is only restricted by the conditions that $C, G, I \geq 0$, and $\lim D_t(1 + r)^{-t} = 0$. Thus, the maximum debt limit $D^M(t)$ is:

$$\sum_{i = t}^{\infty} (1 + r)^{-(i + 1 - t)} Q_i$$

At this debt level, future absorption is restricted to zero in all periods, and national income is fully used for debt servicing. The supply-of-funds schedule is kinked at this point, with perfectly elastic credit at rate r until $D^M(t)$ is reached, and perfectly inelastic credit supply at that level. No interest rate will bring forth loans in excess of D^M. Although it is a trivial case, this kinked supply schedule illustrates that credit ceilings are fully consistent with perfect competition in the loan market. It is simply the case that the market value of all loans for $D > D^M(t)$ must be negative, and therefore such loans will not be made by competitive, value-maximizing financial institutions.

In the case of perfect capital mobility, all domestic investments are undertaken that have a positive present value at the prevailing world interest rate. Importantly, and in sharp contrast to the case with potential default, a rise in domestic savings has *no effect* on domestic investment rates, and therefore results, one-for-one, in a corresponding improvement in the trade balance. We shall see that, under conditions of potential debt repudiation, a rise in savings can actually raise domestic investment so much that the trade balance worsens rather than improves.

Without doubt, the perfect capital mobility assumption is seriously deficient as a basis for current account analysis. There is solid evidence for variations in risk premia on loans to sovereign borrowers, as functions of the borrower's savings and investment rates and overall debt levels. Moreover, there is substantial anecdotal evidence that ceilings on country borrowing are sometimes imposed in the capital markets. One theoretical response to these complicating factors in loan supply has been to assume a supply schedule for total borrowing, with the borrowing rate a rising function of total indebtedness: $r = f(D), f' > 0$. When this approach is pursued, countries become monopsonists in the world loan market, and thus have an incentive to follow particular current account policies. Since increased national indebtedness raises borrowing costs on inframarginal as well as marginal loans, the policy authorities should ration foreign borrowing (through a quota or capital import tax) to limit overall interest costs.

Because $f(D)$ is arbitrarily specified rather than derived, it is likely to be a misleading guide to loan supply. In particular, we shall see that the loan schedule linking r and D will *depend on domestic policies* and will therefore not be invariant to policy changes in the borrowing country. In particular, by raising domestic savings rates, the authorities can shift the supply schedule outward, and thus lower borrowing costs on outstanding debt. There will, in general, be an incentive to subsidize savings.

Borrowing in a Model with Default Risk

In a series of very insightful articles, Jonathan Eaton and Mark Gersovitz (1981a, b, c) describe how the potential for sovereign default can dramatically alter our view of international capital mobility. They consider loans in a noncooperative environment, and argue that a loan ceiling exists for sovereign borrowing that is determined by the effective retaliation that creditors can achieve in the event of a unilateral repudiation of debt. If the possibilities for effective retaliation are good, the debt ceiling will be high, as there is little chance of a default. If there is no way to retaliate, the ceiling is at zero: nothing will be lent. I examine both the noncooperative framework and a cooperative alternative, in which the debtor country can precommit itself to a stabilization package to sustain international lending.

I consider a simple framework in which loans are made in one period that may or may not be paid back in the next. If the loan is defaulted, the creditor retaliates with a cost to the debtor of a fraction λ of national income. λ summarizes all the possible costs of retaliation: trade disruption, exclusion from future borrowing, seizure of assets, and so forth. I assume that the retaliation yields no utility to the creditors (or that the costs and benefits of retaliation cancel), only a loss to the debtor.

For a particular debtor, a given level of debt will lead to default in some circumstances and not in others (depending on second-period income). Creditors will demand a risk premium that depends on the probability of default. Because the possibilities for retaliation are limited, there are some levels of debt that lead to default with certainty. At these debt levels, there is no risk premium that can compensate for the default risk: an absolute *ceiling* of indebtedness must be imposed by creditors when that level of indebtedness is reached. Because of the borrowing ceiling, there is *no presumption* that all investments with positive present value at the world interest rate will be undertaken. The debt ceiling will rise with stronger retaliatory measures, so that it may be in the debtor's interest to *encourage* a strong response to default to raise the debt ceiling and free-up capital inflows.

The default risks can now be usefully formalized. I will start with a case of certainty and then move on to the case of uncertainty.

Suppose national output in periods 1 and 2 is given by Q_1 and Q_2, with $Q_i = Q(K_i)$, and $K_i = K_{i-1} + I_{i-1}$. The social welfare function is specified as $U(C_1, C_2) = U(C_1) + U(C_2)/(1 + \delta)$, where δ is the pure rate of time preference. National indebtedness is equal to the first-period current account deficit, $C_1 + I_1 - Q_1 = D_1$, and the world safe rate of return is given by ρ. In the absence of default, we have the intertemporal budget constraint $C_1 + C_2/(1 + \rho) = Q_1 + Q_2/(1 + \rho) - I_1$ or $C_2 = Q_2 - (1 + \rho)D_1$. In the no-default case, we designate C_2 as C_2^N. With default, there is no second-period debt servicing, but output is reduced in proportion λ: $C_2^D = (1 - \lambda)Q_2$. The default decision depends on whether C_2^D is greater than or less than C_2^N.

Under certainty, banks will agree to make loans up to the point where the country would choose to default; that is, to the point where C_2^D is just less than C_2^N. We must consider two institutional arrangements, which I will label *noncooperative* and *cooperative,* to determine the debt ceiling. In the first case, which is most usual, the loan agreement is reached between the country and the bank before the country's policies with respect to investment and savings in the first period are revealed. In the cooperative setting, the country precommits itself to an investment-consumption plan before a loan is arranged. In this case, the bank's loan limits can be based on the observed first-period policies.

The term *cooperative* is used in analogy to the game-theoretic situation in which players may bind themselves to a particular strategy (and in which the other players recognize the binding constraint). The case in which countries credibly promise certain policies before loans are made may or may not involve true cooperation (in the everyday sense) between banks and the country. The commitment may reflect the fact that certain policies are preset by constitutional rules, or by IMF imposition, or by simple calendar constraints. We will have more to say on the IMF role later.

Now, in either setting, the bank is safe in extending a loan as long as $C_2^D \leq C_2^N$. Since $C_2^D = (1 - \lambda)Q_2$ and $C_2^N = Q_2 - (1 + \rho)D_1$, the loan is safe as long as $D_1 \le \lambda Q_2/(1 + \rho)$. But Q_2 is a function of I_1, so that the loan is safe as long as $D_1 \le \lambda Q_2(K_0 + I_1)/(1 + \rho) = h(I_1)$, with $h' > 0$, $h'' < 0$. Let $I^M(D_1)$ be the minimum level of I_1 such that $D_1 \le h(I_1)$. A loan D_1 will be safe as long as the banks can be sure that $I_1 \ge I_1^M(D_1)$.

In the cooperative setting, the country announces I_1, freeing up loans in the amount $D_1 \le h(I_1)$. Assuming that the borrowing constraint binds (the interesting case for our purposes) the *planner* chooses I_1 to maximize social welfare, subject to $D_1 = h(I_1)$. Formally, the problem is to solve

$$U^c = \max_{I_1} U(C_1) + U(C_2)/(1 + \rho) \qquad (7.4)$$

subject to: $D_1 \le h(I_1)$

$C_1 = Q_1(K_0) + D_1 - I_1$

$C_2 = Q_2(K_0 + I_1) - (1 + \rho)D_1$

We can write the maximum utility level U^c for every level of D_1. This function is graphed in figure 7-1. The optimum is attained at $\hat{D}_1^c$ where the superscript c denotes *cooperative*. Banks will be willing to loan $\hat{D}_1^c$, since by construction, $\hat{D}_1^c \le h(\hat{I}_1^c)$.

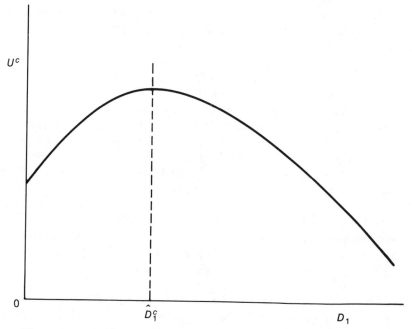

Figure 7-1. Utility and Indebtedness in the Cooperative Case

In the noncooperative (NC) setting, D_1 is set first and then I_1 and C_1 are chosen, given D_1. For given D_1, the planner always evaluates two courses of action, defaulting (D) and not defaulting (ND), and chooses the course with higher utility. Formally:

$$U^{NC} = \max(U^D, U^{ND}) \tag{7.5}$$

$$U^D = \max_{I_1} U(C_1) + U(C_2)/(1 + \delta)$$

$$\text{subject to: } C_1 = Q_1 - I_1 + D_1$$
$$C_2 = (1 - \lambda)Q_2(I_1 + K_0)$$

$$U^{ND} = \max_{I_1} U(C_1) + U(C_2)/(1 + \delta)$$
$$\text{subject to: } C_1 = Q_1 - I_1 + D_1$$
$$C_2 = Q_2 - (1 + \rho)D_1$$

These functions are graphed in figure 7–2. Note that for $D_1 \leq D^*$, the country will not default, while for $D_1 > D^*$ it will. Obviously D_1^* is the credit limit that banks will impose in the noncooperative case. Since $U^{ND}(D_1)$ is rising at D^*, the country will choose to borrow up to D_1^*.

Since the country defaults if and only if $D_1 > D_1^*$, it is a direct implication that:

$$I_1 \geq I^M(D_1) \text{ if and only if } D_1 < D_1^*. \tag{7.6}$$

That is, for $D_1 \leq D^*$ the bank knows that investment will be sufficient to guarantee repayment, while for $D_1 > D^*$, it will be insufficient. Therefore, if we superimpose U^{ND} and U^c as in figure 7–3, we find that they are the same for $D_1 < D_1^*$. Otherwise $U^{ND} > U^c$.[3]

Figure 7–3 allows us to draw the following crucial conclusions. In the noncooperative game, the country reaches $U^{ND}(D^*)$. In the cooperative game, it reaches $U^c(\hat{D})$, which exceeds $U^{ND}(D^*)$. If default is entirely ruled out (for example, by a "world policeman"), it can reach a $U^{ND}(\tilde{D})$, which is the *optimum optimorum*. The possibility of default reduces the country's utility by freezing its credit line. Under certainty, the borrowing country should insist on high penalties for default, for as λ approaches 1, D^* approaches $\tilde{D}$.

It is crucial to understand the role of cooperation in raising welfare. The country is better off to borrow $\hat{D}$ and invest $I^c(\hat{D})$ than to borrow D^* and invest $I^{ND}(D^*)$. But if given the chance to borrow $\hat{D}$ it prefers to invest

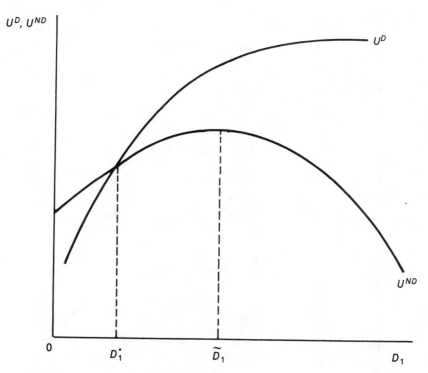

Figure 7-2. Utility and Indebtedness in the Noncooperative Case

less, $I^D(\hat{D}) < I^c(\hat{D})$, and to default. Thus, without a commitment by the country to maintain a high level of investment, the bank will not lend $\hat{D}$.

The importance of the cooperative regime is even more striking when the country enters the first period with *preexisting indebtedness,* which we will denote as D_0. With initial debt the planner's problem is slightly changed. In the cooperative setting the problem is:

$$U_{D_0}^c = \max U(C_1) + U(C_2)/(1 + \delta) \qquad (7.7)$$

$$\text{subject to: } D_0 + D_1 = h(I_1)$$

$$C_1 = Q_1(K_0) + D_1 - I_1$$

$$C_2 = Q_2(K_0 + I_1)$$

$$- (1 + \rho)(D_0 + D_1)$$

(It is actually possible that $D_0 > h(I_1)$ for all I_1, in which case a cooperative solution will not exist.) In the noncooperative case, we again have:

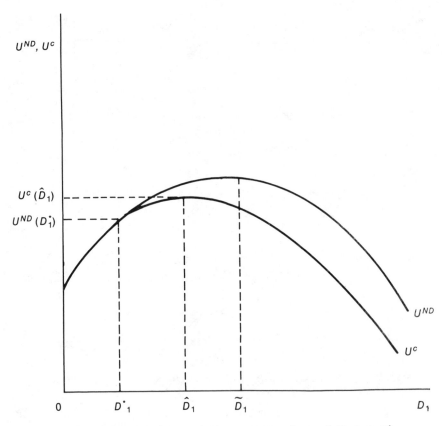

Figure 7-3. A Comparison of the Noncooperative and Cooperative
Solutions

$$U_{D0}^{NC} = \max\,(U_{D0}^{ND},\, U_{D0}^{D}) \qquad\qquad (7.8)$$

$$U_{D0}^{D} = \max_{I_1} U(C_1) + U(C_2)/(1 + \delta)$$

$$\text{subject to: } C_1 = Q_1 - I_1 + D_1$$

$$C_2 = (1 - \lambda)Q_2(I_1 + K_0)$$

$$U_{D0}^{ND} = \max_{I_1} U(C_1) + U(C_2)/(1 + \delta)$$

$$\text{subject to: } C_1 = Q_1 - I_1 + D_1$$

$$C_2 = Q_2 - (1 + \rho)(D_1 + D_0)$$

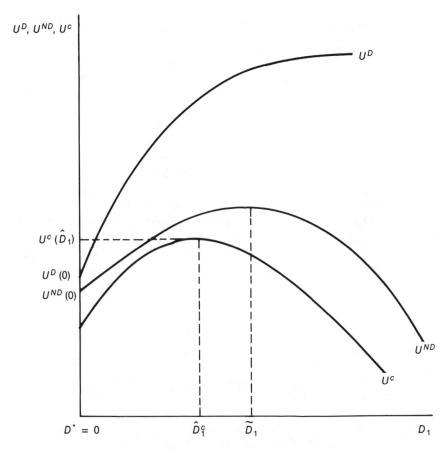

Figure 7-4. The Prisoner's Dilemma in International Loans

Again, let $D_{D_0}^*$ be the cut-off point such that the country defaults if first-period loan D_1 exceeds $D_{D_0}^*$. It is possible that D_0 is sufficiently high so that $D_{D_0}^* = 0$, (in other words the country simply plans to default in the second period, no matter how much it is loaned in the first period).

Suppose that (a) $D_{D_0}^* = 0$; and (b) a cooperative solution exists. The graph of this situation is shown in figure 7-4. This is precisely the prisoner's dilemma alluded to earlier. In the noncooperative case the bank loans nothing, since $U^D(0) > U^{ND}(0)$. A cooperative agreement would allow loans up to $\hat{D}_1^c$, making both the bank and the country better off (since $U^c(\hat{D}_1) > U^D(0)$). The cooperative agreement would precommit the country to a substantial investment program. Again, if the country is absolutely barred from default it can reach $U^{ND}(\tilde{D})$, which exceeds $U^c(\hat{D})$ and $U^D(0)$.

There is another important problem that can occur in financial markets that we must consider. Suppose that banks refuse to issue loans to the country in the first period, even though there is a range of debt for which the country would repay its loan. Since a loan freeze is part of the penalty embodied in λ that attaches to a default, a unilateral freeze on loans reduces the *net* penalty associated with default and makes default more likely. Formally, a freeze on credit reduces $U^{ND}(0)$ relative to $U^D(0)$; with $U^D(0) > U^{ND}(0)$ the country will choose to default. In this sense, a loan freeze by banks in response to a worry about default can be self-fulfilling.

It is important to supplement this analysis with uncertainty, for two reasons. First, it is only through unexpected events that a bank gets trapped holding the bad debt of a sovereign borrower; only with uncertainty (or irrationality) will defaults actually occur. Second, under uncertainty the default option becomes a vehicle for the banks to assume some of the risk of LDC investment projects. It may provide an imperfect form of insurance in a world with incomplete financial markets. I will be carrying out a detailed study of defaults under uncertainty in a many-period model presently. I just touch on the high-lights of that analysis now.

Once uncertainty is added to the model, we find that creditors (assumed to be risk-neutral) will make loans with a positive probability of default, as long as there exists an interest-rate premium that can compensate for the risk. In this case, changes in the penalty for default, λ, affect not only the credit ceiling on loans, but also the risk characteristics of investments from the point of view of both debtor and creditor. Under certainty, high penalties for default make the borrower better off, by raising the country's credit ceiling. Under uncertainty, higher penalties may actually lower the country's welfare. Though the ability to borrow is enhanced, the *insurance* aspect of defaults is diminished, since the penalties for default become more severe. Thus, the $E[U(C_1, C_2)]$ may fall (E denotes *expectation*). In general there will be an optimal λ^* for the debtor country, for which $E[U(C_1, C_2)]$ is maximized subject to the constraint that risk neutral creditors achieve the expected yield ρ. Along with λ^* there is an optimal nonzero probability of default, π^*.

The usefulness of default as a risk-spreading mechanism depends on the alternative financial assets that are available to the debtor country. For instance, if the investment returns depend on easily identifiable exogenous conditions (for example, weather), there may well be an insurance market available to reduce or eliminate risk (for example, hurricane insurance is commonly held by many Caribbean countries). More typically, insurance will not be available for investment where: (1) the *ex post* returns to investment are not easily monitored or (2) unmonitored inputs (for example, labor effort) play an important role in the production process, so that moral hazard precludes full insurance of the project. For similar reasons, foreign equity participation in the investment projects may be unachieveable.

In these cases, default can be important. Of course, defaults provide a very imperfect mechanism for diversifying risk, since the retaliation that follows a default is pareto inefficient (the debtor loses λQ_2, while the creditor welfare, by assumption, is unchanged). Recontracting in the event of default may *not* be a viable option for restoring pareto efficient outcomes moreover—especially if the creditor is unable to verify whether the investment project in fact failed. Because of the inefficiency of default, the debtor country will remain with substantial risks even under optimal contracts with default allowances.

From a regulatory perspective, then, the interesting question is how $E[U(C_1, C_2)]$ and the probability of default vary with the costs of default, λ. Do we perform a service to would-be borrowers by constraining their default option? Does raising λ necessarily reduce the probability of default? In general, there is a welfare trade-off in raising λ: credit ceilings rise, but so do the risks of physical investment for the debtor. There may well exist an interior optimum for λ. Interestingly, the probability of default is not necessarily a strictly decreasing function of λ because a rise in λ tends to increase total indebtedness, and thus the benefits of default as well as the costs.

Now we turn to the historical evidence on defaults, where we shall see the relevance of the preceeding theoretical analysis.

Defaults in Historical Perspective

The concern over LDC debt is anything but new. The history of international capital movements since at least the early nineteenth century is characterized by large-scale borrowing of developing regions, and large-scale defaults. Many of the same debates over prudential standards, government guarantees of foreign loans, rescheduling of debt, and so forth have been pursued for one-hundred-fifty years. And even many of the actors have remained the same. A number of Latin American countries that are still among the most problematic for foreign loans first entered the London bond market upon independence in 1822–1825, and defaulted soon after, setting in train a hundred years of alternating solvency and default. It is good to keep in mind, though, one actor whose perspective has changed: the United States shifted from the world's greatest recipient of capital inflows in the nineteenth century to its greatest creditor in the next, and in the process has been both perpetrator and victim of sovereign defaults.

The striking comparison of pre-1930 and post-1945 international lending lies not in scale, or even sophistication, but in the changing rules of the game. In both periods, the experience is rich, tangled, and contradictory, and governing rules have always involved inexact and evolving standards.

Nonetheless certain broad generalizations are possible. In the earlier period, defaults were a recurrent phenomenon, across countries and over time. Many countries defaulted on debt as many as five times in the course of the nineteenth century. Defaults were typically settled in negotiation with private bondholder committees, on terms that rarely preserved more than a small fraction of the capital value of the original asset. After this partial repayment of debt, the debtor country was typically free to resume borrowing on the international exchanges, subject of course to high risk premia on its debt. Contrary to the popular image of British or American gunboats bearing down on delinquent debtors, true only in a few such spectacular episodes, governments were usually very reserved in debtor–creditor conflicts. The British government rarely allowed its foreign policy goals to be dictated by the fortunes and misfortunes of British financiers. Only in cases where private and foreign policy goals closely coincided, as in midnineteenth-century Egypt and Turkey, did Britain ride the debt situation for larger political ends, ending up with no less than sovereignty in Egypt (1882) for its efforts.

The post-1945 period has thus far operated on a very different basis. At least until the late 1960s, the great bulk of LDC debt (excluding foreign direct investment) was in the form of official bilateral or multilateral loans, or government-guaranteed suppliers credits, often on concessional terms. Thus, debt problems directly involved creditor governments, rather than the private market alone. Typically, debt service problems with official creditors have been handled in negotiations between the debtor country and a multilateral negotiating body of creditor governments, most often in the so-called Paris Club. In this form, creditor governments have often acceded to debt restructuring, grace periods on loan amortizations, and lengthened maturities. But in strong contrast to the earlier experience, they have almost never allowed for an explicit reduction in the principal owed or interest due. Of course, some of the difference with the earlier period is more apparent than real, for when interest rates are already on a concessional basis, a lengthening of debt maturities amounts to a reduction in the market value of liabilities.

Since the reemergence of large-scale private lending, the private creditors have even more strongly resisted the substitution of debt relief for debt rescheduling. In no sense is private debt rescheduling merely a polite phrase for default, as many observers have suggested. The *essence* of the reschedulings has been the preservation of the book value of outstanding debt. While in the nineteenth century, a default settlement often included a conversion of the defaulted bonds to new bonds (at par) with a reduced coupon rate, in the recent period, the debt reschedulings have often included an *increase* in interest rates on the outstanding debt, to compensate creditors for the greater risk of the extended maturities and the transactions costs of rescheduling. Moreover, arrearages and delinquencies on debt payments are capitalized and added to the liabilities of the debtor. Assuming that the rescheduled debt is not ultimately defaulted, the private creditors apparently suffer only small, if any, capital losses in the great bulk of debt reschedulings.[3a]

To a great extent, the difference in pre-1930 and post-1945 experience is the difference in noncooperative and cooperative outcomes. In the former case there was no formal mechanism available for a debtor country to commit itself to particular behavior in return for a loan agreement. The only contract between debtors and bondholders occurred *after* a default, in order to reach a settlement on the outstanding claims. After World War II, the creditor clubs and ad-hoc committees of bank representatives have repeatedly negotiated with debtor countries on the verge of default. Moreover the IMF has played the role of arbiter, in designing stabilization programs for the debtor country that provide the basis for pareto-improving cooperative agreements with private and official creditors. We should not suppose that the stabilization programs are therefore gladly endorsed by the debtor country. The programs have indeed been economically and politically painful—but still less painful than outright defaults.

In the following few pages, I pursue this contrast in historical experience, focusing on some structural features—such as bond-versus-bank debt, official-versus-private credit, and the role of the IMF—that might help to explain the historical shift.

Defaults before World War II: Causes and Remedies

Table 7–7 presents a sampling of sovereign defaults until World War II, to illustrate their frequency and scope. That defaults were a normal and accepted part of the financial system can be judged by two facts: (1) a default in one country typically did little to interfere with the flow of capital to other LDCs and (2) a default usually resulted, after several years, in a formal settlement with bondholders that allowed renewed large-scale borrowing by the debtor. Almost all of the publicly held liabilities of the borrowing countries in this period were in the form of long-term publicly held bonds rather than bank debt. The principal role of the great banking houses in developing-country finance was in underwriting debt, and so defaults rarely had the direct effect of bringing down a banking house. The Baring crisis of 1890 is the stunning exception to the rule, which shows that underwriting itself can be a dangerous business. When an 1888 loan for Argentina was coolly received in the bond market, the Baring Brothers "felt obliged to lend to Argentina through acceptance credits. Falling raw material prices in 1890 made it impossible for the Argentine government to meet these credits

Table 7-7
Periods of Sovereign Default, 1820–1932: Some Examples

Country	Period of Default
Mexico	1827–1870, 1914–end of period
Peru	1825–1849, 1876–1889, 1931–end of period
Venezuela	1834–1841, 1847–1859, 1864–1876, 1878–1880, 1892–1893, 1897–1905
Greece	1827–1878, 1893–1898, 1932–end of period
Portugal	1837–1856, 1892–1902
Turkey	1875–1881, 1930–end of period
Egypt	1876–1881

Sources: See Borchard (1951) and Wynne (1951) in particular, but also Feis (1930), Madden, Nadler, and Sauvain (1937), Kindleberger (1978), and Winkler (1933) for further examples.

Note: The dates are representative of major demarcations between credit worthiness and default. Within many of the intervals, settlements were reached with creditors that restored creditworthiness for a brief period but collapsed shortly thereafter.

as they came due," and the great banking house itself succumbed to bankruptcy (see Kindleberger 1978).

An illustration—in the extreme—of the default cycle that characterized many nineteenth-century countries is provided by Max Winkler (1933) for the case of Guatemala, which I reproduce in table 7–8. Far from a permanent bar to flotation of new debt issues, Guatemalan defaults were regularly renegotiated to permit new borrowing. And though it may appear that bondholders acted irrationally in continuing to hold Guatemalan debt, it must be stressed that these assets carried an enormous risk premium, with yields to maturity often five-hundred basis points above British government consols. Indeed, without a careful calculation it is difficult to know whether the realized return on a century of Guatemalan debt exceeded or fell short of the return on safe assets, even with the history of repeated default.

There is no simple set of factors that underlay most defaults in the early period, with the history recording cases of flagrant economic mismanagement, external shocks (for example, terms-of-trade deterioration), war and war indemnities, crop failures, and failed investment schemes as proximate causes of default. Kindleberger (1977) notes that the least successful loans were those undertaken to maintain real consumption levels in the event of external shocks to income—and that foreign borrowing to match a rise in domestic investment tended to fare more favorably. He also adds, however, that "productive loans in the developing countries are not very productive," so that the distinction between government consumption and investment expenditure is not as sharp as might be supposed.

Table 7-8
The History of Guatemalan Debt, 1825-1928

Year	Debt Status
1825	First loan of £163,000 to Central American Federation contracted at 73 percent, bearing interest at 6 percent per annum.
1827	Guatemala assumes five-twelfths of debt, or £67,900.
1828–1855	Default.
1856	Settlement on basis of loan and arrears being converted into £100,000 5's; Guatemala recognizes one-third of original debt, or £54,433. Interest in arrears estimated and cut down to £45,567. 50 percent of customs given as security.
1863	Private loan of £11,300 for construction arranged in London.
1864	Loan of 1863 defaulted.
1869	Loan contracted for £500,000 at 70½ percent, bearing interest at 6 percent per annum. Sinking fund of 3 percent per annum. Import duties given as security.
1876	All loans defaulted.
1878	⅓ interest due April 1, 1876, on 1869 loan, paid in November 1878.
1884	Settlement made. Because of political disturbances, agreement not carried out.
1887	Loans of 1856 and 1869 and back interest funded into new 4 percent loan; sinking fund of ½ percent applied to semiannual drawings at par; secured on duties levied on each package of foreign merchandise that may be imported into country through any of ports, also on maritime revenues; payments made to a committee composed of representatives of foreign bonds, internal bonds, and railways. Importers to pay pledged revenues to committee.
1888	Terms of 1887 accepted and £922,700 of 4 percent loan created as follows: £100 of 1856 loan and back interest amounting to £62/1/8 exchanged for £144/14 new 4's; £100 of 1869 and £72/10 interest for £152/4; £100 of 1863 loan and £19/11/8 interest for £144/14 of new 4's. Internal debt settled on basis similar to foreign debt.
1894	All loans default and committee suspended.
1895	New arrangement: Internal and external debt exchanged into £1,600,000 new 4's; £100 of 1888 loan exchanged for £75 new bonds. Internals at rate of £80 ($500) for £75 new 4's; noncumulative sinking fund of £15,000 to purchase bonds. Secured by special tax of 6s per quintal of coffee exported; proceeds paid to agents of bondholders.
1895–1896	Negotiations for new loan of £658,500 with Hamburg bankers; secured on excess of coffee warrants after providing for external debt. These new terms were drawn up without consultation with Council.
1897	New arrangement with German bankers, again without consulting Council of Foreign Bondholders.
1898	Duty on coffee, which had been "irrevocably fixed" is reduced—new agreement reached providing for payment of interest on external debt at rate of 2 percent in cash for three years, and 2 percent in certificates that were to be exchanged for 4 percent bonds after June 30, 1901.
1899	Coffee duty again reduced—subsequently raised.
1900	Contract of 1895 again violated.

Table 7-8 continued

Year	Debt Status
1901–1902	New agreement provides for payment of interest due December 1902 and June 1903 at rate of 1½ percent and of later coupons at rate of 3 percent. Arrears funded into new bonds; as security, all customs are pledged. Congress so multilated terms that Committee did not submit it to holders.
1903	New agreement; as security government gives 30 percent of import duty, payable in gold. Agreement not ratified by government; export duty on coffee changed again.
1904	New agreement provides for issuance of new bonds with interest at rate of 1½ percent in 1905; 2 percent in 1906; and 3 percent thereafter. Government refuses to ratify agreement.
1903–1908	Agreement reached with U.S. syndicate that made advances against coffee export duties and import duties payable in gold. Documents deposited with American Legation in Guatemala and holders given right to ask U.S. government for protection in case of violation of terms of Guatemala—thus, special security of 1895 is assigned to others.
1908	New agreement with U.S. syndicate for $5,000,000 loan.
1912	Coffee duty established at original rate.
1913	Arrangement of 1895 resumed on following terms: Government to deliver to bondholders warrants for payment of coffee export duties enough to cover interest for 1913-1914; in exchange for certificates of 1898, government issues £29,656, 4's; for back coupons. Deferred certificates were issued with no interest. At end of four years, bondholders were to deal with government regarding these certificates.
1917	Sinking fund not resumed as provided for in 1913 Agreement.
1919	Resumption of sinking fund.
1924	Railway loan of $3,000,000 contracted at 8 percent.
1925	Additional tax imposed on coffee exported.
1927	Railway bonds issued to the amount of $1,950,000 at 8 percent per annum.
1928	External loan of $2,515,000 issued at 8 percent per annum. New 4 percent external loan for £844,603 issued to take care of deferred interest certificates of 1913.

Source: M. Winkler, *Foreign Bonds: An Autopsy* (Philadelphia: Roland Swain, 1933), pp. 41–44.

The classic case of *consumption loans* are debts to finance war indemnities, as in the Davies and Young Loans to finance German reparations after World War I. An indemnity requires a pure income transfer, which must be matched by a decline in consumption relative to income. A loan may be undertaken to smooth the required consumption decline over time. Effectively the loan is financing a short-term decline in the national savings rate, on the presumption that the savings rate will rise later. But, as we shall see, a drop in the national savings rate is a strong predictor of rising default probabilities. Loans to finance military expenditure or to wage war have the same risky character and help to explain the widespread defaults during the 1820s of a number of newly independent Latin American countries.

Borrowing to finance consumption or military expenditure is no guarantee of default. Indeed, creditors must expect a high enough probability of debt repayment that, when coupled with the risk premium, the expected rate of return on the loan at least matches the return on safe assets. Exogenous shocks, at least partially unanticipated, must precipitate the default decision, unless creditors simply misjudge the debtor's intentions or economic position. The triggering event is often external, such as a recession in the developed countries that reduces export demand and the debtor's terms of trade. As John Madden, Marcus Nadler, and Harry Sauvain (1937) (hereafter MNS) point out, "During the nineteenth century, every major downward swing of the business cycle caused the failure of governments and other foreign borrowers to meet their external obligations" (p. 107). The links of business cycles and default hold clearly in the 1830s, 1870s, and 1890s. Alternatively, an individual country may experience a terms-of-trade shock, such as when the spread of artificial fertilizers substantially reduced the price of Peruvian guano, thus contributing to Peru's default in 1876.

The most significant of all default episodes, in magnitude and in intellectual and institutional legacy, occurred in 1931–1932 in the depths of the Great Depression. Its lessons are still relevant to us for several reasons. The defaults occurred at a time when much of the banking community and public had become convinced that default risk was a thing of the past, and so it is a good antidote to such facile thinking today. Just as in our defaultless era, "Investors in foreign bonds had not suffered any losses for a long time; on the contrary, they had repeatedly made sizable profits. This pleasant state came to be regarded as normal; investors assumed that the world had entered a period of permanent, defaultless prosperity."[4] More importantly, the episode points up one of the potential sources of hazard in international capital mobility: a speculative rush from foreign bonds with no international lender of last resort or forum for debt rescheduling. To explore this episode, it is useful first to survey the wreckage. On the New York bond market alone some or all of the obligations (including national, provincial, and municipal entities) of no less than fifteen Latin-American countries, thirteen European countries, China, and Canada were in default in 1935 (MNS, pp. 308–318). Approximately 39 percent of the par value of all foreign bonds on the New York exchange were in default at the end of that year (MNS, p. 123). On all of the world's exchanges defaults totaled about $22.4 billion at the beginning of 1934 (Winkler 1933, p. xii.) So much for America's first large-scale involvement as a major world creditor!

A major part of the default mechanism in 1931–1932 is typical: the depression in the developed countries sharply reduced the terms of trade of primary producing regions, substantially raising the real value of the debt in terms of national incomes among the debtor countries. As in earlier business cycles, defaults were to be expected, and certainly in greater magnitude in 1931–1932 than earlier—given the severity of the cycle.

Moreover, the incentives to remain solvent also fell. Since the costs of default include a squeeze on trade flows and an exclusion from foreign borrowing, an exogenous reduction in trade or an inability to borrow even *without* defaulting can lower the incentive to maintain debt servicing. Both events seem to have occurred in 1930, about six months *prior* to the onset of widespread defaults. The declines in income in the United States and Europe had already reduced agricultural prices in the primary production regions. On top of this shock came rising trade protectionism in the United States and then elsewhere. The Smoot-Hawley Tariff of June 1930, provided another blow to the terms of trade of the developing countries. More importantly, the capital markets appear to have "shut down" to the developing countries after mid-1930. While about $411 million of new, non-Canadian foreign debt was floated from January to July 1930, only $5 million was floated during the rest of the year. The foreign defaults, led by Bolivia, began six months later on January 1, 1931. Bolivia was soon followed in sequence by Peru, Chile, Brazil, Colombia, and a dozen other Latin-American countries.

The restriction on foreign borrowing is clearly related to a sharp rise in the perceived risk of foreign loans. Risk spreads on foreign debt widened enormously in the second half of 1930, as shown in figure 7–5. Political violence in Brazil was greeted by investors with panic concerning all Latin-American issues, and Latin-American bond prices fell up to 50 percent in the course of a single week (Oct. 3–10, 1930), as shown by table 7–9.

Once the defaults began there was no return. The market environment during 1931 is vividly described in the *Financial Chronicle* (Jan. 16, 1932):

> Foreign obligations, both on behalf of governments and on behalf of corporations, were under taboo all through the year. The financial upheaval through which Europe was passing appeared to have put a complete embargo upon flotations of that description. This was long before the suspension of gold payments by Great Britain and several other countries in September. No foreign government issues of any kind were placed in the United States during 1931 with the exception of $50,422,000 of Canadian municipal issues, and these latter, too, became out of the question when the Canadian dollar suffered such heavy depreciation following the action of Great Britain in passing off the gold standard.

Admittedly, it is very hard to judge whether the market reaction was a rational response to a *fait accompli* of widespread default, or whether the panic itself brought on the default. In markets with multiple equilibria and

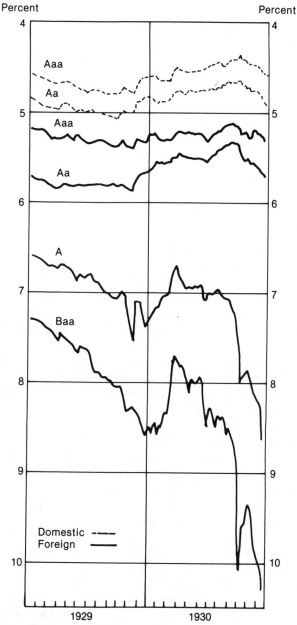

Source: *Moody's Manual of Investments: Government Securities* (New York: Moody's Investor Service, 1931), p. 12. Reprinted with permission.

Note: Each curve is based on average yields to maturity for forty bonds. The list of forty foreign bonds includes twenty government, fifteen municipal, and five corporate issues.

Figure 7-5. Moody's Bond Yield Averages by Ratings/Forty Foreign Bonds Compared with High Grade Domestic (Inverted Scale)

Table 7–9
Latin American Bond Prices, 1930

| Country | Closing Price | |
	October 3	October 10
Argentine 6s	95	54 7/8
Bolivia 8s	76 3/4	66
Brazil 6-1/2s	73	48 1/2
Chile 6s	83 1/2	71
Colombia 6s	66 5/8	58
Uruguay	101	88

Source: *Financial Chronicle,* vol. 131, p. 2264, 1930.

self-fulfilling prophecy, a complete structural model is necessary to find out "what might have been." But since the panic selling of *all* Latin-American bonds seems to have occurred in response to bad news concerning only one debtor, it appears that imperfect information and a bandwagon effect played a vital role in the default process. In either interpretation, the market fell into the no-loan-cum-default box in the creditor-debtor game described earlier.

The remedies to default were as varied as the causes in the period before World War II. Most typically, the default was followed after a number of years by a negotiated settlement between the defaulting government and a private bondholders' committee. In more spectacular cases, military intervention was occasionally threatened or pursued, as when Germany, Great Britain, and Italy blockaded Venezuela in 1902–1903. Not only did the intervention succeed in restoring debt service payments, but an arbitration in the Hague in 1904 awarded priority to the intervening countries over other claimants (including the United States, France, Holland, Belgium, and Spain) on the theory "that they had incurred the expenses of an intervention that resulted in benefits to others as well (Borchard, p. 271). The rewards of a job well done! Ten-to-twenty years later, the United States was active militarily throughout the region in customs house seizures to guarantee debt servicing. The most spectacular of all interventions resulted in loss of sovereignty of the debtor country, as when France installed Maximillian as Mexican Emperor in 1861 after a joint military operation with Britain and Spain. The British occupation of Egypt (1881–1907) followed joint attempts of Britain and France to enforce Khedival debt obligations.

Most authorities concur, however, that "It cannot be said that military action in support of bondholders is now or ever was an important phase of international relations" (Borchard, p. 269).[5] Much more frequently, governments of private creditors did not interfere in default claims, except to prevent discrimination by the defaulting country in favor of creditors of another country. Private bondholders committees carried the burden of negotiation with the defaulting countries. Their main weapon was their power to enforce the exclusion of new debt flotations on the national stock exchanges. More occasionally, the bonds themselves carried explicit default provisions; for example, for arbitration or collateral. Even more rarely, countries have acceded to foreign control or supervision of customs receipts and such in addition to exclusions of further borrowing.

Given these coercive devices, defaults were almost always followed by negotiation between creditors and debtors. A hallmark of such negotiations was an evaluation of the debtor's "capacity to pay", to determine a degree of debt forgiveness for the defaulting country (see Cizauskas 1979). Most frequently, existing debt was consolidated and extended, with a significant reduction in interest and principal due. Interest arrearages were often totally forgiven in the new debt package. Dozens of examples of these settlements may be found in Edwin Borchard (1951, pp. 323–330). More novel types of settlements also merit mention. The Peruvian debt from loans of 1869, 1870, and 1872 was forgiven in return for franchises to the operation of railroad and steamboats in Peru and to certain rights in grain production. Bondholders were assigned pro-rata share in a newly created Peruvian Corporation that took control of these assets.

The Debt Situation since 1945: Reschedulings in Lieu of Default

The period since World War II must be divided into an early and a recent phase. The legacy of the Great Depression defaults sharply restricted the access of developing countries to the private capital markets until the late 1960s. Capital flows until that time were dominated by development loans of multilateral agencies (usually concessional) and supplier credits typically guaranteed by export-import agencies of the creditor countries. There was no shortage of debt difficulties in this period, even with the far more limited scope of loans. But there were also no defaults: governments acting in ad hoc multilateral creditor groups, alongside of the IMF, used both positive incentives and threats to avert defaults, now viewed by the leading nations as a major threat to world economic stability.

From its inception in the early 1950s, the *creditor club mechanism* has offered debtor countries the prospect of debt rescheduling and extended debt maturities in exchange for commitments to a stabilization program to alleviate the debt difficulties; there have been forty-seven creditor reschedulings, involving sixteen countries, during 1946–1980. The stabilization programs that underlie the reschedulings are almost always negotiated between the debtor country and the IMF and allow the debtor to draw loans for balance-of-payments support at concessional rates (technically, the country borrows from its *upper tranche* credits at the IMF, once a stabilization program is approved.)

Both as to the nature of credit relief and the form of the stabilization program, there are consistent patterns that have emerged over time (see IMF [1981a] for discussion). The agreements cover debt falling due within a specified consolidation period (usually one or two years within the date of the rescheduling), and most or all of that debt is rescheduled (or rolled over). Typically the consolidation period includes three intervals: a period prior to rescheduling for which dept payments are in arrears; a period in the future during which debt is unconditionally rescheduled; and a follow-up period, for which the debt will be rescheduled *conditional on the successful completion of an IMF stabilization program.* Frequently, a grace period is allowed, in which no interest or amortization is required. Interest arrearages are *not* forgiven, though they too may be consolidated into new debt obligations. The interest rate on restructured debt is generally left to be negotiated bilaterally between the debtor and creditor countries.

The IMF stabilization programs that underlie the debt rescheduling are similarly systematic and are far more controversial. As described by Manuel Guitian (1981), for example, the stabilization programs typically focus on three factors: a reduction in domestic credit creation, a cut in fiscal expenditure (in part to support the first objective), and a restoration of price incentives in controlled sectors of the economy. The last plank has two purposes: to increase efficiency of production generally and to relieve claims on the budget in the form of subsidies to commodities subject to controlled prices. This set of policy prescriptions has been strongly attacked by many academic economists. We will examine the efficacy of the programs likely in the final section of this chapter.

The list of official debt rescheduling records that many countries participate repeatedly in the Paris Club process. This repetition reflects the narrow consolidation period of rescheduled debt and not any evidence that the earlier stabilization programs have been unsuccessful. The consolidation period is kept short to provide automatically for periodic review of the stabilization efforts.

With the very sharp increase in private sector loans to the LDCs, a substantially more complex environment has emerged. The vulnerability of private debt depends importantly on public sector behavior, and vice versa, so that strategic behavior of the debtor countries, the official creditors, the IMF, and the banks all are interconnected in a complicated game. As one example of this, each creditor is concerned that rescheduled debt not be used merely to pay off the debts of other creditors. The Paris Club regularly requires that a debtor country that reschedules debts to official creditors undertake to reschedule debt to private creditors on comparable terms. The public creditors attempt to prevent the debtor from using the Paris Club rescheduling merely to pay off its private-sector debt.

The recent history of private-capital market transactions shows clearly that banks sacrifice little if anything in asset values in multilateral debt rescheduling. The lesson of the Paris Club is even more decisively true for the private banks: reschedulings are *not* defaults, in that they convey no explicit debt relief except with regard to maturity structure (however, see footnote 3a). With respect to outright debt repudiation, North Korea provides the only case involving private credit in the postwar period.

While we do not have as much public information about private credit reschedulings as we do about the Paris Club undertakings, recent experiences for Jamaica, Nicaragua, Peru, Sudan, Turkey, and Zaire between 1975 and 1980 allow some general points to be made. Most importantly, credit availability to the countries fell when expansionary domestic policies, and often external shocks, led to a significant *fall in national saving rates*. For most of these countries, service payments fell into arrears before the rescheduling, and the private reschedulings were preceded by Paris Club negotiations. In the private reschedulings, the debt restructuring itself provided for grace periods of about three years and total maturities of five-to-seven years. Interest rates were at spreads of 1¾ to 2 percentage points above LIBOR. Importantly, in most cases, the implementation of the rescheduling was made contingent upon successful performance under an IMF stabilization plan.

It is often asserted that banks are too reluctant to declare defaults and that they allow bad debts to accumulate to avoid a debt repudiation. The combination of debt rescheduling and IMF stabilization program can in principle allow the banks to walk the line between default and unchecked debt accumulation. We will investigate in the following section whether the programs have indeed been successful in their assigned task.

The IMF seems to provide a crucial ingredient in arranging a cooperative settlement between creditors and debtors. It remains an open question whether such agreements could be directly reached between the banks and country, without the involvement of an outside institution. The answer seems to be "no," for commercial banks are very wary of undertaking the kind of bargaining and monitoring roles that are central to the IMF. The case of Peru in the mid-1970s provides a case in point, for the banks and Peru tried unsuccessfully to mimic an IMF program without the IMF. The experiment was a debacle, and eventually the IMF had to enter the scene.

Cline (1981) has described this case in some detail:

In March 1976 the Bermudez government sought a large balance-of-payments loan from major U.S. banks, without a prior IMF standby agreement. The government felt that agreeing to IMF conditions would be unacceptable politically, although in its discussion with the banks, the government proposed a program very much like that which might have secured IMF support. Partly out of fear of a more leftist coup if Bermudez lost power, the banks eventually agreed, but only after the regime demonstrated willingness to take unpopular stabilization measures. . . .

The program called for an initial $200 million in loans with a second $200 million to follow after several months, contingent on government adherence to the policy purchase. Signed only by the end of 1976, the package soon demonstrated the frailty of such direct intervention by banks; for reasons of data availability, technical capacity, and political sensitivity, it proved impossible for the banks to enforce their lending conditions, and adverse publicity for the intervention (plus its ineffectiveness) caused the leading banks to resolve that they would not become entangled in similar packages in the future but would rely on the IMF as the monitoring authority.[6]

Prospects for LDC Debt in the 1980s

In light of our theoretical and historical discussion, there are three principal concerns that surround the current debt situation. First, is the threat that Kindleberger (1977) raises that "the problem of developing-country debt today is that the proceeds of loans of developing countries, and even of Britain, France, and Italy in the last three-and-one-half years, have been used to finance consumption and that the recycling has postponed default but cannot be continued indefinitely." (1977, p. 14). He argues that the "analogy of (oil recycling) with reparations recycling is exact," since both involve a fall in savings rates to avoid a necessary fall in real consumption standards, and he then reminds us of the fate of reparations loans. In this gloomy view, we would predict in the coming years either explicit defaults or a steady accumulation of bad debt by banks who continue to loan out of fear of a default.

A second potential concern lies on the opposite end: that the costs of defaults are so large and the effectiveness of debt reschedulings and stabilization programs so consistent that many LDCs are forced to bear extraordinary, and unwarranted risks in the development process. Should defaults or debt relief be encouraged by policy authorities in some cases?

Third, there is the risk that credit supply to the LDCs might suddenly shrink because of a bank failure, an isolated default, a coup, or such with the result of provoking a chain of further defaults and panic. Is the cooperative mechanism strong enough to prevent a clamp-down on foreign loans?

The concern over consumption loans to finance oil imports seems not to be warranted for the LDCs as a whole during 1973–1978. While the timing of sharp rises in LDC indebtedness certainly corresponds to the oil price hikes, there is no logical corollary that the debt is therefore paying for oil imports. Indeed, as I pointed out elsewhere (Sachs, 1981a), the current account deficits for non-OPEC, oil-exporting developing countries rose at least as much relative to GDP as for oil-importing developing countries (table 7–10)! Indeed, the debt/GNP ratio for middle-income oil exporters (excluding Iraq, Saudi Arabia, Libya, and Kuwait) rose from 10.9 percent in 1970 to 24.5 percent in 1980, while it rose from 10.2 percent to only 14.8 percent for the middle-income importers. The LDC debt problem is *not* neatly explained by oil-import dependence.

One clue as to the LDC adjustment process is provided in table 7–11, from the World Bank. The oil-importing LDCs responded to the rise in fuel prices by compressing nonoil imports as a percentage of GDP and expanding exports. Incredibly, Brazil held the dollar value of merchandise imports flat for four years after the oil price increase. In strong contrast to the Kindleberger position, savings rates actually rose in the period. (If the inflation correction mentioned earlier in this chapter is used to adjust the savings data, savings rates would rise even more strongly than in table 7–11.)

The large deficits of the middle-income developing countries arose in this period because very large increases in investment rates exceeded more moderate increases in savings rates—and not because of a fall in savings rates as such. In the aggregate for nine large LDC debtors, the savings-investment relations were as shown in table 7–12. The investment boom, and a matching decline in the OECD, led to a hefty shift in the locus of world investment, as shown in table 7–13. This high rate of capital formation helped to fuel the rapid growth of the middle-income LDCs throughout the 1970s.

Of course, it is not fortuitous that the big debtor countries maintained high savings rates in this period. To a large extent, the high savings rates *permitted* these countries to continue to borrow heavily on the international market, for the reasons explored in the previous section. In many cases, with Brazil the best known, large-scale borrowing in fact followed upon significant domestic financial reforms that raised home-savings rates (domestic savings rose from 21.1 during 1960–1964, to 21.8 during 1965–1969, to 23.8 during 1970–1974, before slipping back to 21.3 for 1975–1977, following the oil shock). Mexico, the Philippines, South Korea, Taiwan, and Thailand were among the large nine borrowers who had large increases in savings rates *after* the 1973 oil shock (comparing 1965–1973 and 1974–1979) (See Sachs 1981a, pp. 234–235).

The large debtor countries enjoy continued access to international loans though many display high Debt/GNP or Debt/Exports ratios. Since they

Table 7-10
Current Account as a Percentage of Gross Domestic Product, Nonoil LDCs, 1973–1979

Category	1973	1974	1975	1976	1977	1978	1979
Net oil-importing countries	−1.9	−5.4	−5.7	−3.7	−2.8	−3.1	−4.0
Net oil-exporting countries[a]	−2.9	−4.4	−7.1	−4.9	−4.4	−4.2	−3.3
All nonoil LDCs	−2.0	−5.2	−6.0	−3.9	−3.0	−3.2	−4.0

Source: *IMF Annual Report, 1980*, table 9, p. 30.

[a]Bahrain, Bolivia, the Congo, Ecuador, Egypt, Gabon, Malaysia, Mexico, Peru, the Syrian Arab Republic, Trinidad, Tobago, and Tunisia.

Table 7-11

Performance Indicators, Oil-Importing Developing Countries (1970-1980)

Item	Percent of Gross Domestic Product			
	1970	1975	1978	1980
Constant (1978) prices				
Fuel imports, net	3.3	2.6	2.8	2.7
Nonfuel imports	21.8	21.0	19.9	20.2
Exports	19.2	19.7	21.1	21.6
Savings	19.9	19.2	20.8	21.5
Current prices				
Current account deficit	2.4	5.1	2.3	4.4
Fuel imports, net	1.0	2.9	2.8	5.2

Source: World Bank, *World Development Report 1981,* p.14

Table 7-12

Inflation-Adjusted Saving, Investment, the Current Account, and National Debt: Averages for Selected LDCs

Item	Average Percent of Gross National Product	
	1965–1973	1974–1979
Fixed investment	20.4	22.6
Saving	20.6	21.9
Current account balance	− 1.8	− 3.1
Net debt	8.5	19.0

Source: Calculated from data in Sachs, 1981a, p. 235.

Note: The nine countries included are: Brazil, Chile, Colombia, Mexico, Peru, Philippines, South Korea, Taiwan, and Thailand. Averages are taken over all available years through 1979.

also have high savings rates, the debt levels reflect high investment and are therefore not a prima facie matter of concern. More generally, a leading banker has stated that developing countries "with good economic management are able to borrow much in excess of any debt-service requirement," giving these countries "strong incentives to pursue policies that maintain their creditworthiness with private banks" (Friedman, 1977, pp. 27, 29). Most reschedulings can be traced to a combination of "bad luck" (for example, excessive government spending in light of the terms-of-trade shift), which shows up as a fall in domestic savings.

Table 7-13
Fixed Investment and GNP, Major Regions, Selected Years, 1960–1978
(percent unless otherwise specified)

Item	1960	1965	1970	1973	1974	1975	1976	1977	1978
Investment of LDCs (billions of U.S. dollars)	8.3	12.2	24.9	91.4	58.1	70.9	76.4	81.2	101.6
Investment of developed countries (billions of U.S. dollars)	160.8	252.7	399.1	677.5	725.5	829.9	957.1	1,175.3	n.a.
Investment of LDCs as a proportion of total investment	4.9	4.6	5.9	5.8	7.4	8.5	8.4	7.8	8.0
GNP of LDCs as a proportion of total GNP	5.6	5.0	5.6	5.9	6.9	7.1	7.4	7.2	7.1
Investment of developed countries as a proportion of their GNP	17.8	19.2	20.0	21.8	21.1	20.0	20.0	20.4	20.9
Investment of LDCs as a proportion of their GNP	15.7	17.7	20.9	21.4	22.8	24.2	23.1	22.4	23.6

Source: The investment and GNP data are from International Monetary Fund, *International Financial Statistics*, series 93e and 99a, respectively. Reproduced from Jeffrey D. Sachs, "The Current Account and Macroeconomic Adjustment in the 1970s," *Brookings Papers on Economic Activity*, 1:1981, Washington, D.C.: Brookings Institution, p. 239. Reprinted with permission.
Note: For a list of the LDCs and developed countries included, see the raw data shown in Sachs, 1981a, tables 8 and 9.

Some examples of investment and savings developments for countries that rescheduled public debt between 1975 and 1980 are found in table 7-14. In all cases, there is some drop in savings rates after 1970-1973, though it is apparently slight for Turkey. In these cases, and in many other similar examples, the extent of bank lending available to the debtor country fell sharply as the savings rate deteriorated. A freeze on new lending, in line with the credit-ceiling model described earlier, seems to take hold before the debt rescheduling process begins. When new loans are unavailable to finance interest and amortization payments, the country typically begins to accumulate arrearages, at which point it signals its need for a debt rescheduling and its willingness to undertake a stabilization program.

An important question for us is whether the stabilization programs in fact stabilize or merely protect the banks from the onus of an explicit default. Very broadly speaking, the record is one of moderate success in restoring creditworthiness—but often at significant political and economic costs to the debtor. Clear examples of success in recent years include Chile and Peru, who have both restored high economic growth and declining external indebtedness relative to GNP. Following its 1975 rescheduling, Chile's Debt to GNP ratio fell from 59.6 percent (1975) to 37.2 percent (1979). Similarly, Peru's fell from a high of 66.3 percent in the year of its rescheduling (1978) to 58.0 percent in the next. And in both cases, real economic activity and savings picked up one year after the rescheduling.

More serious dilemmas exist for countries like Zaire and Sudan, for which stabilization programs have imposed very significant costs on output and growth. In Zaire, for example, real consumption levels and GNP have been declining sharply and continuously since the first rescheduling in 1976. In 1979, the Debt/GNP ratio was a whopping 51.8 percent, though the debt amounted to a mere $3.8 billion. Continued stringent policies will undoubtedly reduce this debt, though at further extreme hardship to the very poor country. In the pre-1930 arrangements, Zaire would have long ago defaulted. And if economic prospects subsequently improved, it would have redeemed a fraction of the value of the debt. Unluckily, Zaire provided the first case of rescheduling of the private banks in the 1970s, and the stand that they took was consequently stern. The IMF should create mechanisms in the future to allow for greater debt relief of such countries.

I close the analysis by returning to an indirect risk in international lending: an event such as a default or bank failure might dramatically shrink the market for international loans. While the system of creditor clubs and IMF oversight probably moderates this risk to some extent, there is no guarantee that the fund could effectively keep private credit lines open in the event of a major panic. Indeed, the market responses in 1974-1975 to the Herstatt and Franklin National Bank failures only reinforce the fears of a major calamity emanating from the credit supply side. As a recent IMF report records:

Table 7-14
The Current Account, Saving, and Investment in Countries with a Debt Rescheduling in 1974–1978

Country and Item	Average, 1970–1973	1974	1975	1976	1977	1978	Year of Debt Rescheduling
			Percent of Gross National Product				
Chile							1975
Fixed Investment	13.2	12.6	10.5	9.0	9.2	n.a.	
Saving	11.5	12.9	−0.2	7.0	5.9	n.a.	
Current Account Deficit	−2.9	−0.8	−6.7	1.4	−3.3	n.a.	
Gabon							1978
Fixed Investment	n.a.	55.8	91.5	n.a.	67.1	n.a.	
Saving	n.a.	63.2	47.8	n.a.	50.7	n.a.	
Current Account Deficit	n.a.	7.4	−43.6	n.a.	−16.4	n.a.	
Peru							1978
Fixed Investment	12.7	15.3	17.5	16.9	14.9	14.5	
Saving	15.6	13.3	9.7	10.9	9.2	15.3	
Current Account Deficit	1.0	−5.8	−10.1	−7.1	−6.2	0.2	

Sierre Leone						1976
Fixed Investment	13.2	12.0	13.4	12.7	11.9	12.8
Saving	13.4	16.3	6.3	4.6	8.2	7.7
Current Account Deficit	-0.4	0.2	-9.7	-7.8	-6.0	-4.7
Turkey						1978
Fixed Investment	17.0	17.7	18.9	22.6	22.7	20.1
Saving	22.8	21.9	21.8	21.7	21.3	22.6
Current Account Deficit	5.0	2.8	-0.5	-1.9	-3.6	-0.1
Zaire						1976, 1977
Fixed Investment	28.4	32.0	28.9	n.a.	n.a.	n.a.
Saving	21.5	19.0	9.5	n.a.	n.a.	n.a.
Current Account Deficit	-10.8	-13.0	-22.8	n.a.	n.a.	n.a.

Sources: All data except that for Turkey are from the International Monetary Fund, *International Financial Statistics*, although no adjustment for inflation is made for these countries. The data for Turkey are from the Organisation for Economic Co-operation and Development, *National Accounts of OECD Countries, 1950–1978* (Paris: OECD, 1980). Reproduced from Jeffrey D. Sachs, ''The Current Account and Macroeconomic Adjustment in the 1970s,'' *Brookings Papers on Economic Activity*, 1:1981, Washington, D.C.: Brookings Institution, p. 246. Reprinted with permission.

n.a.: Not available.

> [T]he bank failures had major consequences on interbank relationships and international lending. Tiering of interbank deposit rates became considerably more pronounced and many small and medium-sized banks withdrew from the market, leaving more of the recycling up to those big banks which tended to receive deposits themselves. Large Japanese banks also retreated from the market because of prudential concerns, particularly on the funding side. Connected with these events was an abrupt hardening of lending terms and a decline in new credit commitments. (IMF, 1980, p. 26)

An important reason that this restraint did not have more serious consequences is that the drop in real interest rates across the board in 1974–1975 far exceeded the rise in spreads on loans to the LDCs, so that overall credit terms improved for those countries for which credit was available.

Some steps were taken in 1974–1975 to protect the capital markets from a chain of bank failures, including the "1975 Concordat of the Cooke Committee" of the *Group of Ten* (and Swiss) central banks, which vested primary responsibility for the solvency of foreign bank branches with the home-country central bank. A second step was a tightening of central-bank supervision over the off-shore portfolios of domestic banks. These steps are useful measures to prevent a breakdown in confidence over the solvency of commercial banks in the international markets. The inability of medium-sized banks to compete on the interbank market in late 1975 is probably vitiated by the clarification and tightening of central bank responsibility. But it seems much less likely that the steps taken in recent years would guarantee continued lending to LDCs in the event of an initial shock that *starts* with an LDC default of debt repudiation. To use the old cliché regarding monetary policy, infusions of central bank reserves in such a case might be like pushing on a string, without guaranteeing continued loans to the LDC.

In Lieu of a Conclusion

This chapter merely raises some of the issues involved in a complicated and controversial topic. I even have ignored one major aspect of the risks of international lending: the vulnerability of the international banking system to a large default or debt moratorium. I have had to handle in a very cursory way the strategic aspects of LDC negotiations with official and private creditors in recent years, which is especially troubling since gaming behavior is at the core of many of the risks to international debt today.

The theoretical analysis stresses that the riskinesses of debt (or the creditworthiness of a sovereign borrower) depends on (1) the overall savings and investment behavior in the borrowing country and (2) the institutional set-up within which loans are extended. On the first point, a sharp rise in indebtedness that reflects high investment rates is far less risky than a comparable increase in debt that is financing a drop in savings rates. For this reason, country-risk indicators such as debt-GNP ratios or debt-service ratios can only tell a partial story; the important criteria for creditworthiness must focus on the reasons for rising indebtedness. On the second point, the IMF has a key role in arranging package deals that commit sovereign borrowers to stabilization programs in return for continued credit flows. When such arrangements cannot be negotiated (as in Poland), the risks of default rise substantially.

With regard to the recent borrowing experience, I have tried to suggest a reason for optimism. One must focus on the underlying economic factors leading to the high levels of borrowing to get a clear view of the dangers therein. Both the ability to repay debt and the disincentives to default rise to the extent that indebtedness reflects high levels of domestic investment rather than low levels of savings. And at least for the major borrowing countries, such a pattern is evident in the 1970s (unfortunately the data for savings behavior after the second oil shock, in 1979–1980, are not yet in). According to the theoretical discussion, this cooccurrance of high investment rates and large lending to the LDCs is not merely fortuitous; rational creditors will raise their exposure on sovereign debt in line with high savings and investment rates of the borrower. In any event, there is no facile relationship between oil-import dependence and deficits in recent years, which is a good thing for the borrowers, creditors, and the international community as a whole.

Notes

1. For good recent summaries, see IMF (1980, 1981a, 1981b), Aronson (1977), World Bank (1981).

2. See Sachs (1981a, pp. 264–268) for a discussion.

3. It is easy to see that $U^{ND} \geq U^c$ for all values of D_1. Both U^{ND} and U^c are the maximum values of $U(C_1) + U(C_2)/(1 + \rho)$ subject to various constraints. The solution for U^c is subject to the same constraints as for U^{ND}, *plus* the added constraint $D_1 \leq h(I_1)$. Since U^c is subject to an added constraint, U^c must be $\leq U^{ND}$.

3a. Theoretical results in Sachs and Cohen (1982), which were derived after the completion of the present chapter, shed added light on the distinction between defaults and reschedulings. In fact, we show that reschedulings are like "partial defaults," in the sense that creditors cannot rationally expect the *full* recovery of rescheduled debt in many cases. Even though there is no explicit write-off of debt in a rescheduling, there is an implicit, partial loss as some of the debt is simply rolled over and over.

4. Mintz (1951), p. 82. The Mintz study offers a brilliant analysis of the international loan market in the 1920s.

5. This paragraph relies on Edwin Borchard (1951).

6. William R. Cline, (1981), pp. 305-306. Reprinted with permission.

References

Aronson, Jonathan D., ed. 1979. *Debt and the Less Developed Countries,* Boulder: Westview.

Bardham, Pranob. 1967. "Optimum Foreign Borrowing." In *Essays on the Theory of Optimal Economic Growth,* edited by K. Shell. Cambridge: MIT Press.

Borchard, Edwin. 1951. *State Involvency and Foreign Bondholders, Vol. 1, General Principles.* New Haven: Yale University Press.

Cizauskas, Albert. 1979. "International Debt Renegotiation: Lessons from the Past," *World Development* 7:199-210.

Cline, William R. 1981. "Economic Stabilization In Peru, 1975-78." In *Economic Stabilization In Developing Countries,* edited by W. Cline and S. Weintraub. Washington, D.C.: The Brookings Institution: 297-335.

Cooper, Richard N. 1981. "Managing Risks to the International Economic System," Cambridge: Harvard University, (Aug.)

Eaton, Jonathan, and Mark Gersovitz. 1981a. *Poor Country Borrowing in Private Financial Markets and the Repudiation Issue.* Princeton: International Finance Section.

————. 1981b. "Debt with Potential Repudiation: Theoretical and Empirical Analysis," *Review of Economic Studies* 48.

————. 1981c. "Country Risk: Economic Aspects," manuscript, Yale University.

Feis, Herbert. 1930. *Europe: The World's Banker, 1870-1914.* New Haven: Yale University Press.

Friedman, Irving S. 1977. "The Emerging Role of Private Banks In the Developing World," Citicorp.

Guitian, Manuel. 1981. "Policies on Access to Fund Resources—An Overview of Conditionality," manuscript International Monetary Fund.

International Monetary Fund. 1980. *International Capital Markets,* Occasional Paper No. 1, IMF: Washington, D.C. (Sept.).

————. 1981a. *External Indebtedness of Developing Countries,* Occasional Paper No. 3, IMF: Washington, D.C. (May).

————. 1981b. *World Economic Outlook,* Occasional Paper No. 4, June.

Kindleberger, Charles P. 1978. *Manias, Phobias, and Crashes.* New York: Basic Books.

————. 1977. "Debt Situation of the Developing Countries in Historical Perspective," Paper for a symposium at the Export-Import Bank on Developing Countries' Debt (April).

Madden, John T., Marcus Nadler, and Harry C. Sauvain. 1937. *America's Experience as a Creditor Nation.* New York: Prentice-Hall.

Mintz, Ilse. 1951. *Deterioration in the Quality of Foreign Bonds Issued in the United States 1920–1930,* New York: National Bureau of Economic Research.

Sachs, Jeffrey D. 1981a. "The Current Account and Macroeconomic Adjustment in the 1970s," *Brookings Papers on Economic Activity,* 1: 1981.

————. 1981b. "The Current Account and the Macroeconomic Adjustment Process," presented at the conference on "Allocational and Structural Consequences of Short-Run Stabilization Policy in Open Economics," Stockholm (Sept.)

Sachs, Jeffrey D., and Daniel Cohen. 1982. "LDC Borrowing with Default Risk," Working Paper No. 925, Cambridge: National Bureau of Economic Research (July).

Winkler, Max. 1933. *Foreign Bonds: An Autopsy.* Philadelphia: Roland Swain.

World Bank. 1981. *World Development Report.* Washington, DC: World Bank.

Wynne, William H. 1951. *State Insolvency and Foreign Bondholders, Vol. II, Case Histories,* New Haven: Yale University Press.

Discussion

Roger M. Kubarych

Regarding Sachs's chapter about LDC debt (ch. 7), I disagree entirely with his conclusion that more defaults can be in the interest of both creditors and debtors. More defaults will increase the perception of risk regarding *all* LDC borrowing and all will be faced with greater risk premiums—including those that have every intention of paying their bills. This result would be unfair.

Current account deficits can be viewed as unsustainably large when lowering them would require a sharp discontinuity in the domestic economy. There is good reason to focus on domestic savings rates as an indicator of economic adjustment capabilities. But other factors are also important, most notably a flexible price structure without too many distortions from large government subsidies, rigid real wage rates, and inappropriate foreign exchange rates.

The big difference between LDC borrowing now, compared to the prewar era, is that much of it is being done through the banking system. This fact has positive elements, particularly regarding the continuity of a banker-client relationship and the potential for a graduated response in the event of debt-servicing difficulties and means that arrangements short of outright default can be worked out to the benefit of both lender and borrower.

But the current system tends to load up too much of the country's lending risk on the banks or other intermediaries, rather than on the final lender (such as an OPEC surplus country). The banks have a comparative advantage in making and servicing loans but not keeping them on their balance sheets. Dispersing these risks more broadly would strengthen the international financial system. Part of the solution is more official lending, either through institutions like the IMF and World Bank or bilaterally by surplus countries. In fact, greater official lending has happened and that is a good development.

New credit instruments are still needed to spread risk more evenly. One idea I have supported (and still do) is *pass-through-type securities* that would enable banks to package existing loans to LDCs and sell the securities to final lenders. Another idea is what I have called *national income equity securities,* where the lender would buy a security whose yield is conditioned

Views expressed are my own and do not necessarily represent those of the Federal Reserve Bank of New York.

245

by the economic performance of the country that is the borrower. The higher the growth rate, the greater the yield—and conversely—so the lender has a direct stake in the good economic performance of the borrower.

Professor Mork's chapter (ch. 6) about the economic impact of a loss of Persian Gulf oil provides a service by giving a rough benchmark for assessing the potential costs of a severe Middle East crisis. My criticism of it is mainly that he has probably overstated the recessionary consequences. Investment would not go down as much as he says because:

1. There could be a large pickup of investment in energy saving equipment, which would be very profitable to operate.
2. Demand for goods and services by the remaining oil producers (largely so-called high absorbing OPEC countries) would grow very quickly, because these are countries that are not able to spend as much as they would like and would probably use their windfall to buy more from the industrial countries. This demand would act as a brake on recession in the industrial countries.

By the same token, the continuing adverse effect of large-scale indebtedness to OPEC that would have to be serviced at higher real interest rates would be lessened because (a) the remaining oil producers would not be saving as much as the Persian Gulf countries do and (b) the Persian Gulf countries would be drawing down existing financial assets to rebuild their economies following the war or other crisis that would have left them without oil revenues.

In the end if Mork's scenario could happen, governments would take steps to ensure that it would not. Policy measures would be taken to ensure that a wage-price spiral were averted, through some form of incomes policy. And compulsory rationing (using the price mechanism but supplemented by quantitative restrictions) would be inevitable.

The interesting question has not been taken up by Mork: namely, in the event of an oil shock of such large magnitude, would the Western alliance be able to cohere, or would the U.S. public (and the Congress) refuse to permit the large-scale oil exports that would be required to keep the allies from turning to the Soviets and/or striking special deals with remaining OPEC producers? If our experience with Alaskan oil is any guide, the prognosis is not very reassuring.

The lesson is that, even if the true magnitude of the oil shock is much less than Mork supposes, there will need to be much greater political leadership displayed than in the past to protect against a divisive, nationalistic scrambling for oil by the consuming countries, with grave consequences for our economies and our alliances.

8

Rescheduling as Seen by the Supervisor and the Lender of Last Resort

Henry C. Wallich

It is about time that the regulators took a look at LDC lending. This is not because the banks have not done a fine job. The banks have done something absolutely amazing. They have moved capital to where it is needed. This would probably not have happened otherwise. I am a great believer in the bathtub theory of capital markets, which holds that the water flows around at the same level no matter which way you pump it and whether you dip into the water with a pail on one side or on the other. I doubt however that the money would have gone round and round and come out at the LDCs.

The banks more or less discovered the LDCs at the same time they discovered rollover credit. These two events made something possible that surely would have been difficult for the official institutions, since they just did not have the resources and could hardly have been involved with them. This would have been very difficult for the traditional bond market to do. That has been limited to very few borrowers for obvious reasons. The banks certainly deserve a great deal of credit for the job they have done.

However, there can be enough of a good thing. One thing that does raise concern is the continuing rapid growth of LDC credit. Gordon Richardson has said that anything financial that grows at 25 percent per year bears watching—and that is the case for LDC credit.

This is to some extent almost like the filling of a vacuum. The discovery that LDCs were creditworthy and that their demands could be handled by medium-term syndicated rollover loans resulted in a disequilibrium in capital markets. That is to say, the stock of such loans was lower than it presumably would have been in equilibrium. When that happens there is typically a very rapid expansion. The problem is how quickly and at what level it stops. In the long run nothing can advance much faster than the overall growth rate of inflation. If the LDCs are increasing their indebtedness at much more than 15 percent, which is perhaps their rate of growth in nominal terms, there is a relative rise in indebtedness. You see this when you look at various measures of debt, including debt service relative to exports, or total debt to GNP. These ratios have been rising, although not at an alarming pace. There are, nonetheless, countries and groups of countries where that

247

is not the case, but on the whole and over the last few years, indebtedness has been creeping up.

U.S. banks have been on the forefront of this movement for some time, but they have been pulled back in recent years. U.S. banks used to provide more than half of total LDC lending. Now it is on the order of 40 percent or slightly less. Banks of other countries have been taking their place. There has been a definite caution on the part of our banks reflecting creeping debt ratios in developing countries. If all the money that they borrowed had been used for investment, debt ratios should have remained fairly stable. If they had plowed all of this capital into growth, one might think that their investment to GNP ratios would have risen, growth would have accelerated, and debt would not have risen, or not have risen much relative to these measures. But, of course, one must fear that some of this money has not been used for investment. Rollover credits are typically balance-of-payments loans. In the old days banks typically lent to LDCs either for very short-term trade financing or for specific investment projects, like the World Bank does.

The typical syndicated Eurocredit is not of that kind. Moreover, it has a maturity of five to ten or twelve years, which is not consistent with the pay-off period of most large, long-term projects. You cannot build a hydro power plant and make it pay over five to twelve years. There is some kind of asymmetry here that leaves one a little uncomfortable. The oil situation has made all the data on LDC exports and debt service seem a little worse than they look because the oil bill preempts, in effect, part of the exports of the LDCs. And if you apply the oil bill first to exports, then measure debt service in relation to the remaining exports, the ratios look less encouraging. Of course, the ratios vary greatly among countries, and a very high ratio is by no means a disaster. It depends on the policies of the country. It depends on the country's ability to turn itself around. I do not want to sound like an alarmist, I just think that the rise in LDC indebtedness ought to taper off. It has not done so and it is worth asking why.

All of which leads me to investigate LDC lending and the responsibilities of regulators with respect to the banks. Why focus on rescheduling? Rescheduling is becoming a more frequent event for banks, and it has not yet been explored thoroughly. It is something that must be examined in terms of what it means for the banks, what it means for the countries, how it has worked, and where it might be leading.

Let me begin by reviewing the arguments why sovereign lending is different from ordinary credit risk. A country is a country is a country. It cannot very well disappear from the surface of the earth. A corporation can very well disappear. You can make a corporation pay out every penny it has and after that it goes into receivership. While you cannot make a country pay every penny that it has, a country can, if it wants, continue paying because there is always room for further belt tightening that will generate enough of a balance-of-payments surplus or reduction in deficit to make that possible. Moreover, a country that shows good debtor discipline will usually have access to credit. Hence, policy is the decisive element on the part of countries.

Thus it is true that countries are different from corporate and other borrowers. They are immortal. Unless they positively repudiate their debt, one can always believe that one can collect from them. This belief is manifested in the fact that even when regulatory systems and accountants and bankers have to make a severe charge against country debt as a result of nonperformance, they typically do not write it off entirely because that seems to imply that the country really has gone out of business. (One exception to that would be Cuba in one instance.)

A certain element that provides reassurance, with respect to a country's ability to pay, is the presence of the International Monetary Fund (IMF). Here is an international institution with very large resources. Its function is by no means to bail out the banks. Its function is to turn a country around if the country is willing to be turned around, and to tell the country what policies it needs to follow in order to make itself bankable again. These are the familiar performance criteria that the IMF imposes in its standby agreements. It aims at an equilibrium exchange rate and limits the amount of foreign borrowing. It limits the amount a government can borrow domestically. It may limit total domestic credit expansion. It may put a ceiling on budget aspects and it may ask for reforms of things such as price subsidies, distortions of prices, and the tax system.

When these measures are undertaken, that is, by and large, an optimal economic position for the country. Politically, however, meeting the IMF standards often is very tough. It may threaten the stability of the country, and, in that sense, a country that faces such a program deserves sympathy. Is it going to be cut off from credit? Is it going to be able to make it on its own? It can do it with the assistance of the IMF. Eventually the country's solvency will be restored. Even though there may be tough conditions they are clearly in the long-run interest of the country. That is what returns bankability to countries. The presence of the IMF in rescheduling agreements makes it possible.

There are other reasons from the point of view of the supervisor for wanting to watch these situations closely. Banks are under a great many pressures to lend to developing countries. One such pressure reflects low domestic bank earnings in many countries. In the international market it is often possible to pick up another syndication and then sell another CD and earn all of five-eighths of one percent. That is an inadequate return, but it is something. Moreover, if the bank is part of the management group, it gets a fee. To some extent interest and fees are substitutes; when a bank or group of banks feels that it needs up-front earnings, it can structure a new loan to produce a lot of fees and a low spread. The fee goes into this year's earnings unless the bank decides to spread it over time.

The pressure on the banks is also considerable because of the alleged liquidity of the Euromarkets. There is always a reason why the Euromarkets are liquid, either the United States has a payments deficit or OPEC is pouring money in. But the fundamental reason why the Euromarkets are liquid is that they are just another part of the domestic market. Offering a little more interest than is offered in the domestic market can, at that interest rate, attract an almost unlimited supply of funds. The elasticity of supply of the Euromarket, at a given rate in the domestic market, is almost infinity. Thus, the Euromarket will, most of the time, appear very liquid.

For the banks, there are other reasons or temptations why these loans should be pushed. There are many collateral advantages to lending to LDCs. One may get a branch there. One may pick up letter-of-credit business and other business. In that way participation in a syndicated credit may become something like a loss leader. The business is done at five-eighths of one percent not because that is a fair rate of return or more than can be made at home but because it is the key to other earnings.

There is also great difficulty for banks not to move with the crowd. What would a bank have done in 1968 or 1972 if it had decided it did not want to get into the international business? It would have had to resign itself to being a smaller bank, though perhaps a more profitable bank.

For a money-market bank, it would have been a very difficult decision not to participate in this upsurge of international lending. It might have meant that the bank would have become an unprofitable bank, a bank with a very low price/earnings ratio, and that its market-to-book-value ratio would have been low. It might have been a takeover candidate.

A little should be said about the history of LDC rescheduling. There are really two tracks. One is for official debt and the other is for private bank debt. The official track has been in operation for a long time. And many respectable LDCs have been rescheduled by their friendly creditors. The official lenders know each other well. It is not a very large group. They are usually government representatives. The procedure has rules that must be followed. For instance, there must be joint negotiations; if there are separate negotiations with different national creditors, somebody may get the inside track and this may lead to trouble. There has to be equal treatment among countries for the same reason. If somebody has an advantage, that will lead to future friction. There also has to be an equal burden imposed on private creditors. That is to say, if there are private lenders on any scale, the official lenders will insist that the general conditions be imposed universally. If that is not done, the banks may pull their money out at the expense of the official lenders who have postponed their claims.

Another principle that has become apparent is that governments will watch for political objectives. Governments may be neutral with respect to economic objectives, for instance, in deciding between rescheduling of interest versus rescheduling of principal. Typically rescheduling of principal is more easily accepted by the creditor than rescheduling of interest. But governments, of course, do have political axes to grind and so their attitudes in a rescheduling will reflect those.

Turning to private rescheduling, we have much less experience as regulators, although the banks seem to have learned pretty quickly what needs to be done. It is a very difficult mechanism because contrary to the official level, where there are a few main creditor countries, there can be hundreds of banks in a major rescheduling. These banks all have to be kept in line. If a single bank, for instance, were to claim default and attach an asset of the borrower, it could create untold mischief because then the loan would be thrown into default. There may be cross-default clauses that throw other loans into default. Suddenly the whole thing could unravel. This has never happened, but great care has been exercised to ensure a favorable outcome.

Most of the loans have contracts underlying them that spell out the rights of the participating banks. Typically there is a majority voting on such things as whether to call a default. But a bank that is outvoted can still take its case to court. It may be dissuaded from taking this action since legally it has to share with all the others anything that it may get out of the borrower. There are additional forms of pressure the banks can bring to bear on each other. But there are often tense moments in these negotiations when somebody appears to be breaking rank.

There is then a question of how to set up national steering committees, each of which would have to keep its own banks in line. These things take a lot of time and work. By now the banks have no doubt developed a pattern. In earlier rescheduling it sometimes took years between the time a problem was recognized and the time when the bank began to talk to the borrower. From there on it could take years until a final settlement was reached.

The banks have learned a number of other things. One thing they have learned is that it is very difficult for them to impose conditionality on a country. They know that it makes no sense to reschedule or to provide new money for a country unless that country changes its policies along the lines that the IMF might counsel. But the banks do not have the power, the means, or even the techniques to replace the IMF. So the situation tends to crumble unless the IMF comes in. There are cases where the IMF cannot come in, such as when the country is not a member of the IMF. In that case, how do you establish conditionality? The banks can propose something, but there is no real way of monitoring a sovereign country. The country may not give the bank access to correct or sufficient information. There is no way of enforcing anything. If the bank has promised to lend a specified amount on a certain date and the country has not performed, then the bank can refuse to pay out that part of the loan. That could happen, but it is a cumbersome way of operating.

The banks have learned that it is important to be specific regarding what happens with shorter term trade credit. There is a temptation to pull out at the expense of the other banks. If that happens, the viability of the whole arrangement may be called in question. The country is dependent on short-term trade credit and if that is not flowing any more, it denotes a very desperate situation for the country. The ability of the country to keep the economy going—to keep essential raw materials flowing, oil, parts, and machinery coming in—is put into question. Consequently, countries often give high priority to paying short-term credit even though medium-term credit may fall into arrears. But when banks do not continue to provide short-term credit, a serious problem is created.

It makes me uneasy when I hear a banker say that if anything were to happen in country X his bank would know how to get its money out. What that means is the bank would stop short-term trade credit, and that is not a good way of proceeding, expect perhaps for that bank. But it is not a good solution for the overall situation, since there is a need to maintain a certain flow of trade credit.

Finally, banks have interests that differ from those of governments and differ from those of other banks. Banks have a strong interest in not having interest payments interrupted. Amortization is not so bad. But if interest is not paid, then the loan has to be put in nonaccrual status. That is a painful thing for the bank to have to show. Hence, the banks will go to much greater lengths than governments will to find some way of not interrupting interest payments. One way to avoid interrupting interest payments is to lend the country the interest. The bank can make a new loan and add that to the old, or else find a way of restructuring the loan that brings the whole thing up to date. Something could be done to make sure that interest service is not interrupted, and it comes down to either a rescheduling or a refinancing. Although banks like to speak of refinancing, which is the more clearly respectable thing, the economics of the two are not very different.

We turn now to the economics of rescheduling. Why is it bad for a bank to have rescheduled loans on its books? After all, the country is going to be there forever. In fact, if the country remains an LDC forever, it will probably be a capital importer forever. That means its debt will grow and grow. It will never repay the debt. But I am not particularly concerned if somebody comes and says that he has discovered that none of this money will ever be repaid. Analogously, neither will the debt of the American Telephone and Telegraph Company be repaid, so long as that is a going concern and a growing corporation. The debt of both country and corporation will keep rising. Is that something terrible? The answer is, of course, in the case of AT&T, there is something behind its liabilities. In the case of a well-managed country there is also something behind its liabilities. In the case of the country, there is a viable economy that can generate foreign exchange and can generate growth. But if that is not the case, there is a difference between the country and the corporation and it becomes a problem when the debt continues to grow.

A bank cannot be satisfied with a situation in which the debt continues to rise, always rescheduling or adding a new debt to an old debt. Rescheduling reduces the liquidity of the bank. After all, the bank presumably had been counting on this cash flow to come in. It makes plans on how to use it. When expected cash is not forthcoming, it has to replace it with something from another source, presumably at some cost. If it turns out that short-term debt is also rescheduled, and therefore will be repaid only over time, the bank loses liquidity even in terms of its balance sheet. It may find it has a greater mismatch of its assets and liabilities. These are costs and risks. Return that depends on the terms of the rescheduling may be relatively low. The banks, of course, try to raise the spread over LIBOR. They do not always succeed. Sometimes they even have to reduce the interest rate. In that case, the difference is paid later, so that interest is never reduced or forgiven. These devices may satisfy generally accepted accounting principles but not an economist.

At the far end of this process, it really could become a kind of Ponzi game. Mr. Ponzi borrows, offering a high interest rate that encourages people to lend to him, thus enabling him to keep paying interest. And, if he can keep it going, he may be able to skim some cream off that game for a long time. Eventually, it will catch up with him. Similarly it will catch up with the country if the country is not growing but the debt is growing.

From the point of view of both the bank and the country, there is a discipline in having to face particular maturities. Indeed companies such as AT&T can incur increasing amounts of debt because they are well-managed, pay their debts on time, and face the test of being able to refund. They incur new debts, but at least whatever the debt, it is serviced punctually. That is really the least that you can ask of a well-managed developing country.

Behind this vision of building up debt, at some point the economist—if not the accountant or the banker—begins to ask himself whether there is not an optimal point for default. At what point would a country that lacks conscience and fails to live up to generally accepted accounting principles find it in its own interest to default? There is a paper at the Federal Reserve Board in which Dick Freeman examines this question. Fortunately he arrives at the conclusion, which is intuitively plausible, that the more anxious a country is to grow, the less likely will it find default to be in its interest. This is because future growth depends very heavily on past credit.

The more the country wants to grow, the less it can rely exclusively on its own savings and the more therefore it needs credit. If the availability or the cost of future credit depends on previous debt performance, then it is not sensible to default. This is not an implausible model, and borrowers should understand it.

A better reason for thinking that countries will not find it in their interest to default is to look at the evolution of countries that once were borrowers and have graduated to become capital exporters. It is likely that all countries in the world, except Great Britain, started out as capital importers and borrowed from Great Britain. Gradually, many of them, like the United States, became capital exporters. They must have gone through a phase in which their trade balance, which must have started out in deficit, went into equilibrium. Their current account would still be in deficit, reflecting the interest on past borrowings. At that point, they would still have been borrowing, but purely to pay this interest. They would not be receiving goods from abroad in excess of the volume of goods they were exporting. At that point, therefore, the country might say: If we are borrowing only to pay the interest, why keep this up?

No country, so far as I know, has ever said that. Those countries that grew to be capital exporters passed through that phase of borrowing only to pay interest and thereafter gradually stopped their net borrowings and began to be net exporters of capital. They passed that phase without a tremor.

Similar developments can and will occur in some of the present LDCs. They will graduate from the ranks of net capital importers. They may still be gross capital importers but also gross capital exporters. They will reach a point where net capital flows are zero and move on to positive net capital outflows. What, then, is the correct role for the supervisor? He should respect the business judgment of the banks.

Nonetheless it might be desirable to move toward setting up reserves against badly rescheduled loans. When a supervisor finds a loan to be doubtful or even substandard, he will classify that loan and he will take it into account in evaluating the capital adequacy of the bank (20 percent against substandard, 50 percent against doubtful). But he is not going to make this appear on the balance sheet, only on the examination report. This does not reduce the bank's capital. It just changes the supervisor's evaluation of whether the capital is adequate.

There is probably no country in the world today where there is a well-defined and overt recognition on the balance sheet of rescheduled loans. There are individual banks that do this, probably for tax as well as for risk reasons. In our environment the Internal Revenue Service is very hard to convince of a need to write anything off unless a clear case can be proven. The loan loss reserve of banks has become much more limited under the

1969 legislation. Furthermore, if a bank held reserves against rescheduled foreign loans, regardless of whether tax deductible or not, there is still the question of how general that treatment would have to be. Can foreign loans be treated differently from domestic loans? If a given procedure were established with respect to foreign loans, would accountants or lawyers decide that it would have to be applied domestically?

It must be recognized that what is being suggested here, that is, allowing banks to hold reserves against rescheduled loans, is not easy to fit into our institutional framework—but this seems to be precisely because internationally there seems to be a clean slate. Other countries do not do anything like this either. It may be possible to get some kind of common action internationally. Usually, that is very difficult in the supervisory field because every country has its own bank legislation and is not going to change that. Therefore, if there is no precedent, perhaps something could be done.

9 Risk and International Bank Lending: A Panel Discussion

Laurie S. Goodman,
H. Robert Heller, and
Arturo C. Porzecanski

The Importance of Diversification in International Bank Lending
Laurie S. Goodman

Few aspects of the international financial system have received more coverage in the financial press than the increased involvement of the largest U.S. and foreign commercial banks in international lending, particularly lending to non-OPEC LDCs. The claims of U.S. banks to non-OPEC developing countries increased from $23.8 billion at the end of 1974 to $47.7 billion at the end of 1977. By end-1980 the figure had further swelled to more than $73 billion and many feared that banks could prudently lend no more to several large LDC borrowers. Meanwhile, foreign bank claims soared from $20 billion at end-1974 to more than $122 billion in December of 1980. This lending is an important link in the recycling process whereby surpluses from oil-exporting countries, in the form of deposits are channeled to less developed countries in the form of loans, to finance their deficits.

The recycling process was an inevitable outgrowth of the first oil shock. A small group of oil-exporting nations (OPEC) accumulated a huge current account surplus in 1974–1977 while both non-OPEC developing countries and industrialized countries ran a deficit in those years. The industrialized countries were able to finance their deficits by attracting capital inflows from the OPEC countries. The non-OPEC LDCs could not attract capital inflows directly from the OPEC countries. Consequently these countries borrowed funds from the financial intermediaries of the industrialized countries who had excess liquidity from the OPEC deposits.

As these large flows of funds occurred, many analysts began to express concern about the risks that banks face as a result of their participation in the recycling process. These concerns escalated after the second round of large oil price increases in 1979–1980. During these years the average price

The views expressed here are strictly my own and do not necessarily represent the opinions of the Federal Reserve Bank of New York.

of a barrel of oil more than doubled from $14 to $32.50 per barrel. The OPEC surplus, having declined from $64 billion in 1974 to $5 billion in 1978, swelled to $120 billion in 1980, with nearly one-half of these flows invested in commercial banks of the industrialized countries. Meanwhile, the deficits of the non-OPEC LDCs, having declined from $38 billion in 1975 to $21 billion in 1977, increased sharply to $65 billion in 1980.

Risks of Recycling

Why are the risks that commercial banks face as financial intermediaries in the recycling process any different from those confronted in ordinary financial intermediation? The purpose of financial intermediation has always been to channel funds from savings surplus units to savings deficit units. However, the role of the largest U.S. and foreign commercial banks in the recycling process has exposed them to two types of risks that had never before posed a problem: fund availability risk and country risk.

Fund availability risk arises because, while governments have always deposited funds in commercial banks, never has such a small group of surplus governments deposited so many funds in relatively few commercial banks over a prolonged period of time. In normal financial intermediation, if a large customer relies upon a bank for its full range of banking services and the customer withdraws all funds, the one bank can borrow more heavily. In the Euromarket, if a major depositor were to withdraw all funds, all banks could not simultaneously borrow more heavily. We would expect fund availability problems to be short run in nature as the depositor would have to move his funds to other investments. This action would change supply, demand, and the relative rates of return in financial markets until an equilibrium situation was reestablished.

The more important risk that emerges from the recycling process is country risk. This risk can be defined as the uncertainties arising from political or economic developments within a country that may influence the ability and willingness of borrowers within that country to meet their obligations. Country risk occurs in normal international financial intermediation but is greatly aggravated by the recycling process, as never prior to the 1974 oil price increases had non-OPEC LDC governments used financial intermediaries for balance-of-payments financing on such a large scale.

Bankers have developed extensive internal procedures to control country risk. The political, economic, and social conditions within each country are reviewed at least twice a year. Based on these evaluations, top management sets maximum exposure limits by country and by area, based on both lending opportunities and country risk considerations. Thus senior bank management attempts to control risk by avoiding an excessive concentration of lending to a particular country.

The three federal bank supervisory authorities—the Comptroller of the Currency, the Federal Deposit Insurance Corporation, and the Federal Reserve System—implemented a new approach to foreign lending at the end of 1978. The basis of this supervisory approach is to emphasize diversification across countries and types of borrowers to avoid excessive concentration of risk. The regulators attempt to highlight concentrations of lending that are large relative to bank capital or country conditions for discussion with bank management.

The Importance of Diversification

Is this emphasis that bankers and regulators place in diversification warranted? Some analysts are concerned that the benefits to banks of loan diversification among non-OPEC LDCs may be very limited, as these countries face a more or less common set of problems. They are particularly concerned about the heavy dependence on imported oil that the non-OPEC LDC must purchase at the world price. Others contend, however, that country-specific factors are far more important, The LDCs are a heterogeneous group of countries. Not only are they at different stages of economic development, but they have very diverse political systems, economic policies, and trade structures. Thus, there are indeed many opportunities for loan diversification.

In my research, I have attempted to examine empirically the importance of the common risks in LDC loans in contrast to country-specific factors. If these country factors are important relative to the common factors, there are substantial opportunities for reducing risk by diversifying lending to many different LDCs. Alternatively, if the common factors are large, the opportunities for reducing risk by lending to many different LDCs will be limited.

Four different proxies were chosen for country risks: growth in exports, growth in the money supply, growth in international reserves, and growth in imports divided by reserves. The growth-of-exports proxy measures, in a crude sense, balance-of-payments risk due to real disturbances. The growth of the money supply serves as a proxy for monetary risk. The final two measures serve as proxies for liquidity risk.

For each proxy, a quarterly time series of observations was compiled for each of the largest borrowers.[1] This data was then utilized to compute the diversifiable and nondiversifiable variance for each of the borrowers.[2] The empirical results are summarized in table 9–1. The results can be easily interpreted. Glancing at the export growth measure for Brazil, 28 percent of the variance is nondiversifiable, whereas 72 percent is diversifiable. That is, 28 percent of the variance is explained by factors common to all countries. The unexplained variance is country specific.

Table 9–1
Empirical Results on Diversifiable Variance

Country	Export Growth 1960–1979		Money Supply Growth 1969–1979		International Reserve Growth 1960–1979		Import/Reserve Growth 1960–1979	
	(Non-DV)	(Div V)	(Non-DV)	(Div V)	(Non-DV)	(Div V)	(Non-DV)	(Div V)
Brazil	28	72	1	99	67	33	58	92
Mexico	26	74	24	76	13	87	45	55
Korea	39	61	2	98	4	96	34	66
the Philippines	13	87	2	98	4	96	10	90
Spain	26	74	8	92	7	93	6	94
Argentina	4	96	69	31	8	92	7	93
Hong Kong	22	78	—	—	—	—	—	—
Greece	37	63	2	98	5	95	31	69
Columbia	7	93	—	—	13	87	13	87
Chile	10	90	2	98	4	96	6	94
Yugoslavia	55	45	2	98	2	98	22	78
Ecuador	7	93	0	100	22	78	12	88
Thailand	1	99	1	99	0	100	1	99
Panama	7	93	—	—	3	97	17	83
Peru	11	89	2	98	2	98	5	95

Note: *Non-DV* = percentage of variance which is nondiversifiable. *Div V* = percentage of variance which is diversifiable.

The results indicate the bulk of the variance is diversifiable as opposed to nondiversifiable although there is always a bit of both. Only six countries (Brazil, Mexico, Korea, Argentina, Greece, and Yugoslavia) had more than 33 percent nondiversifiable variance on one or more of the four risk measures. Only two of the countries (Brazil and Korea) had more than 33 percent systematic or nondiversifiable variance on two or more risk measures.

The four risk proxies each attempt to capture a different aspect of the economy. As such, the independent use of the four proxies may tell different stories for some of the countries. Nondiversifiable variance for a country can be high as measured by one proxy and low as measured by another. For example, Brazil has 28 percent nondiversifiable variance as measured by export growth, 1 percent nondiversifiable variance as measured by money supply growth, 67 percent nondiversifiable variance as measured by international reserve growth, and 58 percent nondiversifiable variance as measured by imports/reserves growth.

Even so, the stories were not very different for most of the countries. Widely disparate results, where systematic variance is more than 50 percent in one proxy and less than 10 percent in another proxy for the same country, occur in only three cases (Brazil, Argentina, and Yugoslavia). Moderately disparate results, where nondiversifiable variance for the highest proxy is between 25 and 50 percent and nondiversifiable variance for the lowest proxy is under 10 percent, occur in four cases (Mexico, Korea, Spain, and Greece). Five of the countries have less than 15 percent nondiversifiable variance in all indexes (the Philippines, Columbia, Chile, Thailand, and Peru).

These results were based on a long-time series. If there were a dramatic increase in nondiversifiable risk as a consequence of the first oil shock, it would render the results less useful. To test for a structural change in the relationship between diversifiable and nondiversifiable risk, the sample period was split at the end of 1973. It was found that in nearly 80 percent of the cases there was no significant difference between systematic risk in the period prior to end-1973 and the 1974-and-after period. In nearly half of the cases when there was a significant difference, it represented a decrease rather than an increase in nondiversifiable risk. Thus the empirical work appears to be fairly robust.

Summary

These results indicate that country-specific risks appear to loom large relative to the common problems faced by non-OPEC LDCs. This conclusion has two important implications. First, it appears the efforts of top bank management and the federal regulatory authorities to emphasize loan diversification is well-placed. Since banks can significantly diversify risks, emphasis should indeed be placed on encouraging diversification and attempting to identify concentrations of lending that are large relative to bank capital.

Second, it appears that the nightmare of bankers, regulators, and journalists that massive LDC defaults will paralyze the U.S. banking system are not warranted on economic grounds. Non-OPEC LDCs are not a homogeneous group, as these results have indicated. Country-specific risks, which are relatively independent across borrowers, are, statistically speaking, far more important to the economic health of the countries than common factors. Indeed, it is misleading to speak of the aggregate exposure of the banking system to non-OPEC LDCs as it implies a much greater uniformity across countries than appears to be the case.

Country Risk and International Bank Lending
H. Robert Heller

The rapid increase in the external indebtedness of the developing countries has generated considerable interest in the risk associated with international lending. In turn, country-risk assessment has assumed increasing significance as a determinant of the willingness to engage in international lending—especially on behalf of commercial banks.

The Importance of Bank Lending for
Developing Countries

During the decade of the seventies the developing countries gained large-scale access to international financial markets. In particular, they were able to obtain ever increasing amounts of loans through the international commercial banking system. During the seventies, the total external debt of the developing countries increased approximately 500 percent, while their debt to international commercial banks increased from $88 billion in 1975 to $265 billion in 1980.[3]

This increased access to foreign capital on commercial terms enabled the developing countries to achieve a rather remarkable growth record. For instance, World Bank data[4] indicate that the low-income developing countries grew at an average annual rate of 3.6 percent during 1970–1978, while the middle-income countries achieved an average annual growth rate of 5.7 percent. These data exclude the capital-surplus oil-exporting countries, which grew even faster at 6.0 percent. In contrast, the industrialized countries were able to achieve only a 3.2 percent annual growth rate during the same period.

What makes this amazing record for the developing countries even more remarkable is that they were able to better the growth record of the industrial countries in all sectors taken separately: agriculture, industry, manufacturing, and services.

Most of those few developing countries that failed to grow during the 1970–1978 period were troubled by noneconomic difficulties. The *World Development Report 1980* lists a total of six countries with declining GDP for that period: Angola, Jamaica, Madagascar, Mozambique, Uganda, and Upper Volta.

1980 was a watershed year for the developing countries in their relationship towards commercial banks. In that year the total assets of developing countries deposited in international commercial banks reached the same level of $250 billion as their total liabilities to commercial banks. By this time, the developing countries had reached equality as lenders and borrowers, thereby erasing their traditional position as net-capital importers through the banking system. Of course, individual developing countries were in a net borrower or lender position, but that is no different from the industrialized countries. In effect, the categorical distinction between developing and industrialized countries was eliminated in 1980 at least as far as commercial bank lending is concerned. The developing countries are from now on just as important on the liability and the asset side of the balance sheet.

Considering this increasing degree of financial interdependence, it is self-evident that a good debt-service record and future debt-service capacity are in the interest of both the borrowers and the lenders. For the borrowing country a good debt-service capacity not only assures continued access to international credit markets, but it will also influence the terms at which that credit will be available. For the lending institution adequate debt-service capacity is also the basis for a mutually advantageous future business relationship. The maintenance of a good debt-service capacity is therefore of importance to both borrower and lenders.

Country-Risk-Assessment Techniques

Much research on the country risk associated with international lending has been conducted during the last decade, and the quantitative techniques employed have become increasingly sophisticated. This is not the place to review the entire literature in detail. Instead, I will briefly describe how country-risk analysis is performed at Bank of America and present some of the conclusions of that work regarding the debt-servicing capacity of various country groups.

Bank of America's country-evaluation system focuses systematically on a country's capacity to service its foreign debt. This includes an assessment of both internal and external influences that are judged to have a potential impact on the country's debt-servicing capacity, including those factors that may be beyond a country's control.

Bank of America's country-risk program utilizes a three-pronged evaluation system. It is composed of: (1) a set of leading indicators pertaining to a country's debt-service capacity; (2) a judgmental economic indicator; and (3) a judgmental political indicator. It was thought that such a system would combine both quantitative and qualitative factors in an optimal fashion.

The Debt-Service Capacity Index

The debt-service capacity index was developed by the bank's economics group, which conducted exhaustive econometric tests utilizing the bank's international economic and financial data bank. This comprehensive data bank covers in detail over eighty countries and contains basic information on virtually every country in the world. In their research, the group was guided by the soundness of the underlying economic theory, the verification of the theoretical hypothesis through empirical research, and the accessibility of data and computational ease.

On the basis of this research, a debt-service capacity model was developed based on the results of economic and statistical analysis. This debt-service capacity model is akin to a set of leading economic indicators and focuses on a country's ability to avoid arrears, reschedulings, and actual default on its foreign debt.

In the estimation procedure the economic characteristics of the countries included in the study for, say, 1974 were correlated with the debt-service record of the country during the following three years (1975–1977) to derive the basic medium-term, (three-years) debt-service-capacity indicator. By applying the formula derived to hard 1979 data, the country's debt-service capacity for 1980–1983 period can then be assessed. The index forms Bank of America's basic debt-service indicator. It should be emphasized that the index is based on actual hard data obtainable and not on economic forecasts that inevitably include already certain judgmental factors.

It was found that a country's ability to service its external debt in a timely fashion is related in a statistically significant fashion to three broad groups of variables: (a) its external liquidity situation, (b) the fiscal and monetary policies pursued, and (c) its economic structure. The analysis showed that external liquidity factors are particularly relevant in an assessment of a country's debt-service capacity over the short-term; that is, over the following year. Similarly the structural factors tend to dominate in the long run, here defined as the next five-year period. While it was expected that the medium-term index would focus on government policy variables, it actually contains a balanced collection of liquidity, governmental policy, and structural variables. Because the medium-term debt-service index is so well-balanced, it was chosen as the basic indicator of a country's debt-service capacity. This debt-service capacity index can also be used to assess the relative debt-service capacity of different country groups and to make comparisons over time.

The Judgmental Economic Indicator

The judgmental economic indicator ranges from A highest rating through F lowest rating and is based on a questionnaire filled out initially by the bank's country or regional managers. The questionnaire focuses on those factors that are thought to influence a country's debt-service capacity but are not adequately covered in the debt-service index. The structure of the questionnaire is flexible so as to permit analysis of all relevant and possibly unique environmental factors while preserving a consistent framework that is common to all countries.

The questionnaire focuses attention on certain areas considered important for the purpose of assessing a country's debt-service capacity. Specifically, the questionnaire calls for an evaluation of the effectiveness of monetary policy, the government's fiscal policy—including the sources and users of funds—as well as the means of financing the government deficit. An evaluation of regulatory policies in the financial sector is also undertaken. An appraisal of the government's attitude towards domestic and foreign investment follows. The government's economic development program is appraised, and the quality of its management is commented upon. The appraisal of the essentially domestic factors covered so far closes with an analysis of the country's economic structure, focusing on the availability of natural resources, the country's labor force, its infrastructure, and the composition of total output.

Turning to mainly external factors, the country's export and import diversification patterns are studied. Next, the country's access to international sources of credit is evaluated and the exchange rate policy is described and analyzed. Certain special regional considerations, such as membership in trade pacts, are then commented upon, and available sources of concessionary finance are identified. The economic questionnaire closes with an open-ended question pertaining to any other important considerations not covered elsewhere and a level-of-confidence indicator.

After the individual country managers have filled out these questionnaires, the responses are collected and collated at divisional headquarters (London, Tokyo, Caracas, or Los Angeles) and actual ratings are assigned to each country on a preliminary basis. These rating suggestions are then forwarded to Bank of America's San Francisco World Headquarters where they are consolidated and checked for global consistency. The worldwide ratings are then reviewed and approved by senior management of the bank including its chief financial-policy council.

The Judgmental Political Indicator

The political judgmental rating focuses on the political factors affecting a country's ability or willingness to service its foreign debts. It focuses on three general areas of concern: governmental control, the potential for social unrest, and external factors. The section on government control begins with an evaluation of the government's effectiveness in formulating a coherent policy regarding important social and political problems. The institutions designed to provide for a resolution of political and social conflict are assessed next. Other factors considered in this section pertain to the orderly succession of government and institutional structures designed to bring competing influences to bear upon government policy. The section evaluating the potential for social unrest as it might influence the country's debt-service ability follows next. The political questionnaire closes with a set of questions regarding external factors including potential security threats, the country's special relations with the United States, and an assessment of relevant regional alliances in which the country might participate. Again, an indication of the level of confidence in the assessment is required.

The procedure in arriving at political judgment ratings is the same as that for the economic judgmental ratings.

It is important to note that the entire process moves from on-site appraisal by bank officers up to senior management review and approval. The one major addition that occurs as the process moves up the organizational hierarchy is the addition of a global perspective.

Country-Risk-Assessment Results

Bank of America's Debt-Service Capacity Index described earlier can be utilized not only to assess the debt service capacity of one country but also of country groups. Such aggregate indicators are helpful if one wishes to make an assessment regarding the overall debt-service capacity of a number of countries or even the world as a whole.

Such an aggregation of Bank of America's basic (medium-term) debt-service capacitator has shown—on average—remarkably little change during the 1970s. As figure 9-1 shows, the index for the world as a whole has deteriorated only slightly from a score of eighty out of a possible one-

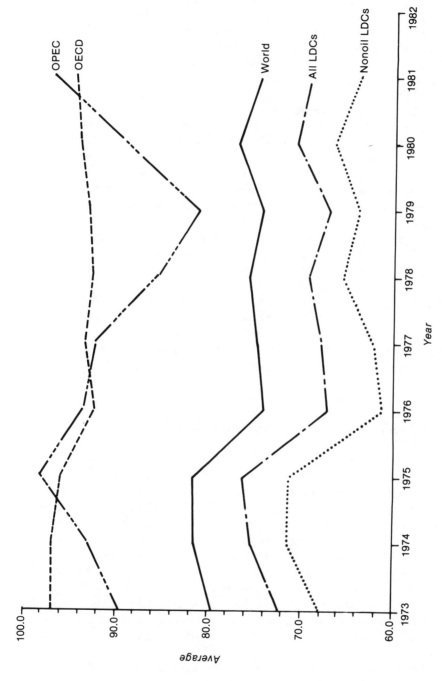

Figure 9–1. Debt-Service Capacity Index

hundred in 1973 to seventy-five in 1981.[5] For all the developing countries the picture is not much different as the Debt-Service Capacity Index changed from seventy-two to sixty-nine over the same period. Even more remarkable is that the nonoil developing countries also showed a remarkable stability in the index, as the index moved from sixty-eight in 1973 to sixty-four in 1981. Given the inherent margin of error contained in such quantitative indexes, these differences are rather minor indeed.

Also, the OECD countries were rather stable in their debt-servicing capacity. For this group of industrialized countries the index changed from ninety-seven in 1973 to ninety-five in 1981. The OPEC group underwent the largest changes. In 1973 its index stood at ninety, then improved in the wake of the first oil price increase to ninety-eight. A period of gradual deterioration followed, which brought the index down to eighty-one by 1979, only to improve again to ninety-seven by 1981 as a result of the second oil price increase.

We may therefore conclude on the basis of this quantitative evidence that the debt-service capacity of the developing countries has remained remarkably good even during the decade of the seventies, which was characterized by very substantial cyclical and structural upheavals in the world economy. Other assessments come to much the same conclusion. For instance, the authoritative IMF report on *External Indebtedness of Developing Countries* finds that "in sum, for developing countries, . . . by the end of the 1970s, . . . the general debt situation does not seem to be substantially different from that at the beginning of the decade."[6]

Some Thoughts on Risk in International Bank Lending
Arturo C. Porzecanski

I would like to share with you my thoughts on the economic and political risks we in the international banking community face when engaged in lending to public and private entities located overseas, and especially in developing countries. I will do this by raising and then answering two main questions. The first is: have these risks increased appreciably over the past three to five years? The second one is: will these risks increase greatly—perhaps even intolerably—over the next three to five years? To be sure, the risks I am referring to are difficult to measure and, consequently, the answers I will provide are necessarily subjective and personal. And yet, this is the kind of perspective I can offer, based on several years of experience as an international economist specializing in country risk assessment with a leading commercial bank.

My answer to the first question is in the affirmative: in absolute terms, the risks involved in international lending have increased over the last few years—although starting from a very low base. However, these risks have not increased relative to the many other risks encountered by the commercial banks, particularly in their domestic operations. I am quite certain, indeed, that if we could survey the top executives of the internationally most active U.S. banks and we could ask them to name their top three concerns, we would find that international lending risks would seldom show up in the list. The level and volatility of interest rates, the existence of legislative constraints to financial intermediation, the future of specific industries—these are the kinds of concerns that are uppermost in the minds of our industry's leaders. And, as I will explain, there are good reasons for this.

However, let me point out first why I believe that the risks have grown in absolute terms. They have done so because the size of our international loan portfolio has increased relative to capital and because our concentration problem has not been eased. The available data compiled by the Federal Reserve System show that for the top nine U.S. banks, loans outstanding to nonoil LDCs—a misnomer since countries like Mexico are still included in this category—rose from $29 billion as of end-1977 to $49 billion as of end-1980. My estimate is that this figure reached $60 billion by early 1982. When measured in relation to the combined capital of these nine banks, lending to nonoil LDCs and whatever risks are associated with it have increased from 156 percent of capital as of December 31, 1977, to 204 percent as of end-1980, and possibly to 225 percent of bank capital as of early 1982.

The loans made by the same nine largest banks continue to be concentrated in few countries: just as they did in 1977, approximately 70 percent of total loans to nonoil developing countries are, as of the end of 1981, to government and private entities in six nations (namely, Brazil, Mexico, South Korea, Argentina, the Philippines, and Taiwan). In other words, a major portion of the leading banks' exposure remains tied up in six countries and it alone is currently equivalent to over 150 percent of the banks' capital base.

The economic and political risks have also grown over time because the international environment has turned increasingly hostile to our debtors. As is well known, high oil prices, slow real economic growth in industrial countries, high interest rates in the Euro-currency market, falling commodity prices, and other factors are impacting ever more adversely on developing countries; and, their ability to service debts contracted earlier with the commercial banks surely is not what it was several years ago.

I hasten to repeat, however, that in my view the risks involved in overseas lending (especially to nonoil developing countries), while higher now than before, are still low relative to other sources of risk. I would like to cite, as an example, one statistic that may explain the absence of grave concern with international lending risks that I sense among top banking executives.

I am referring to our loan loss experience, both in absolute and in relative terms. Consider that while for the ten largest U.S. banks, international earnings as a percent of total earnings have tended to decline somewhat from a peak of 52 percent in 1975 to 47 percent in 1980 (averaging 48 percent during 1975–1980), net international loan losses as a percent of total losses peaked at 29 percent in 1977 and were 15 percent in 1980 (averaging 21 percent throughout 1975–1980). In other words, as far as can be measured through loan charge-offs data, international lending appears to entail much less risk—now as well as several years ago—than does domestic lending. Furthermore, these loan loss statistics reveal that the more industrial Western European economies tend to have a proportionally higher loss record than do the less developed countries. The data suggest that, on the whole, the economic and political risks the commercial banks face in developing countries are less damaging and less significant than the more usual credit risks entailed in lending to mostly private individuals and corporations in industrial societies.

As concerns the second question I raised, namely, whether the risks in international bank lending are likely to increase greatly or perhaps intolerably in the future, my answer is in the negative. I base this opinion on two key facts. In the first place, and despite unfavorable global economic circumstances, the developing countries to which the major U.S. banks have lent significant amounts are making visible progress. They are in the midst of an adjustment process that already is yielding favorable results. For instance, Morgan Guaranty's estimates and projections available for the Conference on Crises in the Economic and Financial Structure of the current account deficit (in the balance of payments) as a percent of Gross Domestic Product for the six developing countries mentioned earlier, show that in four cases the external deficits would be lower in both 1981 and 1982 than they were in 1980. In the remaining two cases, we anticipated at the time of the conference that their current account disequilibria would be smaller in 1982 than in 1981. Of course, further progress is likely to be evident in 1983 when economic growth in the OECD countries, and thus primary commodity prices, will have recuperated.

Additional proof of successful adjustment to a world of high oil prices and high interest rates is provided by the evolution of these countries' exports of goods and services relative to their imports of everything except petroleum and their outflows due to interest payments. The idea here is to highlight the evolution of the other areas of the current account by excluding, for the sake of closer analysis, the two exogenous factors that have blurred and sometimes offset real progress in export promotion and in import containment. According to this *adjusted* and admittedly partial measure of the current account, it is noteworthy that five of the six countries actually are running surpluses of increasing size. Specifically, Morgan Guaranty is anticipating that in 1982, when excluding net oil imports and gross interest payments on their total foreign debt, Brazil will record an external surplus of about 3 percent of GDP, the Philippines will have a surplus equivalent to 2½ percent of GDP, and Korea will register a surplus of almost 7½ percent of GDP. These adjusted current account positions compare quite favorably with 1979 surpluses of a mere 0.5 percent, 2 percent, and 1 percent of GDP, respectively.

Another important fact that leads me to believe that the risks of default will not become widespread is that the countries that are not adjusting successfully, and that are seeking or have sought debt relief, are undergoing a wrenching, traumatic experience that is an object lesson to other countries. I need not remind you of the price (in terms of lost output and investment, high unemployment, and social trauma) that countries with external debt difficulties are having to pay because they have interrupted their access to international capital markets. This high price, in my view, ensures that most borrowers, and particularly the major borrowing countries, will not look upon debt rescheduling or refinancings as easy ways out. The lesson is clear: countries that lose their creditworthiness and do not service their foreign debts promptly and regularly are only getting themselves into deeper trouble. They can refuse to repay according to the original terms of various loan agreements, but surely they cannot force the commercial banks to supply them with the capital (that is, with the new money) that they require to attain high rates of economic growth.

The existing penalties to errant debtors are, in short, a necessary part of a self-regulating mechanism that minimizes, and will continue to minimize, the risks entailed in international bank lending.

Notes

1. These countries include Brazil, Mexico, Korea, the Philippines, Spain, Argentina, Hong Kong, Greece, Columbia, Chile, Yugoslavia, Ecuador, Thailand, Panama, and Peru. All data were taken from the International Monetary Fund's: *International Financial Statistics.* Taiwan was excluded as data were not available on a basis consistent with other countries.

2. The methodology is discussed in detail in Laurie S. Goodman, "Bank Lending to Non-OPEC LDCs: Are Risks Diversifiable?", *Quarterly Review,* Federal Reserve Bank of New York (Summer) 1981. The results and conclusions presented here are abridged from this article.

3. Bank for International Settlements, *Annual Reports,* various issues.

4. World Bank, *World Development Report 1980,* p. 112–113.

5. An unweighted average index score is utilized in these comparisons.

6. IMF Occasional Paper No. 3, Washington, D.C., May 1981, p. 6.

Part IV
Speculative Bubbles

10 Bubbles, Runs, and Gold Monetization

Robert P. Flood and
Peter M. Garber

This chapter is intended as an exposition of recent research in three areas: bubbles, runs, and gold monetization. In particular, we develop a series of simple linear examples designed to illustrate the concepts underlying recent research on bubbles and runs. We will apply these concepts to analyze recent policy proposals to fix the price of gold.

When working with concepts like bubbles and runs, which potentially are very fuzzy, it is important to develop precise definitions at the outset. Therefore, we will expose and discuss first our basic terms and concepts. Later we construct a simple model to illustrate the general ideas presented. Finally we apply these ideas to the policy-relevant problem of fixing the price of gold.

Definitions

Bubbles

The possibility of a market's launching itself onto a price bubble exists when the expected rate of market price change is an important factor determining current market price. While, for years, such a possibility has simultaneously confounded and intrigued economists the recent adoption of the rational-expectations assumption has clarified considerably the nature of price bubbles and has focused widespread professional attention on the problem. The rational-expectations assumption has stimulated progress because its application imposes a precise mathematical structure on the relationship between actual and expected price movements.

With expectations rational in the sense of John Muth (1961), agents' anticipations of actual price movements are mathematical expectations, conditional on an information set that may include some structural knowledge of a particular economic model. Thus, a researcher can determine an expression for agents' expectations by manipulating a proposed model. However, if the expected rate of market-price change influences the

This research was supported in part by National Science Foundation Grant SES–7926807. The views in this chapter are those of the authors and not necessarily those of the Federal Reserve System.

current market price, the researcher using the rational-expectations assumption often cannot produce a unique expression for agents' expectations. In its simplest form, the indeterminacy arises because only one market-equilibrium condition exists; but the researcher requires solutions for two endogenous variables—market price and the expected rate of market-price change.

A bubble can arise when the actual market price depends positively on its own expected rate of change, as normally occurs in asset markets. Since agents forming rational expectations do not make systematic prediction errors, the positive relationship between price and its expected rate of change implies a similar relationship between price and its actual rate of change. In such conditions, the arbitrary, self-fulfilling expectation of price changes may drive actual price changes independently of market fundamentals; we refer to such a situation as a *price bubble*. An explicit definition of market fundamentals depends on a particular model's structure; indeed, the very notion of a bubble can make no sense in the absence of a precise model detailing a market's operation. Without such a model, it is impossible both to define market fundamentals and to isolate the trajectory characteristic of a bubble. We employ specific models to advance exact definitions in the following section.

Many attempts have been made to divert research attention from bubbles through the use of a priori reasoning. Since bubbles cannot exist in some special cases of some models, it is often argued that bubbles should be ignored in all models and in data as well. While the conclusion of such reasoning may be correct, we do not accept the logic of the argument. Just as there are some special cases of models in which bubbles cannot exist in equilibrium there are other perfectly good maximizing models that do not preclude bubbles. Hence, in our view the existence and importance of bubbles is an issue not resolvable at the level of theory. Further, existing empirical work attempting to identify bubbles has turned up mixed results. Flood and Garber (1980) could not reject the hypothesis that no price-level bubble was present in Germany during 1919–1923 hyperinflation. However, Flood, Garber, and Scott (1981) and Burmeister and Wall (1980), do reject the no-bubbles hypothesis for the German episodes. The tests applied in the latter two studies are different from those in Flood and Garber (1980) in that they employ different statistical tests. Thus, one may conclude only that existing empirical work is inconclusive about the relevance of bubbles.

Runs, Panics, and Collapses

Probably through association with the bank panic of 1933 the notion of a *run* in economics is a highly sensitive issue, attributed to mass hysteria rather than to market fundamentals. In their 1978 article Salant and Henderson removed much of the mystery from the economic phenomenon called a run as a predictable event. In Salant and Henderson a run is an event that terminates a price-fixing scheme. For instance some economic agent (perhaps the government) may stand ready to buy or sell a particular item at a fixed price. The viability of such a price-fixing scheme depends on the agent's maintaining a stock of the item. If other agents perceive that the price-fixing regime is temporary; that is, that price will rise eventually, then anticipating capital gains, these agents draw down the stock that backs the price-fixing scheme. If the stock is depleted entirely in one final discrete withdrawal, this event is categorized as a run.

Systematic bank collapses are the most famous examples of the phenomenon. In this instance a bank fixes the price of its deposits in terms of government currency. The bank holds reserves of government currency; and if the depositors fear a possible capital loss on their deposits, they will deplete bank reserves, possibly with one final massive withdrawal, forcing the bank to cease fixing the price of its deposits. Bank runs are studied in detail in Flood and Garber (1981a).

The phenomenon of a currency crisis, prevalent in the 1960s and early 1970s, is closely connected with a run on government foreign exchange reserves. In this instance a government announces a fixed price for its currency in terms of the currency of at least one other country. To make this price-fixing scheme viable the government must hold foreign currency reserves. A government's stock of foreign currency reserves may be depleted slowly through balance-of-payments deficits. If speculators can see no end to the deficits, then they anticipate the eventual demise of the fixed-rate regime. To exploit fully any capital gains associated with the ending of the fixed-rate regime speculators may draw down government foreign exchange reserves in one final massive withdrawal—a run. Such foreign exchange market runs have been studied by Krugman (1979), and Flood and Garber (1981b), and will be studied in the next section.

Bubbles and Runs: Basic Techniques

We will illustrate common techniques used to analyze bubbles and runs in the context of a simple linear example of the market for foreign exchange. The model is drawn directly from Flood and Garber (1981b).

$$\frac{M^d}{S} = \beta - \alpha(\dot{S}/S); \alpha, \beta > 0 \tag{10.1}$$

$$M^s = F + D \tag{10.2}$$

$$\dot{D} = \mu \qquad , \mu > 0 \qquad\qquad (10.3)$$

Equation 10.1 is a semireduced form of the money demand function (see the appendix 10A for a derivation of 10.1). In 10.1, M^d is nominal money demand, S is the exchange rate, $\dot{S} = dS/d\text{(time)}$, α and β are positive constants. Equation 10.2 is the definition of the money supply, M^s. Recall that the supply of high-power money, H, is equal to the right-hand side of the central bank balance sheet. For the Fed this is roughly currency outstanding, C, plus member bank deposits, MBD. Thus, $H = C + MBD$. Since balance sheets must balance, high-power money must also equal the asset side of the central bank balance sheet, which is roughly international reserves, F, plus domestic credit, D. Hence, $H = C + MBD = F + D$. Since we use a high-power money demand function our money supply is high-powered money. Thus $M^s = F + D$, which is equation 10.2. Equation 10.3 states that D is rising at the constant rate μ.

When exchange rates are fixed the central bank must accommodate money demand so F is endogenous. When exchange rates are freely flexible the central bank does not intervene in foreign exchange markets so F is a constant. All of our variables (M, S, $\dot{S}$, F, D, $\dot{D}$,) have an implicit time dimension, which we suppress now but will use when required for clarity.

Flexible Exchange Rates and Bubbles

When the exchange rate is flexible, F is constant and S is endogenous. One may "conjecture" that 10.1–10.3 yields a linear exchange-rate equation of the form $S = \lambda_0 + \lambda_1 M$. When we substitute this conjecture into the model we find that it is a solution for $\lambda_0 = \alpha\mu/\beta^2$ and $\lambda_1 = 1/\beta$. Thus, we have:[1]

$$S(t) = \frac{\alpha\mu}{\beta^2} = \frac{M(t)}{\beta} \qquad\qquad (10.4)$$

where t is a time dimension. Equation 10.4 gives the market fundamentals solution for the exchange rate and this equation is depicted as the solid line in figure 10–1. Given a value of $M(t)$ we locate $S(t)$ on this solid line if only market fundamentals govern S.

However, in addition to the market fundamentals listed in equation 10.4 there may be an arbitrary element in the exchange-rate solution. Hence another trial solution is $S(t) = \lambda_0 + \lambda_1 M(t) + A(t)$, where $A(t)$ is arbitrary. When we substitute this new trial solution into the model we find:

$$S(t) = \frac{\alpha\mu}{\beta^2} + \frac{M(t)}{\beta} + Ae^{(\beta/\alpha)t} \qquad\qquad (10.5)$$

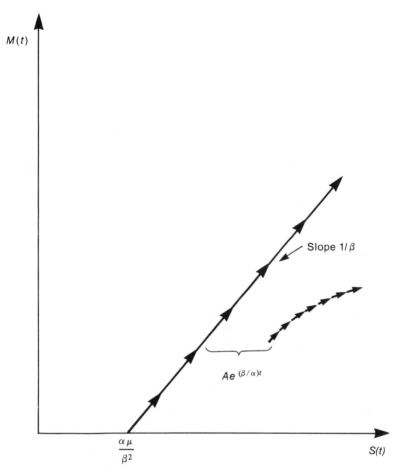

Figure 10-1. Flexible Exchange Rate Solution

where A is an initial value of the arbitrary element $A(t) = Ae^{(\beta/\alpha)t}$. Equation 10.5 is shown for positive A as the dashed line in figure 10-1.

The term $Ae^{(\beta/\alpha)t}$, which is the difference between 10.4 and 10.5 is an exchange-rate bubble. If present for long, such a bubble should be readily recognizable in the data due its high level of acceleration relative to market fundamentals.

We emphasize the point that any positive value of A can result from rational expectations and remain consistent with the model. However, negative values of A are excluded (for this model) since they would imply that S would become negative in finite time. This is an artifact of the linear nature of the model.

Fixed Rates and Runs

When the exchange rate is fixed, F is endogeneous and S is constant at $\bar{S}$. For fixed rates the model 10.1–10.3 specializes to:

$$F(t) + D(t) = \beta \bar{S} \qquad (10.6)$$

We know that D is rising at the rate μ. Thus, since $F + D$ is constant, F must be falling at the rate of μ. However, reserves are finite so the government cannot pay out reserves at a finite rate forever. Eventually the fixed-rate regime must collapse and we will now discuss the final run associated with that collapse.

To study the collapse we first investigate the market for foreign exchange *after* the collapse and then we examine the transition to the postcollapse environment. If there is to be a run on a government's foreign-exchange reserves on some date, T, then on that date government reserves go to zero and the exchange-rate pegging operation must cease in the absence of a change in the policy generating domestic credit. Since in our model such a run is a foreseen event, speculators will force the run to occur at an instant such that the level of the exchange rate will not jump. To understand this crucial point suppose that speculators anticipate a run at date T and expect the exchange rate to jump upward at date T. Since reserves are finite, each individual speculator has an incentive to borrow as much as he can and buy all of the government's reserve stock *at the instant before T*. Since each speculator has an incentive to run the reserves prior to T, the run would take place prior to T. This implies that speculators would not be behaving optimally if they anticipate both a run and an exchange-rate jump on a fixed future date. A speculative equilibrium run can be anticipated for a future date only if no exchange-rate jump is anticipated for that date.

The distinctive feature of an anticipated run on government foreign exchange reserves is a discrete downward jump in reserves and the money supply with no jump in the exchange rate. The money-supply path surrounding the run date, T, is shown in figure 10–2. From date zero until date T the money supply is constant although its components are not. D is rising at the rate μ and F is falling at the same rate. At date T reserves are run and the money supply falls from $M(T_-) = F(T_-) + D(T)$ to $M(T_+) = D(T)$.[2] From date T onward the exchange rate floats and $M(t) = D(t)$, $t > T$. During the floating-rate period we know that in the absence of bubbles, equation 10.4 must give the value of the exchange rate. In particular:

$$S(T) = \frac{\alpha \mu}{\beta^2} + \frac{D(T)}{\beta} \qquad (10.7)$$

With fixed rates we had (from (6)) $\bar{S} = 1/\beta(F(T) + D(T))$. The argument that the exchange rate is not expected to jump at T implies $\bar{S} = S(T)$. Use these facts in 10.7 to obtain:

$$F(T) = \frac{\alpha\mu}{\beta} \qquad (10.8)$$

Equation 10.8 gives the size of the run on government reserves. To find the date of the run, T, we must know when the reserves reach the level $\alpha\mu/\beta$. Since $\dot{F}(t) = -\mu$, we know $F(t) = F(0) - \mu t$. Hence, $F(T) = F(0) - \mu T$. Use this fact in 10.8 to obtain:

$$T = \frac{F(0)}{\mu} - \frac{\alpha}{\beta} \qquad (10.9)$$

Equation 10.9 predicts the date of the run. To use the equation normalize the current instant in time to zero, find current reserves, $F(0)$, and insert $F(0)$ into equation 10.9. The resulting value of T is the amount of time until the run. Notice in 10.9 that $F(0)/\mu$, shown on the horizontal axis in figure

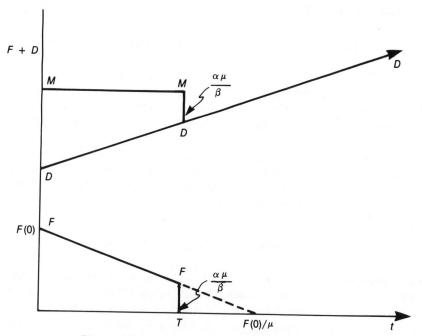

Figure 10-2. Dynamics of Monetary Aggregates

10–2, is the amount of time it would take reserves to go to zero if there were no run. The term $-\alpha/\beta$ is a correction factor that hastens the time of the run in order to avoid a foreseen exchange-rate jump.

The foreign exchange-market run we have studied so far is a run based entirely on market fundamentals. However, bubbles can alter the timing of a run. Suppose that after a run the exchange rate were not governed only by market fundamentals but also contained an arbitrary bubble element. Then, instead of 10.7 we would have:

$$S(T) = \frac{\alpha\mu}{\beta^2} + \frac{D(T)}{\beta} + A(T), \tag{10.10}$$

where

$$A(T + t) = A(T)e^{(\beta/q)t}$$

We may use 10.10, as we used 10.7, to find:

$$F(T) = \frac{\alpha\mu}{\beta} + \beta A(T) \tag{10.11}$$

and since $F(T) = F(0) - \mu T$

$$T = \frac{F(0)}{\mu} - \frac{\beta A(T)}{\mu} - \frac{\alpha}{\beta} \tag{10.12}$$

Equation 10.12 reveals that the arbitrary element, $A(T)$, if positive, will reduce T and thus make the run more imminent. Indeed, $A(T)$ can be set to precipitate the run immediately. This would involve setting $A(T) = [F(0)/\beta] - [\alpha\mu/\beta^2]$. The run on the fixed exchange-rate system would occur even if μ, the growth rate of domestic credit, were set to zero. Therefore, to the extent that a floating exchange-rate system is made unstable and indeterminate by the possibility of speculative bubbles so also is a fixed exchange-rate system unstable.

Gold Monetization: Discipline of Collapse

In the previous section we developed in the context of a simple example techniques useful to the current policy problem of gold monetization. Proponents of gold monetization favor a gold standard because they believe that it forces monetary discipline. Opponents of a gold standard, among other arguments, doubt the government's or the private sector's ability to pick the "right gold price." By the right gold price they mean a price low enough to ensure that all gold is not displaced from private uses but high enough to ensure that a gold standard does not collapse in a run on government gold stocks.

In this section we will examine some current proposals to monetize gold, develop a model of an economy operating a Laffer-Lehrman-type gold standard, and study the anatomy of the collapse of such a standard if gold is priced too low.

Gold Monetization—Policy Proposals

Gold and its price have emerged as frequent topics of both academic and government debate. Public attention focused on the gold market when the price of gold surged briefly to $850/ounce by January 1980; by July 1981, the price collapsed to less than $400/ounce.

These price fluctuations have been coincident with the advent of three lines of thought concerning government gold market policy. First, Salant and Henderson (1978) and Salant (1981) have developed a partial equilibrium gold market model to analyze the interactions between rapid gold-price rises, government gold auctions, and speculative attacks on government gold stocks. Second, Barro (1979) has constructed a model to study money and price dynamics under a version of the historical gold standard. Finally, other economists, led by Laffer (1979) and Lehrman (1980), (1981), have proposed a new monetary gold standard under which the government would maintain a fixed nominal gold price while retaining the freedom to issue money without fixed gold backing. Such a gold standard diverges from the historical gold standard because it does not require a fixed fractional gold backing of each currency unit issued. Rather, it bears a conceptual resemblence to the postwar fixed-exchange-rate regime: governments, which had some autonomy in conducting monetary policy, were constrained by the commitment to hold reserves sufficient to maintain fixed exchange rates.

The concept of gold monetization that we will study here is that proposed by Laffer and Lehrman. In Flood and Garber (1981c) we have studied in detail the Laffer-Lehrman proposal. In particular we investigate the transition to a gold standard, the operation of a gold standard, and a transition from a gold standard. In this section we will examine only the case of an operating gold standard that may be subject to runs on government gold stocks.

As background for our later analysis we now consider the effect on the money stock of a policy to fix the price of gold. If a policy to fix the price of gold is permanently successful, then either currency will dominate gold in private portfolios or portfolio gold and currency will be perfect substitutes. The first case hinges on currency's having a greater convenience than portfolio gold in making transactions. Since the two assets would be permanently fixed in price relative to one another, any purely speculative demand could be equally satisfied by currency balances. Since currency will therefore dominate portfolio gold after the price of gold is fixed, agents will exchange all of their portfolio gold for currency at the fixed gold price. In the absence of sterilizing bond sales, the supply of currency will rise by the value of portfolio gold holdings, thus monetizing existing gold hoards.

Alternatively, if agents perceive that portfolio gold and currency are perfect substitutes, then both the amount of gold that the government must exchange for currency and the ratio of portfolio gold to currency held by the public are indeterminate. However, this indeterminacy is inconsequential; to the extent that portfolio gold is held after price fixing, it exactly fulfills agents' demand for money. Thus, the increase in both supply of and the demand for nominal money at the time of gold's price fixing is identical in both cases.

In summary, when the government fixes the price of gold, the private sector monetizes portfolio gold by cashing in existing speculative hoards, by allowing hoards to fulfill money demands directly, or by a combination of the two. The nature of the government's commitment to exchange gold for currency at a fixed price produces an indeterminacy in the amount of gold exchanged between the government and the public.

Our discussion so far has been predicated on a permanently successful gold-price-fixing policy. However, in U.S. history Schwartz (1981) has documented three gold-price-fixing periods. In each case the price-fixing regime broke down. Therefore, we next construct a model that is useful for studying the collapse of a gold standard.

The Model

The model we will use is an extension of the model of the previous section. It depicts an economy that is already on a gold standard of the type recently proposed for the United States:

$$\frac{M^d}{P} = \gamma - \sigma\left(\frac{\dot{P}}{P}\right) \tag{10.13}$$

$$M^s = \bar{H} + \bar{Q}(R - \bar{R}) \tag{10.14}$$

$$\bar{I} = R + D + G \tag{10.15}$$

$$\dot{D} = v\left[\frac{\delta}{(\bar{Q}/P)} - D\right]$$ (10.16)

Equation 10.13 is a version of the semireduced form money demand function used in the last section (see appendix 10A for derivation). P is the price level, $\dot{P}$ is its rate of change, and γ and σ are fixed positive parameters. Equation 10.14 is the key element linking the gold and money markets. It states that the high-power money supply (M^s) equals $\bar{H}$, the supply existing at the start of the gold standard, plus the money value of any central bank gold sales or purchases since the start of the gold standard, $\bar{Q}(R - \bar{R})$. $\bar{Q}$ is the fixed gold price; R is the physical quantity of gold reserves at the central bank; $\bar{R}$ is the quantity of gold reserves held by the central bank at the time of gold price fixing. Hence, $\bar{Q}(R - \bar{R})$ is the monetary value of government gold market operations and thus gives total money issue due to those operations. Since we assume that the government engages only in gold-market open-market operations the money supply is given by 10.14.

Equation 10.15 states that the fixed total gold stock, $\bar{I}$, is divided among three uses: (1) R, government reserves, (2) D, private consumption and industrial holding, and (3) G, private speculative hoards. While gold's price is fixed we assume private speculative hoards to be zero.[3] However, after a run that collapses a gold standard, G will not be zero.

Equation 10.16 gives the dynamics of consumption and industrial accumulation. Accumulation depends negatively on gold's relative price, $\bar{Q}/P$, and negatively on past gold accumulation, D. v and δ are positive constants.[4] The slow accumulation reflects some costs in quickly transforming raw gold into finished products.

Equations 10.13–10.16 form a system of linear differential equations in the variables P and R. For a permanently viable gold standard the price-level solution of the model is:

$$P(t) = \pi_0 + \pi_1 R(t)$$ (10.17)

where

$$\pi_0 = \frac{\bar{H} - \bar{Q}\bar{R} + v\bar{I}\pi_1}{\beta + (\sigma v \pi_1/\bar{Q})}$$

$$\pi_1 = \frac{\bar{Q}}{2}\left\{-\left[\frac{\sigma v + \beta}{\sigma v}\right] + \sqrt{\left[\frac{\sigma v + \beta}{\sigma v}\right]^2 + \frac{4}{\sigma v}}\right\}$$

and t is a time dimension. This solution is the line PR in figure 10–3. Figure 10–3 also contains the lines $\dot{P}P$ and $\dot{R}R$, these lines show respectively the P,

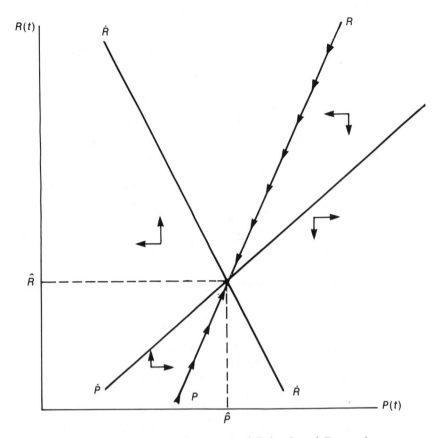

Figure 10-3. Reserve and Price Level Dynamics

R combinations such that $\dot{P} = 0$ and the P, R combinations such that $\dot{R} = 0$. All three lines meet at the model's steady state $\hat{P}$, $\hat{R}$, with:

$$\hat{P} = \frac{\bar{H} + \bar{Q}(\bar{I} - \bar{R})}{\beta + \delta} \qquad (10.18a)$$

$$\hat{R} = \frac{\beta \bar{I} + \delta(\bar{R} - (\bar{H}/\bar{Q}))}{\beta + \delta} \qquad (10.18b)$$

$R(t)$ is a predetermined variable and $P(t)$ is a currently determined variable. History presents the model with a value of $R(t)$, and the model then determines $P(t)$ to be that value of P such that the $R(t)$, $P(t)$ pair lies on *PR*. The steady state price level depends upon the steady state money stock, upon government fiat $\bar{H}$ and gold purchases, and upon the parameters of money and gold demand. Steady state government reserve holdings depend positively on initial gold reserves and negatively on the gold value of initial high-powered money.

At this stage the model is not pertinent for analyzing the collapse of the gold standard. Perhaps the main lesson in figure 10-3 is that gold standard does not ensure the constancy of the price level. Only at the steady state is P constant at $\hat{P}$.

A Run on Government Gold Stocks

In figure 10-3 we have depicted a positive value of $\hat{R}$. However, from equation 10.18b we can see that $\hat{R}$ need not be positive. Indeed if:

$$\frac{\bar{H}}{\bar{Q}} > \bar{R} + \frac{\beta}{\delta}\bar{I} \qquad (10.19)$$

then $\hat{R}$ will be negative. Since it makes no sense for the government to have a negative gold stock the gold-price-fixing scheme must break down. Our task now is to study the anatomy of such a collapse.

As before we begin our study by considering the position of the economy immediately following the collapse. In the postcollapse world the government has exhausted its stock of gold reserves, $R = 0$. With no open-market operations in markets other than the gold market, the postcollapse money supply is $M = \bar{H} - \bar{Q}\bar{R}$, and the postcollapse price level is the constant $P(t) = (\bar{H} - \bar{Q}\bar{R})/\gamma$, $t \geq T$, where T is the collapse date. Further, at the time of the collapse gold price is fixed at $\bar{Q}$. Given our previous argument about prices after expected runs, Q will not jump at the instant after the run.

Thus, the world following a gold run is confronted with a predetermined relative gold price $\bar{Q}/\{(\bar{H} - \bar{Q}\bar{R})/\gamma\}$, which we refer to as $\bar{q}(T)$. In Flood and Garber (1981c) we have laid out in detail the model that governs the gold market after a run. The result we obtained was that for each value of $\bar{q}(T)$ there corresponds a critical value of government reserves, $R[\bar{q}(T)]$, at which a run will take place. This value is:

$$R[\bar{q}(T)] = (1 - e^{v\eta})\bar{I} + \frac{v\delta}{\bar{q}(T)(v - \rho)}[e^{(v - \rho)\eta} - 1] \qquad (10.20)$$

where

$$\eta \equiv \frac{1}{\rho}\ell n[\sigma/\bar{q}(T)\bar{I}]$$

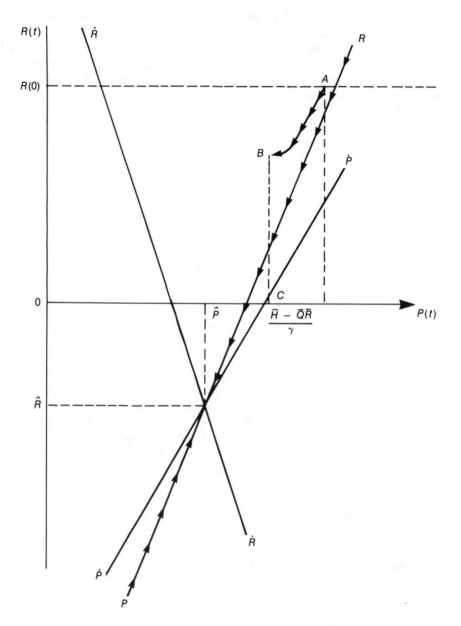

Figure 10–4. Dynamics of a Run on Gold Stocks

and

$\rho \equiv$ the constant real rate of interest.

In figure 10-4 we depict this critical value, $R[q(T)]$, along with other model elements relevant to a run. We know that at the instant following the run we have $R = 0$ and $P = (\bar{H} - \bar{Q}\bar{R})/\gamma$. This is point C on the horizontal axis. Just prior to the run, reserves were $R[q(T)]$ with price still $(H - \bar{Q}\bar{R})/\gamma$, which is point B.

Hence, this economy is at point B at the instant of the run. The economy begins the gold standard with reserves $R(0)$ and there is a unique dynamic path for reserves and prices that goes through point B. This is the path AB. Thus, an economy that inherits $R(0)$ has initial price $P(0)$ and will follow path AB until the run takes place when B is reached. The equation that gives the date of the run is presented in Flood and Garber (1981c). It is a complicated nonlinear expression that can be solved by computer methods given numerical values of the model's parameters.

Some Qualitative Results about Runs

Only one dynamic path goes through point B in figure 10-3. For a given set of the model's parameters the length of the path AB determines the date of the run. This path is always longer the larger is $R(0)$. Hence, as one would expect, for any given gold price larger reserves delay a run.

We have not shown that the run date increases monotonically with $\bar{Q}$. However, we do know (from 10.19) that if:

$$\bar{R} + \frac{\beta \bar{I}}{\delta} \geq \frac{\bar{H}}{\bar{Q}} \tag{10.21}$$

then a run will never take place. Clearly choosing $\bar{Q} \geq [\bar{H}/(\bar{R} + \beta \bar{I}/\delta)]$ will ensure that a run will never take place. Condition 10.21 contains a sufficient condition that conforms with intuition. It is that a run will never take place if:

$$\bar{Q}\bar{R} \geq \bar{H} \tag{10.22}$$

$\bar{Q}\bar{R}$ is the money value of government gold stocks at the outset of the gold standard and $\bar{H}$ is the outstanding high-power fiat stock at the outset of the gold standard. If 10.22 holds, then, the gold standard cannot collapse because there is not enough high-power fiat money to purchase the government gold stock. U.S. government gold stocks are 264 million ounces and the stock of high-power money is \$163.3 billion.[5] Hence any gold price equal to or above \$619/oz. must yield a viable gold standard. Of course \$619/oz. is not the lowest price that will yield a viable gold standard. To find the minimum price we would have to estimate β, δ, and $\bar{I}$.

Concluding Remarks

Until very recently, research involving bubbles and runs was anecdotal in nature. These potentially important economic phenomena were relegated to the realm of the historian. However, the advent of rational expectations forced economists to formulate with precision testable hypothesis concerning bubbles and runs. Research on bubbles is already at the empirical stage. Research on runs is still at the theory stage. However, run-prediction equations, like equation 10.9 or the nonlinear gold run equation in Flood and Garber (1981c) could be implemented at present.

Appendix 10A

In deriving both equation 10.1 and equation 10.13 we start with the following demand function for high-power money:

$$\frac{M^d}{P} = \frac{1}{m}(a_0 - a_1 i + a_2 x) \qquad (10A.1)$$

where m is the high-power-money multiplier, i is the nominal rate of interest, x is the variable summarizing other factors influencing money demand, a_i, $i = 0, 1, 2$ are constants. To derive equation 10.1 we assume purchasing-power parity:

$$P = P^* S \qquad (10A.2)$$

where P^* is the foreign price level, and interest-rate parity:

$$i = i^* + (\dot{S}/S) \qquad (10A.3)$$

where i^* is the foreign interest rate. Use 10A.2 and 10A.3 in 10A.1 to get:

$$\frac{M^d}{S} = \frac{P^*}{m}(a_0 - a_1 i^* + a_2 x) - \frac{P^* a_1}{m}(\dot{S}/S) \qquad (10A.4)$$

For constant P^*, i^*, x, and m we define $\beta \equiv (P^*/m)(a_0 - a_1 i^* + a_2 x)$ and $\alpha \equiv P^* a_1 / m$, which, when substituted into 10A.4, yield equation 10.1 in the text.

To derive equation 10.13 we assume:

$$i = \rho + (\dot{P}/P) \qquad (10A.5)$$

where ρ is constant. Substituting from 10A.5 into 10A.1 yields:

$$\frac{M^d}{P} = \frac{1}{m}(a_0 - a_1 \rho + a_2 x) - \frac{a_1}{m}(\dot{P}/P) \qquad (10A.6)$$

For constant m, ρ, x we define $\gamma \equiv (1/m)(a_0 - a_1 \rho + a_2 x)$ and $\sigma \equiv a_1/m$, which, when substituted into 10A.6, yield equation 10.13 in the text.

Notes

1. Note that μ is not a fixed *percentage* growth rate; it is a fixed level growth rate. Hence, doubling $M(t)$ in equation 10.4 should not be expected to double $S(t)$ as the percentage money growth rate (μ/M) falls with μ fixed.

2. Both M and R are discontinuous at time T. Thus, we use the notation $T_{\pm}$ to indicate right ($+$) and left ($-$) sides of the discontinuity.

3. In Flood and Garber (1981c) we do not require $G = 0$ during the monetized gold period. This is slightly more general but does not alter any of our results.

4. In Flood and Garber (1981c) we have gold accumulation depending on gold's real rate of return. This assumption complicates the model's dynamics but does not alter the position of the steady state, which plays an important role below.

5. U.S. Monetary Base in June, 1981. *Federal Reserve Bulletin,* September 1981, page A14.

References

Barro, R. 1979. "Money and the Price Level Under the Gold Standard," *Economic Journal* March):13–33.

Burmeister, E., and K. Wall. 1980. "Kalman Filtering of Unobserved Rational Expectations with an Application to the German Hyperinflation." Working Paper, University of Virginia.

Flood, R., and P. Garber. 1980. "Market Fundamentals versus Price Level Bubbles: The First Tests," *Journal of Political Economy.* (Aug.). 745–770.

———. 1981a. "A Systematic Banking Collapse in a Perfect Foresight World," N.B.E.R. Working Paper 691.

———. 1981b. "Collapsing Exchange-Rate Regimes and the Indeterminacy Problem." Working Paper, University of Rochester.

———. 1981c. "Gold Monetization and Gold Discipline." Working Paper, University of Rochester.

Flood, R. P. Garber, and L. Scott. 1981. "Further Evidence on Price Level Bubbles." Working Paper, University of Rochester.

Krugman, P. 1979. "A Model of Balance-of-Payments Crisis," *Journal of Money, Credit, and Banking.* (Aug.).

Laffer, A. 1979. "Making the Dollar as Good as Gold," *Los Angeles Times,* Oct. 30.

Lehrman, L. 1980. "Monetary Policy, The Federal Reserve System, and Gold," Working Paper, Lehrman Institute, New York.

———. 1981. "The Case for the Gold Standard." Working Paper, Lehrman Institute, New York.

Muth, J. 1961. "Rational Expectations and the Theory of Price Movements," *Econometrica*. (July):315–335.

Salant, S. 1982. "The Vulnerability of Price Stabilization Schemes to Speculative Attack," *Journal of Political Economy*. Forthcoming.

Salant, S., and D. Henderson. 1978. "Market Anticipation of Government Gold Policies and the Price of Gold," *Journal of Political Economy* (Aug.).

Schwartz, A. 1981. "The Past Role of Gold in the United States." Working Paper, U.S. Gold Commission.

11

Bubbles, Rational Expectations, and Financial Markets

Olivier J. Blanchard and
Mark W. Watson

Economists and financial-market participants often hold quite different views about the pricing of assets. Economists usually believe that given the assumption of rational behavior and of rational expectations, the price of an asset must simply reflect market fundamentals, that is to say, can only depend on information about current and future returns from this asset. Deviations from this market fundamental value are taken as prima facie evidence of irrationality. Market participants on the other hand, often believe that fundamentals are only part of what determines the prices of assets. Extraneous events may well influence the price, if believed by other participants to do so—*crowd psychology* becomes an important determinant of prices.

It turns out that economists have overstated their case. Rationality both of behavior and also of expectations often does not imply that the price of an asset be equal to its fundamental value. In other words, there can be rational deviations of the price from this value—rational bubbles.

The purpose of the chapter is twofold. The first is to characterize the conditions under which such a deviation may appear, the shape it may take and the potential implications of such deviations. The second is to investigate how we can discover such deviations empirically. Some of the chapter is a review of recent work, but much of it is exploratory in nature and will appear a bit tentative. Although this is no doubt due to shortcomings in the authors' thinking, it may also be due to the nature of these bubbles. They present economists and econometricians with many questions to which they may have little to say.

Some may object to our dealing with rational bubbles only. There is little question that most large historical bubbles have elements of irrationality; Charles Kindleberger (1978) gives a fascinating description of many

We are indebted to David and Susan Johnson for research assistance, Jeremy Bulow and David Starrett for useful discussions, and to the National Science Foundation, the Sloan Foundation, and the Harvard Graduate Society for financial support.

historical bubbles. Our justification is the standard one: it is hard to analyze rational bubbles. It would be much harder to deal with irrational bubbles.

Rationality, Arbitrage, and Bubbles

Rationality of behavior and of expectations, together with market clearing, implies that assets are voluntarily held and that no agent can, given his private information and the information revealed by prices, increase his expected utility by reallocating his portfolio.

With many more assumptions, this leads to the standard *efficient market* or *no arbitrage* condition.

Let:

$$R_t = \frac{p_{t+1} - p_t + x_t}{p_t}$$

then

$$E(R_t|\Omega_t) = r$$

or equivalently

$$E(p_{t+1}|\Omega_t - p_t + x_t = rp_t \tag{11.1}$$

p_t is the price of the asset, x_t the direct return. We shall refer to x_t as the *dividend,* although it may take, depending on the asset, pecuniary or nonpecuniary forms. R_t is therefore the rate of return on holding the asset, which is the sum of the dividend price ratio and the capital gain. Ω_t is the information set at time t, assumed common to all agents. The condition therefore states that the expected rate of return on the asset is equal to the interest rate r, assumed constant.

Among the assumptions needed to get equation 11.1 some are inessential and could be relaxed at the cost of increased notational complexity. These are the assumptions of a constant interest rate, no constraints on short sales, and risk neutrality. One assumption is, however, of more consequence: it is that, at least after having observed the price, all agents have the same information. As we shall show, bubbles can exist even in this case and these bubbles would remain even if agents had differential information. The question is, however, whether differential information allows for a larger class of bubbles and whether some aspects of real world bubbles involve differential information. We shall return to this issue—with not much to say—after we define bubbles. (Note also that because of the common information assumption, equation 11.1 is stronger than the usual efficient market formulation, which is that, *for the subset of information common to all agents,* ω_t, the following relation holds:

$$E(p_{t+1}|\omega_t) - p_t + x_t = rp_t$$

Given the assumption of rational expectations and that agents do not forget, so that $\Omega_t \subseteq \Omega_{t+1}$, we can solve equation 11.1 recursively forward, using :

$$E(E\ (\ .\ |\Omega_{t+i})|\Omega_t) = E(\ .\ |\Omega_t), \qquad \forall i \geq 0$$

Thus the following p_t^* is a solution to equation 11.1:

$$p_t^* = \sum_{i=0}^{\infty} \theta^{i+1} E(x_{t+i}|\Omega_t), \qquad \theta \equiv (1+r)^{-1} < 1 \qquad (11.2)$$

p^* is the present value of expected dividends and thus can be called the *market fundamental* value of the asset. (The term is standard in financial markets. It was introduced in economics in a similar context by Robert Flood and Peter Garber [1980]). p^* is, however, not the only solution to 11.1. Any p_t of the following form is a solution as well:

$$p_t = \sum_{i=0}^{\infty} \theta^{i+1} E(x_{t+1}|\Omega_t) + c_t \ = p_t^* + c_t,$$

with

$$E(c_{t+1}|\Omega_t) = \theta^{-1}c_t \qquad (11.3)$$

Thus the market price can deviate from its market fundamental value without violating the arbitrage condition. As $\theta^{-1} > 1$, this deviation c_t must, however be expected to grow over time.[1]

Can this deviation c_t embody the popular notion of a bubble, namely movements in the price, apparently unjustified by information available at the time—taking the form of a rapid increase followed by a burst or at least a sharp decline? The following three examples give paths of c_t that satisfy equation 11.3 and seem to fit this notion.

The simplest is that of a deterministic bubble, $c_t = c_0\theta^{-t}$. In this case the higher price is justified by the higher capital gain and the deviations grow exponentially. To be rational, such an increase in the price must continue forever, making such a deterministic bubble implausible. Consider, therefore, the second example:

$$c_t = (\pi\theta)^{-1}c_{t-1} + \mu_t \qquad \text{with probability } \pi$$

$$= \mu_t \qquad \qquad \text{with probability } 1 - \pi \qquad (11.4)$$

where

$$E(\mu_t | \Omega_{t-1}) = 0$$

How will such a bubble look? In each period, the bubble will remain, with probability π, or crash, with probability $1 - \pi$. While the bubble lasts, the actual average return is higher than r, so as to compensate for the risk of a crash. The average duration will be of $(1 - \pi)^{-1}$. There can be many minor extensions of this example, which also appear to capture certain aspects of bubbles. The probability that the bubble ends may well be a function of how long the bubble has lasted, or of how far the price is from market fundamentals. If π increases for some period of time, c_t will be growing at a decreasing exponential expected rate; if π decreases, the higher probability of a crash leads to an acceleration while the bubble lasts.

In these two examples, the bubble proceeds independently of the fundamental value. There is no reason for this to be true as the last example shows. Consider a war-related stock that pays 1 every period if there is a war, and 0 if there is no war. Suppose a war starts and in each period there is a probability π that the war goes on, a probability $(1 - \pi)$ that it stops forever. The fundamental value is therefore equal to:

$$p_t^* = \sum_{i=0}^{\infty} \theta^{i+1} E(x_{t+i} | \Omega_t) = \sum_{i=0}^{\infty} \theta^{i+1} \pi^i = \theta(1 - \theta\pi)^{-1}$$

Furthermore, it is constant during the duration of the war. The price may, however, increase above p^* in anticipation of future increases during the war. For example, the following bubble might arise:

$$c_t = c_0$$

$$c_{t+i} = (\theta\pi)^{-1} c_{t+i-1} \qquad \text{if there is war at } t+i,$$

$$= 0 \qquad \text{if there is no war at } t+i.$$

This will lead to an increase in the price above its fundamental value initially, a further increase during the war, and a crash in both the fundamental value and the bubble when the war ends.

Now that a definition and examples of bubbles have been given, we may return to the simplifying assumptions made to obtain equation 11.1. What if agents were risk averse? As the last two examples show, bubbles are likely to increase the risk associated with holding the asset. If agents are risk averse, a higher expected return will be required for agents to hold it. Thus, the price will have to be expected to grow even faster than in equation 11.3. If the probability of a crash increases, for example, the price, in the event the crash does not take place, will have to increase faster not only to compensate for the increased probability of a fall but also to compensate for the large risk involved in holding the asset.

What if agents do not have the same information? Each agent will have his own perception of the fundamental value, given by equation 11.3, with the agent's information set Ω_{it} replacing Ω_t. As agents may not have the same fundamental value, they will not perceive the same bubble. There will be agent-specific bubbles, defined as the difference between the price and the agent's perception of the fundamental value. These bubbles must still satisfy the second part of equation 11.3, with Ω_{it} replacing Ω_t: they must be expected to grow exponentially, at rate θ^{-1}. Could it then be that some agents in the market know that there is a bubble while others do not? A typical speculation scheme of the 1920s (Thomas and Morgan Witts 1979) was the creation of a high volume of buying by traders having the reputation of being informed, in the hope of creating additional buying by uninformed traders and a subsequent bubble. If such schemes were consistent with rationality of uninformed traders, we might gain insights on how bubbles start. At this stage, however, we do not know the answer (Tirole, forthcoming, makes some progress in this direction).

Bubbles and Transversality Conditions

The previous section has shown only that arbitrage does not by itself prevent bubbles. Could there be, however, other conditions imposed either institutionally or from market clearing or implied by rationality such that bubbles can in fact be ruled out? This section considers whether such conditions may exist.

As any deviation c_t must satisfy condition 11.3, this implies by successive iteration:

$$\lim_{i \to \infty} E(c_{t+i}|\Omega_t) = +\infty \text{ if } c_t > 0$$

$$= -\infty \text{ if } c_t < 0 \qquad (11.5)$$

This is true even for the last two examples. Although the probability that the bubble ends tends to 1 as the horizon increases, the very large and increasing value of the price if the bubble does not end implies that the expected value of the price increases as the horizon increases.

Condition 11.5 is clearly impossible to satisfy for any asset redeemable at a given price at a given date. For such assets, the price must equal the par value on that date: the deviation must be 0 on that date. Working backwards, the deviation must be 0 today. Thus there cannot be bubbles on bonds, except on perpetuities.

Condition 11.5 also implies that, at least for the model considered here, there cannot be negative bubbles. A negative value of c_t today implies that there is a positive probability, possibly very small, that at some time $t + i$, $c_{t + i}$ will be large and negative enough to make the price negative. If the asset can be disposed of at no cost, its price cannot in fact be negative;[2] rationality implies that c_t cannot be negative today. This argument may, however, be pushing rationality a bit too far. For negative values of c_t, the probability of the price becoming negative may be so small, and the future time so far as to be considered—nearly rationally—irrelevant by market participants.

Apart from institutional boundary conditions, have we exhausted the restrictions imposed by rationality? Bubbles resemble Ponzi games. Ponzi games that grow too fast are inconsistent with rationality. Isn't it the same for bubbles? It may indeed be.

Suppose first that there is a finite number of infinitely lived players—market participants. If the price is below the market fundamental, then it will pay to buy the asset and to enjoy its returns—or to rent it out to agents who enjoy it most in each period—forever (that is, *never* to sell it again). Thus there cannot be a negative bubble. What if the price is above market fundamentals? With short selling, it will pay to sell the asset short forever and thus again there cannot be a positive bubble. The same result arises, however, even in the absence of short selling. The only reason to hold an asset whose price is above its fundamental value is to resell it at some time and to realize the expected capital gain. But if all agents intend to sell in finite time, nobody will be holding the asset thereafter, and this cannot be an equilibrium. (This point is made more rigorously by Tirole [forthcoming].) Therefore, with rationality and infinitely lived agents, bubbles cannot emerge.

As for Ponzi games, what is needed is the entry of new participants. If a market is composed of successive "generations" of participants, then the above arguments do not hold and bubbles can emerge.

This section ends with another set of intellectual speculations. We have shown where bubbles may exist. Can we say where bubbles are more likely to appear? Bubbles are probably more likely in markets where fundamentals are difficult to assess, such as the gold market. If we assume that gold has two uses, one industrial use and the other a precautionary use against major catastrophies, the market fundamentals for gold are the factors affecting future flow industrial demand and flow supply, as well as the determinants of these major catastrophies. These are difficult to assess, at least for the average market participant. He is more likely to base his choice of whether or not to hold the asset on the basis of past actual returns rather than on the basis of market fundamentals. He may hold gold at a high price because gold has yielded substantial capital gains in the recent past. By the same argument, bubbles are less likely for assets with clearly defined fundamentals such as blue-chip stocks or perpetuities.

Real Effects of Bubbles

Until now, we have taken the market fundamentals as given, unaffected by the bubble. Bubbles, however, have real effects and do in turn affect market fundamentals, further modifying the behavior of prices.

Bubbles and Production of the Asset

If the asset is not reproducible, the bubble will simply lead to rents to the initial holders. Many assets subject to bubbles are, however, partly reproducible. Consider for example housing.

Housing can be thought of as an asset composed of two inputs: land and structures. There is an upward sloping supply curve for land. The supply of structures is inelastic in the short run, elastic in the long run. In a well-functioning market in steady state, the price of houses is equal to the present value of housing services—*rents*. In turn, the price and associated return to building structures are such that new housing construction equals the depreciation on the existing stock. (Poterba [1980] formalizes the housing market along those lines, although he does not include land.) Suppose now that a deterministic bubble starts in this market, with agents ready to pay more than market fundamentals. The higher price of housing implies higher returns to housing construction, a larger housing stock in the future, and thus, given an unchanged demand for housing services, lower rents in the future. These relationships imply a decrease in the present discounted value of future rents: the bubble has the effect of immediately decreasing the market fundamental value. What happens over time? The price of housing increases, as the bubble must grow exponentially, leading to a higher and higher housing stock and lower and lower rents. These lower rents are reflected in a lower and lower fundamental value of housing over time, which is simply the symptom of overproduction of housing. The increase in new housing construction may come to an end if land supply becomes entirely inelastic, at which point further increases in the price become reflected entirely in land values. If the bubble is not deterministic but stochastic, the story is identical. When the bubble bursts, the price drops to a level lower than the prebubble level because of the very large housing stock.

Consider finally bubbles in the stock market. Suppose that a firm is initially in equilibrium, with a marginal product of capital equal to the interest rate. In the absence of a bubble, the value of a title to a unit of capital, a share, is just equal to the replacement cost, and the firm has no incentive to increase its capital stock. Suppose that a bubble starts on its shares, increasing the price, say, by 10 percent above market fundamentals. Should the firm invest more or should it disregard the stock valuation? One answer is that it should add to the capital stock until the marginal product has been reduced by 10 percent. When this is done, the market fundamental is decreased by 10 percent, the share price is again equal to the replacement cost, and initial shareholders have made a profit on the new shares issued. The story thereafter is similar to the housing story above, with the fundamental value decreasing while the share value increases. (A more appealing strategy for the firm would be to issue shares and buy shares of other non-bubble firms, therefore avoiding the decrease in marginal product. This strategy is, however, inconsistent with the assumption that the bubble is on titles to capital in the initial firm.) The above answer, however, assumes that the bubble proceeds independently of the actions of the firm. It may well be that the bubble depends on those actions, for example, bursting if the firm issues "too many" new shares. Again here, there are many stories consistent with rationality and the economist has little to say about which one will prevail. It is therefore not clear how firms should react to bubbles on their stock, and this might explain why managers of firms seem sometimes to pay little attention to stock market movements.

General Equilibrium Effects

A bubble on the price of any asset will usually affect the prices of other assets, even if they are not subject to bubbles. The increase in the price of the asset that is subject to a bubble leads initially to both an increase in the proportion of the portfolio held in that asset and an increase in total wealth. The first effect will, if assets are not perfectly substitutable, require an increase in the equilibrium expected return on the asset with a bubble and a decrease in the equilibrium expected return on most other assets. The second effect will, by increasing the demand for goods and possibly for money, lead to an increase in the equilibrium average expected return. The net effect is ambiguous, but it is likely to be a decrease in the price of most of the other assets together with a further decrease in the fundamental value of the asset experiencing the bubble. A bubble on housing or gold may for example depress the stock market.

Bubbles may therefore have many real effects, thus raising a question related to the previous sections. A rational bubble must be expected to grow exponentially. This fact may imply, when the effects on other markets are taken into account, that some other prices may be expected to grow or decrease exponentially as well. Won't this action lead to expected negative prices or some such impossibility, ruling out the existence of a rational bubble in the initial market? The answer is: it depends. If, for example, there exists a perfect substitute for a given asset, available in infinite supply at some—possibly high—price, this prevents a positive bubble on this asset since it puts an upper bound on its price. It is, however, possible to construct general equilibrium models in which bubbles cannot be ruled out.[3]

Looking for Bubbles: I

Bubbles can have substantial real effects. It is therefore of some importance to know whether they are a frequent phenomenom or a theoretical possibility of little empirical relevance.

One strategy is to specify a particular class of bubbles, to assume, for example, that they are deterministic and to attempt to find whether bubbles of this class exist in a particular market. Although this strategy may sometimes be sound (such as in the case of the German hyperinflation studied by Flood and Garber [1980]), bubbles can take many forms and specifying a class general enough to include most forms makes discovery very difficult. A better strategy, and the one we shall explore, is to find evidence of rejection of the no-bubble hypothesis, if possible in the direction of the hypothesis of the presence of bubbles. (Rejection of the null hypothesis of no bubble may be due to phenomena other than bubbles, such as irrationality.)

We therefore have to deal with two problems. The first is to characterize the restrictions on the behavior of the price, p, given the dividend, x, under the null hypothesis of no bubbles. The difficulty here is that even if p and x are observable, we usually have no knowledge about the way information on x is revealed to market participants. Information may come infrequently and in lumps, it may come from variables that the econometrician cannot observe, and so forth. The second problem is to find which of these restrictions are likely to be violated in the presence of bubbles. The difficulty here is the lack of structure on bubbles beyond condition 11.3.

If we only have data on p, and are unwilling to make any assumptions about the process generating x and the information process, there is no hope of showing the presence or absence of bubbles. Recall that p is a sum of two components, market fundamentals and bubbles. We cannot say something about one of these components without knowing something about the other component.

This rather trivial point indicates how difficult it is to prove or disprove the existence of bubbles in a market like gold, where market fundamentals are hard to assess. It also implies that, to make progress we need data on x, or assumptions concerning the generation of expectations of x, or both.

In the next section we consider tests that can be carried out when only data on p are available. These tests are useful only if one is willing to make strong assumptions about x and the information structure. Their usefulness is therefore severely limited. In this section we consider tests that can be used when data on both p and x are available.

Intuition suggests that bubbles may affect the second moments of (p, x) in two ways. By introducing additional noise, they may increase the variance of p. They may also weaken the relation of p to its fundamental determinant x and thus decrease the correlations between p and x. We now consider these two intuitions in turn, making them more precise and operational.

The Variance of p

We must distinguish between the unconditional and the conditional variances of p, given respectively by:

$$V_u \equiv E(p - E(p))^2$$

and

$$V_c \equiv E(p - E(p|\Omega_{-1}))^2$$

Note for future use that although V_c involves $E(p|\Omega_{-1})$, which we do not observe, it is also related, given equation 11.1, to the variance of the excess return since:

$$V_c = E(p(R - r))^2$$

It follows from equation 11.3 that if a stock is subject to a stochastic bubble, its unconditional variance is indeed infinite. This is not, however, necessarily the case for the conditional variance. The excess return, in the presence of a bubble, is given by:[4]

$$p_t - E(p_t|\Omega_{t-1}) = \eta_t + \epsilon_t$$

where

$$\epsilon_t \equiv c_t - E(c_t|\Omega_{t-1})$$

and

$$\eta_t \equiv \sum_{i=0}^{\infty} \theta^{i+1}[E(x_{t+i}|\Omega_t) - E(x_{t+i}|\Omega_{t-1})]$$

so that ϵ_t is the innovation in the bubble and η_t is the innovation in the market fundamental value. If ϵ_t and η_t are negatively correlated, the excess return could have a lower variance in the presence of a bubble. It is probably safe to assume that for most assets the innovations in the bubble are either uncorrelated or positively correlated with the innovations in x, in which case bubbles will increase the variance of the excess return and conditional variance of p.

What are the bounds on the conditional and unconditional variance of p imposed by the hypothesis of no bubble? This question has been analyzed by Shiller (1981), who has derived the maximum values for these two variances given the variance of x. Given that in practice not only the variance but the autocovariances of x can be estimated, it is easy to tighten his bounds by using this additional information. To derive bounds, we need to make some assumption of stationarity. For notational convenience we will assume that x_t has 0 mean (since means are unimportant when calculating variances and covariances) and is generated by:

$$x_t = \sum_{i=0}^{\infty} \sum_{j=1}^{n} a_{ij}\xi_{jt-i} \tag{11.6}$$

where

$$E(\xi_{jt}) = 0, E(\xi_{jt}^2) = 1, E(\xi_{jt}\xi_{kt-i}) = 0, \text{ unless } j = k, i = 0$$

and

$$V(x_t) = \sum_{i=0}^{\infty} \sum_{j=1}^{n} a_{ij}^2 < \infty$$

Although this imposes restrictions on the process generating x, it still allows information on x to come in lumps; the variance of the ξ's conditional on the past need not be constant. We place no restrictions on the distribution of the ξ's other than the moment restrictions.

Given these assumptions, and assuming that Ω contains present and past values of x_t, two upper bounds are easily derived (see Singleton [1980]). The first is an upper bound on the unconditional variance of p: it is attained if agents know in advance the future values of x; that is, if they have perfect foresight. In this case:

$$p_t = \sum_{i=0}^{\infty} \theta^{i+1} x_{t+i}, \text{ so that}$$

$$V_u^{\max} = E\left[\left(\sum_{i=0}^{\infty} \theta^{i+1} x_{t+i} \right)^2 \right] \tag{11.7}$$

The second is an upper bound on the conditional variance of p. This bound is attained if the information set Ω_t includes only current and past values of x_t. In this case:

$$p_t - E(p_t|\Omega_{t-1}) = \sum_{i=0}^{\infty} \theta^{i-1} y_{t+i}$$

where

$$y_{t+i} \equiv E(x_{t+i}|x_t, x_{t-1}, \dots) - E(x_{t+i}|x_{t-1}, x_{t-2} \dots)$$

so that

$$V_c^{\max} = E\left[\left(\sum_{i=0}^{\infty} \theta^{i+1} y_{t+i} \right)^2 \right] \tag{11.8}$$

These upper bounds are likely to be violated when bubbles are present. We can therefore test for bubbles by estimating the actual variances and these upper bounds to see whether they are violated by the data.

Shiller has computed the sample unconditional variance of p and the upper bound given by 11.7, using annual observations from 1871 to 1979 for real prices and real dividends from the Standard and Poor's index. (The data used are deviations from an exponential trend; see Shiller [1981] for details.) The sample variance, $\hat{V}_u$, is 2512, while the sample estimate of the upper bound variance, $\hat{V}_u^{\max}$, is 80, so that these point estimates clearly violate 11.7.

To construct a sample estimate of the upper bound of the conditional variance 11.8, we must first estimate a univariate ARIMA model for the dividend series, x. The best fit is achieved by an $AR(2)$ model:

$$x_t = a_1 x_{t-1} + a_2 x_{t-2} + \xi_t$$

$$= 1.07 \, x_{t-1} - .30 \, x_{t-2} + \xi_t, \qquad \hat{\sigma}_\xi^2 = .796$$

The asymptotic variance-covariance matrix of the estimates is:

$$\text{var} \left(\begin{bmatrix} \hat{a}_1 \\ \hat{a}_2 \\ \hat{\sigma}_\xi^2 \end{bmatrix} \right) = \begin{bmatrix} .0086 & -.0071 & 0 \\ -.0071 & .0086 & 0 \\ 0 & 0 & .0074 \end{bmatrix}$$

Diagnostic checks of the model are:

$$Q(24) = 23.9; \, L(3) = .850; \, L(8) = 3.96$$

The Q statistic is a general test for adequacy of the model, and if the model is correctly specified, is distributed $\chi^2(24)$. $L(3)$ and $L(8)$ are Lagrange Multiplier tests, testing for $AR(3)$ and $AR(8)$ alternatives. If the $AR(2)$ model is correct, they are distributed $\chi^2(1)$ and $\chi^2(6)$. All three tests suggest the $AR(2)$ specification is adequate.

We must now compute an estimate of the right-hand side of equation 11.8. Note that y_{t+i} also follows:

$$y_{t+i} = a_1 y_{t+i-1} + a_2 y_{t+i-2} \qquad \text{for } i > 0 \qquad (11.9)$$

$$y_t = \xi_t; \qquad y_{t+i} = 0 \qquad \text{for } i < 0$$

Multiplying equation 11.9 by θ^{i+1}, and summing from one to infinity yields:

$$\sum_{i=1}^{\infty} \theta^{i+1} y_{t+i} = a_1 \theta \left(\sum_{i=1}^{\infty} \theta^{i+1} y_{t+i} + \theta \xi_t \right) + a_2 \theta^2 \left(\sum_{i=1}^{\infty} \theta^{i+1} y_{t+i} + \theta \xi_t \right)$$

$$\Rightarrow \sum_{i=1}^{\infty} \theta^{i+1} y_{t+i} = (1 - \theta a_1 - \theta^2 a_2)^{-1} (\theta \xi_t (\theta a_1 + \theta^2 a_2)),$$

$$\Rightarrow \sum_{i=0}^{\infty} \theta^{i+1} y_{t+i} = (1 - \theta a_1 - \theta^2 a_2)^{-1} \theta \xi_t,$$

so that

$$V_c^{\max} = \sigma_\xi^2 (1 - \theta a_1 - \theta^2 a_2)^{-2} \theta^2.$$

We have estimates of a_1, a_2, and σ_ξ^2. We need only a value for θ, or recalling that $\theta = (1 + r)^{-1}$, a value for the interest rate. Following Shiller, we assume $r = 5$ percent, so that $\theta = .95$. This gives an estimated upper bound: $\hat{V}_c^{\max} = 9.08$. We now need to compute the sample conditional variance, given by $E(p(R - r))^2$. This also has been computed by Shiller. It is: $\hat{V}_c = 653.83$.

The point estimates again violate the bound. Is the violation significant? We need to compute the variances of the above estimates. Conditional on the value of θ, and assuming that ξ_t is normally distributed, it is straightforward to show that asymptotically: $\text{Var}(\hat{V}_c^{\max}) = 15.13$ and $\text{Var}(\hat{V}_c) = 7843.92$. The asymptotic variance of $(\hat{V}_c^{\max} - \hat{V}_c)$ is thus: $15.13 + 7843.92 - 2 \text{cov}(\hat{V}_c^{\max}, \hat{V}_c)$. We won't calculate the covariance term, but by assuming that $\hat{V}_c^{\max}$ and $\hat{V}_c$ are perfectly negatively correlated, we obtain a lower bound on the covariance term of -344.50. This implies an upper bound on the standard error of $(\hat{V}_c^{\max} - \hat{V}_c)$ of 92.46. Thus the t-statistic on $(\hat{V}_c^{\max} - \hat{V}_c)$ is greater, in absolute value, than 6.97, indicating that the data violate the bound given in 11.8 at any reasonable significance level.

Cross-Covariances of p and x

The intuition that bubbles decrease the relation between p and x can be made rigorous as follows. Assume there are no bubbles, so that:

$$p_t = \sum_{i=0}^{\infty} \theta^{i+1} E(x_{t+i} | \Omega_t)$$

$$= \sum_{i=0}^{\infty} \theta^{i+1} x_{i+i} + u_t; \qquad E(u_t|\Omega_t) = 0$$

Then the unconditional variance of p is given by:

$$V_u = E\left[\left(\sum_{i=0}^{\infty} \theta^{i+1} x_{t+i} + u_t\right)(p_t)\right]$$

$$= \sum_{i=0}^{\infty} \theta^{i+1} \operatorname{cov}(p_t x_{t+i}) + E(u_t p_t)$$

By construction of u_t, $E(u_t p_t) = 0$, so that:

$$\sum_{i=0}^{\infty} \theta^{i+1} \operatorname{cov}(p_t x_{t+i})/V_u = \frac{\sigma_x}{\sigma_p} \sum_{i=0}^{\infty} \theta^{i+1} \rho(p_t x_{t+i}) = 1$$

Under the null hypothesis, the relation of p and x is such that the appropriately weighted sum of correlations between p and x, multiplied by the ratio of the standard deviation of x to the standard deviation of p, is equal to unity. It is likely to be smaller if there are bubbles. Using the same sample, we can estimate this ratio. The two components are:

$$\left(\sum_{i=0}^{\infty} \theta^{i+1} \widehat{\operatorname{cov}}(p_t x_{t+i})\right) = 176.10, \text{ while from above:}$$

$$\hat{V}_u(p) = 2512$$

Again, point estimates strongly suggest rejection of the null hypothesis. We have not carried out a formal test; this could be calculated using spectral techniques as in Singleton (1981). The result is suggestive of bubbles, with the same caveats as above.

Looking for Bubbles: II

We discuss in this section the use of two other types of tests for bubbles: *run tests* and *tail tests*. Both refer to the distribution of innovations in prices, $p - E(p|\Omega_{-1})$, or equivalently the distribution of excess returns $p(R - r)$. A run is a sequence of realizations of a random variable with the same sign.

The bubble component, ϵ_t, of the price innovation appears likely to have both runs and a distribution with fat tails. If bubbles grow for a while and then crash, the innovations in the bubble will tend to be of the same sign while the bubble continues, then of reverse sign when a crash occurs. The runs for the bubble innovation will then tend to be longer than for a purely random sequence, making the total number of runs over the sample smaller. Crashes will produce large outliers so that the distribution of innovations will have fat tails (that is, the distribution will be leptokurtic).

Those are, however, characteristics of the bubble innovations that are not observable. Price innovations that are observable are the sum of the bubble innovations, ϵ, and market fundamental innovations, η. To attribute characteristics of price innovation to bubbles implies imposing restrictions on the distribution of η. We now consider whether these may be reasonable.

Runs Tests

Runs in innovations can only arise from a skewed distribution. If we assume that η has a symmetric distribution, we can then attribute runs in price innovations to bubbles. Is it reasonable to assume that η, the market fundamental innovation, has a symmetric distribution? It may not be, *even if x has a symmetric distribution* as the following example shows. Suppose that:

$$x_t = \xi_{1t} + \xi_{2t-1}, \text{ where } \xi_1 \text{ and } \xi_2 \text{ are independent and white,}$$

with $(\xi_{1t}, \xi_{2t}) \epsilon \Omega_t,$

and $\xi_{1t} \not\in \Omega_{t-1}$

Suppose further that the probability density of ξ_{1t}, $f(\xi_1)$ is skewed to the right and the density of ξ_{2t} is given by $g(\xi_2) = f(-\xi_1)$. In this case x has a symmetric distribution but even in the absence of bubbles

$p_t = \theta(\xi_{1t} + \xi_{2t-1} + \theta\xi_{2t})$ is skewed to the left and
$p_t - E(p_t|\Omega_{t-1}) = \theta(\xi_{1t} + \theta\xi_{2t})$ is skewed to the right.

Even if η is symmetric, runs tests may have only minimal power against bubbles. This is because bubbles do not necessarily generate long runs. Consider the second example of a bubble given earlier in the chapter. If π, the probability of the bubble continuing, is unity, then the bubble innovation is simply μ_t, which could have a symmetric distribution. Even if π is different from one and the distribution of μ is symmetric, we may still find no fewer runs than for a series of independent random variables drawn from a symmetric distribution. If $\pi \neq 0$, the bubble innovation is, in this case:

$$\epsilon_t = \mu_t + c_{t-1}(1 - \pi)(\theta\pi)^{-1} \quad \text{with probability } \pi$$

$$= \mu_t - c_{t-1}\theta^{-1} \quad \text{with probability } 1 - \pi$$

so that:

$$\text{Prob}(\epsilon_t > 0|\epsilon_{t-1} > 0) = \pi\,\text{Prob}(\mu_t > -c_{t-1}(1 - \pi)(\theta\pi)^{-1}|\epsilon_{t-1} > 0)$$

$$+ (1 - \pi)\,\text{Prob}(\mu_t > +c_{t-1}\theta^{-1}|\epsilon_{t-1} > 0)$$

Note that for $\pi = \frac{1}{2}$, this is just:

$$\text{Prob}(\epsilon_t > 0|\epsilon_{t-1} > 0) = \frac{1}{2}\,\text{Prob}(\mu_t > -c_{t-1}\theta^{-1}|\epsilon_{t-1} > 0)$$

$$+ \frac{1}{2}\,\text{Prob}(\mu_t > +c_{t-1}\theta^{-1}|\epsilon_{t-1} > 0) = \frac{1}{2}$$

Thus, for $\pi = \frac{1}{2}$ or $\pi = 1$, a runs test has minimal power against this type of bubble, and it has very low power for values of π close to $\frac{1}{2}$ or 1.

Not deterred by these caveats, we nevertheless calculated the distribution of runs for weekly innovations in the price of gold. We assumed, plausibly, that holding gold during the sample period, 1975–1981, was not providing any direct dividend, so that x_t was equal to zero. In this case, the innovations are given by:

$$p - E(p|\Omega_{-1}) = p(R - r) = p - (1 + r)p_{-1}$$

We used weekly gold prices (Englehart) for the period January 1975 to June 1981. In calculating the innovations we relaxed the assumption of a constant interest rate. The rate of interest that was used was the one-week rate of return on treasury bills that matured at time t.

The results of the runs tests are presented in table 11-1. They reveal no evidence indicating the presence of bubbles. This is somewhat surprising given the increase in prices at the end of 1979. In figure 11-1 we have plotted the excess returns from August 1977 until the end of the sample. The figure clearly shows that the increase in late 1979 and early 1980 was not a steady one. Between the beginning of September 1979 and the middle of January 1980, gold prices rose from \$335 per ounce to \$751 per ounce. During this nineteen-week period, thirteen of the week-to-week excess returns were positive while six of the excess returns were negative.

Tail Tests

The bubble considered above (with $\pi \neq 1$ or $\pi \neq 0$) will at times explode or crash. While the bubble is growing it will generate small positive excess returns, which will be followed at the time of the crash by a large negative excess return. The distribution of innovations for this type of bubble will therefore be leptokurtic. This suggests that a large coefficient of kurtosis for price innovations might indicate the presence of bubbles.

Table 11-1
Runs for Gold Excess Returns—334 Observations

Length	+	−	Total	Expected Total for Random Sequence
1	45	44	89	83.50
2	18	23	41	41.75
3	5	4	9	20.88
4	5	4	9	10.44
5	2	4	6	5.22
6	3	0	3	2.61
7	1	0	1	1.30
8	1	1	2	.65
9	1	0	1	.33
10	1	1	2	.16
11	0	0	0	.08
12	0	0	0	.04
Total	82	81	163	166.96

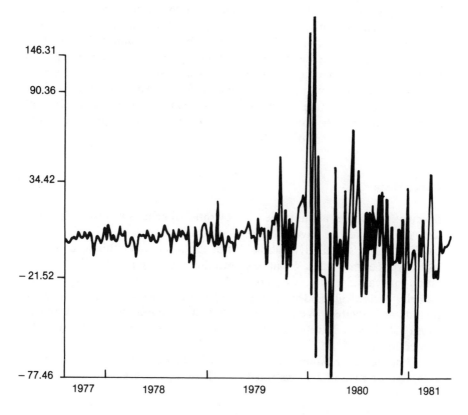

Figure 11-1. Weekly Excess Returns for Gold

Thus, if we assume that market fundamental innovations are not leptokurtic, we can attribute fat tails in excess returns to the presence of bubbles. The problem is, however, the same as for runs. Even if the innovations in x are not leptokurtic, the market fundamental innovations may well be. As Shiller (1981), points out, this will be the case in particular if information about future x's comes in lumps.

Again, despite the caveats, we computed the coefficient of kurtosis for excess returns for our weekly gold series. Because the series was heteroskedastic (see figure 11-1) we computed the coefficient using data from the beginning of the sample to October 1979, and from October 1979 until the end of the sample. The kurtosis coefficients were 7.19 and 6.67, respectively. These are much higher than the normal distribution, which has a coefficient of kurtosis equal to 3. It is also much higher than the coefficient for 25-week treasury bills, whose values over the same periods were 4.30 and 3.36. Whether this is due to fat-tailed fundamentals, to a particular information structure, or to the presence of bubbles is impossible to tell.

The limits of these two types of tests have been emphasized. The results are nevertheless intriguing. The lack of runs suggests that if there were bubbles, they were either very long lived (π close to unity) or short lived (π close to ½, so that the average duration is two weeks). The very high coefficient of kurtosis on the other hand suggests either very leptokurtic market fundamentals or the existence of bubbles.

Conclusions

Speculative bubbles are not ruled out by rational behavior in financial markets and are likely to have real effects on the economy.

Testing for speculative bubbles is not easy. Rational bubbles can follow many types of processes. We have shown that certain bubbles will cause violation of variance bounds implied by a class of rational-expectations models. Empirical evidence is presented that demonstrates that these bounds are violated. We also noted that other alternatives (for example, irrationality) would cause violation of these bounds, and our results must be viewed in light of this.

Other tests for bubbles were suggested when only price data are available. Our discussion demonstrated that these tests may have low power.

Notes

1. This indeterminacy arises not only in arbitrage conditions but in all models in which expectations of future variables affect current decisions. It is the subject of much discussion currently in macroeconomics, under the label of *nonuniqueness*.

2. In some models, such as the model used by Cagan (1956), a condition similar to 11.1 holds with p_t being the logarithm of the price. As a logarithm can be negative, the argument used in this paragraph does not apply.

3. The first example of a bubble-type phenomenon in a general equilibrium model was given by Hahn (1966). In his model, however, bubbles imply that a price becomes negative in finite time. As this is impossible, rational expectations and general equilibrium implications exclude the presence of bubbles in his model.

4. The assumptions of risk neutrality and of a constant interest rate, inessential in previous sections, are essential in this one. The moment tests are only valid if they hold.

References

Cagan, Phillip. 1956. "The Monetary Dynamics of Hyperinflation," in *Studies in the Quantity Theory of Money,* ed. by Milton Friedman. Chicago: University of Chicago Press.

Flood, Robert P., and Peter M. Garber. 1980. "Market Fundamentals versus Price-level Bubbles: The First Tests," *Journal of Political Economy* 88, (Aug.):745–770.

Hahn, F.H. 1966. "Equilibrium Dynamics with Heterogenous Capital Goods," *Quarterly Journal of Economics* 80 (Nov.):633–646.

Kindleberger, C.P. 1978. *Manias, Panics, and Crashes.* New York: Basic Books.

Poterba, J.M. 1980. "Inflation, Income Taxes, and Owner-Occupied Housing." Thesis, Harvard University (March).

Shiller, R.J. 1981. "Do Stock Prices Move too Much to be Justified by Subsequent Changes in Dividends?" *American Economic Review* 71, (June):421–436.

Singleton, K.J. 1980. "Expectations Models of the Term Structure and Implied Variance Bounds," *Journal of Political Economy* 88, (Dec.): 1159–1176.

Thomas, G., and M. Morgan Witts. 1979. *The Day the Bubble Burst.* New York: Doubleday.

Tirole, Jean. Forthcoming. "On the Possibility of Speculation Under Rational Expectations," *Econometrica.*

12 Federal Reserve Margin Requirements: A Regulatory Initiative to Inhibit Speculative Bubbles

Kenneth D. Garbade

Section 7 of the Securities Exchange Act of 1934 gives the Board of Governors of the Federal Reserve System (the board) power to promulgate margin regulations limiting the amount of credit that can be used to purchase stock. Inhibiting speculative bubbles—or the divergence of stock prices from intrinsic stock values—has been the most important goal of those regulations since the mid-1950s.

This chapter examines five aspects of the board's margin requirements. The first section describes the evolution of the intent of Congress that the board should use its regulatory powers to inhibit speculative bubbles in stock prices. The following section discusses the relation between credit-financed speculation and fluctuations in stock prices. The analysis of that section concludes that there is a reasonable basis for believing that bubbles in stock prices can grow and collapse as a result of a pyramiding and depyramiding of credit-financed stock positions. The practical significance of such phenomena for the U.S. stock market is, however, doubtful. As described in the subsequent section, there are both *a priori* and empirical reasons for rejecting the view that speculative bubbles contribute significantly to stock price fluctuations in this country.

The long and continuing history of Federal Reserve margin requirements[1] suggests that, in spite of the arguments advanced in this chapter, the board views speculative bubbles in stock prices as a significant problem that can be controlled through margin requirements. A latter section describes the class of margin requirements best suited to the board's purposes and contrasts those requirements with other types of margin requirements. The final section examines the empirical evidence on the effectiveness of the

This chapter is a revised and condensed version of a staff report on Federal Reserve margin requirements prepared for the Federal Reserve Bank of New York. It expresses only the views of the author and does not reflect the views of the Federal Reserve Bank of New York or the Board of Governors of the Federal Reserve System. The author expresses grateful appreciation to Karen Bradley, Monica Kaicher, Jim McNeil, Mindy Silverman, and the staff of the Board of Governors for their comments on many of the ideas presented here.

board's margin requirements. That evidence provides no support for the proposition that Federal Reserve margin requirements are an important instrument of public policy. At the same time, however, crucial gaps in the evidence preclude an unequivocal conclusion that those requirements should be abandoned.

The Goal of Federal Margin Requirements

Congress has generally recognized two potentially important benefits to federal regulation of securities credit: preventing diversion of the nation's credit resources from productive uses in trade and commerce into speculative activities in the stock market, and inhibiting fluctuations in stock prices that stem from speculation on credit.[2] This section of chapter 12 assesses the contemporary relevance of these two benefits. The analysis concludes that while Congress originally viewed the prevention of credit diversion as the most important benefit, the practical significance of that goal is minimal at the present time. In contrast, while Congress originally may not have viewed stock price stabilization as a major goal, it has clearly acquired that view in more recent years.

Preventing the Diversion of Credit

In passing the Securities Exchange Act of 1934, Congress was acutely aware of the substantial amount of credit devoted to purchasing stock in the 1920s. It was particularly concerned that speculative demands for credit had drained funds from productive uses in commerce, industry, and agriculture, and had increased the cost of credit to those sectors of the economy.

There is little doubt that Congress expected Section 7 of the Securities Exchange Act, and the margin rules promulgated under that section, to prevent the diversion of credit from productive uses in trade and commerce. The House Committee on Interstate and Foreign Commerce, in commenting on a precursor to the Exchange Act, observed:

> The main purpose (of the margin provisions) is to give a Government credit agency an effective method of reducing the aggregate amount of the nation's credit resources which can be directed by speculation into the stock market and out of other more desirable uses in commerce and industry—to prevent a recurrence of the pre-crash situation where funds which would otherwise have been available at normal interest rates for uses of local commerce, industry, and agriculture, were drained by far higher interest rates into security loans and the New York call market.[3]

Whatever may be said of the importance of preventing the diversion of credit in 1934, even a cursory appraisal of recent credit conditions shows that goal has little contemporary significance. During the 1960s and 1970s, security credit averaged about 1¼ percent of the value of all stocks listed on the New York Stock Exchange; about 2 percent of the total credit extended by commercial banks; and about 2 percent of aggregate home mortgage and consumer installment credit. Thus, securities credit is not now of substantial quantitative significance to either suppliers or users of credit, or to the stock market as a whole.[4]

Inhibiting Fluctuations in Stock Prices

Although Congress had some interest in 1934 in the use of margin regulations to inhibit stock-price fluctuations, it does not appear to have assigned a leading role to that objective.[5] Since that time, however, Congress has given significant and increasing attention to the goal of inhibiting price fluctuations that result from credit-financed speculation.

In 1955, for example, a staff report to the Senate Committee on Banking and Currency observed:[6]

> Experience has shown that too much credit may operate to inflate stock prices far beyond underlying values, with harmful effects upon the economy generally. The excessive use of credit for buying and carrying securities accentuates market downswings. Those who hold stocks which are financed by credit may be forced by the lender to sell in order to protect the loan. This can lead to additional selling and as stock prices go even lower, others with stocks financed by credit may be forced to unload. At its worst, this type of chain reaction contains the danger of making a market break more serious and disorderly.[6]

In its 1963 *Special Study,* the Securities and Exchange Commission recommended that Congress amend Section 7 of the Securities Exchange Act to permit the board to regulate credit extended on securities not listed on a national securities exchange. Speaking in support of that recommendation, Vice-chairman Robertson of the Board of Governors specifically cited the destabilizing potential of excessive credit in the over-the-counter markets.[7] Congress concurred and passed the Over-the-Counter Margin Act of 1968.

The Bank Records and Foreign Transactions Act of 1970 made margin credit extended by foreign creditors to U.S. persons subject to board control and provides the most explicit evidence that Congress has been placing greater weight on the goal of market stabilization in recent years. During hearings on that legislation, there was no attempt to argue that foreign credit should be regulated in the interest of preserving the board's control over domestic credit flows. Instead, most commentators took the position that speculation financed with foreign credit could cause excessive fluctuations in stock prices in exactly the same way as speculation financed with domestic credit. The Senate Committee on Banking and Currency, for example, observed that: "One of the purposes of the margin requirements is to prevent destabilizing fluctuations in the securities markets stimulated by the excessive use of margin credit. . . . The objective of preventing destabilizing credit flows can be weakened if U.S. borrowers are free to borrow abroad in excess of the Federal Reserve Board's margin requirements."[8]

How Credit-financed Speculation Might Affect Stock Prices

Credit-financed speculation is commonly believed to exacerbate stock-price fluctuations through a pyramiding/depyramiding process.[9] In the first instance, suppose some optimistic investors believe the price of a particular stock is likely to appreciate substantially. In light of their expectations, those investors will be willing to pay the interest fees on loans used to finance highly leveraged positions in the stock.[10] Their purchases lead to an increase in the stock price. As the price rises, the wealth of the speculators also rises, allowing them to purchase still more of the stock and hence drive its price still higher. Thus, speculators can pyramid their stock purchases and drive the price of the stock above its intrinsic value.[11]

Having financed their purchases substantially with credit, speculators are exposed to the risk of a price decline. Such a decline is especially likely in those cases where a stock has been the object of speculative buying, because other (less optimistic) investors may come to believe that the stock has been overbought. Those investors will begin to sell, and possibly short sell, the stock. As the price of the stock begins to decline, creditors will demand additional collateral on their loans. If speculators can not provide that collateral, the creditors will call their loans and liquidate the collateral securities that they hold. These liquidating sales will lead to further reductions in the price of the stock, further calls for more collateral, and further liquidations. Thus, the depyramiding of leveraged positions in the stock can drive down the price of the stock and may drive it below its intrinsic value.[12]

There are two reasons why it is instructive to scrutinize in more detail this description of the growth and collapse of a speculative bubble in stock prices. First, the conventional description of the pyramiding/depyramiding process is probably incorrect. Second, a more careful examination illuminates those parts of the description that have merit and points the way to further analysis of the practical significance of speculative bubbles in stock prices.

Analysis of Pyramiding

The first step in analyzing the concept of pyramiding is to examine the mechanisms responsible for the increase in stock prices following the first speculative purchases. There are two such mechanisms. First, speculative purchases reduce the supply of the stock available to investors other than the original speculators. Assuming the demand for the stock by those other investors is a decreasing function of price, the reduction in supply will lead to an increase in the equilibrium price of the stock.

The problem with accepting such a supply-reduction argument as the primary force for price increases is that the magnitude of the effect is not likely to be very large. There exists substantial empirical evidence showing that, in the absence of new information, large amounts of a stock can be bought and sold at prices quite close to the prices at which a small amount of the same stock can be bought and sold.[13]

A second mechanism by which speculative purchases can push up the price of a stock is through effects on the expectations of less optimistic investors. Suppose speculative purchases have a small, but nevertheless positive, effect on the price of a stock through the supply-reduction phenomenon described above. When other investors observe that price increase, they may be led to revise upwards their expectations of the future price of the stock. This change in their expectations will lead them to be willing to hold more of the stock at any given price; that is, it will shift outward their demand schedules for the stock.[14] As a consequence of the shift in the demand schedules of nonspeculative investors, the equilibrium stock price will increase further.

The effect of securities price movements on investor expectations has been the subject of several recent studies. Those studies show there is a reasonable basis for anticipating such an effect[15] and that the effect is present even among market makers,[16] who are generally considered to be exceptionally sophisticated market participants.

Price increases that result from changes in investor expectations could lead to further rounds of changes in expectations, shifts in investor demand schedules, and still higher stock prices. Since it is unlikely that all investors will change their expectations by the same amount at the same time, such price increases will typically occur on abnormally heavy trading volumes. This is the basis for the classic symptoms of a speculative bubble: rising stock prices and an unusually heavy volume of trading.[17]

Analysis of Depyramiding

The argument that speculation on credit can lead to price declines through depyramiding can be subjected to a similar analysis. The available evidence suggests that even relatively large sales of stock (when they are not motivated by new information) can be accomplished at prices close to the prices that would be obtained on sales of a more modest size.[18] On the other hand, any price declines that did accompany a liquidation of collateral could depress investor expectations of the future value of a stock. This would lead to an inward shift in the demand schedules of those investors and a further fall in the equilibrium price of the stock. The speculative bubble that had previously fed on cycles of optimism would then collapse under waves of pessimism.

The Practical Significance of the Effect of Credit-financed Speculation on Stock Prices

The analysis of the previous section suggested that changes in investor expectations resulting from stock-price movements is the primary channel through which credit-financed speculation can contribute to the growth and collapse of a speculative bubble. While there is a reasonable basis for believing that such a phenomenon can exist as a general proposition, there are also good reasons for thinking that, in the specific context of the U.S. stock market, speculative bubbles in stock prices are unlikely to be quantitatively important.

The provisions of the Securities Exchange Act of 1934 cover a wide variety of topics, but they generally reflect an intent of Congress to create an environment in which stock prices are reliable indicators of underlying value.[19] Towards that end the Exchange Act provides for registration of publicly held securities, filings of current disclosure documents by issuers of such securities, rules governing proxy solicitations and tender offers, control of trading by corporate insiders, and rules to prevent the manipulation of securities prices. Of particular importance is the on-going program of the Securities and Exchange Commission to provide investors with broader and more detailed information about securities issuers through mandated disclosure.[20]

Empirical studies have shown, with few exceptions, that stock prices are efficient in the sense of reflecting all publicly available information.[21] In light of the vast amount of information now available to investors, it would be reasonable to conjecture that stock prices fluctuate in a narrower band around intrinsic stock values as compared to the behavior of stock prices prior to passage of the Exchange Act, when there was substantially less disclosure by issuers. More particularly, stock analysts now have available more information, on a more timely basis, on which to base their purchase and sale recommendations. This would appear to reduce the likelihood of unreasonably optimistic or pessimistic evaluations and would appear to reduce the incidence of that kind of speculation that the Board's margin requirements seek to control.[22]

Available empirical evidence also suggests that bubbles in stock prices are rare phenomena. The argument that credit-financed speculation can contribute to the growth and collapse of a speculative bubble implies that advances in stock prices ought to be followed by further advances in stock prices (while a bubble is building up), and declines in stock prices ought to be followed by further declines in stock prices (while a bubble is collapsing). The evidence shows, however, that, on average, a stock price increase is equally likely to be followed either by another price increase or by a price decline.[23] In particular, there is no tendency for stock-price increases (decreases) to follow stock-price increases (decreases).

The Design of Margin Requirements for Inhibiting
Fluctuations in Stock Prices Caused by
Credit-financed Speculation

Despite the *a priori* and empirical reasons noted above for believing that speculative bubbles are not an important aspect of the behavior of U.S. stock prices, the board has not left idle its statutory power to promulgate stock margin requirements. To the contrary, the board has exercised that power continuously during the past forty-five years. Before assessing the effectiveness of the board's margin rules, it will be useful to understand the basis for their structure.

Margin requirements generally limit the quantity of stock that can be purchased by an investor with given net worth. For example, when the margin requirement is 80 percent, an investor can acquire a stock position no larger than 125 percent of the equity capital he commits to that position. Similarly, when the margin requirement is 50 percent, an investor can acquire a position no larger than 200 percent of the equity capital he commits. By limiting the stock-purchased-to-equity-capital-committed ratio, margin requirements limit the impact an investor can have on the market.

There are two quite different types of margin regulations currently used in the securities markets. *Maintenance* margins require an investor to maintain, at all times, equity in excess of a specified percentage of the value of his stock position. *Initial* margins, on the other hand, require only that an investor bring forth at the time of purchase equity in excess of a specified percentage of the value of the stock purchased. For the purpose of inhibiting fluctuations in stock prices, initial margin requirements have important advantages over maintenance margin requirements.

Maintenance Margin Requirements

The most important examples of maintenance margin requirements are the margin rules of self-regulatory organizations (SROs) such as the National Association of Securities Dealers, the New York Stock Exchange, and the American Stock Exchange.[24] Those rules require SRO members to monitor the accounts of their customers and to ensure that those accounts maintain a specified minimum net worth. For example, a customer of a member of the New York Stock Exchange must maintain an equity margin not less than 25 percent of the value of stock in his account.

Although a maintenance margin requires an investor to bring forth a minimum amount of capital when he buys stock, it can also lead to forced liquidations of collateral. For example, if the maintenance margin rate is 25 percent, an investor with $10,000 can buy $40,000 of stock. If, however, the value of that stock falls subsequent to his purchase, his broker will make a *maintenance margin call* for additional cash or collateral. If the investor is unable to meet that margin call, the broker will sell some or all of his stock. Such forced liquidations may exacerbate stock-price fluctuations. It is for this reason that the board prescribes an initial margin requirement instead of a maintenance margin requirement.

Initial Margin Requirements

Initial margin requirements, like maintenance margin requirements, require an investor to bring forth a minimum amount of equity capital when he buys stock, but they do not lead to forced liquidations of collateral. In fact, forced liquidations are inhibited when there exists an initial margin requirement in excess of SRO maintenance margin requirements.

The board's initial margin requirement on stock has varied between 40 percent and 100 percent over the past forty-five years. This requirement has been consistently greater than the 25 percent maintenance margin requirement prescribed by the New York Stock Exchange. The difference between an initial margin requirement of, say, 80 percent and a maintenance margin requirement of 25 percent means that the price of a stock bought with the required 80 percent initial equity commitment can fall 73 percent below its purchase price before a creditor will call his loan.

The *equity cushion* created by a high initial margin requirement has the effect of inhibiting forced liquidations of collateral. To the extent an initial margin requirement is unsuccessful in preventing the formation of speculative bubbles, it may at least retard the collapse of such bubbles.[25]

There are two types of institutions that currently impose initial margin requirements on stock purchases: the board and several self-regulatory organizations, including especially the New York Stock Exchange (the NYSE). Although the primary interest of this chapter is Federal margin requirements, it is instructive to compare the breadth and effectiveness of those requirements with the breadth and effectiveness of the NYSE's initial margin requirements.

The Breadth of the Board's Margin Requirements. The board's margin regulations presently cover those securities likely to be of interest to speculators: stock listed on national securities exchanges, stock of comparable character traded in the over-the-counter markets, and related securities such as convertible bonds and put and call options. From a pragmatic viewpoint, the board's margin regulations do not appear to have too narrow a breadth. Substantial differences of opinion among investors as to the future value of a security are most likely for those securities that have the characteristics of a residual claim on earnings and assets, for example, common stock.[26] The policy purpose for insulating the market from excessively optimistic investors is most evident with respect to such securities.

Special Initial Margin Requirements Imposed by the New York Stock Exchange. The board's approach to margin regulation can be termed a *market* approach, because its margin requirements cover virtually all loans to purchase stock that are collateralized by stock. A second, *stock-specific* approach to inhibiting speculation is to impose initial margin requirements only on stocks that actually exhibit speculative characteristics. This approach is taken in NYSE Rule 431. Section d(8) of that rule provides for a Special Initial Margin Requirement on stocks rising rapidly in price on heavy trading volume[27]; that is, on stocks exhibiting speculative characteristics.

The stock-specific approach to initial margin requirements is relatively new. The first instance of the NYSE imposing a special initial margin on stock purchases occurred in December 1964, during an episode of speculative trading in Comsat stock.[28] The most recent instance occurred in September 1978, when such margins were imposed on several so-called gambling stocks, including Bally Manufacturing Corporation, Caesar's World, Inc., and Ramada Inns, Inc.[29]

The Effectiveness of Initial Margin Requirements

Existing empirical evidence does not provide a complete appraisal of the effectiveness of initial margin requirements. The available studies suggest that while initial margin requirements are typically increased following a rise in stock prices, those antecedent stock-price increases were neither generated nor sustained by credit-financed margin buying. The studies do not, however, provide any evidence as to what the subsequent behavior of stock prices might have been in the absence of an advance in margin requirements. In addition, there are not yet any studies that address directly the effectiveness of initial margin requirements in inhibiting the collapse of speculative bubbles. Finally, there are no studies of whether speculative bubbles would be more likely in the absence of any initial margin requirements. This section summarizes the available evidence on the effect on stock prices of an increase in Federal Reserve and NYSE initial margin requirements and summarizes the implications of that evidence for assessing the effectiveness of initial margin requirements.

The Effectiveness of the Board's Initial Margin Requirements

The most thorough tests of the effectiveness of initial margin requirements have relied on the proposition that current stock prices react rapidly to the disclosure of new information that has material significance for future stock prices.[30] Largay and West (1973) used this proposition in a test of the effectiveness of the board's margin regulations. They computed the average percentage change in Standard and Poor's Index of 500 Stocks (the S&P Index) over the thirty days preceding and following an increase in the board's initial margin requirement for stock purchases.[31]

The results obtained by Largay and West are shown in figure 12-1. Three conclusions can be drawn from that figure:

1. The board generally raised margin rates after a period of increasing stock prices. On average, the S&P Index was about 3.4 percent higher on the day margin rates were increased relative to what the Index had been thirty days earlier.
2. On average, the S&P Index fell 0.2 percent on the day a margin rate increase was announced by the board.
3. On average, there was no tendency for the S&P Index to either rise or fall following a margin rate increase.

For the purpose of assessing the effectiveness of the board's margin requirements, the second conclusion is the most important. The *de minimis* size of the fall in the S&P Index indicates that the market did not, on average, consider an increase in the board's margin rates to have any material significance for the future prices of most stocks. If the market believed

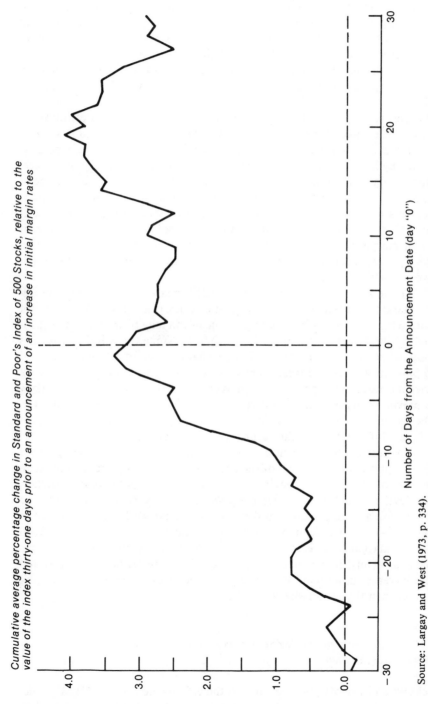

Cumulative average percentage change in Standard and Poor's Index of 500 Stocks, relative to the value of the index thirty-one days prior to an announcement of an increase in initial margin rates

Source: Largay and West (1973, p. 334).

Figure 12-1. Effect of an Increase in Initial Margin Rates by the Board of Governors

otherwise, investors would have changed promptly their expectations of future stock values, and they would have shifted inward their demand schedules for stock. This would have led to an *immediate* fall in the equilibrium level of stock prices. The small size of the average observed price decline indicates that investor expectations were, on average, not changed to any major extent by increases in Federal Reserve initial margin requirements.

This result implies that, while the board raised margin rates following an advance in stock prices, those stock price increases were not typically generated or sustained by speculative margin buying that could be controlled by higher initial margin requirements. (If they were, the announcement of higher margins would have been viewed by the market as leading to a reduction in future demand for stock and would have caused market participants to revise downwards their expectations of future stock prices.) Note that this result could be attributable to either (a) the ineffectiveness of initial margin requirements, or (b) the absence of speculative bubbles in stock prices, or (c) the inability of the board to identify instances of speculative bubbles in stock prices.

Figure 12-1 may appear to suggest that increases in Federal Reserve initial margin requirements stop advances in stock prices even if they do not lead to lower stock prices. While this conclusion may be true, it is not justified by the evidence presented in the figure. Numerous empirical studies support the proposition that stock price changes are, on average, unrelated to past stock price changes.[32] Thus, if one has observed a series of stock price increases in the past, and then asks what level of stock prices is likely to prevail in the future, the answer is: about the same as the current level. The fact that stock prices rose in the immediate past does not, of itself, provide any information on the future course of stock prices.

To illustrate the implications of this proposition for interpreting figure 12-1, suppose we selected all of the dates on which stock prices exhibited an increase of more than 2 percent over the level of prices thirty days earlier. The level of stock prices over the *following* thirty days would show no change, on average, relative to the level on the dates selected. As shown in figure 12-1, the behavior of stock prices following an increase in Federal Reserve margin requirements does not differ significantly from this typical behavior. Thus, that figure cannot be cited as supporting the proposition that increases in margin rates have prevented stock prices from advancing further than they otherwise would have.

*The Effectiveness of the NYSE's Special Initial
Margin Requirements*

Eckardt and Rogoff (1976) examined the effectiveness of the NYSE's Special Initial Margin Requirements with a methodology similar to that used by

Largay and West. They computed the average percentage change in the prices of 264 stocks in excess of the contemporaneous percentage change in the NYSE Composite Index (the NYSE Index) over the nineteen days preceding and following the imposition of a Special Initial Margin Requirement on purchases of those stocks. They divided their sample into two periods: January 1967 to March 1968 (Period I, 95 cases) and April 1968 to June 1969 (Period II, 169 cases).

The results obtained by Eckardt and Rogoff are shown in figure 12-2. There are three conclusions to be drawn from that figure:

1. The NYSE imposes a special initial margin on a stock after a period of rising prices. In Period I, a stock typically increased 26 percent more than the NYSE Index during the nineteen days prior to the imposition of a special initial margin and 19 percent more than the NYSE Index in Period II.
2. On average during Period I, a stock fell in price 3 percent relative to the NYSE Index on the day a special initial margin was imposed on the stock. During Period II the fall was about 1 percent.
3. Following imposition of a special initial margin, there was no tendency for the price of a stock to either rise or fall substantially relative to the NYSE Index.

The most important conclusion that can be drawn from the Eckardt and Rogoff study is that imposition of a special initial margin does not have a substantial effect on the price of the target stock. Thus, even when initial margin requirements are aimed at what appear to be clear cases of speculative trading, they do not alter, to any substantial degree, expectations of future values.

A Caveat

The empirical evidence rejecting the proposition that increases in initial margin requirements have a substantial effect on investor expectations does not necessarily mean that the board's margin requirements are an ineffective instrument of public policy. The available evidence is also consistent with the proposition that Federal Reserve margin rates have never been so low, in the context of prevailing market conditions, as to permit the formation of speculative bubbles in stock prices. It is therefore difficult to conclude with great assurance that Federal Reserve margin requirements do not achieve a legitimate public policy purpose. While *increases* in margin rates have been shown to have virtually no effect on investor expectations, it has not been shown that the *presence* of initial margin requirements makes no contribution to inhibiting credit-financed stock price fluctuations. This gap in the empirical evidence, coupled with a clear Congressional intent that the

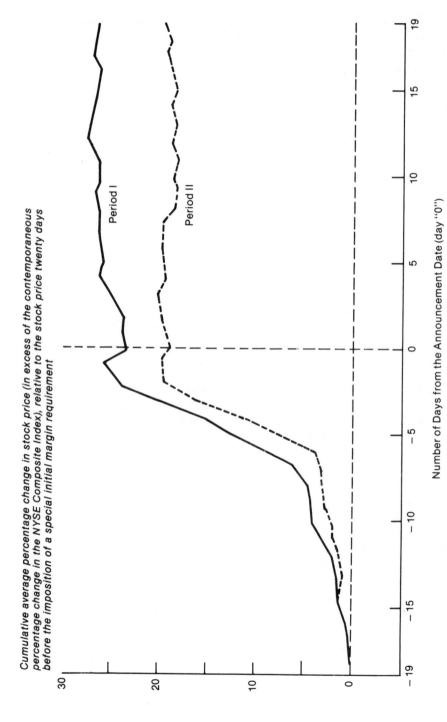

Cumulative average percentage change in stock price (in excess of the contemporaneous percentage change in the NYSE Composite Index), relative to the stock price twenty days before the imposition of a special initial margin requirement

Period I

Period II

Number of Days from the Announcement Date (day "0")

Source: Eckardt and Rogoff (1976, p. 996).

Figure 12–2. Effect of an Imposition of a Special Initial Margin Requirement by the New York Stock Exchange

board should regulate margin credit, may be why the board has continued, and substantially expanded, its regulatory control over margin credit even in the absence of any evidence that its regulations have any positive value.

Notes

1. The board initiated its regulation of margin credit in 1934 when it adopted Regulation T limiting the extension of credit on exchange-listed securities by brokers and dealers. It has since extended its regulations to cover additional creditors and other securities, including: regulation of lending on stocks by commercial banks (1936); regulation of lending on over-the-counter stocks (1968); regulation of lending on stocks by domestic creditors other than banks and broker-dealers (1968); regulation of lending on convertible bonds by commercial banks (1968); regulation of deep-in-the-money over-the-counter call options (1970); and regulation of lending by foreign creditors to U.S. persons (1970).

2. During the debate on the Securities Exchange Act, Congress also noted that margin requirements protect unsophisticated investors from acquiring highly leveraged, and therefore risky, stock positions. However, this investor-protection aspect of margin regulation has been described as a by-product benefit, rather than a primary goal, of the board's regulations. See H.R. Rep. No. 1383, 73d. Cong., 2d Sess. 8 (1934); Climan (1978); and Note (1966). A fourth, and very important, aspect of securities credit regulation is protecting creditors from adverse customer credit risks and protecting investors from creditors who go into default while holding collateral belonging to investors. There is, however, no evidence that Congress considered this a goal of the Federal Reserve's credit regulations. See, for example, H.R. Rep. No. 1383, 73d Cong., 2d Sess. 8 (1934). In any case, the Securities and Exchange Commission and self-regulatory organizations have promulgated rules to achieve this goal. See the SEC net capital rule (17 C.F.R. 240.15c3-1) and customer protection rule (17 C.F.R. 240.15c3-3); Rule 431 of the New York Stock Exchange; Rule 462 of the American Stock Exchange; and Article III, Section 30 of the National Association of Securities Dealers Rules of Fair Practice.

3. H.R. Rep. No. 1383, 73d Cong., 2d Sess. 8 (1934).

4. It could be argued that the minimal aggregate amount of securities credit outstanding during the 1960s and 1970s is a consequence of the board's margin regulations. There is, however, no evidence to support the notion that those regulations effect the volume of such credit. In one investigation, Thomas Moore (1966) found that, over the period from 1947 to 1965, changes in the level of margin rates were only weakly and insignificantly associated with changes in the volume of bank loans used to carry

securities. Each increase of 10 percent in the margin rate was associated with only a $57 million decrease in such loans. Moore's findings were substantially confirmed in a similar study by Jacob Cohen (1966).

5. This has been attributed to a tendency, in the Congressional reports, to equate the effects of excessive credit going into the securities markets with the effects of credit-financed speculation on securities prices. See Comment (1967, n. 66). The Senate report on the Securities Exchange Act did note, however, that "margin purchasers, while their speculations were uncontrolled, affected the national economy in a measure immensely disproportionate to their numbers. Their activities resulted in wide fluctuations in the price of securities, which ultimately imperiled the holdings of bona fide investors of every type." S. Rep. No. 1455, 73d Cong., 2d Sess. 11 (1934).

6. *Factors Affecting The Stock Market,* Staff Report of The Senate Committee on Banking and Currency, 84th Cong., 1st Sess. 41 (1955).

7. Hearings before the Senate Committee on Banking and Currency on S. 1299 and S.J. Res. 160, The Securities Exchange Act Amendments, 90th Cong., 2d Sess. 23 (1968).

8. S. Rep. No. 1139, 91st Cong., 2d Sess. 9 (1970).

9. See, for example, Securities and Exchange Commission (1963, chapter X, p. 33), Climan (1978, pp. 211-213), Ulrey (1975, p. 211) and Note (1966, pp. 1463-1464).

10. Ulrey (1975, p. 216) has observed that, "Brokerage customers have an incentive to increase their buying power by borrowing if they expect stock prices (at least those of selected issues) to rise by amounts that will more than repay the cost of borrowing. Whether or not they forecast correctly, it is reasonable to assume that their decisions are market-oriented and are generally based on expectations of near-term price appreciation."

11. The report of the Senate Committee on Banking and Currency that accompanied an early version of the Securities Exchange Act commented that, "During the boom period a vast and unhealthy volume of credit was sucked into securities markets . . . which made possible the inflation of prices of securities out of all proportion to their value . . . until the bubble burst in October 1929." S. Rep. No. 792, 73d Cong., 2d Sess. 3 (1934).

12. The most famous example of forced liquidation in a declining market was the reduction in brokers' loans from $8.5 billion to $5.5 billion, in ten days, during the stock market collapse that began in late October 1929. Hearings before the Senate Committee on Banking and Currency on S. Res. 84 and S. Res. 56 and S. Res. 97, 73d Cong., 1st Sess. 6437-6438, 6448 (1934) (statement of E.A. Goldenweiser). While it is hard to believe that the stock sales required to reduce brokers' loans by $3 billion did not affect stock prices, it must also be recognized that there has been no investigation of that episode beyond anecdotal recitations.

13. Scholes (1972) and Kraus and Stoll (1972).

14. Friend and Herman (1964, p. 400) have claimed that, "There are both theoretical and empirical grounds for believing that the demand schedule of investors in the stock market is greatly influenced by price movements . . . " See also Kryzanowski (1978) for an empirical analysis of stock price manipulation.

15. Grossman and Stiglitz (1976) and Grossman (1976).

16. Garbade, Pomrenze, and Silber (1979).

17. It should be noted, however, that large price movements on heavy trading volume are hardly *sufficient* to conclude the existence of speculation. Studies show that whenever an issuer discloses material new information, the price of its stock will change substantially (due to the materiality of the information) on unusually heavy trading volume (as investors rebalance their portfolios). See Beaver (1968), Ball and Brown (1968), Brown and Kennelly (1972), and Griffin (1977).

18. See note 13.

19. For example, the House Committee on Interstate and Foreign Commerce observed that, "No investor, no speculator, can safely buy and sell securities upon the exchanges without having an intelligent basis for forming his judgment as to the value of the securities he buys or sells. The idea of a free and open public market is built upon the theory that competing judgments of buyers and sellers as to the fair price of a security brings about a situation where the market price reflects as nearly as possible a just price. Just as artificial manipulation tends to upset the true function of an open market, so the hiding and secreting of important information obstructs the operation of the markets as indices of real value." H.R. Rep. No. 1383, 73d Cong., 2d Sess. 11 (1934).

20. See generally, *Report of the Advisory Committee on Corporate Disclosure to the Securities and Exchange Commission,* House Committee on Interstate and Foreign Commerce, Comm. Print 95-29, 95th Cong., 1st Sess. (1977); and Securities Exchange Act Release No. 14471, "Preliminary Response of the Commission to Recommendations of the Advisory Committee on Corporate Disclosure," Fed. Sec. L. Rep. ¶ 81,505 (February 15, 1978).

21. See Fama, Fisher, Jensen, and Roll (1969), Fama (1970), Pozen (1976), and Sarri (1977).

22. It should be noted, however, that as securities prices come to reflect underlying values more accurately, those prices also convey more information to market participants. This was pointed out by Grossman (1976) and by Grossman and Stiglitz (1976). Thus, the disclosures that enhance market efficiency and may reduce the incidence of speculation also create an environment that fosters the effect of speculation.

23. See Fama (1965), Fama and Blume (1966), and Garbade and Lieber (1977).

24. New York Stock Exchange Rule 431; American Stock Exchange

Rule 462 and Article III, Section 30 of the National Association of Securities Dealers Rules of Fair Practice. Broker-dealers frequently set their maintenance margins at higher levels than required.

25. Ulrey (1975, p. 211) has noted that the purpose of the board's initial margin requirements is "first to limit the magnitude of credit-based buying pressures generated by rising loan values in boom periods and second to provide a buffer between customers' initial equity and the minimum maintenance levels that would trigger widespread margin calls."

26. There have, however, been instances of speculation in Treasury securities. See, for example, U.S. Department of the Treasury (1960).

27. Rule 462(e) of the American Stock Exchange and Article III, Section 30(d) of the National Association of Securities Dealers Rules of Fair Practice also provide for special initial margins but do not specify criteria that must be satisfied before such margins are imposed.

28. Largay (1973, p. 974).

29. See *Wall Street Journal,* September 5, 1978, p. 10; September 18, 1978, p. 4; and October 2, 1978, p. 16.

30. See the works cited in notes 21 and 23, and Dann, Mayers, and Raab (1977).

31. There were twelve such increases over their sample period of January 1, 1933 to January 31, 1969.

32. See the works cited in note 23.

References

Ball, Ray, and Philip Brown. 1968. "An Empirical Evaluation of Accounting Income Numbers," *Journal of Accounting Research* 6 (Autumn): 159–178.

Beaver, William. 1968. "The Information Content of Annual Earnings Announcements," *Journal of Accounting Research* 6 (Supplement): 67–92.

Brown, Philip, and John Kennelly. 1972. "The Information Content of Quarterly Earnings: An Extension and Some Further Evidence," *Journal of Business* 45 (July):403–415.

Climan, Richard. 1978. "Civil Liability Under the Credit-Regulation Provisions of the Securities Exchange Act of 1934," *Cornell Law Review* 63: 206–270.

Cohen, Jacob. 1966. "Federal Reserve Margin Requirements and the Stock Market," *Journal of Financial and Quantitative Analysis* 1 (Sept.): 30–54.

Comment. 1967. "Application of Margin Requirements to the Cash Tender Offer," *University of Pennsylvania Law Review* 116 (Nov.):103–130.

Dann, L.Y., D. Mayers, and R. Raab. 1977. "Trading Rules, Large Blocks, and the Speed of Price Adjustment," *Journal of Financial Economics* 4 (Jan.):3–22.

Eckardt, Walter, and Donald Rogoff. 1976. "100 percent Margins Revisited," *Journal of Finance* 31 (June):995–1001.

Fama, Eugene. 1965. "The Behavior of Stock Market Prices," *Journal of Business* 38 (Jan.):34–105.

Fama, Eugene. 1970. "Efficient Capital Markets: A Review of Theory and Empirical Work," *Journal of Finance* 25 (May):383–417.

Fama, Eugene, and Marshall Blume. 1966. "Filter Rules and Stock Market Trading Profits," *Journal of Business* 39 (Special Supplement, Jan.): 226–241.

Fama, Eugene, Lawrence Fisher, Michael Jensen, and Richard Roll. 1969. "The Adjustment of Stock Prices to New Information," *International Economic Review* 10 (Feb.):1–21.

Friend, Irwin, and Edward Herman. 1964. "The S.E.C. Through a Glass Darkly," *Journal of Business* 37 (Oct.):382–405.

Garbade, Kenneth, and Zvi Lieber. 1977. "On the Independence of Transactions on the New York Stock Exchange," *Journal of Banking and Finance* 1 (Sept.):151–172.

Garbade, Kenneth, Jay Pomrenze, and William Silber. 1979. "On the Information Content of Prices," *American Economic Review* 69 (March):50–59.

Griffin, Paul. 1977. "Sensitive Foreign Payment Disclosures: The Securities Market Impact," in *Report of the Advisory Committee on Corporate Disclosure to the Securities and Exchange Commission.* House Committee on Interstate and Foreign Commerce, Committee Print 95-29, 95th. Cong., 1st Sess.

Grossman, Sanford. 1976. "On the Efficiency of Competitive Stock Markets Where Trades Have Diverse Information," *Journal of Finance* 31 (May):573–585.

Grossman, Sanford, and Joseph Stiglitz. 1976. "Information and Competitive Price Systems," *American Economic Review* 66 (May):246–253.

Kraus, Alan, and Hans Stoll. 1972. "Price Impacts of Block Trading on the New York Stock Exchange," *Journal of Finance* 27 (June):569–588.

Kryzanowski, Lawrence. 1978. "Misinformation and Regulatory Actions in the Canadian Capital Markets: Some Empirical Evidence," *Bell Journal of Economics* 9 (Autumn):355–368.

Largay, James. 1973. "100 percent Margins: Combating Speculation in Individual Security Issues," *Journal of Finance* 28 (Sept.):973–986.

Largay, James, and Richard West. 1973. "Margin Changes and Stock Price Behavior," *Journal of Political Economy* 81 (March/April):328–339.

Moore, Thomas. 1966. "Stock Market Margin Requirements," *Journal of Political Economy* 74 (April):158–167.

Note. 1966. "Federal Margin Requirements as a Basis for Civil Liability," *Columbia Law Review* 66:1462–1485.

Pozen, Robert. 1976. "Money Managers and Securities Research," *New York University Law Review* 51 (Dec.):923–980.

Sarri, Christopher. 1977. "The Efficient Capital Market Hypothesis, Economic Theory, and the Regulation of the Securities Industry," *Stanford Law Review* 29 (May):1031–1076.

Scholes, Myron. 1972. "The Market for Securities: Substitution versus Price Pressure and the Effects of Information on Share Prices," *Journal of Business* 45 (April):179–211.

Securities and Exchange Commission. 1963. *Special Study of the Securities Markets,* House Document No. 95, 88th Cong., 2nd. Sess.

Ulrey, Ann. 1975. "The Structure of Margin Credit," *Federal Reserve Bulletin* 61 (April):209–220.

U.S. Department of the Treasury. 1960. *Treasury-Federal Reserve Study of the Government Securities Market.*

Index

About the Contributors

Olivier J. Blanchard is an associate professor in the Department of Economics at Harvard University. His research is in macroeconomics and he has published extensively on the implications of rational expectations for the behavior of financial markets and the characteristics of the business cycle.

Peter Crawford is vice-president of the Economics Department, Citibank, in charge of economic analysis and forecasts for the United States.

Robert P. Flood is an economist at the Board of Governors of the Federal Reserve System and an associate professor of economics at the University of Virginia.

Kenneth D. Garbade is professor of economics and finance at the Graduate School of Business Administration, New York University. He is the author of *Discretionary Control of Aggregate Economic Activity* (Lexington Books, 1975), *Securities Markets* (1982), and numerous articles in scholarly journals. His major areas of research interest include the analysis of the trading structure of financial markets and the statistical analysis of systems with time-varying parameters. Professor Garbade graduated from the California Institute of Technology in 1968 with the B.S. in physics and history, and from Princeton University in 1975 with the Ph.D. in economics.

Peter M. Garber is an assistant professor of economics at the University of Rochester. He received the Ph.D. from the University of Chicago in 1977.

Laurie S. Goodman is an economist in the International Research Department of the Federal Reserve Bank of New York. She has published numerous articles on international banking and on international financial markets. Prior to joining the Federal Reserve System, Dr. Goodman taught finance at New York University's Graduate School of Business. Dr. Goodman received the Ph.D. in economics from Stanford University.

Jack Guttentag is professor of finance and Robert Morris Professor of Banking at the Wharton School of the University of Pennsylvania. He has been an economist at the Federal Reserve Bank of New York, on the senior staff of the National Bureau of Economic Research, and managing editor of the *Journal of Finance*.

Albert G. Hart is a professor emeritus at Columbia University. He received the Ph.D. from the University of Chicago in 1936 and joined Columbia University in 1946.

H. Robert Heller is vice-president for international economics at Bank of America. He also teaches international financial management at the University of California, Berkeley. He began his career as an economics professor at the University of California, Los Angeles, and subsequently served as chairman of the Economics Department at the University of Hawaii. Subsequently, he was chief of the Financial Studies Division of the International Monetary Fund.

Richard Herring is associate professor of finance at the Wharton School of the University of Pennsylvania. He received the Ph.D. from Princeton University in 1973.

Thomas Ho is an assistant professor of finance at New York University. He received the Ph.D. in mathematics from the University of Pennsylvania in 1978, and has published papers in the *Journal of Finance* and the *Journal of Financial Economics*.

Roger Kubarych is vice-president and deputy director of research at the Federal Reserve Bank of New York.

Thomas Mayer teaches at the University of California, Davis. He is the author or coauthor of *Monetary Policy in the United States, Intermediate Macroeconomics, Permanent Income, Wealth and Consumption, The Structure of Monetarism, Money, Banking and the Economy,* and numerous articles in professional journals. He received the B.A. from Queens College and the Ph.D. from Columbia University.

Allan H. Meltzer is the John M. Olin Professor of Political Economy and Public Policy at Carnegie-Mellon University. He is the author of more than one hundred books and articles on monetary theory and policy. His recent work includes "Keynes' General Theory: A Different Perspective," *Journal of Economic Literature,* 1981 and "Stagflation, Persistent Unemployment and the Permanence of Economic Shocks," *Journal of Monetary Economics,* 1980 (with Karl Brunner and Alex Cukierman).

Knut Anton Mork is a visiting assistant professor of economics at the University of Arizona and was previously a research associate at the M.I.T. Energy Laboratory. Over the last few years, he has conducted extensive research on energy-economy interactions and oil-supply shocks. He was the editor of *Energy Prices, Inflation, and Economic Activity* and has contributed many articles on the subject.

Arturo C. Porzecanski is associate economist, International Economics Department, Morgan Guaranty Trust Company of New York. He is the recipient of the B.A. in economics from Whittier College, and of the M.A. and Ph.D. degrees in economics from the University of Pittsburgh. Dr. Porzecanski has previously served with the International Monetary Fund and the Center for Latin American Monetary Studies (CEMLA). He has published books and articles on international and Latin American economic and political issues.

Jeffrey D. Sachs is an assistant professor in the Department of Economics, Harvard University, specializing in macroeconomics and international finance. Professor Sachs has published numerous articles in academic journals on the macroeconomic effects of the energy-price increases in the 1970s, and on the determinants of international borrowing. He is a research associate of the National Bureau of Economic Research and a member of the Brookings Panel on Economic Activity.

William L. Silber is professor of economics and finance at the Graduate School of Business Administration, New York University. He is also currently a research associate with the National Bureau of Economic Research and an Associate Editor of the *Review of Economics and Statistics.* In the past he has been a senior staff economist with the President's Council of Economic Advisors and has also served as consultant to a number of government agencies.

Ronald F. Singer is an associate professor of finance at New York University, and will be a visiting associate professor of finance at the University of Houston in 1982. His major fields of research interest are in risky bond valuation and corporate financial behavior. He also has authored articles in *The Journal of Finance* and *The Banker's Magazine.*

Richard Sylla is a professor of economics and business at North Carolina State University, Raleigh. An economic historian, Sylla specializes in the development of monetary, banking, and financial institutions in modern economic history. Since 1978 he has been editor of the *Journal of Economic History,* and currently serves as vice-president of the Southern Economic Association.

Henry C. Wallich has been a member of the Board of Governors of the Federal Reserve System since 1974. Prior to that he was Seymour H. Knox Professor of Economics at Yale University. Dr. Wallich has also served as a member of the Council of Economic Advisors.

Mark W. Watson is an assistant professor of economics at Harvard University. He received the Ph.D. in economics at University of California, San Diego, 1980. His fields of interest are time-series analysis and econometrics.

Michelle J. White is Associate Professor of Economics at New York University. She received the Ph.D. from Princeton University. Her research interests are in public finance and law and economics. A recent article on the subject of bankruptcy is "Public Policy Toward Bankruptcy: Me-First and Other Priority Rules," *Bell Journal of Economics,* Autumn 1980.

About the Editor

Paul Wachtel is a professor of economics at the New York University Graduate School of Business Administration. He has been associated with New York University since 1972, shortly after obtaining the Ph.D. from the University of Rochester. Professor Wachtel is also a research associate at the National Bureau of Economic Research. In 1979 he was a visiting economist at the Federal Reserve Bank of New York, and in 1980 a visiting professor at the Hebrew University in Jerusalem. He is the coeditor of the Monograph Series in Economics and Finance published by the Salomon Brothers Center for the Study of Financial Institutions at New York University. He is also coeditor of an earlier conference volume, *Understanding Capital Markets, Vol. II: The Financial Environment and the Flow of Funds in the Next Decade* (Lexington Books, 1977). Recently published articles include "Market Responses to the Weekly Money Supply Announcement in the 1970s," *Journal of Finance* (December 1981) and "Differential Inflationary Expectations – Reply and Further Thoughts on Inflation Uncertainty," *American Economic Review* (June 1982). Professor Wachtel has also published numerous research papers on topics such as the effect of inflation on consumer behavior; demographic change and savings behavior; inflation in the rational-expectations model; and the effect of the money-supply announcement on interest rates.